Design and use of software architectures

ACM Press Books

This book is published as part of the ACM Press Books – a collaboration between the Association for Computing Machinery and Addison-Wesley. ACM is the oldest and largest education and scientific society in the information technology field. Through its high-quality publications and services, ACM is a major force in advancing the skills and knowledge of IT professionals throughout the world. For further information about ACM contact:

ACM Member Services
1515 Broadway, 17th Floor
New York NY 10036-5701
Phone: +1 212 626 0500
Fax: +1 212 944 1318
Email: acmhelp@acm.org

ACM European Service Center
108 Cowley Road
Oxford OX4 1JF
United Kingdom
Phone: +44 1865 382338
Fax: +44 1865 381338
Email: acm-europe@acm.org
URL: http://www.acm.org

Selected ACM titles:

Bringing Design to Software: Expanding Software Development to Include Design
Terry Winograd, John Bennett, Laura de Young, Bradley Hartfield

Software for Use: A Practical Guide to the Models and Methods of Usage Centered Design
Larry L. Constantine and Lucy A.D. Lockwood

Software Requirements and Specifications: A Lexicon of Software Practice, Principles and Prejudices Michael Jackson

Use Cases: Requirements in Context Daryl Kulak and Eamonn Guiney

Mastering the Requirements Process Suzanne Robertson and James Robertson

Software Blueprints: Lightweight uses of logic in conceptual modelling David Robertson and Jaume Agusti

Software Test Automation: Effective use of text execution tools Mark Fewster and Dorothy Graham

Test Process Improvement: A practical step-by-step guide to structured testing Tim Koomen and Martin Pol

Design and use of software architectures

Adopting and evolving a product-line approach

JAN BOSCH

An imprint of Pearson Education

Harlow, England / London / New York / Reading, Massachusetts / San Francisco / Toronto / Don Mills, Ontario / Sydney
Tokyo / Singapore / Hong Kong / Seoul / Taipei / Cape Town / Madrid / Mexico City / Amsterdam / Munich / Paris / Milan

PEARSON EDUCATION LIMITED

Head Office:
Edinburgh Gate
Harlow CM20 2JE
Tel: +44 (0)1279 623623
Fax: +44 (0)1279 431059
Website: www.awl.com/cseng/

London Office:
128 Long Acre
London WC2E 9AN
Tel: +44 (0)20 7447 2000
Fax: +44 (0)20 7240 5771

First published in Great Britain in 2000

© Pearson Education Limited 2000

The right of Jan Bosch to be identified as Author of this Work has been
asserted by him in accordance with the Copyright, Designs and Patents Act 1988.

ISBN 0-201-67494-7

British Library Cataloguing in Publication Data
A CIP catalogue record for this book can be obtained from the British Library

Library of Congress Cataloging in Publication Data
Applied for.

10 9 8 7 6 5 4 3 2 1

Typeset by Pantek Arts, Maidstone, Kent.
Printed and bound in the United States of America.

The Publishers' policy is to use paper manufactured from sustainable forests.

Contents

Preface / ix
Foreword / xi
Acknowledgements / xiii

chapter 1   Software architecture and product lines / 1

The role of software / 3
This book / 9
Software architecture / 10
Software components / 13
Reading guide / 15
Conclusion / 19

PART I   The designing of software architectures

chapter 2   Design of software architectures / 23

Requirements / 27
Architectural design method: overview / 29
Functionality-based architectural design / 33
Assessing quality attributes / 34
Architecture transformation / 36
Concluding remarks / 40
Further reading / 40

chapter 3   Software architectural design: case studies / 41

Fire alarm systems / 41
Measurement systems / 44
Haemodialysis systems / 49
Concluding remarks / 53

chapter 4   Functionality-based architectural design / 54

Defining the system context / 55
Identifying the archetypes / 57

Decomposing the architecture into components / 61
Describing system instantiations / 65
Illustrating functionality-based design / 67
Summary / 76
Further reading / 78

chapter 5   Assessing software architectures / 79

Introduction / 79
Profiles / 82
Scenario-based assessment / 91
Simulation-based assessment / 95
Mathematical model-based assessment / 100
Experience-based assessment / 103
Performing architecture assessment / 104
Concluding remarks / 106
Further reading / 108

chapter 6   Transformation of software architectures / 109

Introduction / 109
The process of architecture transformation / 112
Impose an architectural style / 116
Impose an architectural pattern / 131
Apply a design pattern / 145
Convert quality requirements to functionality / 151
Distribute requirements / 155
Conclusion / 155
Further reading / 157

PART II Software product lines

chapter 7   Software product lines: an introduction / 161

Three types of software architecture use / 162
Decomposing software product lines / 163
Initiating a product line / 166
Applicability of software product-line concepts / 169
Overview / 170
Conclusion/ 174
Further reading / 175

chapter 8   Software product lines: case studies / 176

Axis Communications AB / 176
Securitas Larm AB / 180
Symbian / 183
Concluding remarks / 188

chapter 9   Designing a product-line architecture / 189

Overview / 189
Business case analysis / 191
Scoping / 194
Product and feature planning / 200
Product-line architectural design / 201
Component requirement specification / 208
Validation / 210
Conclusion / 211
Further reading / 213

chapter 10   Developing components: traditional / 214

Component development process / 216
Components and domains / 217
Component interfaces / 220
Component variability /224
Component adaptation / 227
Aspects, constraints and rules / 234
Conclusion / 235
Further reading / 237

chapter 11   Developing components: object-oriented frameworks / 238

Comparing the academic and industrial views / 239
Object-oriented frameworks / 240
Composing independently developed frameworks / 244
Framework component models / 250
Designing frameworks / 256
Conclusion / 257
Further reading / 258

chapter 12 Family-based system development / 259

Requirement specification / 259
Product architecture derivation / 261
Product-line component selection and instantiation / 268
Develop product-specfic components / 273
Product integration / 274
Validation / 278
Packaging and release / 279
Conclusion / 279

chapter 13 Evolving product-line assets / 282

Evolution in software product lines / 282
New product line / 285
Introduction of new product / 288
Adding new features / 291
Extend standards support / 292
New version of infrastructure / 293
Improvement of quality attributes / 295
Post-fielding and run-time evolution / 297
Conclusion / 298
Further reading / 300

chapter 14 Organizing for software product lines / 301

Development department / 302
Business units / 304
Domain engineering unit / 309
Hierarchical domain engineering units / 312
Influencing factors / 315
Conclusion / 317

chapter 15 Industrial experiences / 319

Organization / 319
Process / 323
Technology / 327
Conclusion / 335

References / 336
Index / 345

Preface

Software has entered virtually all parts of society, ranging from basic utilities such as electricity generation and distribution and telecommunications to personal devices such as mobile phones and cars. Whereas traditionally the competitiveness of a company was defined by its ability to construct and maintain mechanical systems, and later on hardware systems, currently it is the ability to develop and evolve software systems efficiently and effectively which is central.

These developments imply an increasing level of responsibility on the software engineering community. With the increase in integration between software systems, failures in one system may have effects which extend beyond the system itself and affect other systems, with possible consequences in the physical world that were not conceivable even a decade ago. On the other hand, software has allowed for unprecedented flexibility and agility in organizations and systems that have many positive effects on society, organizations and individuals.

Despite the success of software, software engineering still has many challenges to address. In particular, the following primary objectives can be identified: to drastically decrease the cost of developing and maintaining software and the time-to-market of new software products and to improve (and manage) the quality attributes of software products.

Although software systems have always had an architecture, during the last decade the notion of an explicit software architecture has been recognized as being important. One can identify three purposes for an explicitly defined software architecture. First, it allows for early assessment of and design for the quality attributes of a software system. Second, the software architecture represents a concrete artefact that can be used for discussions with and between stakeholders. Finally, it defines the architectural components and their interactions, which facilitates reuse in general and software product lines in particular.

This book is concerned with two aspects of software architecture: the design of software architectures and software product lines. In Part I of the book, we present our software architectural design method. This method has been developed and refined through our involvement in a number of software architecture design projects. The three main projects are described as case studies in this book. In Part II of the book, we present the notion of software product lines and the process of adopting and evolving a product-line approach to software development. Again, our approach has been shaped by the co-operation projects that we have had with a number of companies which use software product lines. Consequently, the contents of Part II are shaped by the experiences from these co-operation projects.

Foreword

Our nice little puppy has really grow and now needs a doghouse. A few boards, some two-by-fours and leftover cedar shingles, a handful of nails, and *voilà!* Our puppy has a brand new home. Now, let's say you didn't get it quite right at first, so you made some adjustments along the way, then even more a week later. You could even imagine applying some of these techniques to your house if, like me, you live in an area where most houses are made of wood, but you'd be hard pressed to make a living at it. Some of the fixes along the way may have drastic consequences, or may violate the building codes. Now try taking this 'build and fix' approach to a sky-scraper, and I'm afraid you'd have to completely rethink your strategy.[1]

If you think of the parallel between construction and software development, the fact is that most software today is still developed and built according to the 'code and fix' approach – by writing the code, summarily testing it, and shipping it to the customer to use, or to finish the testing. Also in the software world, all doghouses and most log cabins have already been built, and now companies are mostly tackling the sky scrapers. The 'code and fix' approach does not work and development organizations realize that they need to engineer their software intensive systems.[2] They go from developing 'one-off' systems, to multiple instances, to families of systems or *product lines,* to leveraging their efforts, as you cannot build these sky-scrapers from scratch all the time.

This is where *software architecture* comes into play.

All software intensive systems have an architecture, but, unlike building architecture, this architecture is often hidden, fuzzy, and seems to be produced more by black magic or by accident than by human intent or design. It was only five years ago that Mary Shaw and David Garlan published their book *Software Architecture: Perspectives on an Emerging Discipline*[3] and although this discipline has made some progress, not much has been published since. It has been slow to emerge as a mature software engineering discipline.

---

1 Brooch, G. *et al* (1999) *UML User Guide,* Reading, MA: Addison-Wesley-Longman, pp. 4–5.

2 McConnell, S. (2000) *After the gold rush – Creating a true profession of software engineering,* Redmond, WA: Microsoft Press.

3 1996, Upper Saddle River, NJ: Prentice-Hall.

There are three main aspects where software architecture needs to make progress to establish itself:

- *Architecture representation* – By defining how to represent the architecture of software intensive systems and reaching some industry-wide consensus, we'll be able to communicate architectural designs or blueprints, to reason about them, and to evaluate and compare architectures. This is where the future standard IEEE 1471 on architecture representation will fill a void. This is also a place where the Unified Modeling Language (UML) has a role to play as a uniform notation for architectural blueprints.

- *Architectural process* – By defining the methods to design and assess architectures, focusing on quality attributes (the non-functional or 'afunctional' requirements), and addressing them in a systematic fashion. The architectural design approaches need to be supported by a matching organization that takes architecture as a key function, and understands its value and how it flows into other areas, such as planning, project management, product management, design or deployment.

- *Architectural assets* – By collecting, cataloging, and presenting fragments of successful architectures, or even complete architectures, whether they are called patterns, frameworks, components, mechanisms or standards, we will enable software development organizations to design architecture without re-inventing the wheel. This will also foster better communication across the industry, allowing practitioners to simply name the pattern rather than describing it completely. However, as architectures are usually prized company assets, many companies are reluctant to exhibit their architectural assets in a public forum. They'd rather patent them or carefully hide them in their products.

In this context, we really welcome this book *Design and Use of Software Architectures*, which represents a significant step forward in this discipline. Jan Bosch actually contributes to all three aspects – representation, process, and assets – with a good mix between an academic perspective and an industrial perspective.

Most of Jan Bosch's contribution is on the second point, though: the architectural design process, which is certainly the topic closest to my interests and daily concerns. Method and process are definitely areas where we can say there are many ways to achieve a goal, but at the same time areas where too little has been published yet to allow comparison and evolution. Here Jan Bosch does an excellent job of dishing out engineering wisdom to people who have to design architectures for families of related products, or product lines. This area is especially tough because it goes far beyond the difficulty of getting the architecture right for one system – not an easy undertaking alone. It's compounded with the challenge of getting it right for several systems, many as yet unspecified and, therefore, projecting oneself far into the future, often widely across an organization or even several organizations. The approach Jan develops takes the engineering aspects very seriously as it dedicates a lot of attention to the assessment of the qualities of the architecture, and even driving some design aspects from these qualities.

Many challenges still lie before us in this rather young field of software architecture. One can easily say that there is a lot more we still don't know and can't achieve yet in this domain than what we do and can. This book is an important contribution, a rock placed on the cairn, that one cannot remove nor dismiss easily. I hope that you will enjoy it and learn from it as much as I have. It is a big book, and fortunately there are several paths through it. It is not a boring theoretical manual, as it remains hooked into reality, and is well illustrated with real-life examples – something not very easy to do in the architectural domain; all too often the examples presented on architecture are either too small or too trivial. After all, who needs a blueprint for a doghouse?

This book has also convinced me that we are slowly, but surely, coming to an era where we will assemble systems one component at a time rather than program them again and again, one line at a time, just changing programming language every five years.

Happy reading!

Philippe Kruchten, P. Eng.
Director of Process Development
Rational Software Canada, Vancouver, B.C.

Acknowledgements

This book is, to a large extent, the result of several years of research by the RISE research group at the University of Karlskrona/Ronneby. In particular, the following people (in alphabetic order) have contributed to the research on which this book is based: P.O. Bengtsson, Håkan Grahn, Jilles van Gurp, Lars Lundberg, Michael Mattsson, Peter Molin and Mikael Svahnberg. Several chapters are based on articles which I co-authored with them. Despite the fact that this book has one author, I have used 'we' rather than 'I' to recognize this fact. Together we have shared an exciting journey into the domain of software architectures and I look forward to our continued co-operation in the future!

Parts I and II of the book each contain three industrial cases which are used to illustrate the concepts examined. I would like to thank the following companies and their representatives involved in our projects (in order of their appearance in the book): Securitas Larm AB – Rutger Pålsson, EC-Gruppen – Anders Kambrin and Mogens Lundholm, Althin Medical – Lars-Olof Sandberg, Axis Communications – Torbjörn Söderberg, and Symbian – Peter Molin and Martin Tasker.

The following reviewers have also helped enormously to improve the contents of the book: Lodewijk Bergmans, Maarten Boasson, Robert Nord and Alan O'Callaghan. In particular, I owe a large debt to Lodewijk and Maarten who provided very detailed comments on Parts I and II, respectively.

I am indebted to Philippe Kruchten (Rational Software Corporation) for agreeing to write the Foreword, Juha Kuusela (Nokia Research) for the Nokia Mobile Phones example in Chapter 14, Claes Wohlin (Lund University) for our discussions on the notion of reliability and the staff at Pearson Education, in particular Alison Birtwell, for their help and support during the writing of the book.

Parts of the research reported on in this book have been funded by NUTEK, the Swedish National Board for Industrial and Technical Development (project Dnr. 1K1 p-97-09795), and the KK-foundation, Foundation for Knowledge and Competence Development (project Dnr. 1698-8/95 and Dnr. 2066/96).

Finally, I thank my wife, Petra, and my sons, David and Nathan, for their love, encouragement and support.

CHAPTER 1

Software architecture and product lines

Life as we know it is increasingly dependent on software. Over the decades, software has entered all domains that make up the necessary functions of Western civilization. Virtually any domain has incorporated software to achieve functionality that could not be achieved earlier. Some examples are electricity generation and distribution, telecommunications, modern cars, airplanes and logistic systems. Software is becoming more and more an integrated part of society and if, for some reason, some day all software should stop functioning, the effect on the Western world would be catastrophic. Although people working in technical disciplines have been aware of this fact for many years, it was not clear to the general public until the Y2K problem and its consequences were discussed openly in the media.

A reaction that surfaced in some discussion forums is that, since the failure of software can have such devastating effects, we should decrease our reliance on software by discouraging its use in various contexts. However, this position is fundamentally wrong on at least two counts. First, several experts consider software to be largely responsible for the last decade of economic growth in the world. For instance, software has allowed new organizational forms, such as business process reengineering and virtual organizations, which allow organizations to operate at efficiency levels that are an order of magnitude better than earlier models. In addition, all kinds of devices which increase efficiency would not be available without software – for example, mobile phones, although they contain mechanical and hardware parts, require software as a necessary part of their functioning.

The second reason why the aforementioned position in favour of decreasing the reliance on software is wrong is that this is a natural development. Since the Middle Ages, Western society, in particular, has been increasingly dependent on technology, and each new technology which has been incorporated by society has allowed for higher levels of integration and so efficiency. Although this negatively affects the robustness of society in that the failure of the technology would affect society as a whole, the advantages far outweigh the disadvantages.

However, the critical dependence of society on software does imply increasing responsibility for the software engineering community. With the increase of integration between systems which earlier were stand-alone, the effects of the failure of independent systems may spread well beyond the system itself. On the other hand, to further increase the benefits offered by software, the flexibility requirements of systems are also increasingly important. For instance, the dynamic incorporation of new components or new versions is currently regularly discussed in the domain of embedded systems, traditionally the most rigid of all.

Finally, since software is used in increasingly more systems, thus extending their functionality, and even replacing mechanical and hardware parts, the cost and lead time of software development have to be decreased drastically if we want to exploit the opportunities. Although several approaches have been devised and are under investigation, today as well as during the last decades, the reuse of existing software provides the most likely alternative for achieving these goals.

Reuse of software has been a goal in software engineering for almost as long as the existence of the field itself. Several research efforts have aimed at providing reuse. During the 1970s, the basics of module-based programming were defined and software engineers understood that modules could be used as reusable components in new systems. Modules, however, only provided 'as-is' reuse and adaptation of modules had to be done either by editing the code or by importing the component and changing those aspects unsuitable for the system at hand. During the 1980s, the object-oriented languages increased in popularity, because their proponents claimed increased reuse of object-oriented code through inheritance. Inheritance, different from importing or wrapping, provides a much more powerful means for adapting code.

This book is concerned with two very important developments in software engineering that have one common denominator: *software architecture*. The architecture of a software system is concerned with rationale and the top-level decomposition of the system into its main components and the design process leading to that decomposition. The first development that we discuss in Part I is concerned with the *design* of software architectures. Many of the system properties, in particular quality attributes, such as performance, reliability, maintainability and flexibility, are defined to a large extent by the architecture that is selected for the system. This indicates the importance of an explicit method for the design of software architectures, which is set out in Part I of the book.

Part II of the book is concerned with software product lines, i.e. a set of systems which share a common software architecture and set of reusable components. Software product lines are referred to by some authors as *software system families*. The core element in successful software product lines is the software architecture, which should maximize the benefits of the commonalities between the products in the family while providing sufficient variability for each family member. In Part II, we present all phases in adopting and evolving a software product-line approach, such as the development of the software architecture and components for the family, the instantiation of family members and the evolution of all these assets. Further, we examine a number of organizational models for family-based software development.

In the remainder of this chapter we first discuss the changing role of software in systems. Then, in Section 3, the notion of software architecture is introduced and the industrial and academic interpretations of this concept are compared. Section 4 is concerned with software components and, again, the predominant views in industry and academia are discussed. A reading guide to the book is presented in Section 5. The chapter is then concluded in Section 6.

1 The role of software

As we have noted in the introduction to this chapter, the role of software in systems is changing from a peripheral part to a core part to the primary element of successful systems. Technical systems and organizations increasingly often distinguish themselves in their ability to exploit the possibilities facilitated by software, rather than on the basis of other factors.

The development described above leads to two important consequences. The first is that software is constantly growing in size and complexity, especially with regard to the move from stand-alone to integrated systems, which requires software systems to be able to interact in ways not even thought of a decade ago, such as in Web-based access. This affects the complexity of the system, i.e. there are more interfaces to external systems, requiring more dependencies within the system, but it also affects the absolute size of the software system. As a consequence of this development, the functionality directly related to the application domain is often a relatively small part of the system as a whole. Other types of functionality, such as graphical user interfaces, communication protocols, DBMS-related code, etc. demand considerable development efforts to support the complete system functionality.

The second consequence is that increasingly often both for technical systems and for organizations, software defines the competitive edge. The competitive advantage of a company is no longer in its ability to construct or employ mechanical or hardware systems, but rather in its software. To exaggerate somewhat: everyone can build mechanical systems, almost everyone can build hardware, but very few organizations are able to develop and evolve software in a cost-effective manner and to employ it to its full extent. Two useful examples are Securitas Larm and the role of information systems in business process reengineered organizations.

Securitas Larm AB is one of the organizations that will be used as a case study throughout the book. The company develops and installs fire-alarm systems in a wide variety of contexts, ranging from homes to production sites consisting of multiple plants and hospitals. The major part of a fire-alarm system consists of the sensors and actuators physically located throughout buildings. The parts are not produced by Securitas Larm and can be bought by anyone. The reasons that customers select Securitas Larm for a fire-alarm system is because the company provides an advanced integration system that collects and processes data from all sensors and actuators and presents these in an advanced, graphical interface. In addition, the operator is able to perform many advanced operations and the system can be integrated easily with other building automation systems, such as intruder-alarm and passage-control systems. In essence, the success of the company has been achieved because it has applied software in more advanced ways than its competitors.

A second example is the notion of business process reengineering. Traditionally, organizations have been organized in a functional manner because specialization around function provided the main benefits. However, with the increasing need for agility and effectiveness and the development of information systems, it became possible to structure an organization along its primary business processes. Each process has an associated process team, or perhaps even an individual, that is responsible for the complete process. In most organizations which employ this approach, corporate information systems are not an optional but a necessary part. The process team is simply not able to perform its task without the presence of these information systems and even a temporary failure of these systems is very costly. The advantages of business process reengineered organizations is an enormous increase in flexibility and a decrease in operating cost, often in orders of magnitude. Organizations which dare to take the risk of converting to this organizational model have a considerable competitive edge over their competitors. However, it requires the necessary information systems to be in place.

1.1 Traditional software development

Having established the importance of software in a large variety of systems, it is relevant to characterize the development of software as it is performed in most organizations. In general, software development exhibits the following distinguishing features:

- **One system at a time.** Almost all software development is organized as projects, and the goal of a project is generally a software system that is delivered to a customer, be it internal or external.

- **Focus on delivery.** Part of the project and software-system fixation is a strong focus on delivering the software system before the specified deadline, and all decisions taken during the development process are taken based on the overwhelming priority of delivering on time.

- **Evolution not considered.** Due to the focus on delivering the system, there is little or no consideration of the fact that the system needs to be maintained and evolved for a potentially very long time. For instance, telecommunication and medical systems have lifetimes which are measured in decades.

The features which characterize traditional software development lead to a number of typical problems which pervade the whole of the software engineering industry, though notable exceptions exist:

- **Time and budget.** Despite the strong focus on project deadlines, only a small percentage of the software development projects actually succeed in delivering on time and within budget.

- **System quality.** Many software products have an associated reliability that would not be considered acceptable in any other engineering discipline. If systems are used in contexts where extreme reliability is required, the cost for achieving this quality attribute is substantial.

- **Maintenance cost.** Research has shown that up to 80 per cent of the total system cost is spent during maintenance. Thus, even though most projects are unable to deliver on time and within budget and this is considered to be a major problem by the software engineering community, we are only addressing a minor part of the total system cost.

- **Decreasing competitiveness.** A typical consequence of the high demand for software maintenance is decreasing competitiveness of the companies owning or maintaining the software systems. As more and more staff are busy with maintaining the existing systems, fewer and fewer are concerned with constructing new systems, and this results in a lack of innovative progress within the company and consequent opportunities for competitors.

1.2 Objectives

In the previous section, we have discussed the primary problems that the traditional approach to software development suffers from. Assuming that we agree on the problem analysis, the next activity is to explicitly define the objectives that we would like to achieve. These objectives are, in our opinion, fourfold.

- **Development cost.** The cost of software development for each software product must be reduced drastically. Otherwise, software may not continue to be pervasive in the way it has up to now.

- **Quality.** The quality of software in terms of reliability, but also regarding several other attributes such as maintainability and resource efficiency, is not satisfactory, especially compared to other engineering disciplines. Novel approaches are required to improve the overall quality of software systems against reasonable cost.

- **Time-to-market.** In many software development organizations, especially those producing products, the cost of developing a new system or new version of a system is not a primary issue. Rather the time-to-market or lead-time from defining the requirements until the distribution of the product is much more important. This factor is the primary competitive advantage for many companies and any approach that improves on this is highly relevant.

- **Maintenance cost.** Finally, maintenance cost, even more so than development cost, needs to be considerably reduced. Since we are interested in achieving improvements in orders of magnitude, it seems that a fundamentally different approach is required to achieve this.

In Section 2, we outline the approach which, in our experience, allows software development organizations to achieve these goals, but before we present this approach, we discuss a number of solution approaches that have been proposed traditionally.

1.3 Solution approaches

Already in the late 1960s, an approach to software system construction had been formulated (McIlroy, 1969), which would become the long-standing goal of the software engineering community, i.e. the reuse of existing software through componentization. Reuse of existing software has long been recognized as the most promising approach to achieving the objectives discussed in the previous section. If we are able to develop systems from existing components, development cost decreases, quality increases because the components have been tested in other contexts, time-to-market is shortened and maintenance cost is decreased because changes to the components benefit multiple systems.

Despite the advantages perceived initially, it seems that software reuse has failed to deliver on its promises. Most software development projects are started from scratch without (re-)using assets developed in earlier projects. However, the reuse of software has increased drastically over the decades, but not in the form expected initially by the proponents of software reuse. A wide range of software assets has become available and is used extensively by the software industry. Traditional examples include operating systems, database management systems and compilers, whereas more recent examples include graphical user interfaces, component interconnection standard implementations, Web servers and Web browsers. Although most software engineers do not perceive the use of these software assets as reuse, for each of these examples there was a time when the functionality captured by the component was part of the application code, rather than factored out as a separate component. For operating systems, we have to go back to the 1950s to find that point in time, at least for general-purpose systems, but graphical user interfaces came into existence as independent products during the early 1990s.

The reason why software engineers do not consider the use of these components to be software reuse is that they become part of the infrastructure that is present when developing software products. One can identify a typical lifecycle for such components. First, the functionality is just part of the application code of a software product. Then, at some point, the functionality is identified as a conceptual entity and starts to become modeled as a subsystem in the application code. The third stage is characterized by researchers at universities and research labs who start to develop prototype systems which generalize the functionality captured in a number of subsystems. Fourth, commercial companies, frequently start-ups, identify a marketing opportunity to turn the prototype system into a product. In the fifth phase, the product achieves market-wide acceptance and is used by the majority of software engineers as part of software development. The final step is where the product is incorporated into the infrastructure provided by, among others, companies such as Microsoft. At that point, the product disappears as an independent part of software applications, and is just assumed to be present.

The above examples of components which were developed into commercial products represent successful instances of software reuse. Although it may take considerable amounts of calendar time for a component to evolve through its lifecycle, it does happen for a sizeable collection of useful software products.

Where software reuse has not been as successful, in our opinion, is within software development organizations. Software development organizations generally develop software products in a particular domain. Although the functionality provided by the infrastructure is generally used without further consideration, the reuse of domain-specific software between products is often not established. This may be the result of the organizational structure, the culture among software engineers or lack of domain understanding, but reuse of software representing the core competence of the organization is often very hard. In Fig. 1, this situation is presented graphically. Whereas the use of external components is well established, reuse of software representing the core competence of the organization (the grey area) is often very hard to achieve.

The reason for this situation may be rooted in the over-simplified presentation of software reuse by some of its proponents. The first approaches to software reuse took the, somewhat naïve, 'LEGO-brick' perspective. Components could be plugged together much like children's LEGO bricks and the result would be a useful system. Although this perspective should be appreciated for its simplicity, it is not realistic for anything but toy problems.

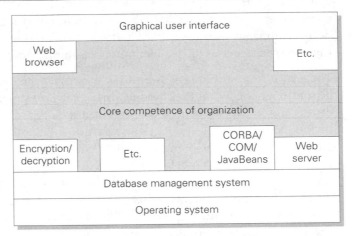

Figure 1 shows a layered diagram. From top to bottom:
- Graphical user interface (containing Web browser and Etc.)
- Core competence of organization
- Encryption/decryption, Etc., CORBA/COM/JavaBeans, Web server
- Database management system
- Operating system

Software product

Figure 1   External components in a software product

Since the first attempts at software reuse, the software reuse community has learned two important lessons, i.e. any successful software reuse programme must be planned, and it must take a top-down approach. To start with the first lesson, one can categorize software reuse into opportunistic and planned approaches. The opportunistic approach assumes that the software engineer selects and combines pieces of software that fit the current problem and adds them to the software product that he or she is working on. Second, the planned approach requires that the organization put explicit effort into developing reusable artefacts which provide the 'right' abstractions and the 'right' level of variability for the software product devised and evolved by the organization. The first lesson is that opportunistic reuse does not work in practice.

An alternative way to categorize software reuse is to bottom-up and top-down approaches. In the bottom-up approach, reusable components, once developed or mined, are added to a (possibly large) collection of assets. Software engineers search their way through these assets looking for suitable pieces. In the top-down approach, on the other hand, assets are developed and presented as parts fitting into a higher-level structure. Assets adhere to predefined provided and required interfaces. The second lesson is that bottom-up reuse does not work in practice.

These two lessons with respect to employing the reuse of software for achieving the objectives discussed in Section 1.2 form the basis of the concepts presented and discussed in this book.

2 This book

The position that we take in this book is that an explicit design and first-class representation of the *architecture* of software systems is the core element in achieving a paradigm shift away from the traditional approach. The approach we propose is twofold; it concerns explicit software architectural design and software product lines. In Fig. 2, the relation between these concepts and to our objectives is presented graphically.

We propose a method for *software architectural design* that includes explicit assessment of quality attributes and design decisions for achieving those quality attributes. The main advantage of the design method is that the software product built in accordance with the software architecture is much more likely to fulfil its quality requirements in addition to its functional requirements. This has secondary effects for the other objectives as well. For instance, the development cost will decrease because system redesigns and reimplementations due to, for example, unsatisfactory performance will require less frequent, since the architecture of the system has been assessed during the architectural design and optimized where necessary. The avoidance of redesign and reimplementation late in the development process improves, for obvious reasons, time-to-market. Finally, during the architectural design, there is an explicit assessment of and design for predicted changes in requirements. Therefore, assuming that the prediction of future needs is appropriate, the incorporation of these requirements will require less effort than in the traditional approach. The design of software architectures is discussed in Part I of this book.

In Part II of the book, we present our approach to the introduction and evolution of software product lines. A software product line consists of a product-line architecture and a set of reusable components that are designed for incorporation into

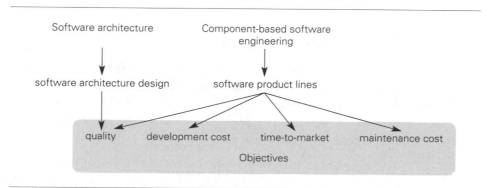

Figure 2   Primary concepts and their influence on main objectives

the product-line architecture. In addition, the product line consists of the software products that are developed using the mentioned reusable assets. Software product lines incorporate software architectural design as an important element, but are also based to a considerable extent on component-based software engineering.

Software product lines address all of the objectives discussed earlier. Quality is improved because the software architecture is explicitly designed and assessed and because the software components are used in multiple products. Development cost of individual software products is decreased since the product is built from the common core defined by the product-line architecture and the reusable components, rather than from scratch. This also leads to a decreased time-to-market for most systems. Finally, maintenance cost is decreased because the major part of each product is shared with other products. Thus, each new or changed requirement that has relevance for more than one product is implemented only once.

At the introduction of the software product line, however, a considerable amount of effort usually is spent on the initial design of the software product line and the shared software components. This has, obviously, negative effects on the objectives, especially on the time-to-market, but only during the conversion to a software product line. When discussing these negative aspects, it is important to consider the long-term consequences of the continued application of the traditional approach.

2.1 RISE research group

The pronoun 'we' has been used throughout this book, although it has only one author. The reason for this is that the concepts and ideas presented in this book have been developed, to a considerable extent, by members of the RISE (Research in Software Engineering) research group at the University of Karlskrona/Ronneby, Sweden. Most of these are or have been my Ph.D. students and the material presented in this book is based on several research articles that have been co-authored by them.

3 Software architecture

The architecture of a software system is concerned with the top-level decomposition of the system into its main components. One can identify three purposes of an explicit representation of the software architecture of a system, i.e. quality attribute assessment, stakeholder communication and software product lines. Below, the various types of use are discussed in more detail.

The software architecture allows for early assessment of and design for quality attributes of a software system. Consequently, the design of the software architecture is located early in the design process lifecycle: it is the first step after the specification of requirements and is followed by later phases such as detailed design and implementation.

Rather than presenting our own definition of software architecture, we will use the definition presented in Bass *et al.* (1998):

> *The software architecture of a program or computing system is the structure or structures of the system, which comprise software components, the externally visible properties of those components and the relationships among them.*

As mentioned earlier, the architecture of a software system is important since it constrains the quality attributes of the system. When selecting a certain software architecture, one imposes theoretical minimum and maximum values on the quality attributes of the system, e.g. performance, reliability or maintainability. Although various models for categorizing quality requirements exist, e.g. McCall (1994), for our purposes here, we categorize these into development quality requirements (e.g. maintainability) and operational quality requirements (e.g. performance and reliability).

Since the software architecture constrains the quality requirements, the driving quality attributes should have a major influence on the architecture of a software system, in some cases, even more than the functional requirements of the system.

A second reason for an explicitly specified software architecture is that it allows for communication between stakeholders early in the development process. In, for instance, Kazman *et al.* (1994), SAAM is presented as a method where all stakeholders of the software product are brought together to validate a software architecture and to discuss and agree upon trade-offs between stakeholders. The method is used as a toll-gate, i.e. the development process cannot proceed unless the stakeholders have accepted the software architecture as appropriate.

A third reason for an explicit software architecture definition is that it defines the shared components in a software product line. The product-line architecture is derived by software products to represent a software architecture for the specific product. Where the product-line architecture and the product architecture are equivalent, components shared within the product line can be used to fulfil those parts of the product requirements. These shared components are instantiated and configured to match the product-specific requirements. The remainder of the product requirements is implemented as product-specific code.

An important issue which we identified during our work projects with industry is that there is a considerable difference between the academic perception of software architecture and the industrial practice. It is important to explicitly discuss these differences because the concepts and techniques presented in this book are based on the *industrial* rather than the academic perspective. It is interesting to note that sometimes the problems which are identified as being the most important and difficult by industry are not identified or are viewed as non-problems by the academic world.

In Table 1, the academic and industrial interpretations of the notion of software architecture are presented. The main differences are related to the definition of architectures, the use of first-class connectors and the use of specialized languages. Research approaches often assumes an explicit definition of the architecture in terms of components and first-class connectors. Often, the use of an architectural description language (ADL) is suggested for verification of system functionality and interface matching and for automatic generation of applications. The practice in industry generally uses only a very high-level and conceptual understanding of the architecture. The experienced software engineers have gained an understanding of interaction between the architectural components and communicate this to novices through informal sketches and references to source code. First-class connectors are not used by our industrial partners, but sometimes *ad-hoc* solutions for run-time binding and adaptation between assets are implemented in ways that can be equated to connectors.

Table 1   **Academic versus industrial view of software architecture**

Academia	Industry
Architecture is explicitly defined.	Mostly conceptual understanding of architecture. Minimal explicit definition, often through notations.
Architecture consists of components and first-class connectors.	No explicit first-class connectors (sometimes *ad-hoc* solutions for run-time binding and glue code for adaptation between assets).
Architectural description languages (ADLs) explicitly describe architectures and are used to automatically generate applications.	Programming languages (e.g., C++) and script languages (e.g., Make) used to describe the configuration of the complete system.

The difference between the perspectives on software architecture by industry and research is very unfortunate as the logical consequence is that research effort in software engineering is spent on addressing issues that are not relevant from an industrial perspective. Many notational approaches, architecture description languages and component-connector models simply do not scale up to the size and complexity of industrial software systems where software architecture plays a role. An additional argument for industry not adopting research results is that they may not provide a sufficient return on investment, in other words the technology does not provide, in practice, the benefits claimed by the researchers who developed the technology. In our own research, we have tried to minimize the gap between our perspective and the state-of-practice by frequent co-operation projects and interaction with industrial partners. Our understanding of the concrete problems industry struggles with has guided us in the selection of research topic to address and the valuation of our ideas.

4 Software components

Especially in software product lines, software components are required to populate the product-line architecture. However, what is a software component? The definition that we use in this book is: *a software component is a unit of composition with explicitly specified provided, required and configuration interfaces and quality attributes.* Our use of the term software component is broader than the traditional definitions, e.g. in Weck *et al.* (1997) and (1998). In those publications, components are required to be subject to composition by third parties without adaptation.

To clarify our position, we discuss three levels of component reuse:

- **Component reuse over subsequent versions of a software product.** This is well–established practice in the software engineering industry and has been used for several decades.

- **Component reuse over product versions and various products.** Using a component in more than one product (or context) is the challenge which the software engineering community is currently addressing. Software product lines are concerned with achieving this type of reuse.

- **Component reuse over product versions, various products and different organizations.** As discussed in Section 1.3, this type of component reuse has succeeded in a number of domains, e.g. graphical user interfaces and Web servers. However, the software engineering profession does not have the maturity today to achieve this type of reuse outside well-established domains. Whereas much of the existing literature on software components addresses this type of component reuse, e.g. Szyperski (1997), the position we take in this book is that we first must learn to handle component reuse within organizations, i.e. software product lines, before we can achieve pervasive component reuse over organizational boundaries.

Our definition of software component addresses the second and third type of component reuse, whereas traditional component literature typically considers the third type. A second difference is that in our projects with industry we have frequently seen the use of object-oriented frameworks as components in software product lines. This is different from the traditional definition of object-oriented frameworks where a framework is used as a monolithic base for application development.

Also with respect to software components, one can identify a difference between the academic and industrial understanding of the concepts. In Table 2, an overview is presented comparing the two views. The academic view of assets is that of black-box entities with a narrow interface. The industrial practice shows that assets often are large pieces of software, such as object-oriented frameworks, with a complex internal structure and no explicit encapsulation boundary. Due to the lack of an encapsulation boundary, software engineers are able to access any internal entity in the asset, including the private entities. Even when only using interface entities, the use of assets is often very complex due to the sheer size of the code. Variations, from an academic perspective, are limited in number and are configured during instantiation by other black-box components. In practice, variation is implemented through configuration, but also through specialization or replacement of entities internal to the asset. In addition, multiple implementations of an asset may be available to deal with the required variability. Finally, academia has a vision of assets which implement standardized interfaces and are traded on component markets. In the attempt to achieve this, there is a focus on asset functionality and formal verification. In practice, almost all assets are developed internally and in the exceptional case where an asset is acquired externally, considerable adaptation of the asset internals is required. In addition, the quality attributes of the asset have at least equal priority, when compared to functionality.

Table 2   **Academic versus industrial view of reusable components**

Academia	Industry
Reusable assets are black-box components.	Assets are large pieces of software (sometimes more than 80 KLOC) with a complex internal structure and no enforced encapsulation boundary, e.g., object-oriented frameworks.
Assets have a narrow interface through a single point of access.	The asset interface is provided through entities, e.g., classes in the asset. These interface entities have no explicit differences to non-interface entities.
Assets have few and explicitly defined variation points which are configured during instantiation.	Variation is implemented through configuration and specialization or replacement of entities in the asset. Sometimes multiple implementations (versions) of an asset exist to cover variation requirements.
Assets implement standardized interfaces and can be traded on component markets.	Assets are primarily developed internally. Externally developed assets go through considerable (source code) adaptation to match the product-line architectural requirements.

| Focus is on asset functionality and on the formal verification of functionality. | Functionality and quality attributes (e.g. performance, reliability, code size, reusability, maintainability) have equal importance. |

5 Reading guide

Providing a reading guide to a book is not easy as it not only depends on the book's contents, but also on the interests of the reader. In this section, we first provide an overview of the organization of the book. Then, we present the most relevant chapters for four categories of readers. As mentioned earlier in this chapter and shown graphically in Fig. 3, this book consists of two parts. Part I is concerned with the design of software architectures and has an explicit focus on assessment of and design for quality attributes. Part II is concerned with software product lines. Since the design of the product-line architecture is of crucial importance for the success of a software product line, the first part of the book provides important concepts (especially used in Chapter 9) for the design of the product-line architecture. Otherwise, the parts are relatively independent.

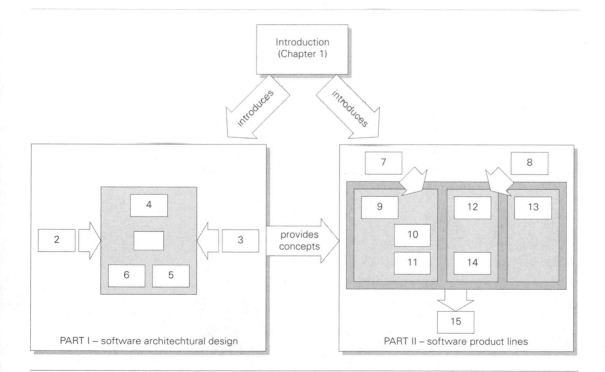

Figure 3   Organization of this book

Part I consists of five chapters (Fig. 4). Chapter 2 introduces our method of software architectural design and provides an overview of the three main phases. Chapter 3 contains three case studies which are used in the later chapters to illustrate the various concepts. Chapters 4, 5 and 6 examine the three main phases of the method, i.e. functionality-based architectural design, architecture assessment and architecture transformation. These chapters form the technical core of Part I (*see also* Fig. 4).

Part II, concerned with software product lines, is shown in Fig. 5, and is organized according to the main phases of the lifecycle of a software product line, i.e. the development of reusable assets, the usage of those assets in product development and the evolution of product-line assets. The first chapter of Part II provides an introduction to the notion of software product lines and contains a more detailed overview. Chapter 8 introduces three case studies of organizations that employ a product-line approach to software product development and evolution. These cases are used in the later chapters to illustrate the concepts presented.

Chapters 9, 10 and 11 discuss the first phase of the software product-line lifecycle, i.e. development of reusable assets. Chapter 9 examines the design of the software architecture for the product line. Chapter 10 looks at the development of traditional components and, among other concepts, those of provided, required and configuration interfaces. Chapter 11 introduces the notion of object-oriented frameworks and discusses their use as components in the software product line.

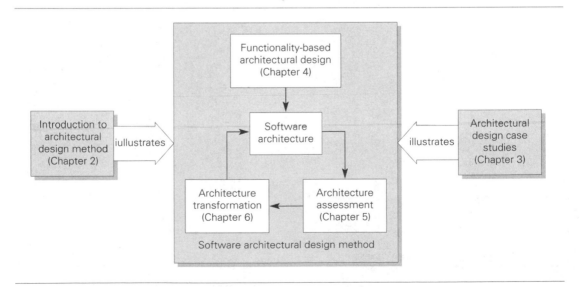

Figure 4   Organization of Part 1

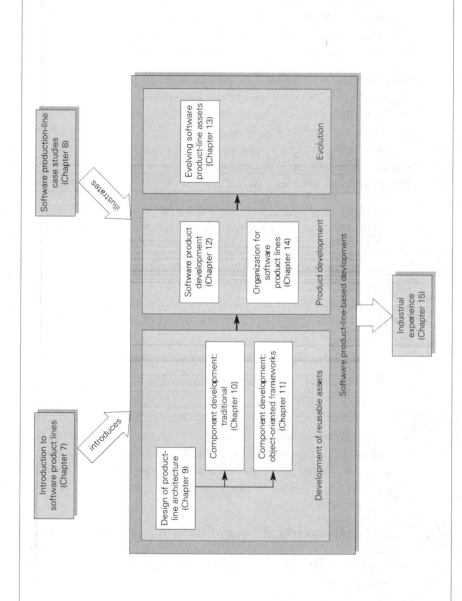

Figure 5   Organization of Part II

Chapter 12 examines the development of software products based on the shared assets developed as part of the software product line. Rather than software development in the traditional sense of the term, software product development is primarily concerned with deriving a software architecture for the product based on the product-line architecture and the instantiation of reusable components. The amount of product-specific software development is generally limited.

Chapter 13 is concerned with the third phase in the software product-line lifecycle, i.e. evolution of the software product-line assets. All assets, the reusable assets as well as the software products, evolve constantly due to the new requirements that originate from various sources. Since, among others, interdependencies exist between products in the family, evolution must be managed more carefully than in traditional software development. The main objective is to maintain an integrated product line while minimizing the limitations imposed on the evolution of individual products.

Chapter 14 is concerned with the organizational structures required for software product-line-based development. We present four organizational models and discuss their applicability and their advantages and disadvantages.

Finally, Chapter 15 discusses the industrial experiences collected from a number of software development organizations which employ product-line concepts in their software development. The experiences are organized according to business, organizational, process and technological issues and provide an insight into industrial practice, which should enable software engineering professionals and managers to deduce the likely effects on their own organizations.

Since not all readers have the same interests, we list below four approaches to reading this book or parts of it.

- **Just the basics.** For those readers who are only interested in the basic concepts presented in this book and who need to focus, for various reasons, on just a few chapters, we propose that you read Chapters 2 and 7. These contain the basic messages concerning software architectural design and software product lines that we seek to convey.

- **Software architectural design.** Part I can be read independently of Part II. For readers only interested in software architectural design and specifically assessment of and design for quality attributes, Chapters 2 to 6 provide the relevant information.

- **Software product lines.** Part II is largely independent of Part I, except for Chapter 9. The design of the product-line architecture is described in terms of the software product-line-specific extensions of the software architectural design method presented in Part I. However, if you are primarily interested in the overall concepts and processes associated with software product lines, Part II is sufficiently independent from Part I to be read separately.

■ **Theory only.** If you are mostly interested in the theoretical concepts presented in the book, then the chapters introducing the industrial cases, i.e. Chapters 3 and 8, can safely be skipped. This may, however, complicate an understanding of the examples presented in the other chapters.

6 Conclusion

Software plays an increasingly significant role in virtually all domains of Western civilization. This implies that the software engineering community must feel more and more responsible for the software that it develops. However, the widespread use of software also facilitates novel approaches which allow for efficiency levels not achievable with traditional technology. Software defines the competitive edge for a wide variety of products, from mobile phone to cars, and, for companies, the IT systems that support their operations.

The traditional approach to software development can be characterized as its focus on one system at a time, delivery deadlines and its lack of focus on evolution. This leads to some typical problems, i.e. failure in keeping to time and budget, unsatisfactory quality, excessive maintenance cost and, consequently, decreasing competitiveness. The analysis of this situation has caused us to formulate four primary objectives, basically to achieve drastic, order-of-magnitude, improvements in the aforementioned problem areas and in the time-to-market for software products.

As stated earlier, the position we take in this book is that an explicit design and first-class representation of the architecture of software systems is the core element in achieving a paradigm shift away from the traditional approach. Our approach is twofold: first, the explicit design of software architectures with a focus on assessment of and design for quality attributes; second, the use of software product lines consisting of a product-line architecture, a set of reusable components and the products that are constructed based on the shared architecture and components. The book is structured into two parts that present our approach to software architectural design and to software product lines, respectively.

We have discussed the notions of software architecture and software component in more detail and compared the academic and industrial perspectives on these concepts. Finally, we presented the overall structure of the book and discussed a few alternative ways of reading this book.

PART I

The design of software architectures

CHAPTER 2

Design of software architectures

In our experience, the most complex activity during application development is the transformation of a requirement specification into an architecture for the system. The later phases also are challenging activities, but, for instance, detailed design and implementation are better understood and more methodological and technological support is available to the software engineer. The process of architectural design is considerably less formalized and little methodological support is available. In industry, the design of a software architecture is often more like art or intuitive craftsmanship than explicit and well-defined engineering.

Although software systems have had architectures since the early days of computers, it has only during recent years been recognized as more important to explicitly specify, analyze and design software architectures. One important factor in this is the fact that quality requirements especially are heavily influenced by the architecture of the system. Architectural design is a typical multiple objective design activity where the software engineer has to balance the various requirements during the design process.

Design of a software architecture is not an independent activity, but is rather one step in the development and evolutionary process of software products. In Fig. 6 this is illustrated graphically. A typical product lifecycle consists of four iterative processes. The outermost one is concerned with the evolution of the requirements on a product during its maturation. Marketing departments, customers and technological advances, identified by engineers, define new and changed requirements on a software product. Thus, the outer iterative process represents the evolution of a product through subsequent versions.

The next process cycle is concerned with iterative product development. For instance, when building one-of-a-kind systems, the customer may not be able to specify exactly what the requirements on the system are. Instead, these are discovered during an iterative development process. Also, when developing mass-market

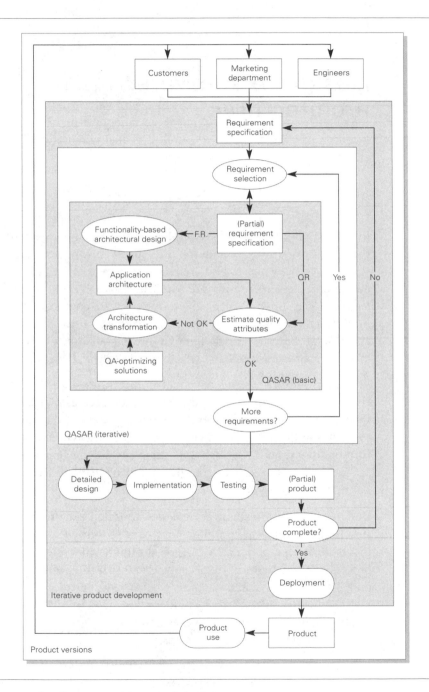

Figure 6   Context of software architectural design

products, the organization may develop several prototypes including part of the product requirements before finalizing the product development and entering the deployment phase.

The two most inner iterative processes encompass the method discussed in this part of the book. The *quality attribute-oriented software architecture design method* consists of two iterative processes: the inner iteration where the software architecture is designed, assessed and transformed for its quality requirements; and an outer iteration where requirement selection is performed.

The outer design method starts from the core product requirements that have highest priority and enters the inner iteration with a subset of the requirements. Based on this subset, a first version of the architecture is developed. The outer iteration is repeated with an extended subset of the requirements until all the requirements have been included for architectural design.

The inner iteration assumes an available set of requirements based on which a software architecture is developed. The focus of the inner iteration is on assessment of and transformation for quality attributes. The design method provides support for an objective, rational design process, balancing and optimizing especially the quality requirements. The method iteratively assesses the degree up to which the architecture supports each quality requirement and improves the architecture using transformations until all quality requirements are fulfilled. This method complements traditional design methods in that it focuses on quality attributes, whereas traditionally the functionality is emphasized.

The basic design method consists of three phases, i.e. functionality-based architectural design, architecture evaluation and architecture transformation. In this chapter, we give a brief overview over the method, and Chapters 4, 5 and 6 describe the method phases in detail.

The software architecture design method does not only define the processes associated with the design of software architectures, but also a number of artefacts that document the architecture and the design decisions that led to the architecture. The artefacts that are developed and evolved are shown in Fig. 7.

The artefacts are divided into two main categories, i.e. the requirement specification and the software architecture. The requirement specification is divided into functional requirements and quality requirements. Functional requirements have an associated priority: typically required, preferred or optional. The quality requirements have an associated scenario profile. The software architecture consists of four artefacts, i.e. the system context, the archetypes, the architectural structure and the design decisions. The system context defines the interfaces the software system has

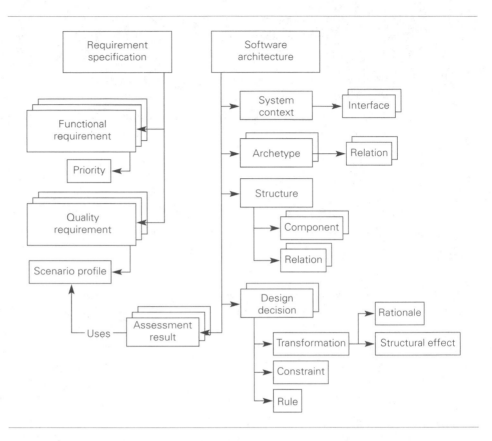

Figure 7   Software architectural design artefacts

to its context. The archetypes represent the core abstractions around which the system is built. The structure represents the decomposition of the architecture into its main components and the relations between those components. Three types of design decisions exist, i.e. transformations, constraints and rules. Each design decision consists of a rationale and a structural effect. In the coming chapters, more detailed specifications of the artefacts will be provided.

The remainder of this chapter is organized as follows. In the next section, we define our terminology for requirements, in particular quality requirements, and describe the notion of profiles and their use in the specification of quality requirements. Section 2 provides a rationale for software architectural design and handling quality requirements explicitly and presents a brief overview of the three main phases in the method. The subsequent sections describe these phases and the chapter is concluded in Section 6.

1 Requirements

Requirement engineering has been studied extensively, e.g. Kotonya and Sommerville (1997) and McCall (1994), and it is not the aim of this book to address the process of identifying and specifying requirements. Instead, the requirement specification is used as an input for architectural design. There is, however, one aspect to requirement engineering that is relevant for software architectural design: the specification of quality requirements. Our experience is that most requirement specifications either do not specify the quality attributes at all, or specify them very unclearly and, consequently, they are not measurable. In the remainder of this section, we first establish a terminology for the various requirement concepts. Subsequently, in Section 1.2 we discuss the specification of quality requirements and the use of, so-called, profiles for this purpose.

1.1 Terminology

In this section we define the terminology related to requirements that we will use throughout the remainder of this book. *System requirements* are defined as the top-level requirement set consisting of software, hardware and mechanical requirements. In this book, we focus on fulfilling the software requirements and ignore other types of requirements. Software requirements can be defined as consisting of *functional requirements* and *quality requirements* (also referred to as system properties). The functional requirements are related to the domain-related functionality of the application. Typically, a functional requirement is implemented by a subsystem or a group of components, i.e. functional requirements are traceable in the architecture. Quality requirements can be categorized as either *development* or *operational* quality requirements. Development quality requirements are qualities of the system that are relevant from a software engineering perspective, e.g. maintainability, reusability, flexibility and demonstrability. Operational quality requirements are qualities of the system in operation, e.g. performance, reliability, robustness and fault-tolerance. Unlike functional requirements, quality requirements can generally not be pinpointed to a particular part of the application but are a property of the application as a whole.

1.2 Quality attributes and profiles

As mentioned in the introduction to this section, our experience is that quality requirements such as performance and maintainability are generally specified rather weakly in industrial requirement specifications. In some of our architectural design projects with industry, the initial requirement specification contained statements such as 'The maintainability of the system should be as good as possible' and 'The performance should be satisfactory for an average user'. Such subjective statements, though well intended, are totally useless for the evaluation of software architectures. Several authors have identified this problem as well. For example, Gilb (1988) discusses the quantitative specification of quality requirements and presents useful examples.

Some research communities, e.g. performance (Smith, 1990), real-time (Liu and Ha, 1995) and reliability (Lyu, 1996), have spent considerable effort on the specification of their particular quality requirement, but the software development industry as a whole has not adopted these techniques. One of the reasons may be that these techniques tend to be rather elaborate and require considerable effort to complete. Since, within an engineering discipline, each activity is a balance of investment and return, these techniques may not have provided a sufficient return on investment, from the perspective of industrial software engineers.

However, when one intends to treat the architecture of a software system that one is working on explicitly in order be able to predict early the quality attributes of the system, it is also necessary to specify quality requirements in sufficient detail. One common characteristic for quality requirements is that stating a required level without an associated context is meaningless. For instance, the statements 'Performance = 200' and 'Maintainability = 0.8' are meaningless.

One common denominator of most specification techniques is that some form of *profile* is used as part of the specification. A profile is a set of scenarios, generally with some relative importance associated with each scenario. The profile used most often in object-oriented software development is the *usage profile*, i.e. a set of usage scenarios that describe typical uses for the system. The usage profile can be used as the basis for specifying a number of, primarily operational, quality requirements, such as performance and reliability. However, for other quality attributes, other profiles are used. For example, for specifying safety we have used *hazard scenarios* and for maintainability we have used *change scenarios*.

Based on our experience, we believe that it is necessary to specify the relevant profiles for the software quality requirements that are to be considered explicitly in the architectural design process. Using the profile, one can make a more precise specification of the requirement for a quality attribute. For example, the required performance of the system can be specified using the usage profile by specifying the relative frequency and the total number of scenarios per time unit.

In Chapter 5, the specification and usage of profiles are discussed in more detail and several examples are presented.

2 Architectural design method: overview

In the software industry, our experience is that quality requirements are generally dealt with by a rather informal process during architectural design. Conventional object-oriented design methods, e.g. Booch (1994), Jacobson *et al.* (1992), Rumbaugh *et al.* (1991), tend to focus on achieving the required system functionality and pay only limited attention to quality requirements. Implicitly, these methods assume that using an object-oriented modeling approach will automatically lead to reusable and flexible systems, thus one could state that the maintainability and reusability requirements are incorporated to some extent. However, only these quality attributes are considered (rather implicitly).

Software engineers in industry, lacking support for the early evaluation of quality requirements, develop systems using the available design methods and measure the quality attributes of the system once it has been built. There are at least two problems with this approach. First, not all quality attributes can be measured before the system is put in operation. For instance, to measure maintainability of a system generally requires up to several years before one can make generalizable statements about the required effort for implementing new requirements. Second, even if one is able to measure a quality attribute once the system has been built, e.g. performance, the effort required to rework the system if it does not fulfil the requirements is generally rather costly. Often, the cost of reworking a system to incorporate the quality requirements after it has been built is one or several orders of magnitude higher than performing the evaluation and transformation of the system design early in the development. The focus on software architectural design currently experienced in the software engineering community can be explained by the above arguments, i.e. explicit evaluation of the architecture of software systems with respect to the quality requirements will minimize the risk of building a system that fails to meet its quality requirements and consequently decrease the cost of system development.

At this point it is relevant to note that many exceptions to the observation exist. In particular, companies that have been working in a particular domain for several years, such as embedded systems, often have remarkable success rates in achieving the quality requirements on their systems. The main explanation for this is that software architects at those companies often have a considerable understanding of the possibilities and obstacles of particular architectural designs in their domain. Since the system architects often are experienced in building systems in the domain, experience helps them to minimize system redesign. However, although this is one of the most successful means for companies to build up a competitive advantage, one can identify at least three disadvantages. First, the design expertise is generally *tacit knowledge*. Thus when the experienced software architect leaves the company, so does the design expertise. In addition, when the organization enters a new domain, the experience base has to be created again through trial and error. Second, since the expertise used as a basis for the design decisions is implicit and design is, to some extent, performed based on 'gut feeling', it is virtually impossible to perform critical evaluations of these decisions. This leads to the situation where a software architect may employ design solutions for addressing a particular issue; but this does not solve that particular problem. We have identified such situations in several industrial organizations, e.g. Häggander *et al.* (1999). In addition, the software engineering community does not benefit from the generated design expertise since it is not made explicit and evaluated. Finally, it complicates the education of software architects at universities since there is no body of knowledge available that can be taught. Consequently, the students have to obtain this by hands-on design experience, hopefully under the guidance of a mentor.

The observations discussed above are by no means novel. Computer science and software engineering research have spent considerable effort on several of the quality requirements. This has led to the formation of several 'quality attribute oriented' research communities that focus on one quality attribute and try to maximize the systems they build with respect to their particular quality attribute. Examples of such communities are those working on real-time systems, high-performance systems, reusable systems and, more recently, maintainable systems. Several of these communities have proposed their own design methods and evaluation techniques. For instance, in real-time systems (Liu and Ha, 1995), in high-performance computing (Smith, 1990) and in reusable systems (Poulin, 1997).

Each of the research communities addresses relevant and important aspects of software systems and to achieve progress in hard problems, one needs to focus and ignore issues outside the focus. However, there is a major problem in this development, namely that, since each research community has a tendency to study a single system quality requirement, it consequently does not address the composition of its solutions with the solutions proposed by research communities studying different quality requirements. Concrete industrial software systems never have only a single quality requirement to fulfil, but generally have to achieve a multiplicity of these requirements. For instance, most real-time systems should be reusable and maintainable to achieve cost-effective operation and usage, whereas fault-tolerant systems also need to fulfil other requirements, such as timeliness and maintainability. No pure real-time, fault-tolerant, high-performance or reusable computing systems exist, even though most research literature within the respective research communities tends to present systems as being such archetypical entities. All realistic, practical computing systems have to fulfil multiple quality requirements.

One may wonder why the above is a problem: if the quality-attribute oriented research communities develop their solutions and guidelines, why not just use the solutions and guidelines in the system currently under design? The answer is that the solutions and guidelines provided for fulfilling the quality requirements tend to be in conflict, i.e. using a solution for improving one quality attribute will generally affect other quality attributes negatively. For example, reusability and performance are generally considered to be contradicting, as are with fault-tolerance and real-time computing. As a consequence, a customer for a system with extreme performance requirements, must accept that the maintainability of the system will be very low, i.e. it is very costly to incorporate new requirements. This observation has been implicitly accepted by the software engineering community, but very few examples of approaches to explicitly handle the conflicts in quality requirements during architectural design exist. Consequently, lacking a supporting method, software engineers in industry design software architectures in an *ad-hoc*, intuitive, experience-based manner, with the consequent risk of unfulfilled system properties.

2.1 Method

As we identified in the previous section, there is a lack of software design methods which explicitly address and balance the quality attributes of a system. In this part of the book, we present our approach to addressing the identified problems, including an architectural design method that incorporates explicit evaluation of and design for quality requirements. The developed approach is part of our research efforts in the domain of software architecture. We report on our experiences with software architectural design, the generalizations we made based on our experiences and the validation of the generalizations that we performed. The software architectural design method presented in this part of the book is primarily based on the design of three software architectures in the embedded systems domain, i.e. fire-alarm systems (Molin and Ohlsson, 1998), measurement systems (Bosch, 1999a) and dialysis systems (Bengtsson and Bosch, 1999a). Members of our research group have been involved in the design of these systems, either while working in industry or as part of a joint research project between our research group and one or more industrial partners. Since these systems will be used extensively as examples, we present the systems and their domains in more detail in Chapter 3.

The architectural design process can be viewed as a function taking a requirement specification that is taken as an input to the method and an architectural design that is generated as output. However, this function is not an automated process and considerable effort and creativity from the involved software architects is required. The software architecture is used for the subsequent phases, i.e. detailed design, implementation and evolution. In Fig. 8, the main steps in the method are presented

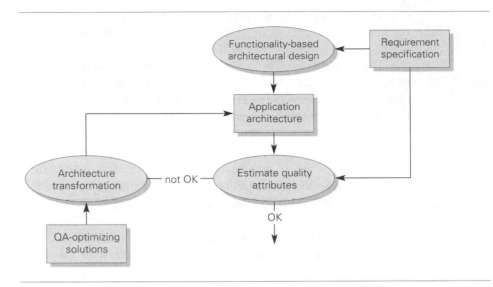

Figure 8   Outline of the core software architecture design method

graphically. The design process starts with a design of the software architecture based on the functional requirements specified in the requirement specification. Although software engineers generally will not design a system less reliable or reusable, the quality requirements are not explicitly addressed at this stage. The result is a first version of the application architectural design. This design is evaluated with respect to the quality requirements. Each quality attribute is given an estimated value, using a qualitative or quantitative assessment technique. The estimated quality attribute values are compared to the values in the requirements specification. If all estimates are as good or better than required, the architectural design process is finished. Otherwise, the second stage is entered: architecture transformation. During this stage, the architecture is improved by selecting appropriate quality attribute-optimizing transformations. Each set of transformations (one or more) results in a new version of the architectural design. This design is again evaluated and the same process is repeated, if necessary, until all quality requirements are fulfilled or until the software engineer decides that no feasible solution exists. In that case, the software architect needs to renegotiate the requirements with the customer. The transformations, i.e. quality attribute-optimizing solutions, generally improve one or some quality attributes while they affect others negatively.

In the remainder of this chapter, the three main steps in the method, i.e. functionality-based architectural design, evaluation and assessment of software architectures and the transformation of software architectures, are described in more detail.

3 Functionality-based architectural design

The first step during software architectural, design is to develop a software architecture based on the functional requirements. Based on the requirement specification, the top-level, i.e. architectural, design of the system is performed. The main issue during this phase is to identify the core abstractions, i.e., the archetypes, based on which the system is structured. Although these abstractions are modeled as objects, our experience is that these objects are not found immediately in the application domain. Instead, they are the result of a creative design process which, after analyzing the various domain entities, abstracts the most relevant properties and models them as architectural entities. Once the abstractions are identified, the interactions between them are defined in more detail.

The process of identifying the entities that make up the architecture is different from, for instance, traditional object-oriented design methods. Those methods start by modeling the entities present in the domain and organizing these in inheritance hierarchies, i.e. a bottom-up approach. Our experience is that during architectural design it is not feasible to start bottom-up since that would require dealing with the details of the system. Instead one needs to work from the top down.

The identification of architectural entities is related to domain analysis methods (Prieto-Díaz and Arango, 1991; Schäfer et al., 1994). However, unlike these approaches, our experience is that the entities resulting from architectural design are generally not found in the domain. A second difference between architectural design and domain analysis is that the architecture of a system generally covers multiple domains.

The assumption underlying our approach is that an architectural design based only on the functional requirements does not preclude the use of transformations for optimizing quality requirements. Some researchers believe that an architectural design cannot be separated in the way proposed in this book. We agree that no pure separation can be achieved, i.e. an architectural design based on functional requirements only will still have values for its quality attributes. However, we believe that an objective and repeatable architectural design method must be organized according to our principles since it is unlikely that an architectural design process does not require iterations to optimize the architecture. Since an architecture based on functional requirements only is more general, it can be reused as input for systems in the same domain but with different quality requirements. On the other hand, it is unlikely that a software architecture that fulfils a particular set of quality requirements will be applicable in a domain with different functional requirements.

Chapter 4 discusses the design of software architectures based on their functional requirements in more detail.

4 Assessing quality attributes

One of the core features of the design method is that the quality attributes of a system or application architecture are explicitly evaluated during architectural design. Traditionally, software engineers implement the system and then measure the actual values for the quality system properties. The obvious disadvantage is that potentially large amounts of resources have been put into building a system that does not fulfil its quality requirements and numerous examples exist to illustrate this point. Being able to estimate the quality attributes of the system during early development stages is important to avoid such mishaps.

The question is how to measure system properties based on an abstract specification such as an architectural design. For obvious reasons it is not possible to measure the quality attributes of the final system based on the architectural design. Instead, the goal is to evaluate the potential of the designed architecture to reach the required levels for its quality requirements. For example, some architectural styles, e.g. layered architectures, are less suitable for systems where performance is a major issue, even though the flexibility of this style is relatively high.

Four different approaches for assessing quality requirements have been identified: scenarios, simulation, mathematical modeling and objective reasoning. For each quality requirement, the engineer can select the most suitable approach for evaluation. In the subsequent sections, each approach is described in more detail.

4.1 Scenario-based evaluation

To assess a particular quality attribute, a set of scenarios is developed that concretizes the actual meaning of the requirement. For instance, the maintainability requirement may be specified by a *change profile* that captures typical changes in requirements, underlying hardware, etc. The profile can then be used to evaluate the effort required to adapt the architecture to the new situation. Another example is robustness where the architecture can be evaluated with respect to the effects of invalid input or exceptional circumstances.

The effectiveness of the scenario-based approach is largely dependent on the representativeness of the scenarios. If the scenarios form accurate samples, the evaluation will also provide an accurate result. Object-oriented design methods use scenarios to specify the intended system behaviour, e.g. use-cases (Jacobson *et al.*, 1992) and scenarios (Wilson and Wilson, 1993). For architectural design, however, two sets of scenarios should be developed, i.e. one for design and one for evaluation purposes. Once a version of the architecture is ready for evaluation, the software engineer can 'run' the scenarios for the architecture and evaluate the results. For instance, if most of the change scenarios require considerable reorganizations of the architecture, one can conclude that the maintainability of the architecture is low.

In our experience, scenario-based assessment is particularly useful for development quality attributes. Quality attributes such as maintainability can be expressed very naturally through change scenarios. In Bengtsson and Bosch (1999b), we present a scenario-based technique which we developed for predicting maintainability based on the software architecture.

4.2 Simulation

Simulation of the architecture using an implementation of the application architecture provides a second approach for estimating quality attributes. The main components of the architecture are implemented and other components are simulated resulting in an executable system. The context in which the system is supposed to execute could also be simulated at a suitable abstraction level. This implementation can then be used for simulating application behaviour under various circumstances.

Simulation of the architectural design is, obviously, not only useful for quality attribute assessment, but also for evaluating the functional aspects of the design. Building a simulation requires the engineer to define the behaviour and interactions of the architectural entities very precisely, which may uncover inconsistencies in the design earlier than traditional approaches.

Once a simulation is available, one can execute execution sequences to assess quality attributes. Robustness, for example, can be evaluated by generating or simulating faulty input to the system or by inserting faults in the connections between architecture entities.

Another frequently used approach to perform assessment of a software architecture is through *prototyping*. Distinct from simulation where the complete software architecture is implemented at a high level of abstraction and is executed in simulated context, prototyping implements a part of the software architecture and executes that part in the actual, intended context of the system. An important difference is that prototyping requires more input from the developing and the availability of the hardware and other parts that make up the context of the software system.

Simulation complements the scenario-based approach in that simulation is particularly useful for evaluating operational quality attributes, such as performance, by actually executing the architecture implementation, whereas scenarios are more suited for evaluating development quality attributes, such as maintainability and flexibility. Nevertheless, the implementation of the architecture in the simulation can be used to evaluate, for instance, maintainability, by changing the implementation according to change scenarios and measuring the required effort.

4.3 Mathematical modeling

Various research communities, such as high-performance computing (Smith, 1990), reliable systems, real-time systems (Liu and Ha, 1995), etc., have developed mathematical models that can be used to evaluate especially operational quality attributes. Different from the other approaches, the mathematical models allow for static evaluation of architectural design models. For example, performance modeling is used while engineering high-performance computing systems to evaluate different application structures in order to maximize throughput.

In our experience, mathematical modeling is primarily an alternative to simulation since both approaches are primarily suitable for assessing operational quality attributes. However, the approaches can also be combined. For instance, performance modeling can be used to estimate the computational requirements of the individual components in the architecture. These results can then be used in the simulation to estimate the computational requirements of different execution sequences in the architecture. Additional examples include checks for potential deadlocks and other behavioural aspects.

4.4 Experience-based assessment

A fourth approach to assessing quality attributes is through experience-based assessment based on earlier experiences and logical argumentation. Experienced software engineers often have valuable insights that may prove extremely helpful in avoiding bad design decisions. Although some of these experiences are based on anecdotal evidence, most can often be justified by a logical line of reasoning.

This approach is different from the other approaches in that the evaluation process is less explicit and more based on subjective factors such as intuition and experience. The value of this approach, however, should not be underestimated. Most software architects we have worked with had well-developed intuitions about 'good' and 'bad' designs. Their analysis of problems often started with the 'feeling' that something was wrong. Based on that, an objective argumentation was constructed either based on one of the aforementioned approaches or on logical reasoning. In addition, this approach may form the basis for the other evaluation approaches. For example, an experienced software engineer may identify a maintainability problem in the architecture and, to convince others, define a number of scenarios that illustrate this.

5 Architecture transformation

Once the quality attributes of an architecture have been assessed, the estimated values are compared to the requirements specification. If one or more of the quality requirements are not satisfied, the architecture has to be changed to cover these requirements also. This requires the software engineer to analyze the architecture and to decide why the property of the architecture is inhibited. Often, the evaluation itself generates hints as to what parts or underlying design decisions cause low scores.

Assessment of the quality attributes is performed assuming a certain context, consisting of certain subsystems, e.g. databases or GUI systems and one or more operating systems and hardware platforms. Whenever a quality attribute is not fulfilled, one may decide either to make changes to the presumed context of the system architecture or to make changes to the architecture itself. In the architectural design method discussed in this part of the book, changes to the architecture are performed as *architecture transformations*. Each transformation leads to a new version of the architecture that has the same functionality, but different values for its properties.

The consequence of architecture transformations is that most transformations affect more than one property of the architecture, generally some properties positively and others in a negative way. For instance, the *Strategy* design pattern (Gamma *et al.*, 1994) increases the flexibility of a class with respect to replacing one aspect of its behaviour. However, performance is often reduced since instances of the class have to invoke another object (the instance of the strategy class) for certain parts of their behaviour. However, in the general case, the positive effect of increased flexibility considerably outweighs the minor performance impact.

Four categories of architecture transformations have been identified, organized in decreasing impact on the architecture, i.e. imposing an architectural style, imposing an architectural pattern, applying a design pattern and converting quality requirements to functionality. One transformation does not necessarily address a quality requirement completely. Two or more transformations might be necessary. In the sections below, each category is discussed in more detail.

5.1 Impose architectural style

Shaw and Garlan (1996) and Buschmann *et al.* (1996) present several architectural styles (or patterns) that improve the possibilities for certain quality attributes for the system on which the style is imposed and are less supportive for other quality attributes. Certain styles, e.g. the layered architectural style, increase the flexibility of the system by defining several levels of abstraction, but generally decrease the performance of the resulting system. With each architectural style, a fitness for each system property is associated. The most appropriate style for a system depends primarily on its quality requirements. Transforming an architecture by imposing an architectural style results in a complete reorganization of the architecture.

Although architectural styles can be merged to some extent, more often a different style is used in a subsystem than at the system level, provided that the subsystem acts as a correct component at the system level. However, if, during design iteration, a second architectural style is selected for a part of the system, it is necessary to make sure that the constraints of the two styles do not conflict with each other.

In our approach, we explicitly distinguish between the components that are used to fulfil the functional requirements and the software architecture of the system that is used to fulfil the quality requirements. In practice, the distinction is generally not as explicit, i.e. the implementation of a component also influences most quality attributes, such as reliability, robustness and performance.

5.2 Impose architectural pattern

A second category of transformations is the use of *architectural patterns*. (Our use of the term 'architectural pattern' is different from that in Buschmann *et al.* (1996); the differences are discussed in Chapter 6.) An architectural pattern is different from an architectural style in that it is not predominant and can be merged with architectural styles without problems. It is also different from a design pattern since it affects the complete architecture, or at least the larger part of it. Architectural patterns generally impose a *rule* (Perry and Wolf, 1992) on the architecture that specifies how the system will deal with one aspect of its functionality.

Architectural patterns generally deal with some aspect of the system's behaviour that is not in the application domain, but which addresses some of the supporting domains, for example the way the system deals with concurrency, persistence, fault-tolerance or distribution. If the software architect decides to implement concurrency using an application-level scheduler that invokes entities that need some active behaviour, then this decision puts requirements on most architectural entities since each entity needs to support a particular interface and needs to limit its execution time to a small and predictable period. Architectural patterns are generally orthogonal to each other and to architectural styles, but they affect most entities in the architecture. Some authors, for example Kruchten (1999), refer to this as an architectural mechanism.

5.3 Apply design pattern

The third class of transformations is the application of a design pattern. This is generally a less dramatic transformation than the former two categories. For instance, an *abstract factory* pattern (Gamma *et al.*, 1994) might be introduced to abstract the object instantiation process. The abstract factory pattern increases maintainability, flexibility and extensibility of the system since it encapsulates the actual class type(s) that are instantiated, but decreases the efficiency of creating new instances due to the additional computation, thereby reducing performance. Different from imposing an architectural style, causing the complete architecture to be reorganized, the application of a design pattern generally affects only a limited number of classes in the architecture. In addition, a class can generally be involved in multiple design patterns without creating inconsistencies.

5.4 Convert quality requirements to functionality

A fourth type of transformation is the conversion of a quality requirement into a functional solution that consequently extends the architecture with functionality not related to the problem domain but used to fulfil the requirement. Exception handling is a well-known example that adds functionality to a component to increase the fault tolerance of the component.

This type of transformation is different from the first three in that it primarily adds functional entities to the architecture which fulfil the particular quality requirement. The existing structure of the software architecture is affected only minimally and instead primarily adds functional entities. The transformations discussed earlier are primarily focused on reorganizing functionality represented by the existing entities.

5.5 Distribute requirements

The final activity of a transformation iteration deals with quality requirements using the *divide-and-conquer* principle: a quality requirement at the system level is distributed to the subsystems or components that make up the system. Thus, a quality requirement X is distributed over the n components that make up the system by assigning a quality requirement x_i to each component c_i such that $X = x_1 + ... + x_n$.

A second approach to the distribution of requirements is to divide the quality requirement into two or more functionality-related quality requirements. For example, in a distributed system, fault tolerance can be divided into fault-tolerant computation and fault-tolerant communication.

The distributing of requirements does not change the structure or functionality of the software architecture that is under design, but it facilitates the breaking down of quality requirements and their assignment to lower-level components. This process is analogous to the process of decomposition of functional requirements during conventional system design.

6   Concluding remarks

In this chapter, we have introduced the architectural design method which is the focus of this part of the book. We started by providing a terminology for requirements in general and quality requirements in particular. Based on that discussion, we introduced the notion of *profiles* and their relevance for the definition of quality requirements. In Section 2, we provided an introduction to software architecture and presented an overview of the architectural design method. In the subsequent sections, we presented an overview of the three main phases in the method, i.e. functionality-based architectural design, architectural evaluation and architecture transformation.

In the following chapters, first three systems are introduced that are used as examples in the subsequent chapters. Then, each of the main phases of the method is discussed in a separate chapter.

7   Further reading

The notion of software architecture is discussed by a number of authors. One of the first books was published by Shaw and Garlan (1996). The book primarily discusses architectural styles, architectural description languages and tools. Buschmann *et al.* (1996) discuss a number of architectural styles ('patterns' in their terminology), design patterns and idioms. Bass *et al.* (1998) provide an overview of the software architectural work performed at the Software Engineering Institute. Hofmeister *et al.* (1999) discuss the design of software architectures and the subsequent system construction based on the architecture.

In our research, we have studied software architectural design extensively. Examples include Bosch and Molin (1999), Bengtsson and Bosch (1999b) and Bosch (1999b).

CHAPTER 3

Software architectural design: case studies

Software architectural design is, similar to most engineering and design disciplines, very hard to discuss at an abstract level. Instead, one needs concrete examples of relevant systems to discuss alternative design solutions and ways of argumentation. In this chapter, we present three examples that will be used throughout this part of the book. All three systems are in the embedded systems domain, but are rather diverse. These systems are not just examples for illustrative purposes: they have been the subject of architectural design projects with various industrial partners and our research group.

1 Fire-alarm systems

The description of fire-alarm systems presented here is based on the work that was performed by TeleLarm AB[1], a Swedish security company. The work originally started in 1992 with the aim of taking advantage of the benefits of object-oriented technology. Concretely, the aim of the project was to develop an object-oriented framework that would be able to handle the large variety of fire-alarm products ranging from small home and office installations to large, complex systems servicing industrial multi-building sites. The first version of the framework was completed in 1994 and, on average, 500 systems per year have been installed at client sites. The experiences from the use of the framework have been very positive in that it has delivered on the two main promises of software reuse: increased quality and decreased development effort. For example, not a single fault has been detected in the framework after beta-testing. Secondly, the software has proved to be easy to modify; a number of changes have been implemented with considerably less effort than expected based on earlier experience.

---

1 During the process of writing this book, the development department at Securitas Larm AB that was involved in the case study was sold to Matsushita, and is now Matsushita Electric Works Fire and Security Technology AB.

During 1996, a second version of the framework was developed and deployed. This version primarily improved the modularization in the framework, extended the domain covered by the framework and improved some dimensions of variability.

The notion of object-oriented frameworks was introduced in Chapter 1 and is important in the design of object-oriented software architectures as well as in the use of software architectures, but in this part of the book we are only concerned with the design aspects of the fire-alarm system framework. The description of the fire-alarm system is based on Molin (1997) and TeleLarm (1996).

1.1 Domain description

The main function of a fire-alarm system is to monitor a large number of detectors and, whenever a potential fire is detected, activate a number of outputs. Several examples of output types exist, including alarm bells, alarm texts on displays, extinguisher systems and automatic alert of the fire department. Detectors, or input devices, cover a wide variety of types, ranging from the traditional temperature and smoke sensors to ultra-sensitive laser-based smoke detectors. The wide variety in input and output devices presents one of the major challenges to the software architectural design.

A second dimension of variability is the range of systems that should be covered by the architecture. At the low end there are very cost sensitive systems that still should fulfil standards and regulations. High-end systems include advanced sensors, a sophisticated high-speed extinguisher control system and a large and complex graphical user interface. For instance, conventional sensors have three externally visible states, i.e. normal, alarm or fault. The advanced sensors instead transmit particle density (smoke intensity) or temperature values to a control unit that deduces, based on the input data and using various algorithms, whether there is an alarm or fault situation.

A third relevant aspect of fire-alarm systems is their highly distributed nature. Detectors and output units are distributed throughout a building and, in the case of high-end systems, over several buildings. The software controlling the fire-alarm system has to monitor all input devices for alarms and, if an alarm occurs, activate the correct output devices.

Because of potential consequences in case of a failure of the fire-alarm system, continuous self-monitoring is part of the system's behaviour. Due to this, one can think of the system as consisting of two levels of functionality, i.e. domain-related functionality and system monitoring functionality.

The platforms for the fire-alarm systems range from small 8-bit micro controller systems to larger 16-bit systems that can be connected to form a distributed network with a capability of up to 10 000 addressable detectors. In addition, the installation owner can configure names and physical locations of detectors, the texts that appear on displays in case of fire and the relations between output devices and detectors, i.e. what output devices are activated when particular detectors indicate an alarm.

1.2 Quality requirements

At the start of the design project, it was identified that the company maintained a family of fire-alarm systems that used different real-time kernels, different hardware and different programming languages. In addition, each system was available in different language versions and with functionality specific for particular countries. The goal of the project was to cover these systems and system variations using a single product-line architecture and component base, i.e. a product-line architecture.

In addition to addressing the variability described above, the system should support a number of other quality requirements as well. The quality requirements are described below.

- **Configurability.** It should be relatively simple to instantiate specific versions of the fire-alarm system. For instance, configuration with country, language and hardware-specific details should be easy.

- **Demonstrability.** Although the architecture can affect reliability of instantiated systems only up to some extent, one can require that the architecture simplify testing and facilitate the demonstration of the reliability of resulting systems. This is particularly important since fire-alarm systems need to be certified by an external certification institute.

- **Performance.** The performance of a fire-alarm system is dependent on the size of the system, the available memory and the CPU processing capacity, making it hard to state absolute performance requirements at the architectural level. However, the architecture and reusable components should be efficient, i.e. not be considerably slower than a system-specific implementation.

- **Maintainability.** The system should be prepared for incorporating new requirements (see below).

Since the maintainability of the architecture and provided levels of configurability are the primary requirements on a product-line architecture, we discuss these aspects in more detail. A list of potential new requirements or requirement categories is presented below.

- **Detector technology.** New types of detectors enter the market continuously. These detectors not only vary with respect to the measured variables, but, more importantly, in the way they interface with the fire-alarm system.

- **Extinguishers.** Extinguisher systems are also evolving constantly due to new technology, but also due to, e.g., new environmental standards.

- **Compatibility.** Several other systems in an organization may need to communicate with the fire-alarm system for, among others things, retrieving data and setting alarm boundaries. In addition, new fire-alarm systems should be able to incorporate legacy fire-alarm systems.

- **Hardware.** Cost plays a major role in the domain of fire-alarm systems. Consequently, new hardware with a better price/performance ratio should be incorporated in the fire-alarm system with limited effort.

- **Man–machine interface.** There is a constant and quick development in technology used to interface with operators. Starting with LEDs and buttons, succeeded by LCD screens and numeric keypads, the current level is to have a graphical, window-based interface. However, the development is towards incorporating multiple media, e.g. audio and video, in the interface with the fire-alarm system.

- **Standards.** Although standards have a tendency to lag behind the industrial practice, they do change on a regular basis and the changes need to be incorporated in the products.

- **User-adapted instantiations.** Large customers often have additional (or even conflicting) requirements on the fire-alarm system that have to be incorporated in their instantiation against limited effort. In addition, when upgrades of the product become available, these customers should have the ability to upgrade while maintaining their additions.

2 Measurement systems

The increasing automation of the production process has begun to address processes beyond the primary production processes. During the last decade, one can recognize an increasing need for automated tools that support the quality control processes surrounding the actual production. The emergence of the ISO9000 quality standards, the quality thinking in general and the increased productivity of production technology requires the quality control systems to improve productivity as well and whereas many factories used manual quality control by personnel, nowadays the need for automated support is obvious. This development has dramatically increased the need for automated measurement systems. The advantages of measurement systems are generally improved performance/cost ratio and more consistent and accurate quality control. This development increased the need for reusability of existing measurement system software. Although these systems, conceptually, have a rather similar structure, in practice the implementation of these systems tends to be somewhat diverse. This is due to the fact that real-time constraints, concurrency and requirements resulting from the underlying hardware strongly influence the actual implementation.

Despite these difficulties, we have, together with our industrial partner, EC-Gruppen, a company located in southern Sweden and developing embedded systems, designed a reference archichitecture and component set for measurement systems that would decrease their software development cost by increasing reuse of existing software and, as an important second requirement, increase the flexibility of running applications. Operators of the measurement systems often need to make some adjustments in the way the measurement system evaluates a measurement item and the system should provide this flexibility. However, traditional systems constructed in C and assembly often have difficulty in providing this functionality. Part of the results of the project are reported in Bosch (1999a) and Bengtsson and Bosch (1998).

2.1 Domain description

Measurement systems are a class of systems used to measure the relevant values of a process or product. These systems are different from the better known process control systems in that the measured values are not directly, i.e. as part of the same system, used to control the production process that creates the product or process that is measured. A measurement system is used for quality control on produced products that can then be used to separate acceptable from unacceptable products or to categorize the products in quality categories. In some systems, the results from the measurement are stored in case in the future the need arises to refer to this information, e.g. if customers complain about products that passed the measurement system.

Although a measurement system contains considerable amounts of software, a substantial part of these systems is hardware since it is connected to the real world through a number of sensors and actuators. The sensors provide information about the real world through the detected impulses. However, whereas traditional sensors were primarily hardware and had a very low-level interface to the software system, new sensors provide increasing amounts of functionality that previously had to be implemented as part of the software. For instance, a conventional temperature sensor would only provide the A/D conversion and the software would need to convert this A/D value into the actual temperature in Celsius or Kelvin and, in addition, had to do the calibration of the sensor. Modern temperature sensors perform their own calibration and immediately provide the actual temperature in the required format. The interface between the sensor and the system is becoming more and more distant from the concrete hardware but also more complex since the amount of configurability of the sensors is increasing.

With respect to the actuators one can recognize a similar development. Whereas the software previously had to be concerned with the actuation through the actuators, modern actuators often only need a set value expressed in application domain concepts such as angular speed or force. For example, to control the open angle of a valve in a traditional measurement system, one would have to generate a 'duty cycle' in software. A duty cycle is the periodic process of sending out a '1' for part of the cycle and a '0' for the rest. The ratio between the time, the output is '1' and the time the output is '0' represents the 'force' expressed through the actuator. For example, a valve is to be open for 70 per cent of the time the system should output a '1' for 70 per cent of the cyclic period and a '0' for the remaining 30 per cent. The implementation of this is often achieved through an interrupt routine that changes the output signal when required. Modern actuators contain considerably more functionality and will generate the duty cycle themselves, requiring only the set value from the software.

These developments in the domain of sensors and actuators change measurement systems from small, single processor systems that are developed very close to the hardware to distributed computing systems, since the more complex sensors and actuators often contain their own processors. However, although the increased functionality of the sensors and actuators reduces the complexity of constructing measurement systems, the increased demands on these systems and the resulting increase in size make the construction of measurement systems a complex activity. The languages and tools used to construct measurement systems ought to provide powerful means to deal with this complexity.

A measurement system, however, consists of more than sensors and actuators. A typical measurement cycle starts with a trigger indicating that a product, or measurement item, is entering the system. The first step after the trigger is the data-collection phase by the sensors. The sensors measure the various relevant variables of the measurement item. The second step is the analysis phase during which the data from the sensors is collected in a central representation and transformed until it has the form in which it can be compared to the ideal values. Based on this comparison, certain discrepancies can be deduced which, in turn, lead a classification of the measurement item. One of the requirements on the analysis phase is that the way the transformation takes place, the characteristics based on which the item is classified and the actions associated with each classification should be flexible and easily adaptable, both during system construction, and also, to some extent, during the actual system operation. In the third phase, i.e. actuation, the classification of the measurement item is used to select the appropriate actions that are associated with the classification and subsequently these actions are performed. Example actions may be to reject the item, causing the actuators to remove the item from the conveyer belt and put it in a separate store, or to print the classification on the item so that it can be automatically recognized at a later stage.

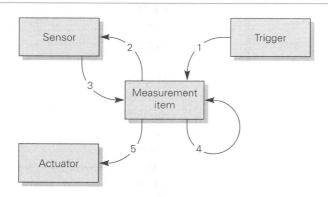

Figure 9   Architecture of a simple measurement system

In Fig. 9, the entities that are typically part of a simple measurement system are shown. The system consists of five entities that communicate with each other to achieve the required functionality. Below, a sequence of events during a normal measurement cycle for an entity is shown:

1   the **trigger** triggers the **measurement item** when a physical item enters the system;

2   the **measurement item** requests the **sensor** to measure the physical object;

3   the **sensor** sends back the result to the **measurement item** which stores the results;

4   after collecting the required data, the **measurement item** compares the measured values with the ideal values;

5   the **measurement item** sends a message to the actuator requesting the actuation appropriate for the measured data.

Based on the above discussion, one can wonder whether the traditional view on measurement systems as a centralized system with one main control loop is still appropriate. During the project, we became convinced that the system should be viewed as a collection of communicating, active entities that co-operate to achieve the required system behaviour. This improves decomposition of the system, decreases the dependencies between the various parts and increases system flexibility. However, decomposing the system into active entities requires processes to be available, or at least simulated, by the underlying operating system.

Another important aspect is the real-time behaviour of the measurement system. Different from many real-time systems, a measurement system is not a periodic system. The real-time constraints in the system are, directly or indirectly, related to the triggering point where a product to be measured enters the system. Although, when running at maximum throughput, this becomes a periodic behaviour, the start is not determined by the clock, but by a physical event. In the ideal situation, the software engineer would specify the real-time constraints on the different activities in the system. Based on that specification, the system would schedule the activities such that the real-time constraints are met or, if it is not possible to schedule all activities, respond to the software engineer with a message. However, in the current situation, the software engineer implements the tasks that have to be performed and performs a test run of the system. Often the system does not meet all deadlines at first and the software engineer has to adjust the system to fulfil the requirements, for instance by changing the priorities of the different processes.

Finally, the requirements on modern measurement systems often result in systems that are no longer confined to a single processor. Distribution plays an increasingly important role in measurement systems. However, the presence of distribution should not require the software engineer to change the basic architecture of the system. The system should just be extended with behaviour for dealing with communication over address spaces.

2.2 Quality requirements

Measurement systems should support the functionality described in the previous section. However, in addition to these functional requirements, one can identify a number of quality requirements as well.

- **Configurability.** The framework should provide reusable components for the construction of measurement systems. This requires a delicate balance between generality and speciality. It also means that the components and decomposition dimensions have to be chosen such that relatively general components from different dimensions can be composed to form specific components that can be used in real systems with minimal extensions.

- **Run-time flexibility.** Although flexibility would be considered to be a positive aspect of any system, the requirements on the flexibility of measurement systems are higher than average. As described, the actual composition of the system from its components, the analysis process and the reaction by the system based on the analysis results need to be easily adaptable during system operation.

- **Real-time constraints.** Since measurement systems often are located at the beginning or end of production lines, the throughput of the measurement system should not restrict the production process. Therefore, real-time constraints on the computation of software components are necessary to achieve the required throughput, but also to synchronize sensing and actuation actions of the measurement system with the physical item that is measured.

3   Haemodialysis systems

Haemodialysis systems present an area in the domain of medical equipment where competition has been increasing drastically during recent years. The aim of a dialysis system is to remove water and certain natural waste products from the patient's blood. Patients who have serious kidney problems, and consequently produce little or no urine, use this type of system. A dialysis system replaces this natural process with an artificial one.

We have been involved in a research project aimed at designing a new software architecture for the dialysis machines produced by Althin Medical. The software of the existing generation of products was exceedingly hard to maintain and certify and management had become convinced that it was necessary to develop the next generation of the dialysis system software independent of the existing software.

The partners involved in the project were Althin Medical, EC-Gruppen and the University of Karlskrona/Ronneby. The goal for EC-Gruppen was to study novel ways of constructing embedded systems, whereas our goal was to study the process of designing software architecture and to collect experiences. As a research method, we used *Action Research* (Apple 1989), i.e. researchers actively participated in the design process and reflected on the process and the results. The results of the research project are reported, among others, in Bengtsson and Bosch (1999a).

3.1   Domain description

An overview of a dialysis system is presented in Fig. 10. The system is physically separated into two parts by the dialysis membrane. On the left side the dialysis fluid circuit takes the water from a supply of a certain purity (not necessarily sterile), and dialysis concentrate is added using a pump. A sensor monitors the concentration of the dialysis fluid and the measured value is used to control the pump. A second pump maintains the flow of dialysis fluid, whereas a third pump increases the flow and thus reduces the pressure at the dialysis fluid side. This is needed to pull the waste products from the patient's blood through the membrane into the dialysis fluid. A constant flow of dialysis fluid is maintained by the hydro mechanic devices that ensure exact and steady flow on each side (rectangle with a curl).

On the right side of Fig. 10, the extra-corporal circuit, i.e. the blood part, has a pump for maintaining a specified blood flow on its side of the membrane. The

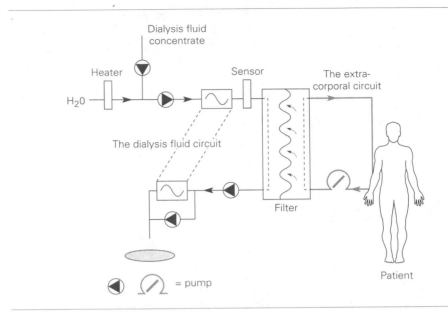

Figure 10   Schematic of a haemodialysis machine

patient is connected to this part through two needles, usually located in the arm, which take blood to and from the patient. The extra-corporal circuit uses a number of sensors, e.g. for identifying air bubbles, and actuators, e.g. a heparin pump to avoid the coagulation of the patient's blood while it is outside the body. However, these details are omitted since they are not needed in this context.

The dialysis process, or *treatment*, is by no means a standard process. A fair collection of treatments exists including, for example, haemodialysis filtration (HDF) and ultra filtration (UF) and other variations, such as single needle/single pump, double needle/single pump. Treatments are changed due to new research results but also since the effectiveness of a particular treatment decreases when it is used too long for a patient. Although the abstract function of a dialysis system is constant, a considerable set of variations exists already. Based on experience the involved company anticipates several additional changes to the software, hardware and mechanical parts of the system that will be necessary in response to developments in medical research.

As an input to the project, the original software architecture and implementation was used. The software had evolved from only a couple of thousand lines of assembly and low-level C code to close to a hundred thousands lines primarily consisting of higher-level control and user interface code. The system runs on a PC-board equivalent using a real-time kernel/operating system. It has a graphical user interface and displays data

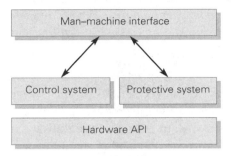

Figure 11   Legacy system decomposition

using different kinds of widgets. It is a quite complex piece of software and because of its unintended evolution, the structure that was once present has deteriorated substantially. The three major software subsystems are the man–machine interface (MMI), the control system, and the protective system (see Fig. 11).

The *MMI* has the responsibilities of presenting data and alarms to the user, i.e. a nurse, and getting input, i.e., commands or treatment data, from the user and setting the protective and control systems in the correct modes.

The *control system* is responsible for maintaining the values set by the user and adjusting the values according to the treatment selected for the time being. The control system is not a tight-loop process control system; only a few such loops exist, most of them low-level and implemented in hardware. Instead the control system is primarily concerned with configuring the system with the appropriate set-values and monitoring the operation of the system.

The *protective system* is responsible for detecting any hazard situation where the patient might be hurt. It is supposed to be as separate from the other parts of the system as possible and is usually implemented as an independent process. When detecting a hazard, the protective system raises an alarm and engages a process of returning the system to a safe state. Usually, the safe state is stopping the blood flow, the dialysis-fluid flow or both.

The documented structure of the existing system is no more fine-grained than this and to do any change impact analysis, extensive knowledge of the source code is required.

3.2 Quality requirements

The aim during architectural design is to optimize the potential of the architecture (and the system built which is based on it) to fulfil the software quality requirements. For dialysis systems, the driving software quality requirements are *maintainability, reusability, safety, real-timeliness* and *demonstrability*. Below, these quality requirements are described in the context of dialysis systems.

Maintainability

Past haemodialysis machines produced by our partner company have proven to be hard to maintain. Each release of software with bug corrections and function extensions has made the software harder and harder to comprehend and maintain. One of the major requirements of the software architecture for the new dialysis system family is that maintainability should be considerably better than the existing systems, with respect to *corrective* but especially *adaptive* maintenance:

■ *corrective maintenance* has been hard in the existing systems since dependencies between different parts of the software have been hard to identify and visualize;

■ *adaptive maintenance* is initiated by a constant stream of new and changing requirements. Examples include new mechanical components as pumps, heaters and AD/DA converters, but also new treatments, control algorithms and safety regulations. All these new requirements need to be introduced in the system as easily as possible. Changes to the mechanics or hardware of the system almost always require changes to the software as well. In the existing system, all these extensions have deteriorated the structure, and consequently the maintainability, of the software and subsequent changes have become harder to implement. Adaptive maintainability was perhaps the most important requirement on the system.

Configurability

The software developed for the dialysis machine should be easily configurable. Already today there are different models of haemodialysis machines and market requirements for customization will most probably require a larger number of haemodialysis models. Consequently, it should be relatively simple to instantiate the product-line architecture for a particular system.

Safety

Haemodialysis machines operate as an extension of a patient's blood flow and numerous situations could occur which are harmful and possibly even lethal to the patient. Since the safety of the patient is a very high priority, the system has extremely strict safety requirements. The haemodialysis system may not expose the dialysis patient to any hazard, but should detect the rise of such conditions and return the dialysis machine and the patient to a state which presents no danger to the patient, i.e. a safe state. Actions such as stopping the dialysis fluid if concentrations are out of range and stopping the blood flow if air bubbles are detected in the extra-corporal system are such protective measures to achieve a safe state. This

requirement has to some extent already been transformed into functional requirements by the safety requirements standard for haemodialysis machines (CEI/IEC
601-2), but only as far as to define a number of hazard situations, corresponding
threshold values and the method to use for achieving the safe state. However, a
number of other criteria affecting safety are not addressed. For example, if the communication with a pump fails, the system should be able to determine the risk and
deal with it as necessary, i.e. achieving safe state and notifying the nurse that a service technician is required.

Real-timeliness

The process of haemodialysis is, by nature, not a very time-critical process, in the
sense that actions must be taken within a few milli- or microseconds during normal
operation. During a typical treatment, once the flows, concentrations and tempera-
tures are set, the process only requires monitoring. However, response time
becomes important when a hazard or fault condition arises. In the case of a
detected hazard, e.g. air is detected in the extra-corporal unit, the haemodialysis
machine must react very quickly to immediately return the system to a safe state.
Timings for these situations are presented in the safety standard for haemodialysis
machines (CEI/IEC 601-2).

Demonstrability

As previously stated, patient safety is very important. To ensure that haemodialysis
machines that are sold adhere to the regulations for safety, an independent certification institute must certify each construction. The certification process is repeated for
every (major) new release of the software which substantially increases the cost for
developing and maintaining the haemodialysis machines. One way to reduce the cost
for certification is to make it easy to demonstrate that the software performs the
required safety functions as required. This requirement we refer to as *demonstrability*.

4 Concluding remarks

The design of software architectures, similar to other engineering disciplines, is
hard to present and discuss without concrete examples. In this chapter, we have
presented three software systems that will be used as examples in the subsequent
chapters, i.e. fire-alarm systems, measurement systems and dialysis systems. All
three systems are in the domain of embedded systems and have to deal with
rapidly developing contexts in terms of requirements, hardware and other technology, and each system has to support considerable variation in terms of the
instantiations which need to be supported by the architecture and its base of
reusable components. For each system, we have provided a domain description and
examined the primary quality requirements.

CHAPTER 4

Functionality-based architectural design

Architectural design is the process of converting a set of requirements into a software architecture that fulfils, or at least facilitates the fulfilment of, the requirements. The method for architectural design presented in this part of the book has a focus on the explicit evaluation of and design for quality requirements, but that does not mean that the functional requirements are irrelevant. Before one can start to optimize an architecture for quality requirements, the first step must be to design a first version of the architecture based on its functional requirements.

The first design phase in the software archictecture design method consists of four main steps. The *first step* is concerned with determining the context of the system under design, the interfaces of the system to the external entities it interacts with and the behaviour the system should exhibit at the interfaces. The *second step* is the identification of the archetypes, i.e. the main architectural abstractions, and the relations between the archetypes. Our experience is that finding these archetypes is very important, especially for the later phases, because they capture the core abstractions of the system. Architecture transformations tend to build additional structures around the archetypes for fulfilling quality requirements. The *third step* is concerned with decomposing the system into its main components and identifying the relations between these components, i.e. the structure of the architecture. The *final step* in functionality-based architectural design is the description of system instances using the archetypes and the system interfaces. Since the architecture, for instance in the case of software product lines, may be required to support a number of different instantiations, these have to be specified explicitly to verify that the system, in addition to the commonality, also supports the required variability.

The assumption underlying our approach to architectural design is that starting from the functional requirements does not preclude the optimization of quality requirements during the later architectural design stages. There are software architects who produce an architectural design based on all requirements, and who believe that design cannot be separated in the way proposed in this book. We agree that no pure separation can be achieved, i.e. an architectural design based on functional requirements only will still have values for its quality attributes. However, our position is that an objective and repeatable architectural design method must be organized according to our principles since it is unlikely that an architectural design process does not require iterations to optimize the architecture. In addition, an architecture based primarily on functional requirements is more general and can be reused as input for systems in the same domain but with different quality requirements. On the other hand, it is unlikely that a software architecture which fulfils a particular set of quality requirements will be applicable in a domain with different functional requirements.

The remainder of this chapter is organized as follows. In Section 1, the definition of the system context is discussed, i.e. the first step in the method. The topic of the subsequent section is the identification of archetypes, and the definition of architecture instantiations is discussed in Section 4. To illustrate this phase of the method, we give a number of examples from the case studies set out in the previous chapter. The chapter is then concluded in Section 6.

1 Defining the system context

'No object is an island', wrote Beck and Cunningham (1989) about a decade ago. The same can be said to be true for software systems in general. All software has to have an interface with one or more external entities. Different from what one may suspect, it is the externally visible properties of a system that matter. All our efforts as software architects and engineers are judged from this perspective, though it is difficult to maintain this viewpoint since virtually all of our efforts are spent on the internals of software systems. The role of the software architect is to convert the requirements of the stakeholder concerning the external visible properties of the system into a software architecture which facilitates the fulfilment of these requirements.

The externally visible behaviour of the system is present at the interfaces to its context. The system may have interfaces to several entities external to itself. The entity at the other end of an interface may be located at a lower level, a higher level or at the same level as the system that we are designing. For a typical system, examples of lower-level entities include network interfaces and sensor or actuator interfaces, whereas peer-level entities are often systems which address a different functional domain, but need to communicate because of system integration requirements. For example, in the case of Securitas Larm, a high-end fire-alarm system has to interface with other building automation systems to achieve more intelligent behaviour. For example, if no humans are supposed to be in one part of the building, the particle-density sensors should be more sensitive then when people who are smoking might be walking around in that part. In the latter case, sensors should not activate

the alarm when temporary peaks in particle density are detected. Higher-level entities may be system integration software, e.g. in the case of the fire-alarm system,
the building automation integration system, or human beings, such as operators of
the system or other users. In Fig. 12 the system context is presented graphically.

Explicitly defining the system in terms of the functionality and quality required on
its interfaces is an important starting point once the requirements have been
defined. It allows one to distribute requirements to the interfaces and to define the
various quality requirements more precisely. Interface-specific requirements allow
for the specification of both operational and development quality requirements.
For example, performance, real-time and reliability requirements can be expressed
in the services provided at the interface. In addition, maintainability and flexibility
requirements can be expressed in terms of the likely changes at the interface.

An additional reason for explicitly defining the system context and boundaries, in
our experience, is that there is a natural tendency to include more and more
aspects during design. When explicit effort is spent on software architectural
design, there generally also is an understanding that this process should be allowed
to take time. When there is no extreme time pressure, software architects, in our
experience, try to extend the domain of the design because each of these extensions will improve the applicability of the architecture and allow for likely future
requirements to be integrated more easily. The problem, however, is that these
extensions increase the design and development cost, resulting in the situation
where the current development project budget is partially used for maintenance
activities in response to likely, but not certain future requirements. Management
may easily react to this development by the imposition of strict deadlines, and not

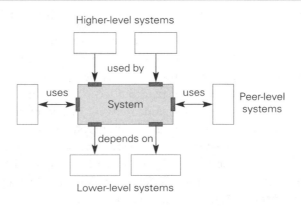

Figure 12   Context of a software system

allow for a sufficiently thought-through architecture. A more fruitful approach to this is to explicitly define the system boundaries and the functional and quality requirements, and to require software engineers to stick to their appointed domain. This approach also allows for the consideration of potential future requirements without their immediate inclusion in the architecture. In this way, the architecture can be prepared for the incorporation of likely requirements, thereby reducing future maintenance cost.

In the case of a software architectural design for a software product line, the definition of the system context is somewhat more complicated since products in the product line tend to have variations in the interfaces they provide. The design of a product-line architecture is discussed in more detail in Chapter 9.

To summarize the discussion in this section, the step of defining the system context is made up of the following tasks:

- define the interfaces of the system to external entities. These entities may be located at a lower level, a higher level or at the same level;

- associate functional and quality requirements with each interface. Both operational and development quality requirements can be associated with interfaces;

- in the case of a software product line, the variability in the interfaces supported by the various products in the product line should be explicitly identified and specified. The cost and resource efficiency of low-end products should not be sacrificed for the requirements of high-end products.

At the end of this chapter, we will present a number of examples that illustrate the concepts discussed in this context.

2　Identifying the archetypes

Once the boundaries for the system have been defined, the next step is to identify and define the core abstractions based on which the system is structured. We refer to these core abstractions as *archetypes*. It is, in our experience, often very beneficial to software architectural design that the architect find a small set of, often highly abstract, entities that, when combined, are able to describe the major part of the system behaviour at an abstract level. These entities form the most stable part of the system and are generally very stable and only changed in very limited ways. Our experience is that even relatively large systems often can be described in terms of a small number of archetypes. However, in later phases, the archetypes are instantiated in a large variety of ways to populate the system.

It is important to note that archetypes are different from subsystems. Whereas subsystems decompose system functionality into a number of big chunks, the archetypes represent stable units of abstract functionality that appear over and over again in the system. In the examples later in this chapter, the difference will be exemplified more clearly.

The identification of archetypes is a difficult process that is largely dependent on the creative insight and experience of the architect or architects. Consequently, it is hard to describe a concrete recipe for finding the right archetypes. The primary starting point is a good understanding of the domains covered by the system and the actual role that the system has to perform in that context. It is important to avoid starting from the concrete instances in the domain and building up generalizations based on those, as was propagated by some traditional object-oriented design methods, i.e. a bottom-up approach. Instead, one should start from a holistic perspective taking the complete system into account, i.e. a top-down approach. In order to increase understanding of particular aspects, the software architect may then address particular domains or parts of the system functionality. Each focusing activity should be finalized by returning to the system level and integrating the newly won understanding with the understanding of the whole system. At that level, the increased understanding of one aspect of the system should be related to the remainder of the system and placed in perspective. The process of increasing understanding of aspects of the system and placing this knowledge in an overall system context is generally highly iterative and may have to be repeated several times, depending on the architect's previous knowledge about the system domain.

During the process of increasing the understanding of the system by repeatedly addressing parts of the system and the system as a whole, the architect will often identify common characteristics between entities in very disparate parts of the system. In other words, it is possible to recognize recurring patterns within the system at various places. The recurring patterns may consist of just a single entity, but may also be a small structure consisting of a handful of entities. These recurring patterns represent potential archetypes and should be recorded. These structures represent the most fundamental structural and behavioural constants of the system and will, later on, be used as the core abstractions around which the system is built.

The patterns identified by the software architect as recurring in different parts of the system are the candidate archetypes that represent the core system abstractions. These candidate archetypes are recorded and form a set. This set is then analyzed to select the most appropriate archetypes for the system. Candidates that are synonyms, or largely overlapping, should be merged. In addition, candidates that are at very different levels of abstraction should be reconsidered. This does not necessarily mean that the more concrete candidate should be removed. Archetypes should be abstract, but should also represent meaningful abstractions in the system. The ambition is to identify the most concrete, most meaningful archetypes that still represent patterns or concepts that appear throughout the system. Finally, when two subsets of candidates exist that represent fundamentally different perspectives on the system, the software architect should choose one of the alternatives and rigorously remove all traces of the alternative. One of the main goals for the architecture is to achieve *conceptual integrity* (Brooks, 1995) throughout the system by using the same fundamental concepts as a basis everywhere.

It is important for the architect to accept that different parts and aspects of the system may require widely different amounts of effort and understanding. At the software architectural design stage, the system as a whole is the subject of study. Thus, when some part or aspect is relatively unimportant for the fulfilment of the requirements of the system, it may only need limited attention from the architect. An example may be logging functionality. Another situation is where the functionality is straightforward and well understood and no challenging quality requirements are associated with the functionality. Depending on the type of system, a graphical user interface may be an example of this category.

The identification of architectural entities is related to domain analysis methods (see e.g. Prieto-Díaz and Arango, 1991 for an overview), but some relevant differences exist. First, although archetypes can be modeled as domain objects, our experience is that these objects are not found immediately in the application domain. Instead, they are the result of a creative design process that, after analyzing the various domain entities, abstracts the most relevant properties and models them as architectural entities. Once the abstractions are identified, the interactions between them are defined in more detail. A second difference between architectural design and domain analysis is that the architecture of a system generally covers multiple domains.

Once one has reduced the archetype candidates to a small and manageable set, the relations between the archetypes are identified and defined. The types of relations are generally domain specific and describe control and/or data flow in the system. The relations should generally not be generic relation types like, for instance, the generalization and aggregation relations in object-oriented modeling. The presence of these relations, especially generalization, between archetypes is suspicious and one should reconsider whether the involved archetypes should perhaps be merged. However, there are cases where this situation is necessary for the archetypes to represent sufficiently concrete, semantically rich entities. For instance, later in this chapter (Section 5.1) we present the example of the fire-alarm system where the specialization relation is used.

One may wonder what the semantics of relations between archetypes is. For instance, within the domain of architecture description languages (e.g. Allen and

Garlan, 1997), architectures are described in terms of components and connectors. The connectors are explicitly modeled entities representing the relations between components. When using a specific architectural style, the connectors are style-specific as well. For instance, in the pipes-and-filters architectural style, the pipes are represented as connectors. However, connectors are not equivalent to relations between archetypes. Instead, connectors represent one way of implementing these relations. When the components implementing two related archetypes provide a good match, the relation may not be represented explicitly but rather through normal message passing. However, if some mismatch between the components exists, then the necessary glue code can be implemented in a connector that then becomes a first-class entity in the implementation.

As we discussed earlier, small groups of related archetypes tend to form system-specific patterns that are applicable in many locations in the system instantiations. The patterns may prove to represent domain-specific patterns that have validity within an application domain, rather than just the system context. It may be relevant to document such domain-specific structures for future use in development projects in the same domain.

Finally, since the process of identifying and evaluating architectures to a large extent depends on the creative insight and experience of the software architect, it is, as mentioned, hard to present explicit guidelines to support the process. In several cases, our experience was that it is hard to decide when the identification and definition of archetypes is done and the team has to move on to the next phase. However, often a consensus develops within the team on when sufficient effort has been spent and the design activity can proceed to the next step. However, during later phases, it may prove necessary to return to this step and rework the archetypes. It is important to allow for this type of iteration and not to force the creative process into a waterfall model too early and easily. In cases when no consensus develops this is often due to differences in understanding of the requirements of the system. In such cases, it may be necessary to proceed with the next steps in order to develop this common understanding. It must, however, be possible to return to this step at a later point when common understanding has evolved and it becomes possible to agree upon the archetypes.

To conclude, the following activities take place during archetype identification:

- the identification of candidate archetypes;

- the selection of a small and stable set of archetypes from the candidates. This may require the exclusion of candidates, but especially the merging of candidates is rather common;

- the identification and selection of relations between archetypes.

3 Decomposing the architecture into components

The identified collection of archetypes captures the most stable and core abstractions of the system domain. However, these abstractions do not represent the architectural structure of the system. Instead, they are generally instantiated in several places in the system in several different concrete forms. Thus, once we have developed a stable set of archetypes, the next step is to define the structure of the software architecture, i.e. its decomposition into components and the relation between these components.

This decomposition of the system into its components does not need to be single level, but may incorporate two or more recursive levels of decomposition for critical parts of the system. As we will discuss in later chapters, the goal of software architectural design is to specify, early in the development process, an architectural structure that allows for the fulfilment of the system requirements. In certain cases, it is required to perform more detailed analysis of critical parts of the system in order to be able to state with sufficient certainty that the system will fulfil its quality requirements.

A second rationale for recursively decomposing the system into its components is that it helps to deal with the complexity of software systems. The complexity of a software system does not have to be the result of sheer size, it can also result from a multitude of interfaces to the system or because of highly prioritized, but strongly conflicting quality requirements. For instance, newer generations of certain types of embedded systems, e.g. hand-held devices, have extreme flexibility and performance requirements. The cost-effective implementation of these conflicting quality requirements is a major challenge for the software engineers involved. To increase the confidence that the system built, based on the software architecture, fulfils its requirements, often rather detailed analysis and prototyping may be required.

The main issue is then, of course, what components to identify and select. Several approaches can be used to identify and select components.

- **Interfaces.** Each of the system interfaces identified in Section 1 should be connected to a component. One typical approach to decomposing a system is by associating a component with each interface. For instance, in the measurement system, three of the five main components are associated with interfaces which the software part of system has to the hardware and mechanical parts, i.e. sensor, trigger and actuator.

- **Domains.** A second source for components is to associate domains covered by the system with components. We can identify two types of domains: application domains and computer science domains. Application domains are typically associated with the problem the software system intends to address. For instance, in the dialysis domain, we can identify the blood domain, the membrane domain and the dialysis concentrate domain. These domains are related to each other, but are identified as different specialities by domain experts. In addition, these domains often lead to a vertical decomposition of the functionality of the system, i.e. components that are at the same level of abstraction and address focused topics.

Computer science domains are areas of competence associated with the solution used to solve the problem. In embedded systems, typical examples include file systems, process schedulers, communication protocols and user interfaces. Computer science domains tend to be organized horizontally, i.e. representing increasing levels of abstraction. Operating systems are the prototypical example. A word of caution is appropriate here. Computer science domains are typically functionally organized and tend to decompose problem-domain abstractions into a number of implemented entities. The advantage of this decomposition is that software engineers tend to understand it easily and frequently standard components are available. However, it may be bad for traceability and has several other potentially negative aspects as well, e.g. decreased maintainability. Therefore, this stage in development may not be the right one in which to decompose the system according to these principles. We refer to Section 2 in Chapter 10 for a detailed discussion of the notion of domains.

■ **Abstraction layers.** A third approach is to decompose the system into a set of abstraction layers, i.e. horizontal layers that implement relevant functionality and simplify the specification of problem-domain functionality at higher levels. Typically, abstraction layers are identified while iterating over the component selection of the system. At first, it is identified that many components need a particular type of functionality, e.g. co-ordinated behaviour. As a second step, it is decided to factor out this common behaviour into a separate component, e.g. a transaction manager. Finally, it is understood that rather than representing this as an application-level component, it is more suitable to represent the functionality as an abstraction layer on top of which the application components are defined.

■ **Domain entities.** A fourth way to identify components is through problem-domain entities. Not all, in fact very few, software systems are concerned with new domains that people have not considered before. Typically, the domain experts for the application domain addressed by the software system have a generally accepted decomposition of systems inside the domain into primary concepts. Such accepted decompositions may be loosely and informally defined by domain experts, there may exist classical literature within the domain that defines the reference architecture and, finally, in certain domains, enforced standards exists that require particular standard system decompositions. One example for which reference literature exists defining the principle of decomposition and behaviour of systems in a domain is control theory. This domain defines a number of typical system structures, e.g. feed-back and feed-forward control structures, and substantial mathematical underpinnings, such as P, PI and PD controllers.

The decomposition defined by the domain experts provides highly valuable input to the identification and selection of components of the system, and software architects are often tempted to select these components right away. However, architects should perform a serious evaluation of the components to make certain that the potential components actually represent the most appropriate decomposition of the system. The problem-domain decomposition was often performed for reasons very different from the automation of the domain, which is generally provided by a software system. In addition, generally accepted decompositions tend to be relatively old and may not have incorporated new technological developments. It is important to recognize that the development of a new software architecture (rather than evolving the existing system) is often chosen based on an identified need to make a clean start. In our experience, such a new start may require a reengineering of the domain understanding as well as architecting a new software system.

- **Archetype instantiations.** Finally, even the identified archetypes may provide valuable input to selecting the components. The archetypes are defined based on the identification of recurring patterns throughout the system. However, that means that in several locations in the system instances of archetypes exist. These archetype instantiations may represent useful components.

  An important advantage of using archetypes is the conceptual integrity that it provides: since the components are all instances of the same archetype, they share common rules, design decisions and structural elements that makes it easier to understand the system as a whole.

Returning to the system decomposition in general, we can identify two fundamental ways of decomposing software systems, i.e. functional decomposition versus entity-based decomposition and problem-domain versus solution-domain-based decomposition. Functional decomposition is concerned with the functions that the system is supposed to provide and performs the primary decomposition of the system according to these functions. A typical analogy can be found in programming languages such as C and Pascal that are organized according to these principles. Entity-based decomposition identifies the primary concepts that can be identified in the system and performs the primary decomposition according to these concepts. The functions relevant for each entity are then associated with the entity. Object-oriented programming languages such as Java, C++ and Smalltalk implement such concepts, as well as component models such as COM, CORBA and JavaBeans.

Along the second dimension we identified the problem domain and the solution domain. Both domains can be decomposed according to the main functions and entities in the domain. For instance, the well-known three-tier architecture for information systems, consisting of a graphical user interface layer, a business logic layer and a data storage layer, is an example of a functionality-based, solution-domain-oriented decomposition. Problem-domain functionality and entities need to be mapped to this architecture, which often requires scattering problem-domain behaviour over the system. Similarly, one can view the standard compiler architecture as a functionally organized, problem-domain-oriented architecture. Finally, a software architecture organized according to control theory principles will be an entity-based, problem-domain-oriented architecture. Finally, a graphical user interface architecture is typically organized according to the entities present in the solution domain. In Fig. 13, the decomposition dimensions and the discussed examples are presented graphically.

Once the components into which the architectural structure is decomposed are identified, the relations between these components need to be established. What relations are present is, of course, as dependent on the actual software system as the components themselves, but a number of guidelines can be provided. In the case of components representing abstraction layers, the components are related to each other according to the levels of abstraction they represent. In the case of components representing domains or domain entities, hints for appropriate rela-

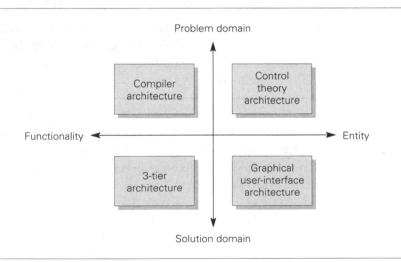

Figure 13   Two dimensions of system decomposition and examples

tions between the components can be found in the domain models. Finally, if components are instantiated archetypes, the relations identified between the generic archetypes generally also apply to the instantiated archetypes. This provides input for defining necessary relations between the components.

In addition to identifying relations based on the origin on which the component is defined, a second approach to finding relations between components is to 'script' usage scenarios (discussed in more detail in the next chapter) for the architecture. Following a logical sequence of execution in the architecture helps to identify what components need to be able to communicate with each other.

At this point, it is important to keep the relations domain-specific and not map them to solution-domain concepts, e.g. a message send, a pipe, etc. Later during the design, the relation will be converted to solution concepts which can be implemented, meaning that it will either be mapped to one of the aforementioned concepts or it will be implemented as a connector component. Finally, it is preferred to keep the number of relations between components minimal, thus no more relations than strictly necessary should be defined. A high connectivity level between components often indicates an architectural decomposition in which functionality is decomposed without adhering to high cohesion/low coupling principles and should be treated as an indicator of a potential problem.

To summarize the discussion in this section, one can identify the following activities during the decomposition of the architecture into its main components:

- **Identification and specification of components.** We have examined the possible sources for the identification of components, including the system interfaces, domains, abstraction layers, domain entities and archetype instantiations. In addition, we discussed the two primary dimensions of system decomposition, i.e. functionality versus entity-based and problem-domain versus solution-domain-oriented decomposition.

- **Identification and specification of relations.** Once the components have been identified, the relations between them need to be identified. We presented some guidelines and hints, based on the origin of the component. In addition, we examined the scripting of usage scenarios for identifying required relations between components.

4   Describing system instantiations

So far, we have been working hard to design a software architecture for the system that we intend to build. We have started by identifying the context in which the system will operate and the archetypes that characterize the 'nature' of the system. In the previous section, we discussed the identification of components and the relations between them. Before continuing to the next phase in the design, i.e. the assessment of the software architecture, it is important to verify that the architecture really is suitable for the system. Design is typically an iterative process consisting of integrating activities addressing the overall system and focusing activities on addressing parts of the system that require particular attention. During this process, it may happen that the software architect is struggling with a particularly hard problem and, in the process, is losing the system-wide perspective. To guarantee that the designed software architecture really covers all the requirements put on the complete system, it is important to verify this before continuing to the next phase.

The approach we take to verifying that the architecture actually fulfils or at least facilitates the fulfilment all system requirements is *to describe system instantiations*. We use the context and the architecture to describe one or more concrete system instantiations. However, this only gives us a rather coarse-grained structure. Therefore, the software architecture needs to be populated with more detailed entities. At the top level, this is generally done by recursively decomposing the components of the system into lower-level components.

The recursive decomposition of the components of the architecture into lower-level components is populated with instantiated archetypes. At the leaf levels of the system, the components are assigned individual instances of archetypes. The generic relations between the archetypes identified during the previous step are instantiated together with the instantiation of the involved archetypes. The assignment of archetypes to components and specification of relations between components allows for a verification of the match between the domain abstractions represented by the archetypes and the concrete system instantiation. If mismatches are identified, this is generally an indication of a problem that needs to be investigated to make sure that no fundamental mistakes have been made, which often prove extremely costly to repair at a later stage.

Product-line architectures generally need to support a wider variety of system instantiations than other software architectures, since the individual products in the family have unique requirements. During the definition of system instantiations, explicit attention needs to be directed to the variation in system instantiation for each product. Although the difficulties of providing the required variability are primarily found in the implementation of the reusable assets, less than careful design of the software architecture can lead to unwanted rigidity in dimensions where flexibility is required. These aspects are described in more detail in Chapter 9.

Describing system instantiations may seem similar to detailed design. Although both activities add detail, their purposes are fundamentally different. System instantiations are developed to verify the architecture against the requirements put on the software system. Detailed design, on the other hand, bridges the gap between the software architecture and the implementation of the system. In addition, a detailed design must be complete, whereas the system instantiation description is used to increase confidence in the architecture and may, therefore, omit details irrelevant for the verification.

In summary, the following activities take place during the definition of system instantiations:

- the components of the software architecture are recursively decomposed into lower-level components;

- each component is either populated with instantiated archetypes that fulfil the functionality required from the system or is represented by an individual instantiated archetype;

- the generic relations between the archetypes are instantiated for the instantiated archetypes and a verification of the match between abstractions and the concrete system decomposition is performed;

- sufficient variability of product-line architectures is verified by the definition of multiple system instantiations, representing different products.

5 Illustrating functionality-based design

In the following sections, we illustrate functionality-based architectural design for the example systems discussed in the previous chapter. Although based on real-world systems, the designs presented here have been modified and simplified for illustrative purposes. Because of this, the designs presented here may seem somewhat small and naïve, but since these designs will be transformed in Chapter 6 to incorporate the quality requirements we are forced to keep the size of the initial designs small.

5.1 Fire-alarm systems

Defining the system context
A fire-alarm system is a relatively autonomous system, but it does provide a number of interfaces to its context. The first issue to decide whether the mechanical and hardware parts of the detectors and alarm devices are part of the system or not. Since we are concerned with the architecture of the software system, we consider those parts to be external and consequently interfaces exist between the *software* system and the physical detectors and alarm devices.

A second issue which we need to decide upon is whether the communication system is part of the system at hand, because the fire-alarm system is highly distributed in nature. In this case, we decide that communication is included as a part since it forms an integral part of the fire-alarm system's functionality.

A second interface of the system is towards the operator of the system, not only in the case of an alarm, but also for activating and deactivating parts of the system and monitoring its behaviour. This amount of variability of the functionality of the interface is very large, but one can identify a number of core issues that need to be retrievable via the operator interface, such as the location of an alarm or fault warning in the building. Part of this interface is the interaction with external contacts that need to be notified when the system enters certain states, e.g. alarm, such as the local fire station.

A third interface, though related to the previous one, concerns interaction with other building automation systems. Other systems may be interested in certain events that take place in the fire-alarm system and may request to be notified. Similarly, the fire-alarm system may want to affect the state and behaviour of other systems, e.g. in case of a fire in a part of the building, the passage-control system may be ordered to unlock all doors in that part allowing people to leave the building without having to use their cards and codes at every door.

In Fig. 14, the interfaces provided by the fire-alarm system are presented graphically. As discussed earlier, in a real design, one would assign functional and quality requirements to the identified interfaces and define the interaction at these interfaces in more detail. However, we leave this step here to avoid exposing unnecessary details of the system.

Identifying the archetypes

When searching for entities that grasp the behaviour of several entities and are still abstract, one can detect a number of candidates. Among these, we will use the following as archetypes:

■ **Point.** The notion of a point represents highest-level abstraction concerning fire-alarm domain functionality. It is the abstraction of the two subsequent archetypes.

■ **Detector.** This archetype captures the core functionality of the fire-detection equipment, including smoke and temperature sensors.

■ **Output.** The output archetype contains generic output functionality, including traditional alarms, such as bells, extinguishing systems, operator interfaces and alarm notification to, e.g., fire stations.

■ **Control unit.** Since a fire-alarm system is a distributed system by nature, small groups of points are located at control units that interact with the detectors and outputs in the group. Control units are connected to a network and can communicate. The latter is of crucial importance since the detector alarms in one control unit should often lead to the activation of outputs in other control units.

In Fig. 15, the relations between the archetypes are shown. As discussed earlier, detector and output are specializations of point and points are contained in control units. Control units communicate with other control units to exchange data about detectors and to activate outputs.

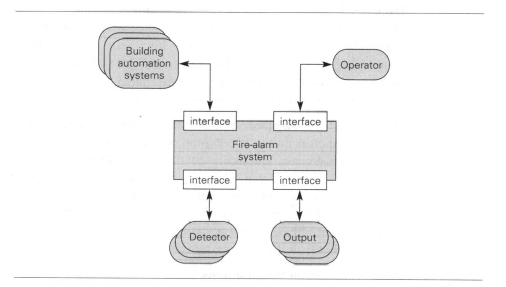

Figure 14   Interfaces of the fire-alarm system

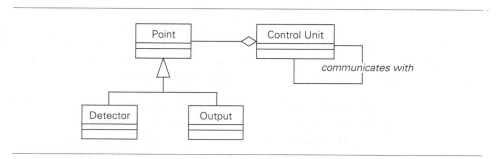

Figure 15   Relations between the fire-alarm system archetypes

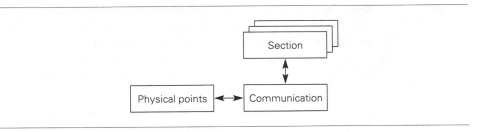

Figure 16   Main components of the fire-alarm system

Decomposing the architecture into components

The first activity in this step is to identify the decomposition of the system into its main components. The actual software architecture is decomposed in six main subsystems. However, since we scaled down the actual system for illustrative purposes, we identify only those subsystems directly related to the identified archetypes for the example fire-alarm system (Fig. 16).

We can see that the physical point component is an instantiation of the *point* archetype, whereas the communication component is typically a component based on a solution domain. The section component is a domain entity in the fire-alarm system domain since it represents a controller and the physical points monitored by it. A section also represents a geographic area where these physical points are responsible for identifying and acting upon alarm situations. The architecture employs an entity-based decomposition and its entities are taken from the solution domain, rather than the problem domain.

Describing system instantiations

To understand the instantiation of the fire-alarm system, we present two system instantiations that are at the two extreme ends of the complexity scale. The first system, shown in Fig. 17, represents a small system that might be found, for example, in a single family house. It consists of a small set of detectors, five smoke detectors in the example, one control unit and two outputs, i.e. a sound alarm and a simple LED-based user interface. The functionality available to the user is to activate or deactivate the system and the feedback from the system is an indication for alarm and one for faults, i.e. internal system errors.

A considerably larger example of an instantiated fire-alarm system is shown in Fig. 18. The fire-alarm system covers a site consisting of two buildings and each building is divided into four sections. Each section is supervised by a control unit. One of the control units has an operator interface as a point connected to it. Since the control units are able to communicate with each other, the opera-tor can monitor the complete system from the control unit to which the interface is connected.

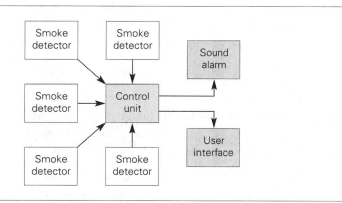

Figure 17   Example: small fire-alarm system instantiation

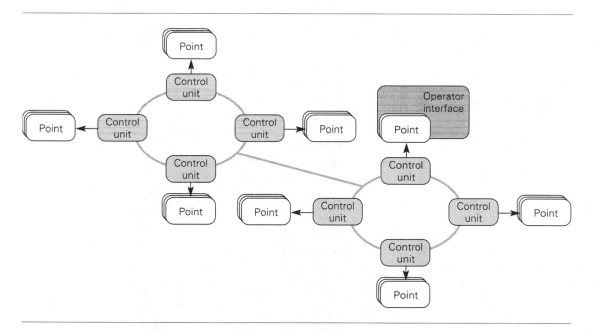

Figure 18   Example: two-building fire-alarm system

5.2 Dialysis systems

Defining the system context

The software part of the dialysis system is needs to interact with the hardware and mechanical parts of the system as well as the users of the dialysis system and other medical information systems. In Fig. 19, the interfaces of the dialysis system are shown graphically. One issue that we had to decide upon at this point was whether we should distinguish between the interfaces to the dialysis fluid circuit and the extra-corporal circuit, or use a traditional division into sensors and actuators. After studying the dialysis domain, we decided to adopt the first alternative, i.e. separate circuits, because the extra-corporal circuit is more highly prioritized for patient safety than the dialysis fluid circuit. Faults in the dialysis fluid circuit do not affect patient safety as long as the blood in the extra-corporal circuit is not affected. Consequently, the system interacts with its context through six interfaces, discussed in more detail below.

The lower-level interfaces of the system are concerned with the sensors and actuators of the extra-corporal and dialysis fluid circuits, respectively. Several quality requirements need to be associated with these interfaces. For instance, the sensors need to support accurate information about the real-world context, thus putting maximum boundaries on the interval between a real-world event and its presence on the sensor interface. Similar requirements are associated with the actuators.

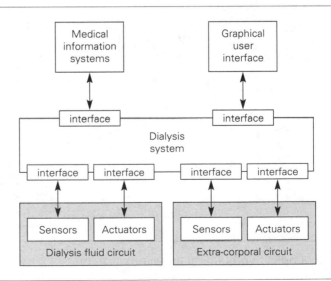

Figure 19   Interfaces of the dialysis system

One higher-level interface is the graphical user interface used by the medical staff supervising the dialysis process. The user interface allows for the setting of operational values, e.g. dialysis fluid temperature and dialysis process characteristics, and provides accurate information about the system operation. Especially in the case of alarm situations, the system should provide up-to-date information and allow for quick and accurate operation. Again, several quality requirements are associated with this interface, though less demanding than for the lower-level interfaces, because it is the responsibility of the system to react to alarm situations by taking the system to a safe state. The medical staff are responsible for solving the identified problems and restarting normal operation.

Finally, the second higher-level interface supports the interaction with medical information systems. This allows for the downloading of patient information, including patient-specific settings of dialysis parameters that can be approved or changed by the medical staff. In addition, it allows for logging of alarms and other dialysis-related information in the patient's file.

Identifying the archetypes

During the design of the software architecture for the dialysis system, we initially identified two archetypes that could be used throughout the system at different levels of abstraction, i.e. the notions of *Device* and *Controller*. At, for instance, the lowest level in the system, an example device is the water heating device. This device takes in cold water and heats it to a level set by the medical staff, normally to around 37 degrees Celsius. The device consists of two lower-level devices, i.e. a temperature sensor and an electric heating element, and is associated with a controller. This can be a simple P controller, but more advanced controllers can be used as well. At the top level, the complete dialysis system can be viewed as a device that is controlled by a controller, which basically is the treatment that the medical staff has selected for the patient. There is a large variety of dialysis treatments that can be applied and various treatments are tried for each patient to identify the one to which the patient (currently) reacts most positively. In Fig. 20, the dialysis system archetypes and their relations are presented graphically.

During subsequent iterations of the architectural design, we identified that a device is generally monitored by a second device, i.e. the *AlarmDetectorDevice*, which is configured with a number of device-specific alarm situations and constantly monitors the device to see whether any of these alarm situations has arisen. If it identifies an alarm situation, it invokes the associated *AlarmHandler* which then takes care of the alarm. Since the alarm detector device also is part of a hierarchy of devices (note the recursive aggregation relation of the *Device* entity), alarms that cannot be handled at the current level are forwarded upwards in the hierarchy.

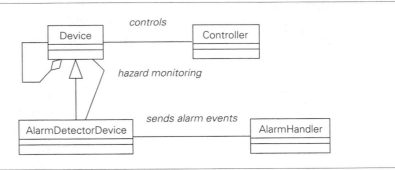

Figure 20   Dialysis system archetypes and their relations

Decompose architecture into components

The decomposition of the software architecture into its main components is primarily related to the interfaces which the system provides to its context. In Fig. 21, the identified components are shown. The external system and user-interface components are directly related to the higher-level interfaces the system has to its context. The hardware abstraction component is a typical abstraction layer that hides the differences between the various hardware elements of the system and increases the abstraction level for the fourth component, i.e. dialysis treatment, which covers the dialysis domain. The hardware abstraction component, for instance, may contain control loops as well. The aforementioned water heating device, for example, is located in the hardware abstraction component. That allows the dialysis treatment component to just set the desired water temperature and leave the details to lower-level components.

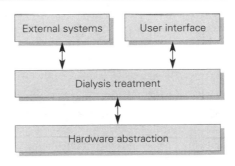

Figure 21   Main components of the dialysis system software architecture

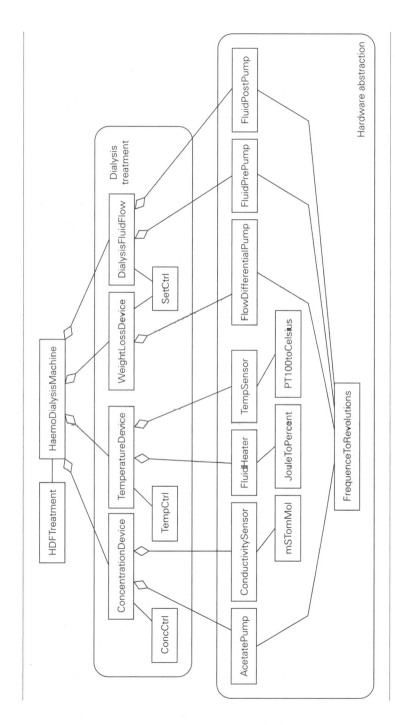

Figure 22 Part of an example of dialysis system instantiation

Describing system instantiations

The final step in the functionality-based architectural design is the description of system instantiations. The rationale behind this step is to verify that the software architectural designed for the dialysis system fulfils all the requirements, rather than just a part of them. Thus, by describing an instantiated dialysis system, it can be verified that the dialysis architecture that we designed covers all the requirements.

A second reason for generating system instantiations is to validate the ability of the architecture to support the differences in configuration that the system may need to support. Even systems that would not be considered to be software product lines are not always instantiated in exactly the same way. Instantiated dialysis systems can primarily vary in two dimensions. The first is the actual configuration of traditional machines used in dialysis clinics. For instance, certain types of dialysis treatments require particular configurations of mechanical components. Some treatments require the concurrent use of two types of dialysis concentrate, rather than one, which requires the addition of an additional pump and sensor to the dialysis machine. The second dimension, actually approaching a software product line, is concerned with dialysis machines used in different contexts than clinics. For instance, some dialysis patients would like to be able to perform the dialysis process at home. Some prototype studies have proposed dialysis machines that are integrated in chairs, for instance. Such alternative physical configurations of dialysis machines, as well as the different contexts, have effects on the actual instantiation of the software system and the software architecture should be able to support these.

In Fig. 22, part of an example of dialysis system instantiation is shown. The figure provides instantiation details for two of the components, i.e. hardware abstraction and dialysis treatment, but does not address the other two components. It can be clearly identified that the lower-level component is used to increase the level of abstraction for the dialysis treatment layer, as was intended in the design.

6 Summary

Architectural design connects the activity of requirements engineering to detailed design by providing a top-level design incorporating the main design decisions. In this chapter, we have discussed the first step in the architectural design process: designing the first version of the architecture based on the functional requirements. The method for architectural design presented in this part of the book has a focus on the explicit evaluation of and design for quality requirements, but that does not mean that the functional requirements are irrelevant. Before one can start to optimize an architecture for quality requirements, the first step must be to design an initial version of the architecture based on the functional requirements.

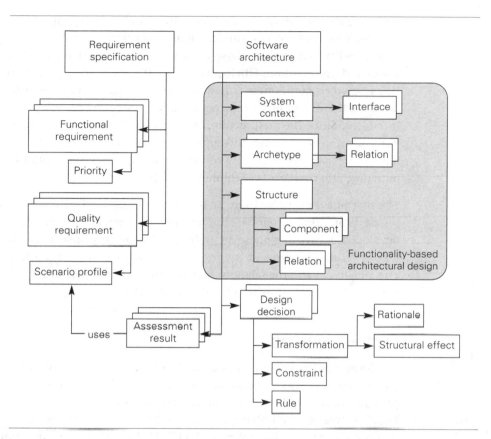

Figure 23   Artefacts developed during functionality-based architectural design

The first design phase discussed in this chapter consists of four main steps. The first step is concerned with determining the context of the system under design, the interfaces of the system to the external entities it interacts with and the behaviour the system should exhibit at the interfaces. In addition, the variability required from the interfaces in different system instantiations is specified. The second step is the identification of the archetypes, i.e. the main architectural abstractions, and the relations between the archetypes. Our experience is that finding these archetypes is very important, especially for the later phases, because they capture the core abstractions of the system. Architecture transformations tend to build additional structures around the archetypes for fulfilling quality requirements. The third step is concerned with decomposing the system into its main components and identifying the relations between them, i.e. the design of the software architecture. We discussed several sources for component identification, e.g. the system interfaces, domains, abstraction layers, domain entities and archetype instantiations. In addition, we discussed the two fundamental dimensions of system decomposition, i.e. functionality versus entity-based and problem-domain versus solution-domain-oriented decomposition. Finally, we treated the identification and selection of relations between components. The final step in functionality-based architectural design is the description of system instances using the archetypes and the system interfaces. Since the architecture, especially in the case of software product lines but also in general, needs to support a number of different instantiations, these have to be specified explicitly to verify that the system, in addition to the commonality, also supports the required variability.

The first phase of the software architectural design method discussed in this chapter develops first versions of a number of artefacts. In Fig. 23, the artefacts developed during this phase are indicated by the grey area. Thus, the system context is defined in terms of the interfaces which the system has to other systems. The archetypes and the relations between them are defined and, finally, the components and their relations are identified and specified.

7 Further reading

Traditional object-oriented design methods are, as we discussed earlier, primarily concerned with the functionality of software systems. Therefore, these methods provide useful input to this phase of the software architectural design process. Booch (1994) and Rumbaugh *et al.* (1991) present well-known object-oriented methods, as well as Jacobson *et al.* (1992). The latter even mention robustness analysis to evaluate the stability of the architecture in the presence of new requirements. In recent years, these methods have merged into the Rational Unified Process (Jacobson *et al.*, 1999). The approach to software architectural design proposed (Shlaer and Mellor, 1997) also contains steps that are related to functionality-based architectural design.

In our research, we have addressed these topics in a number of publications. The design of the fire-alarm system was discussed in a licentiate thesis (Molin, 1997). The dialysis system design was presented in Bengtsson and Bosch (1999a). The notion of archetypes is, to cite two examples, discussed in Bosch and Molin (1999) and Bosch (1999b).

CHAPTER 5

Assessing software architectures

In the previous chapter, we designed a first version of some software architectures, based on their functional requirements. In order to decide whether these architectures fulfil their quality requirements as well, the architectures need to be assessed. In this chapter we discuss a number of different approaches to architecture evaluation that we have found to be useful. These techniques are illustrated using the examples of architectures set out in the previous chapter.

1 Introduction

One of the core features of our software architecture design method presented here is that the quality attributes of a system or application architecture are explicitly evaluated during the architectural design, thus, without having a concrete system available. Although several notable exceptions exist, our experience is that the traditional approach in the software industry is to implement the system and then measure the actual values for the quality system properties. The obvious disadvantage is that potentially large amounts of resources have been put into building a system which does not fulfil its quality requirements. In the history of software engineering, several examples of such systems can be found. Being able to estimate the quality attributes of the system already during early development stages is important for avoiding such mishaps.

However, the question is how to measure system properties based on an abstract specification such as an architectural design. For obvious reasons, it is not possible to measure the quality attributes of the final system based on the architectural design. Instead, the goal is to evaluate the potential of the designed architecture to reach the required levels for its quality requirements. For example, the blackboard architectural style is less suitable for systems where performance is a major issue because there is a considerable overhead associated with the exchange of information between components via the blackboard. However, the flexibility of this style is rather high since it is, in many cases, possible to add components to the system without affecting the existing components.

The assessment of an architecture can have different aims, depending on the situation in which the software architect decides to initiate an assessment and the applicability of the assessment techniques used:

■ **Qualitative assessment.** In the least complicated situation, the software architect is interested in the comparison of two candidate architectures and is concerned with what architecture is more suited for a particular quality attribute. These two architectures may be two completely different alternatives, or they may be two subsequent versions of the same architecture, where the latter has been transformed to improve the assessed quality attribute or another one. For instance, one may assess two architectures for maintainability to decide which of the two is easier to maintain.

  The main disadvantage is that qualitative assessment only gives a 'boolean' answer, e.g. architecture A is more suited than architecture B for a given quality attribute. In the situation where the software architect has two alternative architectures, A and B, and two quality attributes, e.g. performance and maintainability, and one of the architectures is more suited for performance and the other more suited for maintainability, the architect has too little information to make a decision concerning which alternative is more viable. One architecture may be only slightly worse for performance, but considerably better for maintainability, but relative assessment gives no information concerning this.

■ **Quantitative assessment.** In the more complicated case, the software architect is interested in making quantitative statements about the quality attributes of the software architecture. Examples of these are statements about the throughput of the system in terms of transactions per time unit, average response times of individual actions and the maintenance cost of the system per year. If the architect is able to perform quantitative assessments with an acceptable accuracy, then it is possible to compare the assessment results with the requirement specification and decide whether the system will fulfil all its requirements, including the quality requirements, before the system is actually built. In addition, the comparison of alternative architectures or subsequent versions of an architecture becomes much more informed and the architect has quantifiable, objective means to select alternatives.

Although we will discuss techniques in this chapter that allow the software architect to make quantitative statements concerning the quality attributes of the software architecture, one should not underestimate the importance of detailed design and implementation for the quality attributes of the system. We are able to predict these attributes to some extent based on the software architecture, but the accuracy of the figures should be explicitly considered when making design decisions.

A disadvantage of this approach is that although we know what level the architecture provides for the assessed quality attributes, we have no information about the theoretically maximum (or minimum) values for the quality attributes. Thus, we have assessment results that, for instance, predict performance and maintainability levels, but we have no clue whether evolving this architecture or a fundamentally different architecture will provide, potentially, much higher performance and much lower maintenance cost, for example.

■ **Assessment of theoretical maximum.**[1] At the highest level of assessment we assess an architecture both for its present level and for the theoretical maximum (or minimum) for the relevant quality attributes, either for the architecture or for the domain. The gap between present and maximum levels allows us to determine whether evolving the architecture is still useful and whether we need to start making trade-offs between quality attributes and potentially renegotiating with the stakeholders to change the requirement specification, or whether evolving the current architecture or a fundamentally different architecture would be able to incorporate both quality requirements without conflicts.

In our experience, the currently available techniques for architectural assessment allow us to make quantitative statements about quality attributes at the software architectural level (although perhaps not at the level of accuracy that we would like), but we have little means to predict theoretical maximum (or minimum) values for software architectures. However, because of the cost of performing quantitative assessment, in many cases software architects assess qualitatively for deciding between design alternatives.

This chapter is organized as follows. In the next section, the notion of scenario profiles is introduced and explained in detail. These profiles are used for the assessment of quality attributes. Four approaches for assessing quality requirements have been identified, i.e. scenarios, simulation, mathematical modeling and experience-based assessment. For each quality requirement, the engineer can select the most suitable approach for evaluation. Each assessment approach is discussed in a separate section. For instance, Section 6 discusses the use of experience and creative insight of software architects and engineers for experience-based assessment. This section is followed by a discussion of architectural assessment in the broad sense and is concluded in Section 8. Some relevant further reading is considered in Section 9.

---

1. Thanks to P.O. Bengtsson for pointing this out to me.

2 Profiles

Quality requirements such as performance and maintainability are, in our experience, generally specified rather weakly in industrial requirement specifications. In some of our work projects with industry, the initial requirement specification contained statements such as 'The maintainability of the system should be as good as possible' and 'The performance should be satisfactory for an average user'. Such subjective statements, though well intended, are useless for the evaluation of software architectures. For example, Gilb (1998) discusses the quantitative specification of quality requirements and present useful examples.

Several research communities, e.g. performance (Smith, 1990), real-time (Liu and Ha, 1995) and reliability (Lyu, 1996), have developed techniques used for the specification and assessment of their particular quality requirement. Typical for these techniques is that they tend to require considerable effort from the software engineer for creating specifications and predictions. Secondly, since the ambition is to produce detailed and accurate results, these techniques generally require information about the system under development that is not available during the architectural design, but at the earliest during detailed design. Since we are interested in making predictions early in the design process, before the important, architectural design decisions cannot be revoked, other techniques are required that do not require as much detailed information and, consequently, may lead to less precise results, but which give at least indications of the quality of the prediction. Finally, it is important to note that the software engineering industry at large has not adopted the techniques developed by the quality-attribute research communities. One explanation might be that within an engineering discipline, each activity is a balance of investment and return. These techniques may not have provided sufficient return on investment, from the perspective of industrial software engineers, to be economically viable.

When one intends to treat the architecture of a software system explicitly in order be able to predict the quality attributes of the system early in the design process, one is required to specify quality requirements in sufficient detail. One common characteristic for quality requirements is that stating a required level without an associated context is meaningless. For instance, statements such as 'Performance = 20 transactions per second' and 'The system should be easy to maintain' are meaningless for architectural evaluation.

However, one common denominator of most quality attribute specification techniques is that some form of *profile* is used as part of the specification. A profile is a set of scenarios, generally with some relative importance associated with each scenario. The profile used most often in object-oriented software development is the *usage profile*, i.e. a set of usage scenarios that describe typical uses for the system. The usage profile can be used as the basis for specifying a number of, primarily operational, quality requirements, such as performance and reliability. However, for other quality attributes, other profiles are used. For example, for specifying safety we have used *hazard scenarios* and for maintainability we have used *change scenarios*.

Based on our experience, we believe that it is necessary to specify the relevant profiles for the software quality requirements that are to be considered explicitly in the architectural design process. Using the profile, one can make a more precise specification of the requirement for a quality attribute. For example, the required performance of the system can be specified using the usage profile by specifying the relative frequency and the total number of scenarios per time unit.

2.1 Complete and selected profiles

There are two ways of specifying profiles for quality attributes, i.e. the complete and the selected profiles. When defining a complete profile for a quality attribute, the software engineer defines all relevant scenarios as part of the profile. For example, a usage profile for a relatively small system may include all possible scenarios for using the system (perhaps excluding exceptional situations). Based on this complete scenario set, the software engineer is able to perform an analysis of the architecture for the studied quality attribute that, in a way, is complete since all possible cases are included.

It should, at this point, be clear to the reader that complete profiles only work in a limited number of cases. It requires systems to be relatively small and one is only able to predict complete scenario sets for some quality attributes. For instance, in order to predict the maintainability of the system, the definition of a complete profile assumes that one is able to define all changes that will be required from the system during its operation, or during a predefined period of time. It is safe to assume that this is impossible in all but highly artificial situations.

The alternative to complete profiles is selected profiles. Selected profiles are analogous to the random selection of sample sets from populations in statistical experiments. Assuming the sample set is selected according to some requirements, among others randomness, the results from the sample set can be generalized to the population as a whole. One of the major problems in experiment-based research is the truly random selection of elements from the population, because of practical or ethical limitations. However, even if one does not succeed in achieving random selection, but is forced to make a structured selection of elements for the sample set, the research methodology developed for a weaker form of experimentation, known as quasi-experimentation, still allows one to make scientifically validated statements.

The notion of selected profiles makes use of the above principles. Assuming a large population of possible scenarios, e.g. change scenarios, one selects individual scenarios that are made part of the sample set. A complete sample set is what we, so far, have referred to as a profile. Assuming that the selection of scenarios has been done carefully, one can assume that the profile represents an accurate image of the scenario population. Consequently, results from architectural analysis based on the profile will provide accurate results for the system and not just for the profile. Obviously, the actual selection of scenarios is not random because these are created by a software architect. Therefore, we have to spend explicit effort on making sure that the scenario profile is as representative as possible. In the next section, we discuss our approach to this.

2.2 Defining profiles

The most difficult issue in defining a profile is, of course, the selection of scenarios that become part of the profile. Since these scenarios are selected and defined by software engineers and other stakeholders, it is hard to claim that this process is random. In our experience, totally unsupported selection and definition of scenarios leads, in some cases, to situations where particular types of scenarios, e.g. changes to the user interface, become overrepresented. To address this, we divide the process of profile specification into two main steps:

■ **Definition of scenario categories.** The first step in profile specification is the decomposition of the scenario 'population' into a number of smaller populations that cover particular aspects of the system. For instance, in the case of usage profiles, one may identify different stakeholders of the system, e.g. local user, remote user, operator, etc. To give a second example, in the case of maintenance profiles, one may identify changes to the different interfaces to the context of the system, e.g. the hardware, the communication protocols, the user interface, etc. In our experience, we normally define between four and eight categories, but this is heavily dependent on the type of system and the intentions of the software architects in defining the profiles.

■ **Selection and definition of scenarios for each category.** In the second step, the software architects select, for each category, a set of scenarios that is representative for the sub-population. Of course, we have moved the problem of representativeness one level down from the profile as a whole to the category. However, we have found, when dealing with a particular category, e.g. hardware changes in a maintenance profile, that it is considerably easier to cover all relevant aspects in that category. In addition, even if the scenarios within a category are not representative, the resulting profile will still be closer to the ideal compared to not using categories. Finally, in our experience, we select and define up to ten scenarios per category for quality attributes that are crucial for the system and three to five scenarios for important quality attributes.

The fact that humans are part of the process of selecting scenarios and categories can be considered a weakness, especially compared to automated random selection. However, it is not possible to perform random selection for the definition and the alternative is to not use scenarios and architecture analysis at all. As discussed in the introductory chapter, we know where the lack of assessment early in the design process leads.

Once the categories and scenarios that are part of the profile have been selected and defined, the next step is to assign weights to the scenarios. The weights have slightly different meanings for different profiles, e.g. in the case of a usage profile, the weight indicates the relative frequency of executing a particular scenario whereas, in the case of a maintenance profile, the weight indicates the predicted relative likelihood of a particular change scenario.

There exist many different approaches to assigning weights to scenarios. For instance, scenarios can be rated on a scale from 1 to 10 or 1 to 100 or an approach using (−−, −, 0, +, ++) can be used. We have no preferences on the particular approach to use, but we do require that the approach used is quantifiable and that the weights can be converted to relative weights.

For example, assume that the scenarios in a profile have been rated on a scale 1 to 10. Once all weights have been assigned, we calculate the relative weight by adding the scores of all scenarios to achieve a total X. The relative weight of each scenario is then calculated as assigned weight divided by X. This results in a number between 0 and 1 and indicates the relative importance of the scenario in the profile. The sum of relative weights of all scenarios in the profile is, obviously, 1. Later in this chapter, we will describe how the weights are used in the assessment of architecture.

Finally, we have studied alternative approaches to defining scenario profiles (Bengtsson and Bosch, 2000). We identified three approaches to creating profiles, i.e. individual creation, group creation and prepared group creation. In the last case, an individual first prepares a profile and then meets in a group to merge the respective profiles to create a group profile. In the experiment that we performed, it turned out that the use of prepared groups for creating scenario profiles is the preferable approach. It leads to the most representative profile and the variation between the prepared group profiles was considerably smaller than for the other approaches.

2.3 Quality attribute profiles

We have, up to this point, implicitly indicated that each quality attribute has an associated profile. Although this is true for several system attributes, some profiles can actually be used for assessing more than one quality attribute. In this section, we briefly describe the most important quality attributes and their associated profiles.

Several categorizations of quality attributes exist (see e.g. McCall (1994) for an overview) and no categorization exists that is widely accepted within the software engineering community. Because of this, we have selected five quality attributes that we believe can be considered as the most relevant from a general software system engineering perspective. For each quality attribute, we first present a description of the attribute. Then, the profile used for the assessment of the attribute is described. Finally, we discuss the architecture description data that is required for the assessment of the attribute. In Chapter 2, we introduced the artefacts developed during the software architectural design process. The architecture description data associated with the quality attributes extends some of these artefacts with relevant information or estimations. For instance, for maintainability, the assessment technique that we discuss requires estimates of the number of lines of code for each component. This information is added to the component definition artefact. Below, the selected quality attributes are described in more detail.

Performance

The general efficiency with which the system performs its functionality, measured in throughput, i.e. number of use scenarios per time unit, or the response time of use scenarios, is generally considered to be a very important property of any software system. Especially in large systems, the architecture plays a central role in achieving high performance, since performance bottlenecks are not caused by the actual computation related to the domain functionality, but are due to context switches, synchronization points, dynamic memory management, communication overheads, etc.

- **Profile:** usage profile describing either a complete or selected set of functional scenarios, describing a particular instance of system usage by one of the users. Scenario categories generally decompose the use scenario space based on user types and/or system interfaces. Scenario weights represent the relative frequency of the scenario.

- **Architecture description data:** the architecture should contain, in addition to the base information concerning component and component functionality, the system behaviour in response to the use scenarios in the profile, the required computation at each component, the average (and worst-case) delays due to e.g. synchronization and the general overhead in the system. This information can be generated by the software architects based either on estimations or on historical data from existing systems.

Maintainability

Similar to performance, maintainability is also a quality attribute fundamentally affected by the architecture of a software system. The way the system functionality is decomposed into components leads to highly different efforts in response to requirements changes. This is because a requirement change may lead to a local change in one architecture, but may cause changes in several components in another architecture. There are considerable cost differences between the two examples, due to the additional effort of changing more than one component, but also due to the increased architecture erosion and other effects. Finally, there are requirement changes that have so-called architectural impact, i.e. they require the structure of the architecture to be changed. It should be possible to incorporate all likely requirement changes without changes to the software architecture since changes with architectural impact tend to be prohibitively expensive.

- **Profile:** maintenance profile, consisting of change categories and change scenarios. Change categories tend to be organized around the interfaces the system has to its surroundings. Generally, the hardware and operating system, the interface to other systems the system under design is intended to communicate with and the user interface to each of the user types tend to become change categories. The change scenarios describe concrete requirement changes that lead to changes to the software. The relative weight of a scenario indicates its relative likelihood, i.e. the chance that the scenario (and the scenarios it represents) occur during a time period. Note that since we assume that multiple requirement changes may take place during this time period, it is not impossible that, change scenarios that are particularly likely to occur will happen several times. This does not mean that the concrete change scenario happens more than once (the requirement change can only be incorporated once), but that multiple concrete scenarios may occur from the set represented by the change scenario. Since these scenarios are assumed to have a similar impact, it does not matter for the assessment which concrete scenario is counted.

- **Architecture description data:** as we will see in the examples later on in the chapter, change scenarios are evaluated with respect to their impact on the architecture. For the assessment technique discussed in this chapter, we calculate impact in terms of number of lines of code that have to be changed. In order to determine this, the estimated size of the architectural components in terms of lines of code needs to be available for maintainability assessment.

Reliability

More than the quality attributes described earlier, reliability is a function of several factors, including the architecture, the detailed design, the implementation, the education and experience levels of the people involved, etc. During architecture assessment, we are, naturally, primarily concerned with the architectural dimension of reliability. The architectural aspect of reliability is concerned with component interaction during operation and the effects of component errors on the system reliability as a whole. Use scenarios that use multiple components will have a lower reliability than use scenarios using fewer components since the combined component reliabilities lead to lower use scenario reliabilities.

■ **Profile:** usage profile, where the use scenarios are evaluated with respect to the component reliabilities, resulting in use scenario reliabilities. Based on these reliabilities and the relative weights, a system reliability can be calculated.

■ **Architecture description data:** in addition to the knowledge about the architectural components and information about component interaction in response to each use scenario, the software architect needs component relia-bility data. This data can be based either on historical data or on estimations. In addition, the reliability data can be converted into component requirements. The component designers and implementers then need to assess component reliability and make sure that the required levels are achieved.

Safety

Safety is concerned with the negative or even destructive effects the system under design may have on entities in the real world. It is, consequently, not concerned with the system functionality (this is what the reliability of the system is concerned with), but with the negative effects the system may have on the real world. The effects may be physical, e.g. a dialysis machine not detecting air bubbles in the extra-corporeal blood flow, but need not be, e.g. a banking system performing incorrect money transfers, thereby damaging customers and/or the banking corporation itself. In addition, the safety requirement is supposed to detect both internal system errors and incorrect system input.

■ **Profile:** hazard profile, containing hazard scenarios, i.e. situations where not detecting a fault may lead to negative or disastrous consequences. The hazard categories can be organized according to certification documents, as is the case for medical systems, the interaction points of the system with the real world or the critical system components, whose failure may lead to hazard situations.

■ **Architecture description data:** safety is often an issue in embedded systems, i.e. systems including mechanical, hardware and software parts. Since safety is primarily a system attribute and the software safety is derived from the system safety, the relation between system architecture and the software architecture should be explicit and clear.

Security

The security of a software system is concerned with three main issues, i.e. secrecy, integrity and availability. Secrecy is compromised when confidential information becomes available to unauthorized entities. Integrity is threatened when the attacker attempts to illegally alter parts of the system. Finally, availability can be attacked through so-called denial-of-service attacks. Security is not just an issue for military (intelligence) systems, but is relevant for most business and governmental systems since most organizations have both the right and the obligation to keep data inaccessible for all but authorized users. In particular, intentional attempts at access by unauthorized entities can take many forms, including attacks at the level of the system hardware, but there is definitely an architectural component in security. One issue is that security should preferably be handled consistently throughout the system, another that 'compartmentalization' needs to be handled at the system level. Finally, software security is part of system security, which in turn may be part of other security schemes.

- **Profile:** the content of the security profile is determined by the aspect of security that should be assessed, i.e. secrecy, integrity or availability. For instance, for authorization, the profile can be divided into at least a 2×2 matrix using the categories, unintentional versus intentional unauthorized access attempts and internal versus external unauthorized access attempts. In addition, all system interfaces can be used for categorization. The usage profile may be used as a secondary profile to provide information on the actual usage of the system.

- **Architecture description data:** the required architectural data also depends on the aspect of security that is to be assessed. For instance, when assessing availability, the execution times of security-related operations may be required to determine the behaviour of the system under attack.

2.4 Example

To illustrate the selection and definition of a profile, we use the dialysis system as an example. As described in Chapter 3, one of the driving quality attributes for the dialysis system is *maintainability*. The company had learned the hard way the importance of developing maintainable software. In Table 3, a summary of the maintenance profile for the dialysis system is shown. Six change categories are presented, i.e. changes driven by the market, the hardware, safety regulations, medical

Table 3   Dialysis system maintenance profile

Category	Scenario description	Weight
Market driven	C1 Change measurement units from Celsius to Fahrenheit for temperature in a treatment.	0.043
Hardware	C2 Add second concentrate pump and conductivity sensor.	0.043
Hardware	C3 Replace blood pumps using revolutions per minute with pumps using actual flow rate (ml/s).	0.087
Hardware	C4 Replace duty-cycle controlled heater with digitally interfaced heater using per cent of full effect.	0.174
Safety	C5 Add alarm for reversed flow through membrane.	0.087
Medical advances	C6 Modify treatment from linear weight loss curve over time to inverse logarithmic.	0.217
Medical advances	C7 Change alarm from fixed flow limits to follow treatment.	0.087
Medical advances	C8 Add sensor and alarm for patient blood pressure.	0.087
Com. and I/O	C9 Add function for uploading treatment data to patient's digital journal.	0.043
Algorithm change	C10 Change controlling algorithm for concentration of dialysis fluid from PI to PID.	0.132
	Sum	**1.0**

advances, communication and I/O and, finally, algorithm implementation. For each of the scenario categories, one or a few scenarios are presented. Each scenario has an associated weight, which is normalized. The example is discussed in more detail in Bengtsson and Bosch (2000).

2.5 Summary

The definition of profiles for the quality attributes considered most relevant for the software architectural design allows for concrete and precise description of the meaning of statements about quality attributes. For instance, a maintenance profile describes what changes are most likely to occur and should be easy to incorporate.

For instance, using the profile as input, the software architect is able to optimize the architecture for the most likely changes, thereby improving the maintainability of the system.

In order to achieve the above situation, however, the software architecture needs to have two important tools available, i.e. techniques to assess the quality attributes and techniques to transform the architecture to improve its quality attributes. These two issues are the subject of the current and next chapter, respectively.

The software architect can decide to define a complete scenario for a particular quality attribute, but often this is not feasible and one is required to define a selected profile. The definition of a selected profile for a quality attribute consists of the following steps:

- **Define scenario categories.** As a first step, the scenario population for the quality attribute is divided into categories. In our experience, we have used four to six categories for the systems that we have assessed, but this depends on the type of system.

- **Define scenarios.** For each category, a set of scenarios is selected by the software architect which cover the category as well as possible. In our projects we have used up to ten scenarios for a detailed assessment and three to five for obtaining a good indication. Again, this depends considerably on the type of system and the goal of the assessment.

- **Assign weights.** Each scenario is assigned a weight indicating its 'likelihood'. For instance, in the case of performance, the weight denotes the relative frequency of the scenario, whereas in the case of maintainability, the weight expresses the chance that this change scenario occurs. No approach to assigning weights is enforced, but, as a minimum, the weights should quantifiable.

- **Normalize the weights.** To simplify the use of the profile in the assessment techniques described in the subsequent sections, the weights of the scenarios may be normalized. However, this is not necessary for all assessment techniques.

3 Scenario-based assessment

In the remainder of this chapter, a number of approaches to architectural assessment are discussed. The approaches have different advantages and disadvantages, but tend to complement each other. In this section, we discuss scenario-based assessment of software architectures.

Scenario-based assessment is directly dependent on the profile defined for the quality attribute that is to be assessed. The effectiveness of the technique is largely dependent on the representativeness of the scenarios. If the scenarios form accurate samples, the evaluation will also provide an accurate result. Scenario-based assessment of functionality is not new. Several object-oriented design methods use scenarios to specify the intended system behaviour, e.g. use-cases (Jacobson *et al.*, 1992) and scenarios (Wirfs-Brock *et al.*, 1990). The main difference to the object-oriented design methods is twofold. First, we use scenarios for the assessment of quality attributes, rather than for describing and verifying functionality. Second, in addition to usage scenarios, we also use other scenarios that define other quality attributes, e.g. change and hazard scenarios.

If, however, the software architect decides to use traditional use-cases during the architectural design and the usage profile is a selected profile, it might be important to define the use-cases independently from the usage profile. The reason is that the architectural design will, most likely, be optimized for the set of use-cases. If the set of use-cases and the usage profile are the same, then one can no longer assume that the assessment of the architecture based on the profile is representative of the scenario population as a whole. Finally, depending on the system, it may be necessary to develop new scenarios for evaluative purposes if the design is iterated a number of times.

Scenario-based assessment can be used for comparing two architectures and for an absolute assessment of a single architecture. The main difference is the amount of quantitative data and estimates necessary to perform the assessment, which is considerably larger in the latter form. Below, we will first describe the absolute assessment and then discuss how one can scale down the approach for comparative assessment.

As shown in Fig. 24, scenario-based assessment consists of two main steps: impact analysis and quality attribute prediction.

■ **Impact analysis.** As an input to this step, the profile and the software architecture are taken. For each scenario in the profile, the impact on the architecture is assessed. For a change scenario, the number of changed and new components and the number of changed and new lines of code could be estimated. For performance, the execution time of the scenario could be estimated based on the path of execution, the predicted component execution times and the delays at synchronization points. The results for each scenario are collected and summarized.

■ **Quality attribute prediction.** Using the results of the impact analysis, the next step is to predict the value of the studied quality attribute. For performance, the scenario impact data can be used to calculate throughput by combining the scenario data and the relative frequency of scenarios. For maintainability, the impact data of the change scenarios allows one to calculate the size in changed and new lines of code for an average change scenario. Using a change request frequency figure that is either estimated or based on historical data, one can calculate a total number of changed and new lines of code. Using historical data within the company or figures from the research literature, the software architect can calculate the maintenance cost by, for instance, multiplying the number of work hours per maintained line of code by the total number of maintained lines of code.

To illustrate scenario-based assessment, we present maintainability assessment and an associated maintenance profile as an example. We use the dialysis system example discussed in Chapter 3 and the maintenance profile presented in Table 3. For each of the change scenarios in the maintenance profile, an impact analysis is per-

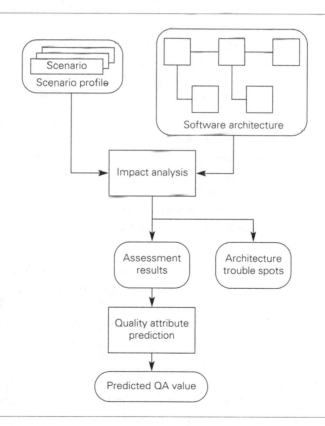

Figure 24   Scenario-based assessment process

formed. In this case, the changed code is expressed in the percentage of lines of code affected in an existing component. The component sizes are taken from a small prototype that was constructed as part of the joint research project with the involved companies, i.e. EC-Gruppen and Althin Medical. The result of the impact analysis is shown in Table 4.

Using the impact analysis data, we can calculate the average number of lines of code (LOC) for a change scenario:

$$0.043*60 + 0.043*127.5 + 0.087*350 + 0.174*10 + 0.217*100 + 0.087*190 + 0.087*350 + 0.087*120 + 0.043*290 + 0.132*100 = 145 \text{ LOC/Change}$$

Assuming a number of change requests per year of 20 and an average productivity of 1 LOC/hour (which is high for medium-sized and large systems, where studies have shown a productivity of 0.2 LOC/hour (Henry and Cain, 1997)), one can calculate a maintenance effort for the architecture of:

20 change requests * 145 LOC/change request * 1 hour/LOC = 2800 hours

This equals about 1.5 person working full-time on the maintenance of the software system. Note that these figures incorporate all maintenance-related activities, including updating the requirement specification, design documents and user documentation, the actual design and implementation, regression testing and testing of the new functionality and the deployment of the software.

As mentioned earlier, scenario-based assessment can also be used for the comparison of two or more alternative architectures. In that case, the quantification of impact data is less important and no prediction of quality attributes is done. Instead, for each architecture, impact data is collected, which can be, for instance, on a (––, ..., ++) scale and summarized. Using this model, each architecture is assigned a score and the software architect can select the most appropriate architecture by comparing the scores. However, the disadvantages of qualitative assessment discussed in the introduction remain.

Finally, in our experience, scenario-based assessment is particularly useful for development quality attributes. Quality attributes such as maintainability can be expressed very naturally through change scenarios. Although operational quality attributes, such as performance, can be assessed using this technique as well, we have discovered that other assessment techniques are sometimes preferable.

Summarizing, scenario-based assessment can be used both for relative (or comparative) and absolute assessment. It consists of two major steps, i.e. impact analysis, taking the software architecture and the profile as input and generating impact data, and quality attribute prediction, using the impact data to make a statement

Table 4   Impact analysis per scenario

Scenario	Affected components	Volume
C1	HDFTreatment (20% change) + new Normaliser type component	$0.2*200+20 = 60$
C2	ConcentrationDevice (20% change) + ConcCtrl (50% change) + reuse with 10% modification of Acetate Pump and ConductivitySensor	$0.2*100+0.5*175+0.1*100+0.1*100 = 127.5$
C3	HaemoDialysisMachine (10% change) + new AlarmHandler + new AlarmDevice	$0.1*500+200+100 = 350$
C4	Fluidheater (10% change), remove DutyCycleControl and replace with reused SetCtrl	$0.1*100 = 10$
C5	HDFTreatment (50% change)	$0.5*200 = 100$
C6	AlarmDetectorDevice (50% change) + HDFTreatment (20% change) + HaemoDialysisMachine (20% change)	$0.5*100+0.2*200+0.2*500 = 190$
C7	See C3	$= 350$
C8	new ControllingAlgorithm + new Normaliser	$100+20 = 120$
C9	HDFTreatment (20% changes) + HaemoDialysisMachines (50% changes)	$0.2*200+0.5*500 = 290$
C10	Replacement with new ControllingAlgorithm	$= 100$

about the level of the quality attribute. In the case of comparative assessment, the phase of quality attribute prediction does not lead to a figure, but to a ranking of alternative architectures.

4   Simulation-based assessment

The assessment technique discussed in the previous section is rather static in that no executable dynamic model is used. An alternative is *simulation-based assessment* in which a high-level implementation of the software architecture is used. The basic approach consists of an implementation of the components of the architecture and an implementation of the context of the system. The context, in which the software system is supposed to execute, should be simulated at a suitable abstraction level. This implementation can then be used for assessing the behaviour of the architecture under various circumstances.

Once a simulated context and high-level implementation of the software architecture are available, one can use scenarios from the relevant profiles to assess the relevant quality attributes. Performance, for example, can be evaluated by executing the usage profile in the simulated context and architecture and collecting information about the throughput and response time to system events.

The process of simulation-based assessment consists of a number of steps:

■ **Define and implement the context.** The first step is to identify the interfaces of the software architecture to its context and to decide how the behaviour of the context at the interfaces should be simulated. It is very important to choose the right level of abstraction, which generally means removing most of the details normally present at system interfaces. For instance, for an actuator in the context of the system requiring a duty cycle to be generated, the simulated actuator would accept, for example, a flow or temperature setting.

Especially for embedded systems where time often plays a role, one has to decide whether time-related behaviour should be implemented in the system. For instance, when increasing the effect of the heater in the dialysis system, the actual water temperature will increase slowly until a new equilibrium is met. The software architect has to decide whether such delays in effects between actuators and sensors should be simulated or not. This decision depends on the quality attributes that the software architect intends to assess and the required accuracy of the assessment.

Finally, for architecture simulation as a whole, but especially for the simulation of the system context, one has to make an explicit balance between cost and benefit. One should only implement at the level of realism required to perform the assessments one is interested in.

■ **Implement the architectural components.** Once the system context has been defined and implemented, the components in the software architecture are constructed. The description of the architectural design should at least define the interfaces and the connections of the components, so those parts can be taken directly from the design description. The behaviour of the components in response to events or messages on their interface may not be specified as clearly, although there generally is a common understanding, and the software architect needs to interpret the common understanding and decide upon the level of detail associated with the implementation.

Again, the domain behaviour that is implemented for each component as well as the additional functionality for collecting data is dependent on the quality attributes that the software architect intends to assess. For some quality attributes, additional architecture description data need to be associated with the components. For instance, in the case of performance assessment, estimated execution times may be associated with operations on the component interfaces. In that case, generally a simulated system clock is required in order to be able to calculate throughput and average response time figures.

■ **Implement profile.** Depending on the quality attribute(s) that the software architect intends to assess using simulation, the associated profile will need to be implemented in the system. This generally does not require as much implementation effort as the context and the architecture, but the software architect should be able to activate individual scenarios as well as run a complete profile using random selection based on the normalized weights of the scenarios.

For example, in virtually all cases, the use profile needs to be implemented. The software architect generally is interested in performing individual use scenarios to observe system behaviour, but also to simulate the system for an indefinite amount of time using a scenario activator randomly selecting scenarios from the profile.

■ **Simulate system and initiate profile.** At this point, the complete simulation, including context, architecture and profile(s), is ready for use. Since the goal of the simulation is to assess the software architecture, the software architect will run the simulation and activate scenarios in a manual or automatic fashion and collect results. The type of result depends on the quality attribute being assessed.

It is important to note that for several quality attributes, the simulation will actually run two profiles. For instance, for assessing safety, the system will run its use profile in an automated manner, and the hazard scenarios will, either manually or automatically, be activated. Whenever a hazard scenario occurs, data concerning the system context is collected. For example, in the dialysis system example, all values relevant to the safety of the patient, e.g. blood temperature, concentrate density, air bubbles, heparin density, etc. are collected from the simulation to see if any of these values, even temporarily, exceed safety boundaries.

■ **Predict quality attribute.** The final step is to analyze the collected data and to predict the assessed quality attribute based on the data. Depending on the type of simulation and the assessed quality attribute, excessive amounts of data may be available that need to condensed. Generally, one prefers to automate this task by extending the simulation with functionality for generating condensed output or using other tools.

To give an example, for performance assessment, the system may have run tens (or hundreds) of thousands of use-scenario instances and collected the times required to execute the scenario instances. All this data needs to be condensed to average execution times per scenario, and perhaps include a standard deviation. This allows one to make statements about system throughput, scenario-based throughput and average response times of individual scenarios.

Simulation of the architectural design is not only useful for quality attribute assessment, but also for evaluating the functional aspects of the design. Building a simulation requires the engineer to define the behaviour and interactions of the architectural entities very precisely, which may uncover inconsistencies in the design earlier than when using traditional approaches. In our experience, it is extremely useful to be forced to express exactly what the functionality of an architecture component should be. Simulation has been used in all three example systems described in Chapter 3 and the experiences have been very positive. Although there is an overhead involved in the implementation of, especially, the system context, our experience is that the advantages easily outweigh these.

The fact that an executable specification of the system is available early in the design process often proves to be highly relevant. It is important to note that it is possible to have a simulation of the system available during the whole design process. This is achieved through iterative refinement of the simulated context and the system implementation. Using this approach, the software engineers working with the system iteratively detail the design and the context in which the design operates until the context is no longer simulated, but the actual context. If this level is achieved, the system implementation is also complete. It is possible to use parts of the actual system context early in the design and use simulated parts where the system is not sufficiently detailed yet. Although our experience is that this approach is very interesting for, especially, the implementation of embedded systems with high availability and strict safety requirements, it is outside the scope of this book.

Another frequently used approach to perform assessment of a software architecture is through *prototyping*. Distinct from simulation where the complete software architecture is implemented at a high level of abstraction and is executed in a simulated context, prototyping implements a part of the software architecture and executes that part in the actual, intended context of the system. Prototyping is, similar to simulation, most often used to assess an operational quality requirement, for example, performance, that is of crucial importance to the success of the system. An important difference is that prototyping requires more input from the development and the availability of the hardware and other parts that make up the context of the software system. In return for the additional effort, one obtains a more accurate and stronger validated assessment result.

Simulation and prototyping complement the scenario-based approach in that simulation is particularly useful for evaluating operational quality attributes, such as performance of fault tolerance by actually executing the architecture implementation, whereas scenarios are more suited for evaluating development quality attributes, such as maintainability and flexibility.

Simulation can be used for the assessment of reliability in two ways. First, using component reliability figures, one can simulate component failures during automated execution of the usage profile and collect reliability figures for the architecture based on this data. Secondly, some research results have shown that correlations exist between the reliability of specifications and the systems implemented based on those specifications. For instance, in Zhao (1997), it has been shown that the prediction of the reliability from the design is almost as good as the predictions from the implementation. This points to the fact that the reliability is built into the system early and so emphasizes the need to get early estimates. Thus, the reliability of the architecture implementation in the simulation gives an indication of the reliability of the final system.

Although simulation is primarily suited for the assessment of operational quality attributes, the implementation of the architecture in the simulation can be used to evaluate development quality attributes, such as maintainability. Once the simulation is available, the software architect can then implement scenarios from the maintenance profile and measure the required effort and identify the affected components and the extent of change. Using this data, one can extrapolate the required effort for the complete system.

Finally, the accuracy of simulation-based assessment depends on a number of factors. First, the accuracy of the profile used to assess the quality attribute. Second, it is dependent on how well the simulated system context reflects real-world conditions. Finally, it depends on the relation between architectural implementation and implementation of the final system. Consequently, the factors influencing accuracy are considerably more numerous than for scenario-based assessment, but the early availability of an executable implementation of the system has, as we have said, several advantages as well.

In Fig. 25, the graphical interface of a simulation of a measurement system is shown. The system is a beer can inspection system consisting of a trigger identifying cans entering the system via the conveyer belt, a camera that obtains an image from each can and an actuator that is able to remove cans which do not fulfil the requirements from the conveyer belt. We used this simulation, among others, for predicting the throughput of the system. We assigned estimated execution times to the operations of the components involved in the normal system operation, ran the simulation and measured various performance characteristics.

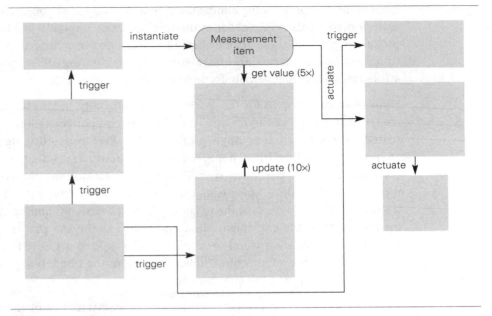

Figure 25   Simulation of a beer-can inspection system

In summary, simulation-based assessment makes use of an executable model of the software architecture and a simulation of the context of the system. Using the model and its context, one can execute the profile for the quality attribute that is to be assessed. Using the data collected during profile execution, one can predict the level of the quality attribute for the software architecture. The simulation-based assessment process consists of the following steps:

■ define and implement the context;

■ implement the architectural components;

■ implement profile;

■ simulate system and initiate profile;

■ predict quality attribute.

5   Mathematical model-based assessment

Various research communities, e.g. high-performance computing (Smith, 1990), reliable systems (Lyu, 1996), real-time systems (Liu and Ha, 1995), etc., have developed mathematical models that can be used to evaluate especially operational qual-ity attributes. Unlike the other approaches, the mathematical models allow for static evaluation of architectural design models. For example, performance model-ing is used while engineering high-performance computing systems to evaluate different application structures in order to maximize throughput. Using, for instance, queuing network theory (Smith, 1990), the software engineer can develop a mathematical representation that can be analyzed.

Mathematical modeling is an alternative to simulation since both approaches are primarily suitable for assessing operational quality attributes. However, the approaches can also be combined. For instance, performance modeling can be used to estimate the computational requirements of the individual components in the architecture. These results can then be used in the simulation to estimate the com-putational requirements of different use scenarios in the architecture.

The process of model-based assessment consists of the following steps:

- **Select and abstract a mathematical model.** As mentioned in the introduc-tion, most quality attribute-oriented research communities have developed mathematical models for assessing 'their' quality attribute. The models are gen-erally well established, at least within the community, but tend to be rather elaborate in that much, rather detailed, data and analysis is required. Consequently, part of the required data is not available at the architectural level and the technique requires too much effort for architectural assessment as part of an iterative design process. Thus, the software architect is required to abstract the model. This may result in less precise prediction, but that is, within limits, acceptable at the software architecture design level.

- **Represent the architecture in terms of the model.** The mathematical model that has been selected and abstracted does not necessarily assume that the system it models consists of components and connections. For instance, real-time task models assume the system to be represented in terms of tasks. Consequently, the architecture needs to be represented in terms of the model.

- **Estimate the required input data.** The model, even when abstracted, often requires input data that is not included in the basic architecture definition. This data, then, has to be estimated and deduced from the requirement specification and the designed software architecture. For instance, real-time task models require data about, among other things, priority, frequency, deadline and com-putational requirements of tasks and information about the synchronization points in the system.

■ **Predict the quality attribute.** Once the model is defined, the architecture is expressed in terms of the model and all required input data are available, the software architect is able to calculate the resulting prediction for the assessed quality attribute. In some cases, for instance in non-trivial performance assessments based on the performance engineering method developed by Smith (1990), a more advanced approach may be required.

The software metrics research community has developed a variety of product metrics of which at least part can be used for the assessment of software architectures. Validation of several of these metrics has shown correlation to quality attributes. For instance, McCabe's cyclomatic complexity metric (Fenton, 1996) has shown correlation to the maintenance cost of software systems. However, it is important to note that correlations are statistical relations, meaning that though true on the average, a metric does not have to predict accurately for the software architecture at hand.

Unlike the two aforementioned assessment techniques, not all types of mathematical model-based assessment make use of profiles. For instance, structural metrics, e.g. the aforementioned McCabe's Cyclomatic Complexity metric, base their values solely on the actual structure of a software design. This means that the assessment technique provides an immediate translation from the software architecture to the quality attribute, without incorporating the actual meaning of the quality requirement as specified by the customer. Other approaches do employ the profile in their assessment. For instance, real-time schedulability analysis models base the task model on the usage profile.

To give an example, in Alonso *et al.* (1998) an illustration of assessing the timing properties of a software architecture is presented. The mathematical model used by the authors is rate-monotonic analysis (RMA). Whereas RMA traditionally is used for relatively small, stand-alone and embedded systems, the authors applied the method for assessing a distributed software architecture. Their approach requires the architecture to be expressed in terms of the RMA model, i.e. the architecture is described in terms of events (periodic, irregular, bounded, bursty and unbounded) and reactions to events, expressed in terms of actions and resources. Actions make use of resources and are described by a number of attributes, i.e. priority, usage, atomic and jitter tolerance. Finally, the timing requirements need to be specified, i.e. the hard, soft and firm deadlines of the various events.

Based on the information described above, the rate-monotonic analysis method takes in the following steps. First, the connections between components are determined. Second, a physical model of the system is described based on provided resources. Third, components are allocated to resources. Fourth, the interconnections are modeled based on the resources. Finally, priorities are assigned to the tasks. Based on these artefacts, conventional rate-monotonic analysis can be performed to determine the real-time properties of the software architecture.

To conclude, mathematical model-based assessment provides an alternative primarily to simulation-based assessment in that these models are primarily available for operational quality attributes. Which assessment technique to choose depends upon at least two factors. First, no appropriate mathematical models may be available for the relevant quality attributes. Second, the development of a complete simulation model may require substantial effort, but if the model is used to assess more than one quality attribute, the effort can be divided over the attributes. Mathematical models are unique for each quality attribute.

6 Experience-based assessment

In the previous sections, we have discussed three approaches to *quantitative* architectural assessment. The reason we stress these approaches is because we hope to progress the state of the art towards quantitative, objective assessment rather than the current state of practice, which often is subjective and qualitative. However, it is by no means our intention to diminish the value of architectural assessment through objective reasoning based on earlier experiences and logical argumentation. On numerous occasions, we have encountered experienced software architects and engineers who provided valuable insights that proved extremely helpful in avoiding bad design decisions. Although some of these experiences are based on anecdotal evidence, most can often be justified by a logical line of reasoning.

One can identify two types of experience-based assessment. The first type is the informal, *ad-hoc* assessment by the software architects themselves performed as part of the normal design process. The second type of assessment is performed by external software architectural assessment teams. In that case, during the design process (often during the later stages), an external assessment team will evaluate the available assets to make sure that a system built on the designed architecture will fulfil its quality requirements. The results generated by the assessment team represent some kind of audit and may be used by management external to the project to decide upon its continuation. An external architecture assessment may be initiated by management, but in the organizations that have reported on its use, even the software architects within the project itself may initiate an external assessment. This can be done to confirm that the architecture is developing in the right direction or because the architecture has reached a critical point where a decision between two (or more) alternatives needs to be taken. In the latter case, the rationale is that consulting competent architects outside the project will increase the chance of a correct decision being taken.

Experience-based assessment is different from the other approaches in that the evaluation process is less explicit and more based on subjective factors such as intuition and experience. The value of this approach should, nevertheless, not be underestimated. Most software architects we have worked with had well-developed intuitions about 'good' and 'bad' designs. Their analysis of problems often started with the 'feeling' that something was wrong. Based on that, an objective argumentation was constructed based either on one of the aforementioned approaches or on logical reasoning. In addition, this approach may form the basis for the other evaluation approaches. For example, an experienced software engineer may identify a maintainability problem in the architecture and, to convince others, define a number of scenarios which illustrate this.

To give an example, during the design of the fire-alarm system architecture, it was identified that the system is inherently concurrent. Consequently, it was necessary to choose a concurrency model. Earlier experience by some team members in small embedded systems had shown that fine-grain concurrency with a preemptive scheduler could be error-prone considering the possibility of race conditions. The argumentation by those team members convinced the team as a whole and led to a transformation of the architecture that was later named the 'point pattern' (Molin and Ohlsson, 1998). In the next chapter, the point pattern and the associated architecture transformation are discussed in more detail.

7 Performing architecture assessment

So far, in this chapter, we have primarily discussed techniques and approaches that can be used as part of architecture assessment, but we have not shown how these parts are integrated in a full-scale process of architecture assessment. Although the reader may have deduced this from the discussion in this and previous chapters, we will here explicitly define the main steps in architecture assessment.

First, one should observe that architecture assessment is an iterative activity that is part of an iterative design process. Once the architecture is assessed for the first time, it will enter the transformation phase, assuming it does not already fulfil all its requirements. After transformation, the architecture will, again, be assessed for its quality attributes.

The first time the architecture is assessed, or possibly even before functionality-based design is performed, the profiles for the relevant quality attributes should be defined. It is important to notice that it is generally not feasible nor useful to assess all or many quality attributes. As in any engineering discipline, the benefit should outweigh the cost for each activity. Since both the definition of the profile and the repetitive assessment process are time-consuming activities, only those quality attributes should be selected for explicit assessment that are crucial for system success and for which it is unclear whether they will be fulfilled.

Once the relevant quality attributes have been selected and the profiles for these quality attributes have been defined, the next step is to select an assessment technique. As a general rule, our experience is that development quality attributes are generally most easily assessed using a scenario-based approach, but a mathematical or metrics-based model can also be used. Operational quality attributes can be assessed using either simulation-based assessment or a mathematical or metrics-based model. Both the selection of the assessment technique and the concrete implementation of it are influenced by, among other things, the goal and required accuracy of the assessment. In certain cases, one may decide to use two techniques to assess the same quality attribute. This allows the software architect to cross-reference results and to increase confidence in the assessment or, alternatively, to investigate inconsistencies.

The above steps are generally performed once during architectural design, for instance the first time an assessment of the architecture is performed. During the design iterations, the actual architecture assessment is performed during every iteration and for each quality attribute. Assuming that one is able to achieve quantitative predictions for each quality attribute, the result is a table containing, for each version of the architecture, the required level, the predicted level and an indication for each quality attribute. The indication may simply show that the attribute is or is not fulfilled, but possibly also that the attribute needs to be renegotiated with the customer or that a generally negative relation exists to another quality attribute.

To conclude, the process of architecture assessment can be divided into two components: a part that is performed once and a part that is executed for every design iteration:

- select the relevant quality attributes and define the required levels;

- define a profile for each quality attribute;

- select an assessment technique for each quality attribute.

For each design iteration:

- perform the quality attribute assessment for the current version of the architecture;

- assemble the results and decide upon continuation, renegotiation or termination of the design project.

8 Concluding remarks

Assessment of software architectures is the process of predicting quality attributes of the system developed based on a software architecture. We have identified three different goals with architecture assessment. First, *qualitative assessment* is used to compare two alternative architectures. Although useful, the disadvantage of qualitative assessment is that when comparing alternative architectures for more than one quality attribute, one has only 'boolean' data to base the selection on. Second, the software architect can perform *quantitative assessment* resulting in statements about the quality attributes for the assessed architecture expressed in numbers. This allows the software architect to decide whether the requirements are met by the assessed architecture. However, quantitative assessment provides no means to determine the theoretical limits for the architecture and the distance between the current level and the theoretical maximum or minimum. The third possible goal of architecture assessment is to determine the theoretical maximum of a software architecture for a particular quality attribute. In our experience, techniques are available for the first two assessment goals, but no work, to the best of our knowledge, is currently available with respect to the third goal.

The actual meaning of quality requirements in the requirement specification is often rather vague and imprecise. In this chapter, we propose to define scenario profiles that define the meaning of quality requirements more precisely. Two approaches to defining profiles exist, i.e. complete profiles and selected profiles. The first defines all relevant scenarios for a particular quality attribute, whereas the second selects a limited number of scenarios from a large population of possible scenarios. To structure the selection process, scenario categories are defined to divide the population into parts.

We have presented four architecture assessment techniques, i.e. scenario-based, simulation-based, mathematical model-based and experience-based architecture assessment. The scenario-based approach assesses the impact of the scenarios in the profile and predicts the quality attribute based on the impact data. Simulation-based assessment develops an abstract system context that is simulated and a high-level implementation of the architecture. Generally, for practical reasons, the profile that is used for the assessment is also implemented. During the simulation, relevant data is collected and the quality attribute can be predicted using the collected data. The software architect can use an, often adapted, mathematical model developed by one of the quality-attribute research communities. The adapted model can be used to predict the quality attribute. Finally, we have discussed the importance of experience in software architecture assessment and design. This experience can be used for experience-based assessment where the software architects from within the project, alternatively external assessment teams, perform an assessment of the architecture that leads to a conclusion in terms of the architecture fulfilling its requirements and a set of recommendations.

Although our goal is to improve the state of practice by providing objective and quantitative means to reason about architectures, it is explicitly not our intention to diminish the value of experience and creative insight in the architectural design process. Experienced and creative software architects and engineers are a necessary ingredient of any successful software development project.

The artefacts developed during this phase of the software architectural design process are primarily concerned with assessment results. In Fig. 26, the assessment results are marked by a grey box. However, a second aspect not shown explicitly, but highly relevant to the software architect is that the assessment of the software architecture provides indications about problem areas in the architecture, as we dis-

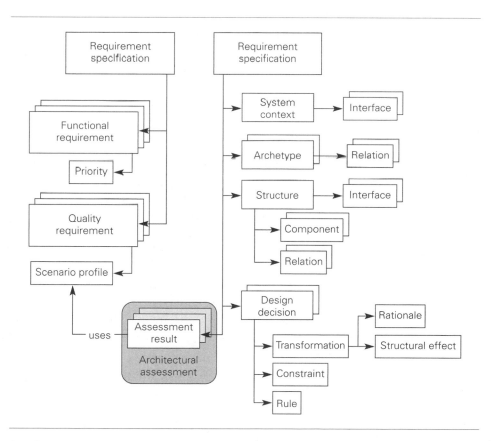

Figure 26   Artefacts developed during software architecture assessment

cussed earlier. These indications are used by the software architect to select the appropriate transformations, as discussed in the next chapter.

Finally, we have briefly mentioned the overall process of software architecture assessment. This process can be divided in two parts. The first part is performed once during the design of a software architecture and includes activities such as selecting and defining the relevant quality attributes, developing the associated profiles and selecting an assessment technique for each quality attribute. The second part of the process is performed for each iteration of the architecture and consists of performing the assessment for the relevant quality attributes, collecting the results and deciding upon the continuation, renegotiation or termination of the design project.

9 Further reading

The assessment of software architectures is discussed by several authors. The book by Bass *et al.* (1998) considers the notion of architectural reviews and looks at various approaches to performing these reviews. Kazman *et al.* (1994) present SAAM, a scenario-based technique for the assessment of software architectures. Boehm (1996) discusses the conflicts between various quality attributes, whereas Alonso *et al.* (1998) discuss the application of rate-monotonic analysis to the software architectural level to determine the real-time properties. Smith (1990) examines the notion of performance engineering and gives relevant information for assessing a software architecture for its performance characteristics. Poulin (1997) discusses the principles of measuring software reusability.

In our research, we have studied the assessment of software architectures. In Bengtsson and Bosch (2000), we present the results of an experiment to determine the best approach, from three alternatives, to define scenario profiles. Bengtsson and Bosch (1999b) present a scenario-based technique for the assessment of maintainability of a software architecture, and Bengtsson and Bosch (1998) discuss assessment of both reusability and maintainability during software architectural reengineering. In van Gurp and Bosch (1999), we discuss the use of Bayesian belief networks for the assessment of software architectures. Finally, in Grahn and Bosch (1998) there is a discussion of simulation techniques for assessing performance of software architectures.

CHAPTER 6

Transformation of software architectures

The approach to architectural design presented in this book consists of three major phases: functionality-based architectural design, architecture assessment and architecture transformation. In the previous chapters, the first two phases were explained. In this chapter, the notion of transforming an architecture to improve one or more of its quality attributes is discussed. We identify four types of architecture transformations that can be used to change the properties of the system. The transformations are illustrated using the examples of software architectures discussed in earlier chapters.

1 Introduction

In functionality-based architectural design, the structure of the system is determined by the application domain and the functional requirements. The identified archetypes and the system instances described using the archetypes are based on the software architect's perception of the domain. The perception of the software architect is largely based on the culture in which the architect lives and the education that he or she has received. Consequently, it is likely that other software architects and engineers will share the perception of the software architect who designed the initial version of the architecture. The fact that domain understanding is shared among, at least, the software engineering community is an important property of functionality-based design, since it allows for easy communication between members of the community. Thus, when software development based on the software architect's design is initiated, it is relatively easy for the software architect to explain the important concepts underlying the design. In addition, if the software architect disappears during the development, the people taking over will have an easier task to understand the architectural design and maintain its conceptual integrity (Brooks, 1995). Finally, during maintenance, software maintainers will have an easier understanding of the constraints, rules and rationale underlying the architecture, and thereby be able to maintain its conceptual integrity and, consequently, to slow down the software ageing process.

Thus, the functionality-based design of the architecture is based on domain analysis that is formed by the culture and education and, to some extent, it is shared by, at least, the software engineering community. As mentioned, this has important advantages. However, there is an important issue which has remained implicit: the functionality-based architectural design may not fulfil the quality requirements of the system! Performance, maintainability and other quality attributes of the architecture may not be satisfactory.

Assessment of the software architecture, as discussed in the previous chapter, is performed to collect information on the quality attributes of the architecture so that these can be compared to the requirements. If one or more of the quality requirements are not satisfied, the architecture has to be changed to improve the quality attributes. This is the process of architecture transformation, which is the topic of this chapter.

Architecture transformation requires the software engineer to analyze the architecture and to decide due to what cause the property of the architecture is inhibited. Often, the assessment generates hints as to what parts or underlying principles cause low scores. The assessment of the quality attributes is performed assuming a certain context, consisting of certain subsystems, e.g. databases or GUI systems and one or more operating systems and hardware platforms. Consequently, whenever a quality attribute is not fulfilled, one may decide either to make changes to the presumed context of the software architecture or to make changes to the architecture itself.

If it is decided that the software architecture, rather than the context or the requirement specification, should be changed, the architecture is subjected to a series of one or more architecture transformations. Each transformation leads to a new version of the architecture with the same domain functionality, but with different values for its properties.

The consequence of architecture transformations is that most transformations affect more than one property of the architecture, generally some properties positively and others in a negative way. For instance, the *strategy design pattern* (Gamma *et al.*, 1994) increases the flexibility of a class with respect to exchanging one aspect of its behaviour. On the down-side, performance is often reduced since instances of the class have to invoke another object (the instance of the strategy class) for certain parts of their behaviour. In the general case, however, the positive effect of increased flexibility considerably outweighs the minor performance impact.

We have identified four categories of architecture transformations, organized in decreasing impact on the architecture, i.e. imposing an architectural style, imposing an architectural pattern (or mechanism), applying a design pattern and converting quality requirements to functionality. One transformation does not necessarily address a quality requirement completely. Two or more transformations might be necessary. In the sections below, each category is discussed in more detail.

Although the transformation of a software architecture is necessary to fulfil its quality requirements, there are two important disadvantages to changing the functionality-based architectural design. First, the transformed architecture will not be as close to the shared understanding of the domain, requiring software architects and engineers to spend more time trying to understand the 'philosophy' underlying the architecture. For instance, the functionality-based architectural design of the measurement system consists of four components. The object-oriented framework that we designed for the measurement system domain consists of more than 30 components. These components have been added through architecture transformations improving the quality attributes, but not changing the domain functionality represented by the architecture. Second, the design tends to blow up the number of components. Most transformations will take one or a few components and reorganize the functionality by dividing it over more components. To use the aforementioned strategy design pattern as an example, the pattern transforms one (class) into at least three classes, i.e. the original class without the factored out behaviour, the abstract strategy class defining the interface and, at least, one concrete strategy class providing one variety of the factored out behaviour. Since most transformations increase the number of components in the architecture, it easily becomes the case that an elegant and simple functionality-based architectural design is transformed into a large and complex set of components which bears no visible relation to the initial architecture. During the complete architectural design process, it is of crucial importance to keep things as simple as possible and to search for conceptual integrity, a notion hard to quantify but understood by every software engineer (Brooks, 1995).

One may wonder whether the architectural design method presented in this book is not making design overly complicated. It is important to observe that we defined this method based on a number of architectural design projects that we have been involved in. Generally, researchers from our research group formed an architectural design team with software architects from the companies with whom we worked. We have tried to reflect the way the team and its members perform architectural design. Based on the experiences from the projects, we have made the *implicit* architectural design process, as we experienced it, *explicit*.

A second problem that we seek to attack in our explicit approach to architectural design is that *ad-hoc* architectural design approaches tend to lead to mismatches between the perceived problems and the actual problems and between problems and the solutions selected to address those problems. In several industrial architectural designs we have seen the use of styles, patterns or other solution technology which did not match the problems, such as unfulfilled quality requirements, that the project members were trying to solve. Subsequently, further analysis showed that the quality requirements which the project members were trying to solve were not the problematic quality attributes of the architecture. Converting the *ad-hoc*, implicit architectural design approach into an architectural design method which explicitly organizes the process into a number of well-defined steps will help to avoid the problems described above.

Finally, a note on the level of detail that should be achieved during architectural design. This is a function of the size of the system, the quality requirements and the required level of certainty. If the system is very large, architectural design is unable to penetrate the challenges of the individual parts of the system. The quality requirements, however, are the most important factor in deciding on the level of detail. The *goal of architectural design* is to develop a software architecture which, with a sufficient level of certainty, will fulfil all of its requirements, including the quality requirements. Thus, if the quality requirements are very challenging and close to the boundary of the technical capabilities, architectural design needs to go into considerable detail regarding the critical parts of the system, e.g. down to the behaviour of individual classes. The important issue is not to avoid performing design tasks normally considered to be part of detailed design, but to make sure that the final system will fulfil its quality requirements in addition to its functional requirements.

The remainder of this chapter is organized as follows. The next section considers the process of transforming a software architecture. Section 3 and onwards discuss the categories of architectural transformations that we have identified. Section 7 discusses the balancing of requirements for the software architecture and the requirements for the components that are part of the architecture. The chapter is concluded in Section 8, and accompanied by a section on interesting material on the topic.

2   The process of architecture transformation

Before describing the categories of architecture transformation techniques that we have identified, we present a process of architecture transformation that seeks to put these categories into a context. Transforming the architecture according to an architectural style or a design pattern is not an independent event, but occurs as part of a larger process of problem identification, solution selection and solution application.

The first step in the process is to identify what quality requirements are not fulfilled by the current version of the software architecture. In addition, information about the discrepancy between the assessed level of the quality attribute and the requirement is collected. Based on the difference between assessed level and the requirement for each quality attribute and their relative importance, we define a ranking of the quality attributes. The ranking indicates what quality attributes should be addressed first. As mentioned earlier, we address only those quality attributes during the assessment and transformation process which have been selected by the software architect as having crucial importance for the success of the system. In our experience, usually up to about five attributes are addressed. Finally, the assessed and required levels for the quality attributes that are fulfilled are also noted. This information is used later on in the selection of transformations.

Although some quality requirements and types of transformations affect the complete software architecture, several requirements and transformations are more local in nature. For instance, in the case of the dialysis system, the reaction time of the system to hazard situations is critical, but the response time to most user-interface commands can be much more relaxed. This results in different parts of the architecture having different associated quality requirements. Consequently, different local transformations are necessary for different parts of the software architecture.

The following steps of the process are, in principle, repeated for each quality attribute. However, since transformations affect more than one quality attribute, decisions concerning the selection of transformation will be based on all the relevant quality attributes.

The second step is to identify, for the quality attribute currently addressed, at what components or locations in the architecture the quality attribute is inhibited. The assessment performed in the previous phase has led to a quantitative prediction, but while assessing the architecture the software architect normally gets several hints on what components represent bottlenecks for the quality attribute. In our experience, when performing impact analysis during scenario-based maintainability assessment, there often is one (or a few) components that play a role in multiple scenarios. For some reason, the functionality captured by that component is sensitive to requirement changes. Such kinds of indications often give valuable input into what aspects of the architecture need to be changed.

The third step is the selection of a transformation that will solve the identified problem spots in the architecture. Generally, several different transformations can be used, differing in scope and impact, but also in their effects on the other quality attributes. For the selection of the most appropriate transformation, it is important to explicitly analyze the effects of the transformation on the other quality attributes. Based on this analysis, we select the transformation that does not affect any unfulfilled quality attributes in a negative manner, but only quality attributes for which there is a satisfying (positive) difference between the assessed and required level. For instance, if the system performance is well satisfied by the current architecture, it is acceptable to select transformations that improve maintainability at the expense of performance. However, if both are currently not fulfilled or the assessed level is very close to the required level, one should search for other alternatives.

The fourth and final step in the process is to perform the transformation, meaning that the functionality is reorganized according to, e.g. the selected style or pattern, and that the description of the architecture is updated to incorporate the changes. It is important to keep a record of the versions of the software architecture, the assessed levels for each of the relevant quality attributes and the rationale for each transformation. This is both useful when it proves necessary to backtrack to an earlier version since the team reached a dead-end in the design and for future reference by software engineers doing detailed design, implementation or software maintenance.

In the remainder of this chapter, we look at four activity categories of transformations that can be imposed on a software architecture, i.e. impose architectural style, impose architectural pattern, apply design pattern and convert quality requirement to functionality. In Fig. 27, these transformations are presented graphically. We identify two dimensions based on which the transformations can be distinguished. The first is the scope of the impact. Certain transformations affect the software architecture as a whole, causing changes at several locations. Other transformations are more local in their effects and affect only one or a small set of components. The second dimension is the type of transformation. Some transformations primarily restructure the existing components, e.g. by splitting components, adding and replacing relations, etc. Other transformation types primarily extend the existing software architecture with additional functionality and components. As a conse-

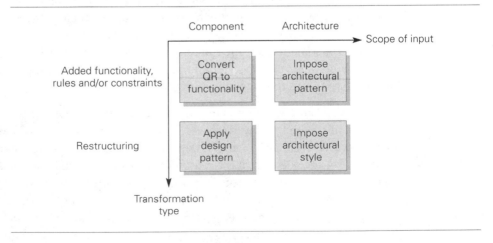

Figure 27   Taxonomy of transformation categories

quence, often additional rules and constraints are imposed as well. The four categories of transformations span the two-dimensional space that is created by these two dimensions.

Although the taxonomy in Fig. 27 suggests a clean separation between the transformation categories, deciding for a particular transformation in what box it belongs may not be straightforward in all cases. One can identify a number of reasons for this. First, some transformations, e.g. the model-view-controller, can both be used locally for a small set of components, i.e. the observer design pattern (Gamma *et al.*, 1994), but also as the main structuring style for a complete system, i.e. the model-view-controller architectural style (Buschmann *et al.*, 1996). Thus, the same mechanism is used at multiple levels of abstraction. Second, there has been some inconsistency in the use of terminology. Particular transformations can, in some systems, only be used locally whereas in other systems the transformations are used as the main structuring principles of systems. The architects and engineers working with these systems will undoubtedly disagree on the appropriate location of the design transformations in the taxonomy. However, from our perspective, the important issue here is not the actual mechanism that is used to accomplish, e.g. the fulfilment of a quality requirement, but rather the problem that is to be addressed and the intent the software architect has regarding its solution.

The architectural design method presented in this part of the book assumes an objective and quantitative approach. It presents a picture of an idealized software architectural design process because the technology for several aspects of the method is currently not available or has not been disseminated to software industry. For instance, for some quality attributes no validated assessment techniques are available. In addition, for several of the transformations discussed in the remainder of this chapter, the exact effect on the quality attributes of a software architecture is not obvious. Part of this is due to the fact that performing a design, basically any design, is fundamentally a creative process that cannot be formalized and automated. However, many parts surrounding the creative process can and should be formalized in order to become objective and, potentially, automated. Thus, the method presented here is as much a vision of how we would want to perform software architectural design as it is a viable way of working today. However, at times it requires one to resort to qualitative reasoning or experience-based decisions.

To conclude, the software architecture transformation process consists of four major steps:

- identify the QAs that are not fulfilled;
- for each QA, identify the locations where the QA is inhibited;

- ■ select the most appropriate transformation;

- ■ perform the transformation.

3 Impose an architectural style

The first category of architecture transformation is concerned with imposing an architectural style on the software architecture. Shaw and Garlan (1996) and Buschmann *et al.* (1996) present several architectural styles[1] that improve the possibilities for certain quality attributes for the system the style is imposed upon and are less supportive for other quality attributes. Certain styles, e.g. the layered architectural style, increase the flexibility of the system by defining several levels of abstraction, but generally decrease the performance of the resulting system. With each architectural style, there is an associated fitness for the quality attributes. The most appropriate style for a system depends primarily on its quality requirements.

Transforming an architecture by imposing an architectural style results in a complete reorganization of the architecture. Often virtually all architectural components are affected and the assignment of functionality to the components is reorganized. In addition, the original connections between the components are often affected. Consequently, imposing an architectural style is a transformation with a major, architecture-wide impact.

Although architectural styles can be merged to some degree, styles are not orthogonal in the sense that they can be merged arbitrarily. If a second architectural style is selected for a part of the architecture, it is necessary to make sure that the constraints of the two styles do not conflict with each other or are at least dealt with. A typical example of a software architecture using two styles is the compiler example in Perry and Wolf (1992) where the standard pipes-and-filters compiler architectural style is complemented with a blackboard style. The blackboard contains data which need to be accessible by multiple filters. Although the resulting software architecture contains both styles, constraints of both styles are violated. This is acceptable if it is a conscious decision and the conflicts are dealt with, but it generally affects conceptual integrity and complexity negatively.

The more common case is where a subsystem uses an architectural style that is different than the style used at the system level. This use of different architectural styles leads to fewer conflicts between styles, provided that the subsystem acts as a correct component at the system level. However, when considering conceptual integrity, our experience is that where one is able to use the same archetypes and

---

1 Buschmann *et al.* (1996) use the term 'architectual patterns', but we use that term for another category of transformations.

organizing principles at all levels of the system, this is preferable. The same is the case for using the same style throughout the system.

In our approach, we explicitly distinguish between the components that are used to fulfil the functional requirements and the software architecture of the system that is used to fulfil the quality requirements. In practice, the distinction is generally not as clear-cut, i.e. the implementation of a component also influences most quality attributes, such as reliability, robustness and performance.

3.1 Styles and quality attributes

Architectural styles have been discussed at length in other publications (see e.g. Buschmann *et al.* (1996) and Bass *et al.* (1998)), though the suitability of styles for the various quality attributes is not always discussed to the same extent. In this section, we briefly consider the most fundamental styles that are generally recognized.

Pipes and filters

The pipes and filters of this style can be viewed as analogous to a chemical plant, in which the filters initiate chemical processes on the material transported through the pipes. The pipes-and-filters style assumes a dataflow network where data flows through the pipes and is processed by the filters. The most well-known instance of this style is implemented in the Unix operating system, in particular the associated command shells. A second example is the standard compiler architecture taught in virtually every computer science study programme. In a standard compiler, the scanner, parser, optimizer and code generator form the filters, whereas pipes transport, for instance, character and token data.

There exist many varieties of pipes-and-filter implementations and definitions. Variations include pipeline (linear), systems without feedback loops (a-cyclic) and arbitrary (cyclic graph) (Shaw and Clements, 1997). The common denominator is that the filters operate asynchronously and have little or no state. However, filters do exchange data through pipes and, consequently, some synchronization occurs in that manner. The way data is transported through pipes can be pushing, pulling or asynchronous. In the first approach, entry of data by the source filter will activate the sink filter. This is typically useful when the system is processing data from an external source. The opposite occurs for the pulling approach, where the sink filter activates the source filter. This typically occurs in a compiler where the parser will ask for tokens from the lexer. Finally, when using the asynchronous approach, the pipe will store data entered by the source filter until the sink filter requests this, thereby decreasing the synchronicity in the system.

The application of each style to transform a software architecture has an associated effect on the quality attributes of the architecture. However, the actual effect depends as much on the type of system modeled by the software architecture as it does on the selected style. Nevertheless, we discuss below the general effects of the pipes-and-filters style on the quality attributes.

- **Performance.** The advantage of the pipes-and-filters style from a performance perspective is that the filters form excellent units of concurrency, allowing for parallel processes which generally improve performance, assuming that it is used with care. In addition, since the pipes connect the components, the interface for each component is very narrow, reducing the number of synchronization points.

  The advantage of the pipes-and-filters style discussed above may, however, turn into a disadvantage for performance as well. If each filter only performs a very small unit of computation for each unit of data, the style will lead to many context switches and copying of data, which affects performance negatively.

- **Maintainability.** The maintainability of a pipes-and-filters system also has two sides. On the positive side, the configuration of filters is generally very flexible, allowing for even run-time reorganization of pipes and filters. Thus, as long as new requirements can be implemented by new filters and reorganization of the network, maintainability of this style is very good.

  The disadvantage is that requirement changes often affect multiple filters. A typical example are syntax changes or extensions in a compiler. These are generally orthogonal to the compiler components and, consequently, require changes to the lexer, parser, optimizer and code generation component. Especially in larger systems, the disadvantage of this style is that real-world entities represented by the system are decomposed and part of the functionality of multiple filters. Our experience is that, for the systems that we have worked with, the majority of requirement changes affect more than one filter and that, consequently, the pipes-and-filters style is not particularly suitable for maintainability.

- **Reliability.** The reliability of a pipes-and-filters system is dependent on its topology and, as a result, it is hard to generalize. However, since the pipes-and-filters style assumes that each external event causes computation in a series of filters, one may deduce that the reliability may be less than in styles where most events lead to computation in only one, or perhaps a few components. The series of filters requires each filter to deliver the specified result in order for the system to be successful, i.e. analogous to an 'and'-function in boolean logic. In other styles, the primary component handling the event may still be able to deliver a result even if some of the secondary components used by the primary component fail.

- **Safety.** The line of reasoning used for reliability also holds for safety. The fact that correct computation is dependent on several components increases the chance that some failure will occur. Thus, in cases where passivity of the system may cause hazardous situations, this results in decreased safety. On the other hand, the fact that the output of the system generally will occur through one or a few filters allows for local verification of reasonable output values.

- **Security.** Pipes-and-filters systems generally have small and explicitly defined input and output interfaces and a well-defined component topology. This means that access to the system is only available through the defined interfaces, where identity verification, authorization and encryption/decryption can be performed. The same technique can be used at the component level in systems where information of different security levels is present.

Layers

The layered architectural style decomposes a system into a set of horizontal layers where each layer provides an additional level of abstraction over its lower layer and provides an interface for using the abstraction it represents to a higher-level layer. As a consequence, an atomic task at the highest level of abstraction is decomposed into a number of tasks at the lower-level layer, which in turn is decomposed into yet lower-level tasks, thus forming a hierarchy of tasks which become smaller and simpler as one descends the hierarchy.

Probably the best known example of a layered architecture is the OSI seven-layer model for communication protocols (Tanenbaum, 1988). In Fig. 28, the layers of the OSI standard are presented. Each layer is at an abstraction level higher than the layer below it, and deals with one particular aspect of communication and builds upon the lower-level aspects to be available.

Several variants of the layered style exist. The pure style allows layers to call only their immediate subordinate layer. Assuming this fits the application domain, this leads to the lowest level of dependency between layers. The relaxed style exists in two forms. In the first, each layer can invoke all lower-level layers, rather than just the layer immediate below it. In the second form, the layer can invoke higher-level layers.

In Fig. 29, the two discussed examples are presented graphically. In example (a), higher-level layers are allowed to invoke all lower-level layers. This obviously increases the coupling between the layers, but either the nature of the problem or quality attributes may require this solution. In example (b), lower-level layers are allowed to invoke the next higher layer, thus creating bi-directional communication between the layers. Again, coupling between the layers is increased. Finally, if it is necessary to mix examples (a) and (b), i.e. all layers may call all other layers both upwards and downwards, this is a strong indication that the layered style is not appropriate for the system under design and alternatives should be investigated.

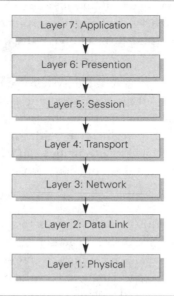

Figure 28   The OSI seven-layer model for communication protocols

Imposing a layered style involves at least the following steps. First, the identification of a number of abstraction levels and representing them as layers. Second, the assignment of components to the layers and, finally, the remodularization of components that contain functionality belonging on different levels. The latter may result in a real-world entity being represented in multiple layers, which has a negative effect on maintainability, but this may be outweighed by the advantages. A

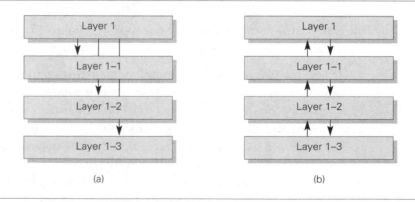

Figure 29   Examples of the relaxed layered style

typical example is the three-tier architecture in business applications, where the lowest level provides persistence and atomic transactions, the middle layer provides the business logic and the top layer provides presentation and user interaction. Despite its advantages, especially in client-server type applications, it does cause a real-world entity to be represented in all layers of the architecture.

We examine below the relation between the layered style and the selected quality attributes.

- **Performance.** The layered style organizes computational tasks based on level of abstraction, rather than their computational relation. This generally causes functionality related to an external event or request to be divided over multiple layers, for instance, in the case of communication protocols, over all layers. As a consequence, the computation in response to the external event covers multiple layers as well, requiring several switches of method context. This leads to decreased performance and experience has shown that the layered architecture does cause a performance penalty when used. Consequently, communication protocols are generally not implemented according to the OSI seven-layer model, but rather in a reorganized fashion avoiding the disadvantages associated with passing several layer boundaries.

  With respect to concurrency, there is an important point to make. The naïve approach to adding concurrency to a system built in the layered style is to assign to each layer its own thread of control. In general, this does not lead to an increase in performance, but may even lead to decreased performance, due to the number of switches of task context required to react to a single event. The alternative approach is to assign to the events processed by the layer stack their own thread of control and to implement the layers in a re-entrant fashion. This generally leads to an increase in performance.

- **Maintainability.** Maintainability of a system is influenced by the way requirement changes affect the system. If most changes can be implemented by changing one or a small number of components or by adding a new component, then the maintainability of the system will be high. Assuming that the way the functionality of a layered system is assigned to its layers is done in an appropriate way, the maintainability of a layered system is generally relatively high. Layers have few dependencies on other layers, allowing for replacement of a layer without changing its superior and subordinate layer. If, however, the functionality of the system is not organized according to the expected requirement changes, maintainability may be compromised since several layers will need to be changed for requirement changes.

■ **Reliability.** Similar to the pipes-and-filters style, the layered style requires computation in all or most layers for each external event or request. Due to this, failure of one layer may cause the system as a whole to fail. Consequently, the reliability may be lower than when using some of the subsequent styles. On the positive side, a higher-level layer may contain functionality for handling faults occurring at its lower-level layer. Because the higher-level layer has a better overview of the ongoing computation, it may be able to deal with failures the lower-level layer would not have been able to manage on its own.

■ **Safety.** Most of the safety issues discussed for the pipes-and-filters style are relevant to the layered style. In addition, the layered style allows for the introduction of layers in between the existing layers. That allows, for instance, for the insertion of safety monitoring layers between the domain software and the device drivers. This can be used to determine whether the values read from and sent to the hardware and mechanical parts of the system are reasonable.

■ **Security.** The layered style supports security rather well due to the fact that all computation starts at the top level or at the bottom level, as in the case of communication protocols. This allows for the insertion of security layers performing authorization and, possibly, encryption and decryption of data.

Blackboard

The blackboard style originated in the domain of artificial intelligence, where it was used as a data or knowledge-sharing mechanism between a number of intelligent entities. The computational model used by the blackboard style assumes a central data repository and a set of active components surrounding the data repository. The components scan the blackboard for data items that they are able to take as input; they then take these items from the blackboard, process them and place the results on the blackboard. Different from the styles discussed earlier, the control flow of the system is not explicitly designed, but evolves as the components are able to execute. Consequently, giving different priorities to the components generally affects the control flow.

The blackboard style was initially typically used in cases where no overall solutions to a problem were available, and there were only elements that addressed one aspect of a problem. The solution elements are implemented as components that roam the blackboard for problem pieces that they know how to handle. This may result in multiple components selecting a data element and trying to process it. Often, however, this results in all but one component failing to process the data. More recently, the blackboard style has also been used in cases where there exist overall solutions, but where the solution may change so often due to changing requirements that it is more feasible to use a blackboard and let the components dynamically arrange the composition of solution elements into an overall solution.

For instance, the fire-alarm system uses a blackboard style to achieve real-time and performance-quality attributes. However, the components communicating with the blackboard and the blackboard data are static and the control flow is hard-wired in order to fulfil, especially, the real-time requirements. Finally, to present a widely known example, systems that employ a database subsystem make use of the blackboard style at least to some extent. The database removes the connections between the components in the system, in that most components can work independently towards the database and communicate through the additions and changes made to the data in the database.

The simplest form of blackboard system employs a single central data repository, but more complex forms exist in which multiple repositories are organized according to type of data or location in a distributed system. In the more complex cases, some of the components move data between repositories, possibly after having processed it.

Finally, in addition to the blackboard and the components processing data elements on the blackboard, a control component may be present that determines in what order the processing components can access the blackboard and compute. The control component may activate processing components according to a predefined schedule or inspect the blackboard to determine what processing component would be most suitable to activate next.

The effect of using the blackboard style on the quality attributes is difficult to describe due to the wide variety of ways this style can be used. However, below we present some general guidelines:

- **Performance.** Although one can build blackboard-based systems with high performance, generally performance is not one of the strong points of this style. One can identify two main reasons for this. First, considerable amounts of computation may be spent on behaviour that is not related to the application domain, such as roaming the blackboard, or behaviour that is redundant, e.g. multiple components trying to process a data element. Second, because there is no explicitly defined control flow, but, in the best case a control component that attempts to optimize the flow, computation is generally not performed in an optimal order, leading to decreased performance for the critical paths in the system.

  Nevertheless, examples of blackboard-based systems with high performance do exist. For instance, in Boasson and de Jong (1997) an architecture is presented that consists of a highly structured blackboard with a fixed and identifiable set of data fields, a set of tasks with specified interfaces, in terms of what data fields are read and what fields are written, and, finally, a control component that contains an optimized and hard-coded control flow. This architecture is, for example, used in simulation systems where timing and performance are very important. The 'factored-out' control can be optimized late in the development process to obtain the highest refresh rates while keeping all simulated entities synchronized.

- **Maintainability.** A considerably stronger aspect of the blackboard style is maintainability. The blackboard allows for easy, even dynamic, addition and removal of types of data as well as the number of instances of the type. Since processing components are independent of each other, components can be added and removed without having to change other processing components. Depending on how it is constructed, the control component is the only element in the system that would need to be changed in order to incorporate changes in the processing component set. However, one can define control components that use meta-models to capture what types of data are present on the blackboard and what data each processing component needs in order to carry out its task. In that case, the control component is able to incorporate some types of new processing component without having to be changed.

  However, for blackboard-based systems it is also important to note that naïve design may lead to systems that are hard to maintain. Likely requirement changes should be incorporated by changing or adding, preferably, a single component. In addition, blackboard-based systems that hard-wire many of the aspects of the system, such as the example simulation system discussed earlier, will be harder to maintain than very flexible systems.

- **Reliability.** The reliability of blackboard-style systems has two sides to it. On the one side, the independence of the processing components and the fact that the control component iteratively activates the various components increases reliability since it makes the system more tolerant to faults and robust with respect to invalid data on the blackboard. However, on the other side, there is no central or explicit specification of the system behaviour, which may make it hard for the system to identify that certain responsibilities are not fulfilled. The control component plays an important role in addressing this problem.

- **Safety.** The fact that the system has no central or explicit specification of overall system behaviour may also compromise safety in safety-critical systems. Processing components may write incorrect data on the blackboard that can lead to potentially dangerous external actions. Since all components, at least in the pure model, may read and write all data, one component may compromise both safety and reliability.

- **Security.** The fact that the blackboard style employs a central data storage that can be accessed by all components in the system and the ability of the system to dynamically incorporate new components may lead to security problems if no precautions are taken. On the other hand, having all classified data in a single location simplifies the control of access.

Object-Orientation

The object-oriented style (Shaw and Garlan, 1996) organizes the system in terms of communication objects. Objects are entities that contain some state and operations to access and change this state. Whereas the state and operations are encapsulated by the object, the signatures of the operations are accessible on the interface of the object. Operations can be accessed by sending messages to an object. A message causes the activation of an operation, which may lead to changes to the internal object state and messages to other objects. Messages are synchronous in that the object sending a message waits until it receives a reply and only then continues with its own computation.

Several models extend the basic object-oriented style with various aspects. The concurrent object-oriented style, for example, assumes all objects to be potentially active and an object sending a message to another object will delay the thread sending the message, but other threads may be active within the object.

Although objects do not need to be aware of the sender of a message, an object is required to have the identity of an object it intends to send a message to. Since objects, in the course of their computation, generally need to send messages to several other objects, each object is required to maintain references to its acquaintances. Consequently, an object-oriented system can be viewed as a network of connected objects.

The object-oriented style, similar to the other styles, affects the quality attributes of the system. These effects are discussed below:

- **Performance.** The performance of object-oriented programming has received considerable attention in the literature, especially in comparison to conventional structured programming. Although new object-oriented languages, at their introduction, generally are less efficient than traditional languages, this disadvantage is generally largely removed at subsequent versions. Typical examples are C++ and Java. However, using the object-oriented style as an organizing principle at the architectural level is even less controversial since it is generally accepted that a system needs to be broken down into components. The question is just whether these components should be filters, layers, objects or of yet another type.

  The performance of systems based on the object-oriented style is very much dependent on the principles the designer used to define the objects, but there is not necessarily a fundamental conflict. For optimal maintainability, objects should be selected so that the most likely requirement changes affect as few objects as possible. For optimal performance, objects should be selected so that the most frequent use scenarios cause computation at as few objects as possible, since performing context switches between objects is expensive. Since requirement changes often affect the use scenarios, the optimal system organization for maintainability and for performance may actually be very close to each other. In our experience, we have seen several examples of this.

One important note to make is that, similar to the layered style, the naïve way of adding concurrency to an object-oriented system is to use the homogenous approach, i.e. each object has its own thread of control. This is generally not optimal if there are many objects in the system due to the large number of context switches and synchronization points for each use scenario. Instead, threads should be attached to external events that cause considerable amounts of computation in the system.

■ **Maintainability.** The object-oriented programming paradigm became popular due to claims of increased reusability and maintainability. In our work with industry, we have seen many examples of cases where these claims were actually fulfilled. However, the main issue in achieving maintainability in object-oriented systems is modeling the right objects. As discussed in the previous section, the likely change scenarios should affect the system as little as possible, and preferably lead to the definition of a new subclass or a new type of object aggregation.

One reuse inhibitor is the fact that an object requires references to the objects it sends messages to, i.e. its acquaintances. If the types and number of acquaintances are hard-coded in the class specification, changes will always require the class specification to be changed. The implicit invocation style discussed later addresses this problem.

■ **Reliability.** The object-oriented style is not particularly positive or negative with respect to reliability. One disadvantage that could be mentioned is that fault handling generally has to be managed inside the object, due to the encapsulation. This may make it harder to have fault handling at higher levels in the system, where more information is available. However, the fact that the system is modeled in terms of relatively independent entities is positive for reliability, since other objects cannot change the state of the object, except through the operations on the interface of the object.

■ **Safety.** One of the basic organizing principles of the object-oriented style is that real-world entities should, as much as possible, be represented as objects. As a consequence, the real-world entities that may compromise or assure safety are also modeled as objects. The fact that each real-world entity has a one-to-one correspondence to a system entity is positive for safety since the system entity is better suited to identify hazardous situations and react to them than an organization where the behaviour of the system entity is divided over multiple entities.

- **Security.** The object-oriented style both encapsulates and fragments the data contained in the system, being positive and negative aspects, respectively. Authorization of access to the system may be simplified by the fact that system interfaces generally will be represented by objects.

Implicit invocation

The fact that an object in the object-oriented style needs to know the identity of an object it sends a message to increases the dependencies between objects which leads to a more rigid organization, with consequent negative effects on maintainability. To address this, a style developed based on the object-oriented style has recently become more popular: *implicit invocation* (Shaw and Garlan, 1996). The implicit invocation style organizes the system in terms of components that generate events, possibly containing data, and that consume events. Components register their interest in receiving events of certain types and, depending on the type of system, publish their ability to generate certain types of events. An event handling mechanism implicitly present within the system handles all generated events and delivers the events to interested components. The JavaBeans standard (JavaBeans, 1997) is a typical example of the implicit invocation style.

Events received by components are bound to operations much in the same way as messages are bound to operations in the object-oriented style and lead to computation within the component and, possibly, the generation of new events. The main differences between events and messages are that events are asynchronous, i.e. the component generating an event continues its computation immediately after sending the event, and that events are undirected, i.e. the identity of the receiving component or components is unknown to the sender of the event.

Systems built on the implicit invocation style can vary in a number of aspects. The first is whether an event, in the case of multiple consumers, should be sent to one or to all components. In the case of observing components, all components should receive the event, but in other cases only one component should consume the event, that is receive it and remove it from the system. A second aspect is whether events of certain types generated by different components should be treated as equal. For example, assume two button components in a graphical user-interface environment. Both buttons can be clicked, leading to the generation of a 'clicked' event. However, the system behaviour in the case of a clicked event from button 1 should be different from that in response to a clicked event from button 2. Three alternative solutions can be chosen. First, rather than using the clicked event, one defines two events, i.e. 'button1_clicked' and 'button2_clicked'. This solution allows one to treat similar events independently from the generator of the event, but forces components to incorporate system specifics, e.g. the name of system-specific events. The second solution is to generate a 'clicked' event, but to attach the identity of the generating component to the event. This solution also allows the system to treat all events of a certain type as equal, but the components need to contain system specifics, e.g. component identities to be able to exhibit different behaviour, dependent on the component generating the event. Finally, one may choose to not broadcast events in a system-wide manner, but to explicitly configure the system in terms of what components will receive events generated by what other components. This solution allows components to be generic since they need not incorporate system specifics, but an explicit system configuration is required to connect components.

One can identify a relation between the implicit invocation style and the blackboard style in that both avoid explicit specification of the control and data flow. The control component may exhibit some influence on the control flow, which is similar to the implicit event handler which may prioritize certain event types over others. Consequently, the quality attributes are, to some extent, similarly affected by both styles.

■ **Performance.** The event handling mechanism requires a certain amount of computation that is unrelated to the actual domain functionality, thus negatively affecting performance. In addition, component communication where an answer is required from another component requires two events to be sent and processed and may lead to fragmentation of logical operations into multiple implemented operations, which is negative both for performance and for maintainability. These negative effects can be addressed to some degree through explicit system configuration, since it removes the implicit, central event handler required otherwise.

■ **Maintainability.** The implicit invocation style allows for run-time addition, removal and replacement of components, in addition to easy compile-time flexibility. Whether this leads to high maintainability is dependent on the modeling of components, similar to the object-oriented style. Likely change scenarios should lead to changes in one or only a few components.

■ **Reliability.** The reasoning with respect to reliability is similar to the object-oriented and blackboard styles. One advantage with respect to the object-oriented style, however, is that the implicit invocation mechanism can also be used for broadcasting events indicating faults, which may be used for system-wide fault handling.

■ **Safety.** See the object-oriented style.

■ **Security.** See the object-oriented style.

Concluding remarks

In this section, we have examined five architectural styles that can be imposed on a software architecture. We have discussed the effects of using these styles on the quality attributes of the software architecture. It is important to observe that the actual effect is dependent not only on the style, but also on the type of system and on the way the style is imposed on the architecture. Our intention in the discussion was to avoid making absolute statements, but instead to clarify how different uses of the style may affect the quality attributes. Finally, even if an architectural style generally affects a particular quality attribute in a positive or negative manner, it is possible to address this using different transformations or by careful detailed design. For instance, some studies carried out by members of our research group, (e.g. Häggander and Lundberg, 1998) have shown that performance problems in object-oriented systems are largely due to the excessive use of dynamic memory for object creation and deletion (in C++). These problems, however, can be easily handled by either selecting a smarter memory-handling library or by adding memory pools to the system and requesting objects from the memory pool rather than creating them. This can lead to up to an order of magnitude of difference in performance when compared to a naïve implementation. Thus, software architects should not avoid selecting styles that affect some of the driving quality attributes negatively, but select the style based on its positive effect on quality attributes that are hardest to achieve and its negative effect on quality attributes that are easiest to affect later in the design. Finally, many systems use more than one style. Although one can argue that this reduces intuitiveness, using more than one style may be the best way to achieving the quality requirements.

3.2 Example

To illustrate the imposition of an architectural style on the system, we use the fire-alarm system presented in Chapter 3. The functional architecture of the fire-alarm system can be represented as shown in Fig. 30. During the architecture assessment phase, the performance and real-time characteristics of the system were evaluated. Since each output depends on a potentially large collection of inputs, the output will request the status at each sensor it depends on. This involves sending a request to the sensor via the communication loop, waiting for the answer and processing the answer to determine whether the output should activate. The result of the evaluation was that the response time of the system in case of a fire would be far above the maximum required in international standards. Obviously, this assumed the use of the intended hardware, i.e. a small 8-bit processor and a very low bandwidth network.

To address the evaluation results and to improve the performance and real-time attributes of the architecture, it was decided to impose a blackboard style on the software architecture. The blackboard would not contain sensor values, but rather deviations. *Deviations* are put on the blackboard only by those inputs that are in a state different from normal. An output only needs to investigate the blackboard in order to establish its behaviour. The resulting software architecture is shown in

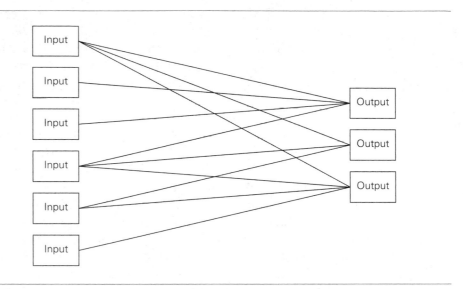

Figure 30   Functional view of the fire-alarm system

Fig. 31. The consequence of this transformation was that the response time of the system was well below the required levels, as was as the performance, in terms of refresh rates for the inputs.

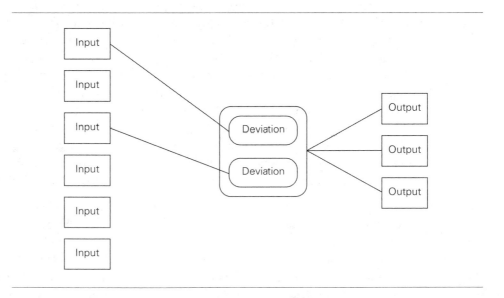

Figure 31   Fire-alarm system architecture based on the blackboard style

4 Impose an architectural pattern

In the previous section, imposing an architectural style was presented as a way to transform a software architecture and improve its quality attributes. A second category of transformations is the imposition of an *architectural pattern*.[1] An architectural pattern (sometimes referred to as an architectural mechanism) is different from an architectural style in that it is not predominant and can be merged with architectural styles without problems. It is also different from a design pattern, discussed in the next section, since it affects the complete architecture, or at least the larger part of it. Architectural patterns generally impose a *rule* (Richardson and Wolf, 1996) on the architecture that specifies how the system will deal with one aspect of its functionality, e.g. concurrency or persistence.

An architectural pattern generally does not reorganize the fundamental components of the architecture, but rather extends and changes their behaviour, as well as adds one or a few components that contain functionality needed by the pattern. The architectural pattern, however, constrains the behaviour of the components in the software architecture, or at least those components that are affected by it, and generally does not allow the use of another architectural pattern which addresses the same aspect.

As we have said, architectural patterns deal with one aspect of the behaviour of the system. Generally this aspect is not in the application domain, but rather in the 'computer science' domain. Examples of aspects include the way the system deals with concurrency, persistence, synchronization, transactions, distribution, run-time binding, real-time behaviour and graphical user interfaces. However, these are just examples of aspects and other aspects may be relevant for particular systems.

For each aspect, several architectural patterns exist that can be used to deal with the aspect. For instance, in the case of concurrency, one can decide to use a concurrent operating system with preemptive tasks, a real-time kernel with non-preemptive tasks or one can implement an application-level scheduler as part of the system and integrate handling of concurrency in the software architecture. Each solution has its advantages and disadvantages and the optimal choice depends on the system requirements.

In the next section, we discuss architectural patterns for the aspects that we mentioned earlier in this section. In Section 4.2, we present an example of the imposition of an architectural pattern.

---

1 Note that our use of the term 'architectural pattern' is different from its use in Buschmann *et al.* (1996).

4.1 Architectural patterns and quality attributes

Architectural patterns impose a rule on the system that requires one aspect to be handled as specified in the architectural pattern. In this section, we describe some examples of architectural patterns for the primary aspects that most systems have to deal with. The effect of each architectural pattern on the quality attributes is also briefly described.

Concurrency

Many applications have a need for simulating parallelism even on a single processor system. But even in distributed systems, generally more threads are required than available processors. This has to be incorporated into the architecture by adding an architectural pattern for handling concurrency. Several solutions are available for achieving concurrency, depending on the requirements and type of system. The use of a particular architectural pattern imposes a rule on the system, since each pattern requires the components to behave in a particular way in order to create, synchronize and remove units of concurrency. Below, we briefly describe the most common approaches to incorporating concurrency into a software architecture.

■ **Operating system processes.** Assuming that the system will function on top of a general-purpose operating system, processes will be available that allow components to concurrently run in separate address spaces. The use of processes to contain components requires additional functionality, or even components, to handle the communication between components. Several models for communication between processes are available, including streams, shared memory areas and message passing.

– Although concurrency will generally increase **performance** for systems that are I/O-bound, the use of processes has disadvantages for components that exchange much data as a result of the necessary copying of data between processes. Even if shared memory areas are used, this often requires additional specific code to handle the shared memory which is different from the implicit use of local memory.

– **Maintainability** is influenced positively by the increased separation of components. Modeling components as processes requires the components to be more autonomous. On the other hand, additional functionality and, possibly, additional components are required for the communication and synchronization between components. This increases both the distance to the conceptual, domain-based model and the size of the system. Since maintenance costs are directly related to system size, this leads to decreased maintainability. In addition, if groups of objects are modeled as processes, the difference in intra-process communication and inter-process communication will make the organization of components more rigid since moving a component from one process to another will require changes to the way the component communicates with its related components. Conceptual integrity is affected negatively as well since the required system decompositions are present for achieving suitably sized chunks of concurrency, rather then domain-related decomposition. Finally, the use of operating system processes does not allow for intra-component concurrency.

- The fact that the system is organized as independent processes is positive for **reliability** since the failure of one component and its associated process leaves the other components in operation. A disadvantage is that communication between components is more complicated, increasing the likelihood of communication failures.

- The fact that the failure of one component generally leaves other processes unaffected is positive for **safety** as well. In addition, the ability to restart processes that have failed allows for relatively quick recovery of the system in response to failures.

- **Security** is influenced positively since achieving access to one process will not automatically lead to access to the other parts of the system. On the other side is the fact that classified data may be fragmented throughout the processes.

- **Operating system threads.** In addition to processes that are relatively heavy-weight and create separate address spaces, most general-purpose operating systems support threads. A thread, or light-weight process, does not create a separate address space, but executes in the same address space as the other threads. If the handling of external events should be the source of concurrency, rather than the components, threads are a more suitable model than processes. Also, if the level of concurrency should vary dynamically, threads provide a more flexible solution than processes. However, threads can access components simultaneously, leading to racing conditions, if not controlled by appropriate synchronization mechanisms.

  - Compared to a single-threaded solution, the use of threads generally increases **performance**. Also, when compared to processes, threads require, except for synchronization, no additional overhead for communication between components, since the components remain in the same address space. However, in the case of multi-processor machines, studies have shown (e.g. Häggander and Lundberg, 1999) that the performance of thread-based applications is lower than similar process-based applications. This is due to the fact that the threads operate in the same address space and processors are delayed by conflicts due to simultaneous access of memory locations in the same proximity.

- Threads may access components simultaneously and to avoid race conditions, synchronization mechanisms have to be added to the components. This is negative for **maintainability** not only because of the additional code that is required, but also due to the additional complexity of multiple threads in a single address space. To optimally employ concurrency, synchronization is only added where it is absolutely necessary, which may lead to complex schemes that are defined based on knowledge of the control flow. Incorporating new requirements in the system may invalidate these schemes, but since the assumptions are very much implicit and often not well documented, this easily leads to incorrect synchronization. This is further complicated by the fact that concurrent applications are notoriously difficult to debug, leading to increased maintenance cost, since testing and corrective maintenance are part of maintenance.

- Threads that fail will generally not affect other threads directly, but failed threads may leave parts of the system in an inconsistent state. In addition, through setting invalid pointers and endless loops, threads may cause problems for other threads. Finally, the aforementioned increased complexity of the system due to synchronization will affect **reliability** negatively.

- Threads can be used to facilitate the implementation of monitoring tasks that, among others, may identify the failure of high-priority threads controlling safety-critical parts. Since the monitoring thread, upon identification of a failure, can control the system in order to reach a safe state, **safety** is improved, compared to the single-threaded solution, where the complete system would become passive. The use of a separate process for monitoring system behaviour may be preferred due to the higher independence. However, the increased complexity of using threads affects reliability, and consequently, safety negatively.

- The use of threads has no major effects on **security**.

■ **Non-preemptive threads.** Processes and threads in general-purpose operating systems are often preemptive, i.e. the system may preempt tasks at any point, based on clock interrupts. The disadvantage, especially in embedded and time-critical systems, is that synchronization mechanisms are required and that it is hard to make any statements about the timing of system behaviour. An alternative approach is the use of non-preemptive threads, i.e. threads that give up the processor through an explicit statement. This gives more control to the software engineer since it is known what behaviour is executed as an atomic unit. However, it also requires more responsibility since not giving up the processor due to, e.g. an infinite loop, will stall the system.

- In single-processor systems, non-preemptive threads may provide the highest **performance** in terms of, especially, throughput, since the delays at synchronization points are not present. The response time to high-priority events is determined by the size of the atomic units of computation defined by the software engineers. A high-priority event will be scheduled immediately after the current task gives up the processor, whereas the preemptive thread model would allow for immediate execution.

- Although no explicit synchronization mechanisms are put into the code that affect **maintainability** negatively, the design of the code, and sometimes even the architecture, is influenced by the fact that tasks have to release the processor at frequent, but safe locations in the code. This may lead to a less intuitive code, affecting maintainability negatively since it becomes harder to understand.

- The main negative influence on **reliability** is the fact that one task failing to release the processor may stall the complete system. Embedded systems often employ watchdog mechanisms in hardware, but these will just reboot the system, not handle the failure.

- Also **safety** is affected negatively by the ability of one task to stall the system. In cases where passivity from the system may lead to hazardous situations, non-preemptive threads are generally less suitable.

- **Security** is not affected substantially.

- **Application-level scheduler.** The last architectural pattern that we will discuss with respect to concurrency is the use of an application-level scheduler. This approach is typically used in embedded systems with very tight resources in terms of memory and CPU cycles. Rather than incorporating a real-time kernel or other operating system, the management and scheduling of tasks is performed at the application level, as part of the system. Whereas non-preemptive threads give the software engineer control on when to reschedule, but not on what task to run next, this pattern allows the software engineer to control the scheduling of tasks as well. This, obviously, also leads to increased responsibility for the software architects and engineers since both aspects are now handled by the software architecture.

A typical instance of this pattern is described in Molin and Ohlsson (1998). In their model, the system contains a scheduler and a set of active objects that have a tick() method on their interface. The tick method of each active object is invoked periodically by the scheduler. The method performs the necessary tasks it requires and subsequently returns to the caller, i.e. the scheduler. The cycle time for the system is the sum of the execution time of all tick methods plus some minor overhead by the scheduler. If the cycle time is too long for some active objects, these objects can be put twice into the list, so that they are invoked twice during each cycle, although the total cycle length, obviously, increases. An application-level scheduler allows for the highest level of control by the software engineer, but also imposes the responsibility for the correct operation of the system with respect to concurrency fully on the shoulders of the engineer.

- Since there is no overhead from the operating system or kernel, except for some minor overhead for the application-level scheduler, **performance** is generally very high using this model. Resource efficiency is maximized at the expense of additional development time, since the software architect and engineers are responsible for task management and scheduling. A disadvantage may be, similar to non-preemptive threads, that the response time of the system to high-priority events is not optimal, although this can partially be handled by using interrupt routines.

- As mentioned above, this pattern maximizes resource efficiency at the expense of development time, system size (in terms of system-specific code) and system complexity. This has a negative impact on maintainability. Otherwise, the disadvantages are the same as for non-preemptive threads.

- See the above section concerning non-preemptive threads for the effects on **reliability**, **safety** and **security**.

In summary, although not more than one of the architectural patterns discussed above can be applied to a component, it is possible to use different patterns for different levels of the system. For instance, the system can be decomposed at the top level into a small number of processes, but, within the processes, concurrency is achieved by using, e.g. non-preemptive threads. In addition, one can identify a direct relation between control over the behaviour of the system and the responsibility that is put on the software architect.

Persistence

The second aspect for which we will discuss architectural patterns is persistence and transactions. Since transactions are generally used in combination with persistence we discuss these topics together, rather than separately. Persistence is the ability of data to survive the process in which it was created. This allows data to be stored on permanent storage and read from this storage by other processes, at later points in time. With the emergence of object-oriented systems, the ambition expanded from persistent data to include persistent objects as well. This creates a number of challenging problems, especially with respect to object references. The first problem is that it is not always clear whether an object reference points to a part object, that should be saved together with the object containing the reference, or that the reference points to an acquaintance and thus should be rebound when the object is recreated from storage. The second issue is how to bind object references when recreating objects from permanent storage. This requires objects to have permanent identities, if the reference should be bound to the same object. However, in several cases, it is not the identity, but rather the capabilities of an object that determine whether it can be bound as an acquaintance of a recreated object. In that case, other rules for rebinding object references apply. Two architectural patterns for achieving persistence will be discussed, i.e. the use of a database management system and application-level persistence handling.

Transactions describe operations covering multiple data elements or objects that should be handled atomically. Generally, transactions should fulfil the ACID properties, i.e. atomicity, consistency, isolation and durability. These properties are primarily useful for the traditional database applications, such as banking and accounting systems. However, for several of the new types of systems, such as those for computer-aided design or Internet-based systems, not all properties are relevant or even useful. For instance, in computer-aided design systems often object-oriented databases are used that allow for versioning of objects. In such systems, even objects that are part of ongoing 'transactions', i.e. that are under design, can be accessed for reading, new versions of the object can be created and multiple versions of an object can be merged on later occasions. Some computer-supported software engineering environments support such approaches as well. In the afore-mentioned systems, the isolation property is not just useless, but even counter-productive. As an alternative, in real-time systems, rather than the isolation property, the durability property may be irrelevant. Transactions may be used to co-ordinate actions on two or more devices, e.g. two valves that need to close or open synchronously for correct system behaviour. In summary, although transactions provide important functionality for achieving correct system behaviour, it is important to understand what properties one is aiming to achieve when using the transaction mechanism. We describe two architectural patterns for achieving transaction-like functionality: a database management system and application-level transaction management.

Before we look at the architectural patterns and their relation to quality attributes, it is important to note that persistence and transactions are really two independent aspects of a system and can be used independently of each other.

■ **Database management system.** A database management system (DBMS) extends the system with an additional component, but also imposes rules on the original architecture components. Both for persistence and for transactions, the entities that should be persistent and/or part of transactions need to be extended with additional functionality to support these aspect. In addition, components need to handle requests from other components in accordance to the rules imposed by the DBMS.

– Despite the fact that a DMBS requires considerable resources in terms on primary and secondary memory, **performance** of these systems often very high. For instance, ObjectStore (1993) claims to be able to provide access rates to persistent data that are as high as data access to transient data, while providing the advantages of databases, i.e. persistence and transaction semantics. In general, the many years of effort spent in optimizing the internal implementation of DBMSs has removed much of the overhead that was present in early systems, although this is primarily the case for larger systems in which much data is moved around. The primary disadvantage of using a DBMS, especially in embedded and real-time systems, is the amount of resources required by the subsystem. In addition, since DBMSs generally are optimized for large amounts of data, considerable overheads may be incorporated in handling small amounts of data under real-time constraints.

Transaction management is, obviously, incorporated in database management systems. However, transactions, and in the case of non-ACID transactions even the transaction semantics, have to be specified explicitly in the system code and the quality of the implementation influences performance considerably. Transaction conflicts cause restarts of transactions, which invalidate possibly considerable amounts of computation.

– The effect of using a DBMS on **maintainability** depends to a large extent on the types of changes that have to be incorporated into the system and on the type of database, i.e. relational or object-oriented, that is used in the system. Assuming that most applications are at least object-based, the use of a relational database requires a transformation process to take place each time data is stored and retrieved. The manual transformation is sensitive to changes in the structure of the objects, thus requiring considerable effort. Changes to transaction semantics are also costly, especially since the transaction code is embedded in the code of the various system entities.

– Writing database interaction code is often rather complex, which is negative for **reliability**. On the other hand, DBMS functionality has generally rather high reliability since it is extensively tested and used by many users.

– **Safety** is not affected significantly by the use of a database management system.

– Most database management systems have means for authorization as part of their functionality, which is a positive aspect with respect to **security**.

■ **Application-level persistence and transaction handling.** The use of a database management system requires, as mentioned earlier, considerable amounts of resources in terms of primarily memory management, but also other resources, such as performance, for certain systems. For embedded and other systems with small resources, this overhead may be unacceptable. Secondly, a system may only need some of the functionality provided by a database management system, e.g. persistence, but no transactions, or co-ordinated action through the use of transactions, but no roll-back. Using only a part of a full-fledged DBMS with associated resource requirements may not be a feasible solution in such situations.

The alternative approach is to incorporate the required persistence and transaction functionality as part of the system, rather than by using a third-party DBMS product. To achieve this, the software architect and engineer may make use of language and operating system features, such as serialization of objects in the Java language and semaphores or some other synchronization mechanism that is part of most operating systems. The advantage of this approach is that only the functionality required for the system is implemented.

– It is difficult to make statements about the **performance** of systems using application-level persistence and/or transaction implementation, since it heavily depends on the amount of functionality required by the system, the quality of the implementation and the characteristics of the system usage. However, assuming a reasonable implementation, performance should not be worse than when using a DBMS, while avoiding the resource requirements.

– Similar to performance, the effect of using application-level persistence and transaction handling on **maintainability** depends on the implementation. However, assuming that the amount of code required to implement the functionality is larger than the DBMS interaction code and the fact that this code is distributed over all components requiring persistence or transaction semantics, it is reasonable to assume that this has a negative effect on maintainability.

– For **reliability**, a similar line of reasoning holds: a larger amount of system-specific code distributed over the system results in lower reliability, due to the increased complexity of the software.

– The negative effect of this architectural pattern on reliability has negative effects on **safety** as well. However, the fact that the persistence and transaction functionality is present at the system level allows for application-specific failure handling, which may well improve safety.

– Since persistence and transaction semantics have no explicit relation to authorization and other security issues, no major effects of this architectural pattern on **security** are expected.

Distribution

One of the observations with respect to the current state of practice in systems development is that distribution is becoming ubiquitous. Most systems consist of parts distributed over multiple nodes or need to communicate with other systems via networks. Consequently, distribution is an integrated part of most systems.

The problem of distribution consists of two major aspects. The first is the way in which entities connect to each other. This can be achieved through predefined addresses and connections or, more flexibly, through a central broker. The second aspect is the actual communication between remote entities. Again, several solutions exist, including remote procedure calls and remote method invocation, distributed streams, a Web interface, etc. Finally, one way to deal with distribution is by making it transparent, that is the system entities are unaware of their acquaintances being remote or local. Although much of the functionality related to distribution is transparent in today's approaches to distribution, components are often aware of acquaintances being distributed or not, both when binding and when communicating.

The solutions used to achieve distribution in a system are typically architectural patterns since they require all entities in the system that are concerned with communication over address spaces to follow the same set of rules and constraints. Below, we discuss two architectural patterns that are typically used in the context of distributed systems, i.e. brokers and remote method invocation.

■ •**Brokers.** Brokers provide functionality for distributed components to find each other. A client component sends a message to the broker requesting a reference to a server component that fulfils certain requirements. These requirements include the component name and its interface, but possibly also other aspects, such as the state or the location of the component. CORBA is one of the best known broker architectures, but other alternatives exist, such as DCOM/AxtiveX (Szyperski, 1997). However, as presented in Buschmann *et al.* (1996), one can even implement the broker as an architectural pattern at the system level, meaning that the broker is part of the system rather than of the infrastructure supporting the system.

It is important to note that not using a broker requires the system to hard-code the remote references and port addresses to at least each distributed part of the system in order to be able to communicate between the distributed parts.

– The broker is used to connect distributed entities at run-time. Typically, a broker provides a reference which is then used during the life of the component requesting the reference. Exceptional situations, i.e. the reference losing validity due to, e.g. a system crash, may require the component to invoke the broker again for a reference, but generally this happens only occasionally.

However, **performance** is affected by using a broker architecture, since all communication to non-local entities has to pass through the middleware layer which imposes some overhead.

- As mentioned above, the alternative to using a broker in a distributed system is to hard-code references between machines in the code or configuration files. This is negative for **maintainability** since relocation of services in the system requires an explicit effort for each client depending on that service, whereas in a broker architecture no effort would be required.

- The broker architecture affects **reliability** both positively and negatively. On the positive side, the broker disconnects logical services from physical locations. This allows for clients to connect to a service that has failed and restarted on a different node in the network. On the negative side, the broker itself is a central entity in the network and when it fails, the complete system may cease to function. However, generally brokers have back-ups that take over when the primary broker fails, thus reducing this weakness.

- A general property necessary for achieving **safety** is that it is easy to determine the behaviour of the system in critical situations. The broker architectural pattern breaks a large system down into a set of smaller, but communicating systems, thus complicating the prediction of system behaviour. However, depending on the type of middleware implementation, the broker may allow the system to dynamically reconfigure itself, which improves safety since clients of a failing service may dynamically connect to a new service, thus maintaining system behaviour.

- The broker is a central point for handing out references to system services. This allows for authorization at that point which is positive for **security**. Secondly, services need to register at the broker before they can be found by the clients. The broker can perform security checks for registering services so that trusted clients do not use untrusted services. However, once references have been exchanged, the broker is not involved in the continued communication between system entities, thus security is not influenced by the broker architectural pattern.

■ **Remote method invocation.** Distribution has two primary aspects, i.e. finding remote entities and communicating with these entities. The broker architectural pattern is concerned with the first aspect, but for the latter aspect a remote communication mechanism is required. Traditionally, remote procedure calls were a typical communication mechanism between address spaces, but with the emergence of object-oriented programming languages, the use of remote method invocation as in Java (for URL see end list of references) becomes a more relevant alternative. However, it is possible to make use of, e.g. sockets, for communication. The disadvantage is that this requires application-level 'interpreters' of the data that perform the work typically done in, for instance, the Java RMI layer. The latter depends, however, on the type of architectural style used for the system.

– Naturally, the **performance** of a remote method invocation compared to a local invocation is much lower. However, the use of distribution may be necessary for the system at hand or has advantages that outweigh the performance loss on a (small) subset of the method invocations. Even compared to other distributed communication mechanisms, remote method invocations may be slow, due to the overheads associated with, among other things, the marshalling and demarshalling of the arguments. Therefore, it is important to explicitly investigate the type of distribution mechanism needed for the system. For instance, if the domain model assumes a flow of data, rather than random access patterns, a stream-based solution, with less overhead for 'flattening' data, may be preferable from a performance perspective.

– Assuming that the acquaintance handling, i.e. selection and binding, is separated from the actual functionality, the **maintainability** of a system using remote method invocation is likely to be good. This is because no distinction has to be made between communicating with remote and local entities, allowing for flexible reallocation of objects. Generally, it has to be noted that the use of distribution is negative for maintainability since it increases the system size and because the code associated with distribution tends to be mixed with other code, which complicates changing either the distribution code or the other code related to, e.g. domain functionality.

– The use of remote method invocation has, compared to other distribution mechanisms, no major effects on **reliability**, **safety** or **security**.

Graphical user interface

It may be surprising to the reader to find the topic of graphical user interfaces (GUIs) on the list of architectural patterns. The interface of the system to its users may as well be considered a functional requirement and, up to a considerable extent, it is. However, the GUI is concerned with presenting and controlling the domain functionality which requires the entities representing the domain functionality to provide interfaces that support this. Thus, deciding upon a particular approach to incorporating means to obtain domain data and controlling behaviour imposes constraints.

One can identify two main approaches to incorporating interactivity in systems, i.e. model-view-controller (MVC) (Krasner and Pope, 1988) and presentation-abstraction-control (PAC) (Buschmann *et al*. 1996). Both consist of a model (abstraction), a view (presentation) and a controller (control), but the way these components are organized is different. The MVC architectural pattern adds a view and a controller component to the current architecture, which is considered to be the model since it contains the domain functionality. Both the view and the controller interact with the model and the controller governs the view as well. The PAC pattern organizes the architecture into a hierarchy of co-operating agents that internally consist of a presentation, an abstraction and a control component. The control component is the primary external contact for the agent as well as the internal co-ordinator that interacts with both the abstraction and the presentation components. However, these components do not directly interact with each other. Below, we briefly describe the effect of using these patterns on the quality attributes.

- Although it depends on the type of system and the implementation, user-interface functionality requires, potentially considerable, computational resources, thus affecting **performance** negatively. The MVC pattern tends to result in large numbers of update messages between the model and the view components. In addition, the access of data in a view may require several messages to different parts of the model component. The control component in the PAC pattern tends to be the bottleneck for communication since all messages need to pass this component. Especially requests that travel up and down the hierarchy often experience considerable overhead.

- The primary reason for using these patterns is to improve **maintainability** and **flexibility**. The intention is that by separating the domain model from the presentation of the domain model and from the control of the system, each component can evolve independently, thus simplifying maintenance. Although this is the case, there are a few negative aspects to consider as well. Both patterns increase the complexity of the system since functionality related to domain concepts is divided over different components, e.g. domain and control functionality. In addition, the view and the controller in the MVC pattern often are connected rather intimately, which complicates changing one component without affecting the other. Finally, the PAC pattern tends to result in a complex control component that is hard to change.

- Compared to a traditional approach in which GUI functionality is mixed with domain functionality, the advantage of the MVC and PAC architectural patterns is that computation related to the application domain, to a large extent, takes place independent of other types of computation. This is positive for **reliability** since failures in one part of the system do not automatically affect other parts. A negative aspect is that the increased complexity of the system tends to decrease reliability.

■ The relative independence of the system components is also positive for **safety**. The central role of the control component in the PAC pattern, however, partially neutralizes this because the failure of the control component will often cause the failure of the presentation and abstraction components.

■ The controller in the MVC pattern can, relatively easily, be extended with authorization functionality, which is positive for **security**. Due to its organization, this is slightly less easy in the PAC pattern, but if all access to the system starts at the top agent, the control component of that agent can be extended with authorization functionality.

4.2 Example

An example from the fire-alarm system domain is related to concurrency. In the functional architecture in Fig. 31, it is assumed that reading of inputs and potentially generating corresponding outputs take place concurrently. Assuming that light-weight preemptive threads are used, this solution can be evaluated with respect to efficiency and reliability. The cost of threads, due to the large number of context switches and the fact that preemptive threads are error-prone since they may cause racing conditions when accessing shared data, necessitates investigation of other solutions.

To address this, we decide to make use of an application-level scheduler and the notion of a periodic component. A *periodic component* is an interface containing a *tick* method that is regularly activated by the scheduler. Concrete components implement their own *tick* method that defines one slice of the periodic execution of an 'active' component. The degree of concurrency achieved by this solution depends on the 'thinness' of the largest slice. This design rule is an example of an architectural pattern that influences the complete architecture since all inputs and outputs are affected.

In Fig. 32, the result of the transformation is shown. Both the input components and the output components are extended with behaviour that supports the application-level schedule, e.g. a *tick* method. Other extensions may be necessary as well. For instance, the periodic nature of the *tick* method and the associated constraint on the amount of computation that can be executed for each invocation may require more complex calculations to be divided into multiple, smaller units that are executed in a series of invocations rather than just one. In addition, each active component needs to register itself at the scheduler in order to be invoked periodically. The constructor or initialization operation of each active component needs thus to be extended accordingly. After initialization of the fire-alarm system, control is handed to the scheduler which will invoke the *tick* method of each active component in the set. If a small number of components needs a higher scheduling

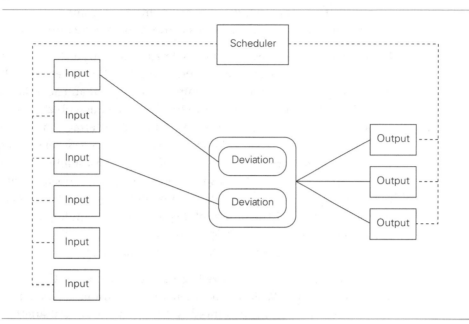

Figure 32   Application-level scheduler for the fire-alarm system

frequency, this can be achieved by adding the same component twice to the set, e.g. in the beginning and halfway through the (ordered) set. In that case, it will be invoked twice per set iteration. However, this should be used highly restrictively because it decreases the overall response time of the system.

5 Apply a design pattern

In the previous sections, we have discussed architecture transformation techniques that have an architecture-wide impact, i.e. the imposition of a style or architectural pattern.

A less dramatic transformation is the application of a design pattern on a part of the architecture. For instance, a *strategy* pattern (Gamma *et al.*, 1994) might be introduced to separate a concrete algorithm from a component. The strategy pattern increases maintainability, flexibility and extensibility of the component since it allows for the easy replacement of the concrete algorithm used to perform a certain task, but it decreases the efficiency of the component due to the additional interaction between the domain component and the strategy component, and thereby reduces performance and predictability. Different from imposing an architectural style, which causes the complete architecture to be reorganized, the application of a design pattern generally affects only a limited number of components in the architecture. In addition, a component can generally be involved in multiple design patterns without creating inconsistencies.

Design patterns have received a considerable amount of attention in the literature both in books (e.g. Gamma *et al.*, 1994, and Buschmann *et al.*, 1996) and conference proceedings (e.g. the PLOP conferences: Coplien and Schmidt, 1995; Vlissides *et al.*, 1996; Martin *et al.*, 1998). Patterns have been described for a variety of problems, including persistence, distribution, user interfaces, reactive systems and processes, but also for specific domains, such as business objects, hypermedia and transport systems. These patterns, generally, describe a solution that improves reuse and maintainability, while, to some degree, sacrificing operational quality attributes, such as performance and real-time behaviour, and understandability, i.e. patterns often make the design of a system more complex. However, exceptions exist: some patterns, e.g. Flyweight (Gamma *et al.*, 1994), improve other quality attributes, such as performance and resource efficiency.

Design patterns can be categorized in many different ways. Gamma *et al.* (1994) use a two-dimensional classification, where one dimension is class and object patterns and the second dimension addresses creational, structural and behavioural patterns. Buschmann *et al.* (1996) use a different classification and define the following categories: structural decomposition, organization of work, access control, management and communication.

In the next section, we present a few general-purpose design patterns and discuss the effect of these patterns on the quality attributes. Since design patterns make local rather than architecture-wide transformations, the quality attributes are not affected as much by a design pattern either. An example of applying a design pattern is presented in Section 5.2.

5.1 Design patterns and quality attributes

Design patterns are used to improve quality attributes. Patterns do not change the functionality of the system, only the organization or structure of that functionality. Consequently, when applying a design pattern, it is important to consider the effects on the quality attributes. In this section, we briefly discuss three of the classic design patterns presented in the Gang of Four (GoF) book (Gamma *et al.*, 1994): the façade, observer and abstract factory patterns. The primary difference between the presentation of design patterns in the GoF book and other publications and in this book is the fact that we explicitly treat the use of design patterns as transformations taking an architectural design from one version to the next, rather than presenting patterns as static structures.

Façade

The façade design pattern is used to provide a single, integrated interface to a set of interfaces in a subsystem. Façade defines a higher-level interface that simplifies the use of the subsystem. The structure of a subsystem incorporating the façade design pattern often looks like the representation in Fig. 33. The subsystem is defined as a component containing the entities that are part of the subsystem. The function of the subsystem component is basically twofold. The first is the co-ordination between the entities in the subsystem, whereas the second function is to provide an integrated interface to clients of the subsystem. Below, the effects of the façade pattern on the quality attributes are discussed.

- The **performance** of the architecture employing the façade pattern may be reduced due to the indirection in the communication between external and internal components, but also due to the co-ordinator role the facade plays within the subsystem.

- The façade decreases the coupling between external components and components inside the façade. The decreased dependency is positive for **maintainability**. However, the evolution of the internal components often leads to many changes at the façade interface.

- The reduced complexity of interaction between subsystems may be positive for **reliability**, i.e. rather than n-to-n, the connections are reduced to n-to-1. However, the façade interface may easily grow complex, which affects reliability negatively.

- The façade pattern has no major effects on **safety**.

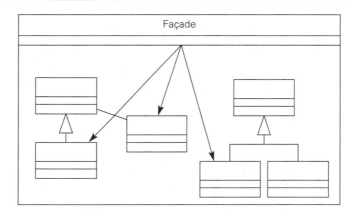

Figure 33   Structure of the façade design pattern

■ The fact that the façade pattern provides a single point of access to the sub-system functionality is positive for **security** since, among other things, authorization can be performed more easily.

Observer

The observer design pattern deals with the situation where several components depend on state changes in another component; when the component changes state, all its dependants are notified. The observer pattern is widely used in object-oriented systems since it significantly decreases the dependency between an object and its dependent objects.

The structure of the observer pattern is shown in Fig. 34. The abstract classes of *Subject* and *Observer* define the roles involved in the pattern. The subject represents an component (object) observed by a number of observers. The subject defines attach and detach methods for dynamically accepting and removing observing components. In addition, it implements a *notify* method that will invoke the *update* operation on all observing components. Concrete components reuse the behaviour defined by these roles and provide a concrete implementation for the *update* method at the observing component and the operations necessary for fulfilling the requests of the observing components on the interface of the subject component. The quality attributes are affected as discussed below by the pattern.

■ The observer pattern avoids the situation where dependent components poll the component for state changes, which is positive for **performance**. However, the pattern updates, by default, all dependent components, possibly leading to

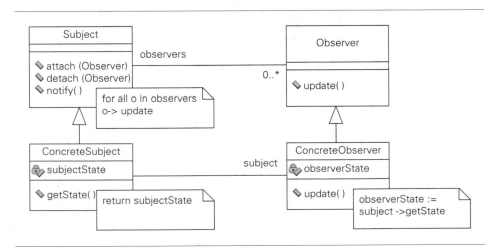

Figure 34   Structure of the observer pattern

unnecessary computation. The situation where the subject would send the data that the dependent component requires whenever a relevant state change took place and the dependent component currently was interested in state changes would be more efficient, but also increase the dependencies between the subject and the observers.

■ Compared to alternative approaches, such as discussed above, the **maintainability** of the observer pattern is positively influenced. Observing components can be dynamically added and received without changes to the system.

■ The decreased dependencies between the subject and the observers is generally positive for **reliability** since a failure at one of the observing components does not affect the other components, assuming that the failure is handled appropriately.

■ **Safety** and **security** are not notably affected by the pattern.

Abstract factory

The abstract factory pattern provides an interface to creating a family of related objects without specifying their concrete classes. Often when using reusable software, such as object-oriented frameworks, selecting one type of component in part of the framework restricts the selection of component types in other parts of the framework. The typical example is user-interface frameworks. When one selects an X-windows component such as a window, one is required to select all component types from the X-windows sub-hierarchies. If one explicitly used the names of the component types, this would complicate the use of the software for different platforms or the evolution of the software since replacing a component type with an updated one will require the software engineer to replace the name of the component type at all points of usage. When the abstract factory pattern is used, the name of the component type is only used in the factory. In Fig. 35, the structure of the pattern is shown. Since the abstract factory pattern is only used when instantiating objects, it affects the quality attributes even less than the design patterns discussed earlier. This is discussed in more detail below.

■ The abstract factory pattern requires more computation for the creation of new components, which affects **performance** negatively. However, once the component is created, the pattern does not play a role, so the impact on performance is minimal in most systems.

■ Since explicit references to component types are avoided in the majority of the code and concentrated in the factory components, **maintainability** is improved. Evolving the system by adding new component types will result in a single point of change, rather than many changes distributed throughout the code.

■ **Reliability, safety** and **security** are not affected by the pattern.

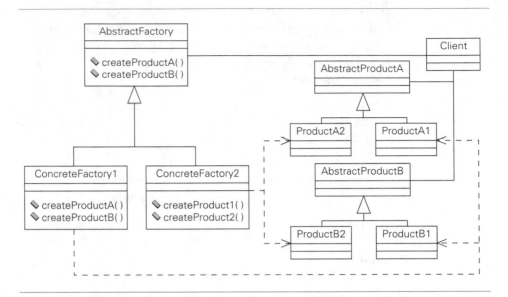

Figure 35   Abstract factory design pattern

5.2 Example

To illustrate the use of design patterns, an example from the measurement system architecture is used. Sensor components represent physical entities that measure some aspect of the real world. The relation between the physical entity and the software representation in the form of the sensor component needs to be maintained. In general, one can identify three alternative approaches to achieving this. The first is to wait for a client to ask for the value of the sensor. At that point the sensor communicates with its real-world counterpart, calculates the value and returns it to the caller. The second approach is for the sensor to periodically request the current value from the real-world sensor and store the calculated value. Clients requesting the value will then receive the stored value, which may be slightly outdated. Finally, the real-world entity may notify its software representation whenever it changes state, e.g. through an interrupt. When notified, the sensor component retrieves the new data and calculates the new value, which is stored and sent to a client whenever it requests the value.

The problem is that the approach to use depends on the situation, and the approach may vary independently of the domain functionality of the sensor. To avoid maintainability problems, we made use of the strategy design pattern which factors out the different update approaches as separate update strategies. Upon instantiation, but even at run-time, the sensor is configured with a particular update strategy which is used by the sensor. The resulting structure is shown in Fig. 36.

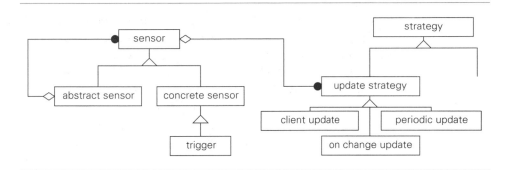

Figure 36   The strategy pattern applied to the sensor component

6 Convert quality requirements to functionality

In Section 2, we presented a taxonomy of architecture transformations. The fourth transformation category discussed in this section is concerned with local additions of functionality, constraints and rules. Architectural styles and design patterns primarily reorganize the existing functionality in new structures in order to improve the quality attributes of the architecture. However, this is not always sufficient. Often, it is necessary to extend the system with additional functionality not concerned with the application domain but primarily with improving the quality attributes.

The fourth and final category of transformation is the conversion of a quality requirement into a functional solution that consequently extends the architecture with functionality not related to the problem domain but used to fulfil the requirement. Although this type may require minor reorganizations of the existing architecture, the primary effect is the addition of new components and functionality. Exception handling is a well-known example that adds functionality to a component to increase the fault tolerance of the component.

Many examples of this type of transformation exist, but we have traditionally not necessarily considered these examples as quality attribute-improving transformations. In the next section, two examples are discussed, i.e. self-monitoring and redundancy. Section 6.2 presents an example of this type of transformation.

6.1 Converted quality requirements

As mentioned, the category of transformation discussed in this section primarily extends the existing functionality to the architecture. In this section, we discuss two examples of this type of transformation.

Self-monitoring

Although an architecture may provide the required functionality under ideal circumstances, it often is unclear how well it handles unexpected situations, such as failing components, hardware that breaks and external systems that go down. To address this, one solution is to add self-monitoring to the system. Analogous to the architectural patterns for GUI, i.e. MVC and PAC, two alternatives exist. One can add a layer on top of the system that monitors the behaviour of the system, similar to the base layer of the system that monitors relevant behaviour in the real world. Alternatively, the self-monitoring behaviour is modeled as a hierarchy that mirrors the existing component hierarchy. Independently of the alternative chosen, the behaviour of the monitoring includes not just identifying and reporting problems, but generally also actions to solve the problems. The effect of adding self-monitoring functionality to the architecture on the quality attributes is discussed below.

- Self-monitoring adds an additional subsystem (either logically or virtually) to the architecture that requires computational resources, but is unrelated to the application domain. Consequently, sometimes there is a considerable **performance** impact.

- The subsystem for self-monitoring increases the system size which has an immediate negative effect on **maintainability**. However, there is an additional effect as well: the code related to the application domain has to be mixed with the code for monitoring in order to detect erroneous situations. This increases the complexity of existing architecture, with corresponding effects on maintainability.

- Although this transformation has a negative impact on both performance and maintainability, **reliability** is definitely improved. The ability of the system to detect problems and take counter-measures is increased.

- The same line of reasoning holds for **safety**. The ability to detect potentially hazardous situations increases the likelihood that the system, or part of it, can be brought to a fail-safe state.

- Self-monitoring can be used to identify errors, but also to detect suspicious patterns of behaviour, which could be used for improving **security**. However, this type of application is less frequent than the earlier two.

Redundancy

To increase the fault tolerance of software, the notion of redundancy, originating from hardware, has also been applied to software. Since it serves little purpose to use multiple copies of the same software module, different implementations of the same requirement specification are required, i.e. N-version programming (Storey,

1996). N-version programming is often complemented with recovery blocks, allowing the system or a module, upon the detection of an error, to abort and return to a system or module state saved earlier at a recovery point. Typical computation consists of creating a recovery point, for each version of a module, computing the results and testing the values for acceptance, and finally accepting the values as correct data, allowing the module to create the next recovery point. An alternative approach is to order the implementations as primary, secondary, etc. and to execute the, e.g. secondary, version only if the acceptance test for the, e.g. primary, version failed.

- The **performance** of the system is seriously decreased using N-version programming, especially when using the first approach. However, this can, at least partially, be addressed by using a multi-processor system and executing the versions in parallel on different processors.

- Obviously, N versions of the same module will also need to be changed when the requirements change, thus having a considerable impact on **maintainability**. In addition, the use of recovery points complicates the code considerably.

- Obviously, the primary reason for using redundancy is to increase the **reliability** and the **safety** of the system. The risk of the system failing due to software errors is decreased considerably.

- Redundancy has no major effects on **security**.

6.2 Example

In the example fire-alarm system, there are quality requirements related to self-monitoring and availability. In certain cases, detected faults should be handled using hardware redundancy, whereas in other cases problems should be indicated to the fire brigade or the persons responsible for system maintenance. These requirements are, at least, partially fulfilled by transforming them to functional requirements similar to the basic alarm requirements. The corresponding architecture extended with entities dealing with self-monitoring is presented in Fig. 37. The elements in the grey area in the figure are fault inputs and outputs. The fault inputs constantly monitor the elements of the system, rather than the 'real world', i.e. the fault inputs monitor sensors and actuators for defects and handle anomalies found similar to the way the basic system handles fire alarms.

The solution described in Fig. 37 is a typical case where a logical additional layer is added to the system for self-monitoring (grey area in the figure). In the dialysis system, we used an alternative approach. As discussed in Chapter 4, the primary archetype in the dialysis system architecture is the *Device*. As shown in Fig. 38, each domain device

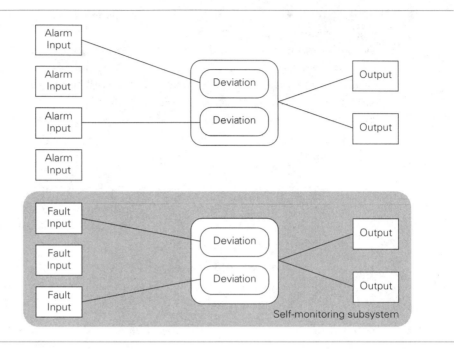

Figure 37   Self-monitoring in the fire-alarm system architecture

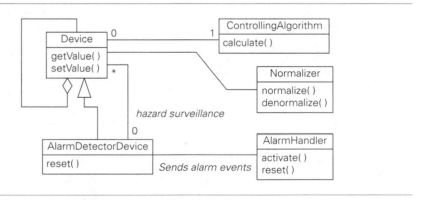

Figure 38   Self-monitoring in the dialysis system architecture

may have one or more alarm detector devices associated with it that monitor for potentially hazardous situations. Once an alarm has been detected, the alarm detector device activates an appropriate alarm handler by sending an alarm event.

7 Distribute requirements

In the previous sections, we discussed four categories of architecture transformation that improve, or at least affect, the quality attributes of the architecture, while leaving the domain functionality intact. However, the architecture can only facilitate the fulfilment of quality requirements. The design and implementation of the components are of crucial importance for the quality attributes of the final system. The increased awareness of the importance of an explicit design of the architecture of a software system has not decreased the importance of the components that make up the architecture.

Consequently, the final activity of each architecture transformation deals with quality requirements using the *divide-and-conquer* principle: a quality requirement at the system level is distributed to the subsystems or components that make up the system. Thus, a quality requirement X is distributed over the n components that make up the system by assigning a quality requirement x_i to each component c_i such that $X=x_1+ \ldots +x_n$. A second approach to distributing requirements is to divide the quality requirement into two or more functionality-related quality requirements. For example, in a distributed system, fault tolerance can be divided into fault-tolerant computation and fault-tolerant communication.

Fire-alarm systems are often implemented as a distributed system where one CPU-based system controls one building. Several such systems communicate with each other and the basic requirement is that an alarm detected on one system should be indicated on all other systems. This requirement can be achieved by enforcing a copy of the 'blackboard' to be available on all systems. This distribution can be effectuated by means of communication software operating at a lower layer and assuring that consistent copies of the blackboard are distributed throughout the system. The quality requirements stating how well the fire-alarm system should cope with communication problems is assigned to the communication software, effectively distributing a system requirement to a system component.

8 Conclusion

The design of software architectures as proposed in this book consists of three main phases: functionality-based architectural design, assessment of the quality attributes of the software architecture and transformation of the architecture to improve the quality attributes that do not fulfil the requirement specification. In this chapter, we have discussed the final phase, i.e. architecture transformation.

Architecture transformation is concerned with rearranging the software architecture designed according to the domain model and the functional requirements and extending it with additional components which address quality attributes rather than functional requirements. In this chapter, we have discussed four categories of architecture transformation. The first category is the imposition of an architectural style, such as a pipes-and-filters or layered architectural structure. Although architectural styles can be merged, styles tend to be predominant in the architecture and merging should be performed with care. The second category is the imposition of an architectural pattern (also referred to as architectural mechanism). An architectural pattern is different from a style in that it is not predominant, but can be merged with most styles and other architectural patterns. An architectural pattern declares system-wide design rules on how an aspect of the software architecture is solved, such as concurrency or persistence. The third category of architecture transformation is the use of a design pattern. Design patterns do not have an architecture-wide impact, but tend to have more local effects. Although many design patterns have been proposed, most patterns improve reusability and maintainability while sacrificing the performance and real-time attributes. The final category of architecture transformation is the conversion of a quality requirement into functionality. Different from earlier categories that primarily focus on rearranging the existing functionality, this category mainly extends the software architecture with new functionality. Examples of the category include self-monitoring and redundancy.

The artefacts developed during the phase of software architecture transformation are, obviously, the design decisions and, in particular, the transformations. However, transformations generally have structural effects on the software architecture. Therefore, a second type of artefact that is developed during this phase is subsequent versions of the software architecture. In Fig. 39, the artefacts developed during architecture transformation are presented graphically.

Finally, it is important to understand that the discussed architecture transformations are part of a larger process that starts with identifying what quality requirements are not fulfilled. Subsequently, for each quality attribute, the inhibiting factors and locations in the architecture are identified. Thirdly, the most appropriate transformation is selected and, finally, the transformation is performed. Generally, the software architecture is subject to multiple transformations that need to be combined to lead to an integrated result. As a last step, the architecture's components need to be annotated with quality requirements that are required for the software architecture to fulfil its quality requirements. The system as a whole will only function as predicted if the components provide their required quality levels as well as the architecture.

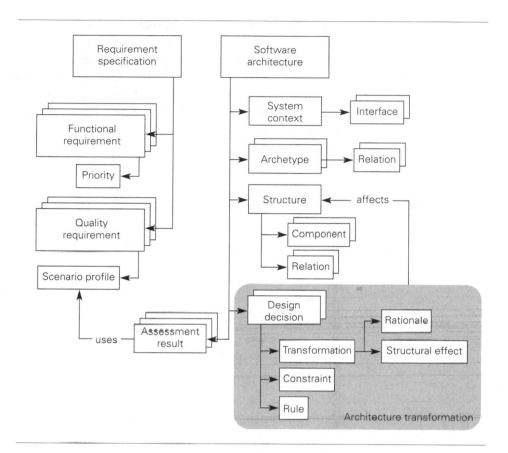

Figure 39   Artefacts developed during software architecture transformation

9   Further reading

Design of software for fulfilling quality requirements, rather than functional requirements, has been performed implicitly for as long as we have developed software. However, the actual codification of design structures and their associated benefits and liabilities has occurred primarily during the last decade. The work on design patterns, most notably Gamma *et al.* (1994) and Buschmann *et al.* (1996), represents a very successful instance of this effort. Bass *et al.* (1998) discuss quality requirementoriented design of software architectures, but primarily focus on architectural styles and unit operations. Finally, the various quality-attribute centred research communities have studied design solutions appropriate for their particular quality attribute. For instance, Smith (1990) does not just discuss the assessment of a software design for performance, but also design solutions to improve performance of a system.

In our research, we have also studied the notion of design for quality attributes. In Bengtsson and Bosch (1998) we illustrate the process of iteratively improving a software architecture through a number of architecture transformations. In another paper (Lundberg *et al.*, 1999), we present guidelines for selecting among a number of architectural styles. Molin and Ohlsson (1998) present a number of design patterns specific for the domain of embedded systems. Finally, in Bosch (1999a) the software architecture for the measurement system is presented, as well as the rationale behind the design decisions.

PART II

Software
product lines

CHAPTER 7

Software product lines:
an introduction

Reuse of software has been a long-standing aim of the software engineering community. Already at the end of the 1960s, the notion of constructing systems by composing components was discussed as the most promising approach to addressing the software crisis (e.g. McIlroy, 1969). During the 1970s, several module-based approaches to achieving reuse were proposed and during the 1980s, object-oriented programming proposed the use of classes as units of reuse. However, all these efforts only provided reuse at the level of individual, often small-scale, components that could be used as the building blocks of new applications. The much harder problem of reuse at the level of large components that may make up the larger part of a system, and of which many aspects can be adapted, was not addressed by the object-oriented paradigm in itself. This understanding led to the development of object-oriented frameworks, i.e. large, abstract applications in a particular domain that can be tailored for concrete applications. As a parallel development, the notion of component-oriented programming developed as an approach to software reuse (Szyperski, 1997).

The efforts to achieve software reuse have led to the general acceptance of two importance lessons. The first is: opportunistic reuse, sometimes referred to as 'code scavenging' or 'code salvation', is not effective in practice; a successful reuse programme within an organization must be a planned and proactive effort. Secondly, bottom-up reuse, i.e. the composition of arbitrary components to construct systems, does not function in practice; successful reuse programmes are required to employ a top-down approach, i.e. components are developed that fit into the higher-level structure defined by a software architecture. However, particularly in the presence of existing components that need to be incorporated into the product line, the process may consist of some bottom-up design decisions as well. For instance, the decision to employ a third-party component, such as a communication protocol or an encryption/decryption component, will have effects on the design of the product-line architecture.

As we said in Part I of the book, during the 1990s, it was possible to identify an increasing awareness of the importance of explicitly defined software architectures. When combining software architecture and component-based software development, the result is the notion of software product lines, which is the topic of this second part of the book. In this chapter, we present an overview of the concepts and processes relevant in software product lines, whereas the subsequent chapters discuss the various parts and aspects of this approach in more detail.

The remainder of this chapter is organized as follows. In the next section, the various types of use of a software architecture are discussed. Section 2 looks at dimensions along which a software product-line approach can be decomposed. Four approaches to initiating a product line are discussed in Section 3, and Section 4 discusses the domain of applicability for product-line concepts. Section 5 contains an overview of the remaining chapters in this part of the book and the chapter is concluded in Section 6.

1 Three types of software architecture use

In the previous part of the book, we have been concerned with the design of software architectures that fulfil their quality requirements. However, for what purpose was the architecture defined? Why did we spend all this effort on the initial architectural design, the architecture assessment and the architecture transformation? From our perspective, an architecture may be used for three main purposes, viz. for an individual software system, as a product-line architecture or as a standard architecture used for a public component market. Below, each type of architectural use is discussed in more detail.

The software architecture for an individual software system is part of the normal development cycle, preceded by requirement elicitation and specification and followed by detailed design, implementation, validation and deployment. The software architectural design method presented in the first part of the book is intended for and directly applicable to this type of system.

The second type of use for a software architecture is as a product-line architecture, i.e. the common architecture for a set of related products or systems developed by an organization. Since we believe that a product-line-based approach to software development is the most promising technique for achieving increased productivity, time-to-market and software quality, we will focus on software product lines in the remainder of this book. However, the software architectural design method presented earlier cannot be applied directly to product-line architectures since it does not take the required variability and differences between the various products sufficiently into account. In Chapter 9, some complements to the architectural design method are presented which cover specific aspects of the product-line architecture.

The final type of software architectural use is the standardization for a particular domain that may be used by component developers and users as a means to agree on functionality covered by components, provided and required interfaces and dependencies between components. Szyperski (1997) refers to this type of architecture as a *component framework*. In order for a component market in a particular domain to succeed, one necessary ingredient is that a generally agreed upon software architecture is present. The software architecture may be the result of a standardization process or it may be a *de facto* standard dictated by an organization with a dominant role in the market segment. An example of the first are the special interest groups at the Object Management Group (OMG) that define domain standards in a number of domains, e.g. medical information systems. An example of a *de facto* standard is the Microsoft Visual Basic environment that has served as a platform for a market of third-party Visual Basic controls.

In summary, although there are three types of uses for software architecture, the focus in this part of the book will be on the use of the software architecture for the domain of software product lines. The primary argument for selecting this particular perspective is that we believe that, on the one hand, the case of developing an individual system is an activity that, except for the design of the software architecture, is reasonably well understood. On the other hand, our experience is that reuse of components over organizational boundaries is still very difficult and happens relatively infrequently. However, the use of an architecture for a set of products or systems used within an organization is a difficult but feasible process that has been or is being adopted by several companies.

2 Decomposing software product lines

In the previous section, we decided to restrict ourselves to the domain of software product lines. In this section, we describe three dimensions in which the concepts included in software product lines can be decomposed. These dimensions are: (1) architecture, component and system; (2) business, organization, process and technology; and (3) development, deployment and evolution. We will describe each of the dimensions in more detail below.

The first dimension we will discuss divides the product-line domain according the primary assets that are part of the reuse-based development. This approach is taken in, for instance, Jacobson *et al.* (1997). We describe these topics below in more detail.

- **Architecture.** The first main asset of the product line is the software architecture. The main activity is to design an architecture for the product line that covers all the products in the product line and includes the features that are shared between products. Jacobson *et al.* (1997) refer to this activity as 'application family engineering'.

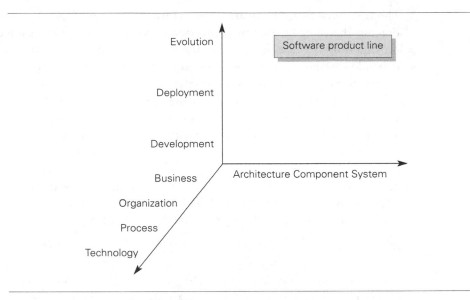

Figure 40   Three decomposition dimensions of software product lines

■ **Component.** The second set of assets in the product line are the components that have been as identified in the architecture. The product-line architecture identifies the components and the variability required from the components. However, these components need to be developed once the functionality and the variability have been specified. These components tend to be relatively large entities, i.e. up to 100 KLOC or even more, and are typically more like object-oriented frameworks than classes in object-oriented systems. Jacobson *et al.* (1997) refer to this phase as 'component system engineering'.

■ **System.** The final set of assets comprises the systems constructed and based on the product-line architecture and its components. This activity requires an adaptation of the product-line architecture to fit the system architecture, which may require the removal or adding of components from/to the architecture, the adding or removal of relations between components, the development of system-specific extensions to the remaining components, the configuring of the components for the system and the development of system-specific code. Jacobson *et al.* (1997) refer to this phase as 'application engineering'.

The second dimension according to which one can decompose the product-line architecture is according to the different views on the organization. The SEI workshops on product-line architectures (Bass *et al.*, 1997 and 1998) use this decomposition to describe issues related to product-line architectures. These views are discussed in more detail below.

- **Business.** All activities that take place within an organization should, in the end, be justified in terms of business benefits. With respect to the product line, one important aspect is that generally a considerable investment is required to convert from a product-oriented, one-at-a-time approach to a software development approach which is reuse-oriented and product-line based. The design of the product-line architecture and the development of the components is generally rather costly and, more importantly, will generally delay the time-to-market of the products currently in the pipeline.

- **Organization.** At least the traditional approach to software product lines suggests the use of a domain engineering unit responsible for the development and evolution of the product-line architecture and the reusable components. Alternative approaches do not necessarily employ domain engineering units, but generally do have effects on the organization. For instance, reusable components are developed by domain engineering projects, components have associated responsible persons, etc. Thus, the conversion to reuse-based software development has organizational effects as well, and these need to be addressed.

- **Process.** The third aspect of software product lines is the processes that go on within a reuse-oriented organization. The fact that a product-line architecture and a set of reusable components are available has considerable effects on the processes associated with product or system development. In addition, there are, among others processes, product-line-specific processes with respect to the design of the product-line architecture and the development of the reusable components.

- **Technology.** The final aspect of a reuse-oriented organization is concerned with the technology used to support the reuse-based development of software. In this book, we use the notion of technology in a rather wide form, including the assets of the organization, e.g. the reusable components. However, the technology or techniques used in the development of and with reuse are also included, e.g. the concept of object-oriented frameworks, assessment techniques for maintainability and other quality attributes, etc.

The third decomposition along which one can describe the domain of software product lines is based on the lifecycle of each of the assets in the organization. The phases are discussed in more detail below.

- **Development.** For each of the main assets, there is a point at which it is developed initially either from scratch or based on legacy code. The product-line architecture, the set of components and the set of products are all developed initially at some, generally sequential, point in time. There are several aspects which are specific to this phase in the lifecycle of these assets.

■ **Deployment.** The product-line architecture and the components are deployed (or instantiated) during product development. Even the product is used, once it is developed, but generally there is no software engineering relevance to the use of the product, so we consider it beyond the scope in this context. However, the use of the product-line architecture and the components does not imply simply copying the shared assets. The product-line architecture needs to be adapted to represent a useful product architecture and the components need to be configured, adapted and extended for their use in the product.

■ **Evolution.** Finally, all three main assets evolve constantly because the requirements on the products also evolve. These changing requirements have effects on the product-line requirements, i.e. these evolve as well. These requirements cause the architecture to evolve, causing the components to evolve. Based on this, the product can evolve as well since the extended functionality in response to the product requirement is available. Although initial development and evolution are rather related, there are several differences which justify differentiating these two phases in the lifecycle of assets.

In this part of the book we will use the decomposition presented last as the primary one and the other dimensions as secondary decompositions. This division is chosen because it represents the phases which a company adopting the approach based on a product-line architecture would go through sequentially.

3 Initiating a product line

Software product lines do not appear accidentally, but require a conscious and explicit effort from the organization interested in using the product-line approach. Basically, one can identify two relevant dimensions with respect to the initiation process. First, the organization may take an evolutionary or a revolutionary approach to the introduction process. Secondly, the product-line approach can be applied to an existing line of products or to a new system or product family that the organization intends to use to expand its market. Each case has an associated risk level and benefits. For instance, in general, the revolutionary approach involves more risk, but higher returns compared to the evolutionary approach. In Table 5, the characteristics of each case are briefly described.

Evolve an existing set of products into a product line

In this case, the organization maintains a set of existing software products, but without exploiting the commonalities between them. Once the benefits of a software product-line approach have been identified, the conversion from individual products to a product line is performed in an evolutionary manner. This requires, as a first step, the development of a product-line architecture based on the product architectures. Secondly, during the evolution of the products that are to be part of the

Table 5   Two dimensions of product-line initiation

	Evolutionary	Revolutionary
Existing product line	Develop vision for product-line architecture based on the architectures of family members. Develop one product-line component at a time (possibly for a subset of product-line members) by evolving existing components.	Product-line architecture and components are developed based on a super-set of product-line members' requirements and predicted future requirements.
New product line	Product-line architecture and components evolve with the requirements posed by new product-line members.	Product-line architecture and components developed to match requirements of all expected product-line members.

product line, components are identified that implement requirements of more than one product. Starting with the most important components, a product-specific component is generalized to incorporate the requirements of multiple products and the products are adapted to use the shared component rather than their individual components. During the evolution of the software products, more and more components are converted from product-specific to product-line components, and the product-line components are extended to cover the requirements of more and more products in the family. Using this approach, the organization slowly converts from a product-based approach to software development based on product lines.

The advantage of the evolutionary approach is that risk is minimized in two ways. First, since the up-front investment is decomposed into small steps for each component, the pay-off of sharing components gives a quick return of investment and the investment itself is relatively small. Second, the products in the family continue their normal evolution, albeit at a somewhat slower pace, whereas the revolutionary approach generally stops all but cosmetic evolution of the products in the family until the product-line architecture and components are in place. The disadvantage is that the total amount of investment until the product-line architecture and components are completely in place is larger than when using the revolutionary approach. This because much work on components done during the conversion is only performed to support temporary requirements.

Replace an existing set of products with a software product line
The evolutionary approach generally requires a considerable amount of time for the conversion from a set of independent products to a product line. For several reasons, this period may be too long, requiring an alternative approach. The preferable way

is then to completely replace the existing set of products by a product-line architecture and set of components. In this case, development on the existing products is basically halted and all efforts are directed towards the design of the architecture and development of the components in the software product line. Legacy software employed in the products may be incorporated in the components, but only when it matches the architectural design and the component requirements. Unlike the evolutionary approach, the goal is to develop a new platform that does not suffer from the problems present in the existing set of products.

The advantages of replacing an existing set of products with a product line are especially the shorter conversion time and the generally smaller total investment required for developing the architecture and component set for the family, when compared to the evolutionary approach. The primary disadvantages are the increased risk level, due to the large initial investment that may prove useless if important requirements change, and the delayed time-to-market of the first products developed based on the product-line architecture.

Finally, an important factor in the decision to either evolve or replace a set of systems is the presence of mechanical and hardware parts. If systems, in addition to software, contain considerable pieces of mechanics and hardware, the product-line approach needs to be synchronized to all three aspects. Especially if considerable differences exist in the mechanical and hardware parts of the products, it is generally harder to adopt an evolutionary approach and replacement of the existing systems may simply be the only alternative.

Evolving a new software product line
An organization may decide to enter a new domain by developing a set of new products located in that domain. Again, one can identify two possible approaches to this: evolutionary and revolutionary. The evolutionary approach incorporates the requirements of each new product into the product-line architecture and the component set. The approach is primarily concerned with keeping all functionality common to the products in the product line and minimizing the product-specific code.

The advantage is similar to evolving an existing set of products: the up-front investment is smaller and the time-to-market of the first products in the new domain is sooner. In addition, since the company is entering a new domain, generally little experience is available. Introducing the software product line in an evolutionary fashion will simplify the correction of initial mistakes. The disadvantage is that the requirements of new products in the domain may have an architectural impact and so the incorporation of these requirements may be rather costly.

Develop a new software product line
The final point in the matrix is the development of a complete product-line architecture and set of components before developing the first product in the new

domain. This requires the software architects and engineers to elicitate all requirements that the products in the family may demand. Based on this requirement 'super-set', the architecture and its components are designed and developed.

The advantages are, obviously, that once the product-line architecture and associated component set are in place, new products can be developed very rapidly and the total investment will be smaller than in the evolutionary approach. The disadvantage is primarily concerned with risk: especially because the organization is entering a new domain and, consequently, the domain requirements may be hard to get complete and correct, the architecture and component set may not support the system construction as well as expected.

4 Applicability of software product-line concepts

The notion of a product line using a shared architecture and set of components is directly applicable to organizations that develop and market systems or products. However, these organizations represent only a subset of all organizations developing software. Other types of organizations include, e.g., software consultants developing software on a project basis for other organizations or IT departments that develop IT support systems. These kinds of organizations generally are more project than product-oriented, which makes it harder to apply the concepts presented in this part of the book.

Nevertheless, many of the principles can be employed even in such project-based organizations. For instance, even most software consultant organizations tend to perform projects in a particular domain, e.g. services in mobile telecommunications systems or applications for hand-held computers. This commonality between projects allows for the development of a software architecture and a set of components that can be used for subsequent projects. However, since the amount of commonality between projects is often not as great as between the products in a product line and are less predictable as well, the amount of software shared between projects may be less. The benefits, however, may still be well worth the effort, especially with respect to the future evolution of systems developed in the projects.

An important issue that needs to be addressed in the case of software consultant organizations is the copyright of the software developed. In standard contracts, the client organization generally obtains the copyright on the developed system and the organization that developed the software loses it. In order to employ the software product-line approach, it is necessary that the developing organization retain the right to use and evolve the software that it developed for its client, even though the ownership can be non-exclusive. To achieve this situation, the organization often has to offer benefits to its clients, such as a reduced price for the initial system or subsequent versions.

In the case of IT departments within organizations, the product-line approach can also provide considerable benefits, provided that the supported applications have some degree of commonality. In this situation, copyright of the software is not an issue, but the requirements from the departments may be more diverse than necessary. In such cases, it is important to increase the commonality between the different applications by (re-)negotiating the application requirements to create a common base that is as wide as possible. If the departments are organized as profit centres which pay for their IT services through an internal bookkeeping system, then illustrating the benefits for the departments involved in the case of accepting the homogenized requirements will generally be helpful. These benefits do not just involve a decreased cost of the initial system, but also the inclusion of new features. Development of a new feature in the common software will automatically become available for all departments, rather than just for the department that ordered it.

In summary, one can identify three primary issues that determine the applicability of the product-line approach, i.e. the amount of commonality between the systems that would be included in the potential software product line, the negotiability of requirements and the ownership of software assets. If these three aspects are fulfilled to a sufficient extent, the software product-line approach can be applied successfully. However, there are several other issues that influence success or failure as well, such as cultural issues both at the customer and at the development ends.

5   Overview

Software product lines offer a highly promising approach to achieving the reuse of software within an organization. In this part of the book, we discuss the development, usage and evolution of a software product line. Below, we present a brief overview of the topics discussed in the subsequent chapters.

To illustrate the topics, we present three cases in the next chapter. The first case is Axis Communications AB, a developer of networked devices such as storage servers, scanner servers and camera servers. The second case is Securitas Larm AB, also discussed in the previous part of the book. In this part, we will focus on the aspects specific to software product lines. Finally, we discuss Symbian Ltd, which develops and maintains the EPOC operating system for hand-held devices and is the main competitor of Microsoft's Windows CE and the Palm operating systems.

5.1   Development

When the decision to initiate a software product line has been taken, the first step is the development of the product-line software architecture that supports the functional and quality requirements of the products included in the family. This phase includes activities such as scoping, commonality and variability analysis, architectural design and verification. The architectural design method presented in the previous part of the book is used for the design of the software architecture, but it is embedded in a number of other activities.

Once the software architecture of the product line has been designed, the subsequent phase is the development of the components that make up the common part of the product line. We discuss two types of components, i.e. traditional components as presented in contemporary literature (e.g. Szyperski, 1997) and object-oriented frameworks. In our work with various industrial software development organizations, we have identified that object-oriented frameworks are frequently used as components in software product lines. One reason for this is the high level of configurability that can be provided by an object-oriented framework. This suits the notion of software product lines very well, since it allows for the easy configuration of components for individual products.

The development of software products based on the product-line architecture and components could be viewed as the third phase in development. However, since the focus in this part of the book is on software architectures and reusable components, we discuss product development in the next part, i.e. deployment.

5.2 Deployment

The software architecture and set of reusable components that are part of the software product line are deployed during product development. The intention is that the effort required for the development of products should be decreased drastically by using the architecture and components as a basis. Software architecture deployment is concerned with configuring the product-line architecture based on the product requirements, leading to a software architecture specific to the product. The configuration includes the addition and removal of components and relations in the architecture.

The second phase is concerned with the instantiation of the product-line components that will be used in the product under development. The instantiation may consist of two parts, i.e. straightforward configuration of the component and the development of product-specific component extensions. Configuration includes activities such as parameter setting and defining input specifications to code generators. The development of product-specific component extensions occurs typically when using a white-box framework as a component. In that case, the component architecture and its generic behaviour have been defined, but the product-specific code needs to be added by the software engineers developing the actual software product.

The final phase is concerned with the development of product-specific software. The product-line components do not necessarily implement all product requirements. The subset of the requirements that is not fulfilled by the product line must be implemented as product-specific software. This software is not part of the shared product-line assets, but only included in the source code for the specific product.

When using the evolutionary approach to developing a software product line, the product-specific software may provide useful hints about likely useful extensions to the functionality supported by the reusable parts of the software product line.

5.3 Evolution

Once the first versions of the product-line architecture, the set of components and the set of products have been developed, the evolution of all these assets will become the primary activity. Evolution is, to some degree, similar to development, but the presence of software assets is a major complicating factor. The evolution is initiated by new requirements on existing products and by new products that need to be incorporated in the software product line. Evolution caused by the new requirements takes place on all assets, i.e. architectural evolution, component evolution and product evolution. Architectural evolution is concerned with changes to the components that make up the product-line architecture, changes to the relations between these components, etc. Component evolution is concerned with the incorporation of new and changed requirements on the component functionality which generally affects the component internals, but may also affect the component interface, which causes effects on the architectural level.

Product evolution may express itself in two ways. Traditionally, products evolve through subsequent versions that incorporate new requirements. During recent years, a new type of product evolution can be identified, i.e. run-time evolution. Systems or products that have been shipped to customers can be upgraded with new components or new versions of existing components. However, each individual instance of the software product may have its own configuration of older and new component versions. Run-time evolution is also referred to as dynamic architectures.

5.4 Artefacts

As a result of the processes described in the previous sections, several artefacts are developed. In Fig. 41, an overview of these artefacts is provided. The artefacts are divided into two main categories, i.e. the artefacts shared by the product members in the product line and the product-specific artefacts. The shared artefacts consist of the results of the business case analysis, the product-line requirements and the feature graph. In addition, artefacts include the product-line architecture, one or more reference contexts and the structure of the software architecture in terms of

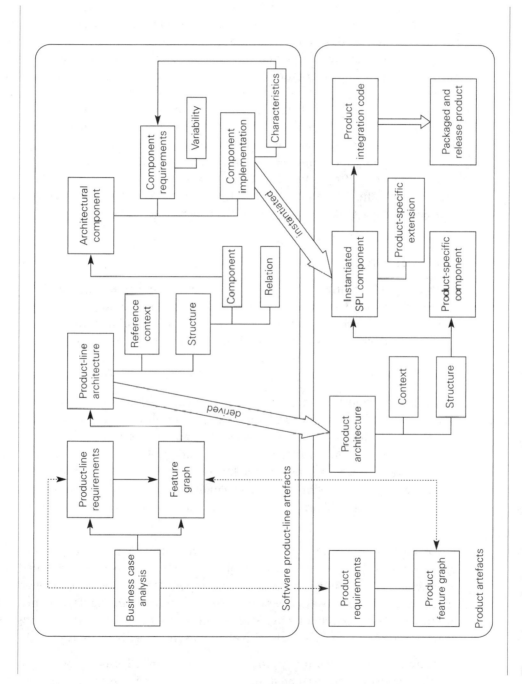

Figure 41 Software product-line artefacts

the components and the relations. In Chapter 2, several additional artefacts associated with a software architecture were described. These are relevant in a software product-line context as well, but have been excluded from the figure. The product-line architecture defines a number of architectural components with associated component requirements and zero, one or more component implementations. Each component implementation has associated characteristics, describing its suitability for particular products. The product-specific artefacts consist of product requirements and a product feature graph. In addition, a software architecture for the product derived from the product-line architecture is defined, including a description of the context and the structure. Based on the architecture, one or more instantiated component implementations from the software product line, potentially configured with product-specific extensions, and zero, one or more product-specific components are present. Finally, the product integration code and the packaged and released product form product-specific artefacts.

6 Conclusion

Software product lines represent one of the most promising approaches to increased reuse of software, increased quality and decreased maintenance cost. Traditional approaches to software reuse assume the reuse of third-party software components, which has not resulted in pervasive software reuse. The software product-line approach represents a less ambitious, organization-wide reuse of software assets which has been proven successful in several organizations.

The software product-line approach can be organized along three dimensions. The first is the asset dimension, in which the product line is described in terms of the software architecture, the set of reusable components and the set of products. The second dimension is concerned with the various views that one can have on a product line. These views include the business view, the organizational view, the process view and the technology view. Finally, the third dimension is organized around the primary phases of a product line, i.e. initial development, deployment and evolution.

There are four alternative approaches to reach a software product-line approach, organized according to two orthogonal issues. The first issue is concerned with whether the product-line architecture and component set is created in a revolutionary or an evolutionary way. The second issue has to do with the development of a product-line architecture for an existing set of products, replacing the existing software, or for a new set of products, also known as the 'greenfield approach'.

Although the product-line approach has been applied especially by product-developing organizations, the applicability of the underlying concepts is wider than just products. Even software consultancy organizations and IT departments in large organizations can benefit from the ideas presented in this part of the book.

Finally, the software product-line approach will be described in detail in the following chapters. These chapters are organized according to the phases of a product line, i.e. development of the architecture and component set, deployment through product development and evolution of the assets. The conceptual discussion is complemented by an examination of the experiences of some companies which have used a product-line approach for several years.

7 Further reading

One of the first books in promoting a software product-line approach is Jacobson *et al.* (1997). As we discussed earlier, the authors use the notions of application family engineering, component system engineering and application engineering. A second book discussing software product-line engineering is Weiss and Lai (1999). Although Bass *et al.* (1998) is a book on software architecture in general, the notion of software product lines is discussed as well. The proceedings of the ARES workshop (van der Linden, 1998) presents a variety of research results in the domain of product lines. The Fraunhofer Institute performs research on software product lines, such as the PULSE method (DeBaud and Knauber, 1998).

CHAPTER 8

Software product lines: case studies

To illustrate the software product-line approach, three cases are featured in this chapter, which will be used in later chapters. The first case is that of Axis Communications AB, a developer of networked devices. The second case is that of Securitas Larm AB, also discussed in Chapter 3, a developer of safety and security products. In this chapter, the focus is on the product-line aspects of the fire-alarm system family, rather than the software's architectural design aspects. Finally, Symbian Ltd is the third case. Symbian has developed the EPOC operation system for wireless information devices.

1 Axis Communications AB

We present Axis Communications in this section. First, the background of the company is presented. Subsequently, we present the product line and, in Section 1.3, the technology which the company uses. Finally, the organization and the development and evolution processes are discussed.

1.1 Company background

Axis Communications started business in 1984 with the development of a printer-server product that allowed IBM mainframes to print on non-IBM printers. Up until then, IBM had a monopoly on printers for its computers, with the consequent price setting. The first product was a major success which established the company. In 1987, the company developed the first version of its proprietary RISC CPU which allowed for better performance and cost-efficiency than standard processors for their data-communication-oriented products. Today, the company develops and introduces new products on a regular basis. At the beginning of the 1990s, object-oriented frameworks were introduced into the company and since then, a base of reusable assets has been maintained, upon which most products are developed.

1.2 Product family

Axis develops IBM-specific and general printer servers, CD-ROM and storage servers, network cameras and scanner servers. The latter three products, in particular, are built using a common product-line architecture and reusable assets. In Fig. 42, an overview of the product-line and product architectures is shown. The organization is more complicated than the standard case with one product-line architecture (PLA) and several products below this product line. In the Axis case, there is a hierarchical organization of PLAs, i.e. the top product-line architecture and the product-group architectures, e.g. the storage-server architecture. Below these, there are product architectures, but since generally several product variations exist, each variation may have its own adapted product-specific architecture, because of which the product architecture could be referred to as a product-line architecture. However, for the purposes of this part of the book, we use the term *product-line architecture* for the top level (or two top levels in the case of the storage and printer-server architectures) and *product architecture* for the lower levels. The focus of the case study is on the marked area in the figure, although the other parts are discussed briefly as well.

Axis maintains a product-line architecture and a set of reusable components that are used for product construction. The main components are a framework provid-

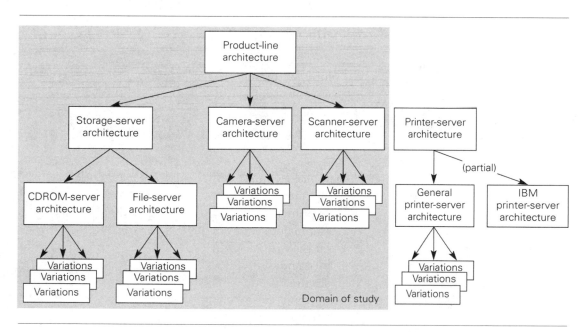

Figure 42   Product-line and product architectures in Axis Communications

ing file-system functionality and a framework proving a common interface to a considerable set of network protocols, but also smaller frameworks are used such as a data-chunk framework, a smart pointer framework, a 'toolkit' framework providing domain-independent classes and a kernel system for the proprietary processor providing, among other things, memory management and a job scheduler. In total, Axis employs more than ten object-oriented frameworks. In Fig. 43, the organization of the main frameworks and a simplified representation of the product-line architecture is shown.

The size of the frameworks including the specializations is considerable, whereas the abstract frameworks are rather small. The abstract design of the file-system framework is about 3500 lines of code (LOC). However, each specialization of the framework, implementing a file-system standard, also is about 3500 LOC and since the framework currently supports seven standards, the total size is about 28 KLOC. In the protocol framework, the concrete specializations are much larger. The

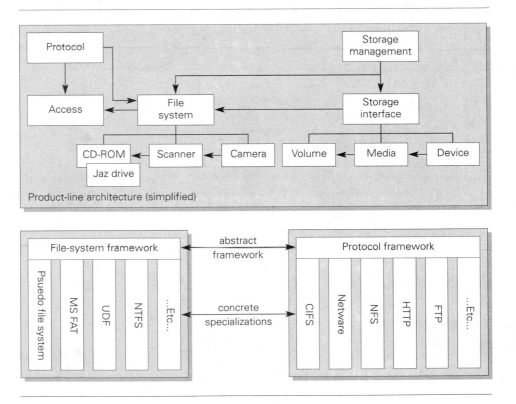

Figure 43   Overview of the main frameworks used in Axis products

abstract protocol framework is about 2500 LOC. The framework contains three major specializations, i.e., Netware, Microsoft SMB and TCP/IP, and a few smaller specializations operating on top of the aforementioned protocols. The total size of the framework is about 200 KLOC, due to the large size of concrete specializations. For example, the implementation of the Netware protocol is around 80 KLOC.

In addition to the frameworks and the product-line architecture, the other smaller frameworks are part of most products and each product contains a substantial part of product-specific code. A product can, consequently, contain up to 500 KLOC of C++ code.

1.3 Technology

Axis makes considerable use of relatively advanced software engineering methods and techniques. As mentioned, the object-oriented paradigm is used throughout the organization, including more advanced concepts such as object-oriented frameworks and design patterns. Also, it makes use of peer review of software, collects test metrics, performs project follow-ups and has started to put effort into root-cause analysis of problems identified after products have been put in operation in the field.

Configuration management is performed by a system developed in-house that is built on top of SCCS. The system manages the source code, the product descriptions, the tools, documentation, tests and other relevant data.

1.4 Organization

Initially, all software engineers were part of a development department. A number of years ago, this department was reorganized into a number of business units. The reorganization was in part caused by the identified need to increase the focus on individual products. More recently, the business units have been 'divisionalized', i.e. each business unit has received more independence. Each business unit has responsibility for a product or product category, e.g., storage servers. The product-line architecture and its associated assets, however, are shared between the business units and asset responsibles are assigned to guide the evolution.

1.5 Processes

Evolution of products, the product-line architecture and the reusable assets constitute a major challenge. The hardware of products evolves at a rate of 1–2 times per year. Software, being more flexible, has more frequent updates, i.e., 2–4 major updates per year depending on the product. Since the products are equipped with flash memory, customers can, after having obtained the product, upgrade (for free) by downloading and installing a new version of the software. The evolution is caused by changing and new requirements. These requirements originate from customers and future needs predicted by the business unit. The decision process involves all stakeholders and uses both formal and informal communication, but the final decision is taken by the business unit manager. The high level of involvement of especially the engineers is very important due to the extreme pressure on the time-to-market of product features. If engineers were not committed to this, it might be hard to meet the deadlines.

The evolution of the product-line architecture and the reusable assets is controlled by the new product features. When a business unit identifies a need for asset evolution, it will, after communicating with other business units and the asset responsible, basically proceed and extend the asset, test it in its own context and publish it so that other business units can benefit from the extension as well. Obviously, this process creates a number of problems, as discussed in later chapters, but these have so far proven to be manageable.

2 Securitas Larm AB

As for the previous case, we first present the background of the company, Securitas Larm, then the system family and the technology which the company uses. Finally, the organization and the development and evolution processes are discussed. (Please note that during the process of writing this book, the development department at Securitas Larm AB, which was involved in our case study, was sold to Matsushita and is now Matsushita Electric Works Fire & Security Technology AB.)

2.1 Company background

Securitas Larm AB, earlier TeleLarm AB, develops, sells, installs and maintains safety and security systems such as fire-alarm systems, intruder-alarm systems, passage-control systems and video-surveillance systems. The company's focus is especially on larger buildings and complexes, requiring integration between the aforementioned systems. Therefore, Securitas has a fifth product unit developing integrated solutions for customers including all or a subset of the aforementioned systems. In Fig. 44, there is an overview of the products.

2.2 Product family

Securitas uses a product-line architecture in its fire-alarm products – in practice this is only for the EBL 512 product – and traditional approaches in the other products. However, due to its success in the fire-alarm market, the intention is to expand the software product line in the near future to include the intruder alarm and passage-control products as well.

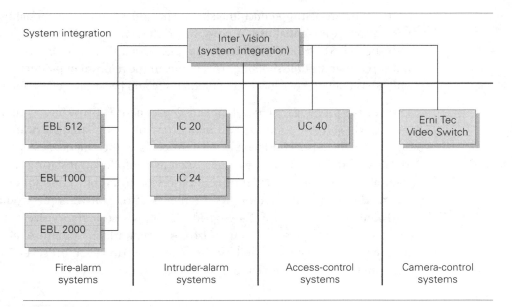

System integration

Figure 44   Securitas Larm: product overview

The products of Securitas are rather different from the products mass-produced by Axis. A fire-alarm system, for example, requires considerable effort in installation, testing, trouble-shooting and maintenance and the acquisition of such a system generally initiates a long-term relationship between the customer and Securitas. Consequently, the number of products for Securitas is in the order of magnitude of hundreds per year, whereas for Axis the order is in the tens of thousands per month.

2.3 Technology

Although originally a traditional embedded systems company employing C and assembly code, Securitas Larm identified the benefits of object-oriented technology early. This was in part the result of the REBOOT Esprit project (Karlsson, 1995). During the early 1990s, the company developed a monolithic object-oriented framework using C++ for the domain of fire-alarm systems. A later generation reorganized the monolithic framework into a hierarchical structure of smaller frameworks and added substantial amounts of functionality. In the terminology of this book, the company introduced an explicit product-line architecture and developed the components in the architecture as object-oriented frameworks.

Unlike most other approaches where the product-line architecture and components only contain the functionality that is shared between various products, the shared assets in the fire-alarm product line aim at encompassing the functionality in all fire-alarm product instantiations. A powerful configuration tool, Win512, is associated with the EBL 512 product that allows product instantiations to be configured easily and supports in trouble-shooting. This results in the removal of product-specific code, which has immense benefits for maintainability and backward compatibility.

Some of the problems the development department is concerned with are the following. No suitable tools for automated testing of updated software have been found, but there is a considerable need. In general, the engineers identify a lack of tools support for embedded systems, such as compilers translating the right programming language to the right micro processor. It has proven notoriously hard to accurately predict the memory requirements of the software for products. Since hardware and software are co-designed, the supported memory size has to be predicted early in the project. To minimize cost, one wants to minimize the maximum amount of memory supported by the hardware. However, on several occasions, early predictions have proven to be too optimistic.

2.4 Organization

Initially, the software and electronics engineers were located in the business units organized around the product categories. However, due to the small size of the engineering group in each business unit, generally a handful, and the fact that similar work was being performed in the business units, it was decided to reorganize development into a development department which acts as an internal supplier to business units responsible for the marketing, installation and maintenance of the products. Thus, all product development at Securitas Larm is organized in a single development department.

Finally, since each product area has an associated organizational product unit and the development department acts as an internal supplier to these product units, benefiting from the commonalities between the different products has proven nearly impossible, despite the considerable potential.

2.5 Processes

The development department uses a number of software engineering techniques and methods. Peer and team reviews are used for all major revisions of software and for all critical parts in the systems. Since the organization is ISO9000 certified, the decision and development processes are documented and enforced. System errors that appear after systems have been put into operation are logged and the counter-measures are documented as well.

3 Symbian

The third case we describe in this chapter is Symbian, the developer of the EPOC operating system. As we will see, the Symbian case is different from the other two in the sense that the products developed by the company are not final products. Instead, Symbian's products are used by EPOC licensees to develop their own products, typically wireless information devices such as communicators and smartphones.

3.1 Company background

The landscape of wireless information devices such as mobile phones has been changing dramatically for several years already. This was identified early on by the main developers of mobile phones, such as Ericsson, Nokia and Motorola. Symbian was formed in 1998 out of the software unit of Psion, i.e. Psion Software. It is owned by Ericsson, Matsushita, Motorola, Nokia and Psion, but it licenses the EPOC operating system and application suite to other organizations as well, such as Philips.

Psion was founded in 1980, and initially focused on game programming, but it soon entered the hand-held device arena with an organizer in 1984. In 1990, it was one of the first to develop and market a mobile computer, but it was ahead of its time and did not become a commercial success, despite its technically advanced level. The EPOC operating system was primarily developed during the 1990s. The first major version was a 16-bit implementation, but in 1994 the first 32-bit version of the operating system was available. It was primarily used for Psion's own product line, including, among others, the Series 5 range, the Siena and Series 3 range, the Organizer and corporate hand-held terminals.

As mentioned earlier, Symbian was formed in June 1998 out of Psion Software as an independent joint venture between Ericsson, Nokia, Motorola and Psion. The mission of the joint venture is to set the standard for mobile wireless operating systems and to enable a mass market for wireless information devices. The approach Symbian takes to achieving this vision is to develop a complete software platform, including an operating system, application frameworks, applications and development tools for wireless information devices. This software platform is licensed by a wide range of wireless-industry leaders. The aim is to promote standards for the interoperation of wireless information devices with, for example, wireless networks and content services. (See Tasker (2000) for an overview.)

The creation of core software and standards, and the support by its owners, who combined have a market share of around 80 per cent in the mobile phones market, allow for a large market for wireless information devices based on the EPOC operating system and application set. This market is, and most likely will continue to be, large enough for the owners of Symbian and others to compete with their own devices and for third-party software developers to develop applications for these devices.

3.2 Product family

Unlike the first two cases described in this chapter, Symbian does not develop products that can be deployed directly in the home or business contexts. Instead it develops the core software for wireless information devices. This core software is licensed to licensees who develop their own products based on the provided core.

Products can be viewed as originating from two sources: hand-held PCs and mobile phones. The former are in the process of being extended with wireless communication functionality, whereas the second category is being extended with functionality normally expected from personal computers. Since the products have rather different characteristics depending on their origin, the core software needs to be adapted for the specifics related to the user interface.

The identification of the various types of devices has led to the definition of so-called 'device families'. Currently, three device families are recognized, i.e. a landscape display communicator (640 × 200 pixels and upwards), a portrait display communicator (approximately 320 × 240 pixels) and a smartphone family. Communicators are defined as *information-centric products* with voice capability. Typically, a communicator is equipped with a keyboard, it supports seamless linking with PCs, printers and the Internet and has, in general, a richer functionality than a smartphone. Smartphones are defined as *voice-centric devices* with information capability. These devices typically provide functionality to browse the Internet, and to receive and send faxes, SMS and email. Some smartphones have (or will have) scheduling and contact management software built-in.

Initially, Symbian had defined two smartphone device families, i.e. devices with approximately a 200 × 200 pixel display and devices with a switchable landscape and portrait display (320 × 120 pixels). However, the requirements from the various licensees were more diverse than those supported by these two families. In response, the two device families were replaced with a (more general) platform for smartphones.

Associated with each of the device families is a device family requirement definition (DFRD) which defines the specifics of the family members. In addition, for each family, a reference device exists for which Symbian guarantees correct behaviour and retains responsibility for errors. The reference device is defined in co-operation with the licensees. Licensees are required to adapt the EPOC operating system and application set to their particular device and are responsible for solving any problems resulting from differences between their device hardware and the reference device.

3.3 Technology

Although one might easily focus on the operating system, EPOC really is an operating system, application framework and application suite. It is optimized for use in wireless information devices and for hand-held, battery-powered, computers. EPOC also includes connectivity software for synchronization with data on PCs and servers. EPOC can be decomposed into four main parts:

- **Core:** the core components provide the APIs and runtime environment on which all other components are built. Core components include the base, i.e. a run-time kernel, supporting multi-tasking, power management, and support for an efficient client-server architecture, engine support, i.e. fundamental APIs for data management, and the graphical user interface functionality.

- **Comms:** communications components provide the APIs, drivers, link and higher-level protocols for a wide range of communication and data interchange requirements.

- **Languages:** EPOC includes a run-time environment for Java to JDK 1.1.4 specification including AWT, and both a run-time and development environment for OPL, a Basic-like rapid application development language.

- **Applications:** the engines and GUIs which directly implement end-user applications.

In Fig. 45, three of the main parts are shown. Each application is divided into a GUI, a view and an engine part dealing with different aspects of the application functionality. Separating the GUI and engine allows for the easy adoption of the engine of an application in different device families. In general, one can say that the design of EPOC is heavily influenced by the, at times conflicting, quality attributes which the system should provide. The primary quality requirements include robustness, resource efficiency, reliability and ease of use. The price for this is the relatively high complexity of the software. In particular, the variability required from the components for use in multiple DFRDs is a main contributing factor.

3.4 Organization

Symbian is organized functionally into six main units, i.e. development, programme management, technical consulting, design and technology, marketing and sales, and finance and operations. As may be expected from a technology-focused company, the main part of the staff is located in development. Programme management is responsible for the device family requirement definitions and defines the technical 'roadmap' for each DFRD. However, it co-operates extensively with the other units. In Fig. 46, the organization is presented graphically.

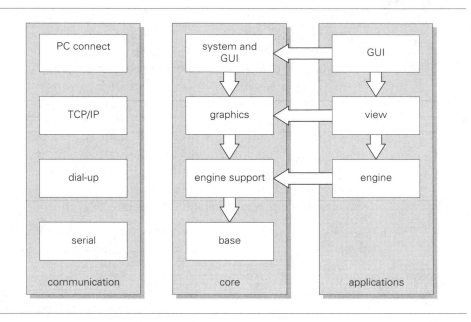

Figure 45   Main components of EPOC

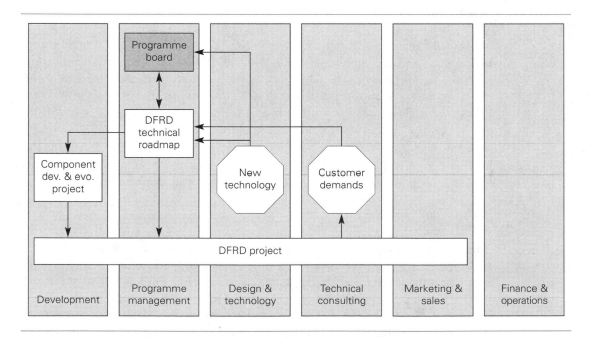

Figure 46   Processes in the Symbian organization

Development contains most of the software engineering staff and performs the actual software development. The development unit is organized in smaller units, called groups, and each group is responsible for a subset of the components that make up EPOC. In addition to these groups, there are groups which are responsible for each DFRD, i.e. the integration and configuration of the operating system, the application platform and an application set for one specific device family.

The EPOC deliverable for each device family requirement definition is developed and evolved as a project cross-cutting the organizational units, i.e. staff from most units are involved in the project.

3.5 Processes

Symbian makes use of two types of projects: domain engineering and DFRD projects. Domain engineering projects are typically concerned with developing new versions of EPOC components, and even new components. DFRD projects are concerned with developing the next version of an EPOC delivery for a particular DFRD. In Fig. 46, the organization and some of the processes are shown. Component development and evolution projects are initiated based on the technical roadmap of one or more DFRDs. The results of the component projects are used in the DFRD projects. Unlike component projects which are internal to the development department, DFRD projects involve staff from most departments in the company. The delivered EPOC version for the DFRD is used by the licensees to develop their own products, possibly with the help of the technical consulting staff. This leads to the identification of requirements which may be incorporated in the technical road map for the DFRD. A second source of new requirements is the identification of new technology which facilitates new types of functionality for the wireless information devices and must be incorporated. The consequences may be DFRD-specific, but frequently, they affect all EPOC products. In the latter case, this becomes an issue for the programme board that decides how and when to incorporate support for the new technology. In the case of conflicts between program boards, another body exists for resolving these. Since different EPOC products may have conflicting requirements on the components, these conflicts must be resolved.

4 Concluding remarks

In this chapter, we have looked at three case examples of companies which employ a software product-line approach to their software development, i.e. Axis Communications, Securitas Larm and Symbian. The products developed by these companies lie primarily in the domain of embedded systems, in the sense that they all include hardware and mechanical parts. In the remainder of this part of the book, these cases will be used to illustrate the concepts discussed. Due to the limitations on the information which the companies involved have been willing to make public and the space available in the book, many details have had to be omitted.

CHAPTER 9

Designing a product-line architecture

Changing the software development in an organization to a software product-line approach requires fundamental changes to the organization and the processes. The advantages of adopting this approach are, as described earlier, decreased development and maintenance cost and time-to-market and increased software quality. However, as with any change, there is risk involved that needs to be assessed. In addition, the products that are planned to be part of the product line need to exhibit sufficient commonality and it should be possible to handle the variability in a modular fashion.

In this chapter, we set out the first phase in the conversion from a product-based to a product-line-based approach: the design of the software architecture for the product line. In the next section, an overview is given of the steps that make up this phase. Section 2 discusses business case analysis, and scoping and feature and product planning are discussed in Sections 3 and 4, respectively. The design of the software architecture for the product line is described in Section 5. The definition of component requirements is discussed in Section 6, and the verification of the resulting architecture in Section 7. The chapter is concluded in Section 8.

1 Overview

The first step in the process of converting to a product-line approach must be to perform an analysis of the business case. The analysis should indicate whether the advantages promised by the proponents of this approach are also valid in the concrete case of this particular organization. Subsequent steps include scoping, feature planning, software architectural design, component requirement specification and verification. The steps are briefly described below.

- **Business case analysis**. Before making a commitment to a new approach to product development, one should have verified to a sufficient level of certainty that the software product-line approach will pay off. In addition, the selection of either a revolutionary or an evolutionary path to convert from a products-based to a product-line-based organization should be made after a business case analysis of the alternatives.

■ **Scoping.** An activity highly related to business case analysis is determining the products and the product features which should be included in the software product line. It may not be beneficial or even desirable to include all products and features in the software product line, especially not from the start. Scoping is concerned with selecting, based on the results of the business case analysis, the products included in the product line and, secondly, what features are shared in the product line and handled specifically for each product.

■ **Product and feature planning.** Once the initial scoping of features supported by the product-line architecture has been defined, it is important to spend some effort on identifying the characteristics of subsequent versions of the product-line architecture. Independently of using an evolutionary or a revolutionary approach to the introduction of the product-line approach, there will be continuous development of the product-line architecture in terms of the features and products it supports. Since incorporating new, but anticipated, features is generally considerably easier than other features, it is important to develop a plan for feature incorporation. This plan can then be used by the software architects to prepare the product-line architecture for the future inclusion of these features.

■ **Design of the product-line architecture.** The main step in the process is, of course, the design of the software architecture for the product line. All other activities discussed in this chapter support of this activity. Software architectural design has, however, been discussed at length in the earlier part of the book. Consequently, in this chapter, we primarily address the activities that are specific to designing a software architecture that should cover or be easily extended for a line of products, rather than just address the specifics of a single product.

■ **Component requirement specification.** The software architecture dictates a set of components that implement the required behaviour. This activity is concerned with specifying the requirements for each of the components. The next development phase is the design and implementation of the components that make up the software product line. However, for developing a component the software engineer has to know what functional and quality requirements the component should fulfil, in what products it will be used and how it will be instantiated for each product, i.e. its configurability.

■ **Validation.** Finally, before entering the next activity, i.e. component development, it is important to validate that the product line supports all features defined during scoping, that it can be easily instantiated for each of the products in the product line and that planned new features can be readily incorporated.

In the subsequent sections, the activities will be discussed in more detail, addressing the business, organizational, process and technological aspects of the particular activity.

2 Business case analysis

The analysis of the business case aims at identifying the benefits of adopting the product-line approach as compared to the approach currently used within the organization. One can identify three primary reasons for adopting the product-line approach, and these are discussed below.

- **Cost.** The cost associated with developing and evolving a line of products is so high that the profitability and so the competitiveness of the organization is affected negatively. To address this, the common parts of the products are captured by the shared assets that make up a product line. In addition to the common parts only having to be developed once for the product line, the quality of the common parts tends to be higher, leading to decreased corrective maintenance. In addition, new requirements that are relevant for more than one family member have to be incorporated once rather than for each product.

- **Time-to-market.** Especially for the many organizations developing software products, the cost associated with product development often does not really play a primary role. The most important aspect is the time-to-market, i.e. the amount of time needed to convert a set of requirements into a reliable product that can be shipped. Since the products developed by the organization are often related, the product-line approach allows the developers to obtain the traditional features from the product-line assets and only develop the features unique to the product. This consequently reduces time-to-market considerably.

- **Staff.** A more recent development is that software development organizations are simply unable to hire additional staff, despite the fact that there are considerable funds and projects available. Assuming that the organization's goal is to expand its line of products, the traditional strategy of adding business units with newly hired staff will not be an alternative. Instead, alternative approaches have to be employed. The product-line approach, again, provides a highly attractive route which allows the existing staff to develop, support and evolve a larger set of products. This, however, requires that the competence level of the staff be such that they can be trained to apply the product-line principles in practice.

The analysis of the business case should start with a clear understanding of what aim the organization intends to achieve by converting to a product-line approach. The three rationales above are not fully orthogonal and other reasons for adopting a product-line approach may exist, so that more than one may be selected as relevant.

Separate from the rationale (i.e. cost, time-to-market or staff) the business case analysis consists of a number of steps. First, it is important to analyze the current situation. Second, a prediction of the future cost and benefits should be made based on the assumption that software development continues using the traditional means. Third, we must analyze the investment required to convert to a product-line approach. Finally, a prediction of the future cost and benefits using the product-line approach should be developed. The mentioned cost and benefit factors can either be pure financial figures, development effort, i.e. man hours, calendar time or a logical combination of factors. The future predictions should be based on some goal or set of goals that the organization intends to achieve. Examples of such goals may be decreasing the cost of incorporating new features for the existing product set, decreasing the time-to-market of new products by half or introducing new products without additional staff. Based on these four results, one can base conclusions about the viability of the product-line approach to achieve the overall goals of the organization.

■ **Analysis of current situation.** This step is primarily concerned with a strengths and weaknesses analysis of the current approach to software development. In addition, the intention is to collect a set of key figures that are used for the later steps. The relevant key figures depend, among others, on the organization and the rationale, i.e. cost, time-to-market or staff, but examples of these include average effort per maintenance request, average effort per new feature and average effort per new product.

■ **Prediction of future cost and benefit using current approach.** Based on the strengths and weaknesses analysis and the key figures, it is generally possible to define a reasonably accurate prediction of the future of the organization, in terms of the ability to achieve the goals, the cost and benefit of each of the goals and the conflicts between the goals. For instance, for one organization the goal may be to extend existing products with new features and to introduce a number of new products. The prediction may show that the current amount of staff is insufficient to achieve both goals. Finally, an accurate prediction generally requires additional information on the effects on market share, profit per sold unit, etc.

■ **Investment analysis to convert to product line approach.** The product-line approach generally requires a reorganization of software development, the development of a product-line architecture, the development (or mining and consequent adaptation) of a set of components and the development (or mining and reengineering) of product-specific code. The effort required for achieving this needs to be calculated as well as the effects on evolution of existing products and the shipping dates of new products currently in the development pipeline.

■ **Prediction of future cost and benefit using product line approach.** Based on the key figures and under the assumption of an available product-line architecture and component set, one can develop a prediction of the ability of the organization to achieve its goals as well as the cost and benefit of achieving those goals. For instance, in the aforementioned organization where the currently used approach did not allow for the introduction of new features in existing products and the introduction of new products, the product-line approach may enable both goals to be fulfilled. This is because the features already implemented can be reused directly by the new products and the features developed for the new products may be relevant for existing products as well.

■ **Conclusion.** It should, in principle, be easy to derive a conclusion based on the above data: there is a prediction for each approach and the prediction with the biggest $ figure wins. In practice, however, it is generally considerably more complicated than this. There is an immediate delay in the evolution of existing products and the introduction of new products during the conversion to a product-line approach which will affect the short-term results negatively. In addition, there is a certain amount of risk involved in adopting new technology, meaning that the long-term prediction of the product-line approach should be corrected with respect to the risk. Thus, the conclusion to adopt the product-line approach should be a strategic decision taken at a sufficiently high level in the organization, e.g. top management, and with considerable involvement of software architects and engineers and project and business unit managers.

The above is by no means intended to be complete or valid in all contexts. Product families (or product lines) have been studied in other fields, such as mechanical engineering and economics, fairly extensively and we refer to publications in especially the field of economics for reasonably complete and validated decision models. However, it is important to note that the results of using complex models are only as accurate as the input of data into them. Thus, if the key figures or the predictions have considerable error margins, it may be just as well to use relatively simple, straightforward techniques.

Scoping

As we have seen, the activity of scoping is concerned with the selection of product features that are to be included in the product-line architecture. It is important to perform a careful selection since the features included in the product-line architecture are relatively inexpensive to develop and evolve in terms of cost per product, since they are generally included by multiple products. On the down side, features that are part of the product-line architecture may be detrimental for products not including them. The feature may be difficult to implement as optional. This will require additional resources for those products, such as memory or performance, compared to the situation where the feature was not provided for in the product-line architecture. Even if the feature is optional, the feature may still leave its traces in the remaining parts of the product and its quality requirements may affect the overall architecture. Because of the potential conflicts between features, scoping is not only concerned with selecting the features incorporated in the product-line architecture, but also what products, built using those features, should be included in the product line.

The scoping activity can be decomposed into several steps, which include candidate product selection, candidate feature selection, feature graph specification, product-line scoping and the specification of product-specific requirements. In the section below, we first discuss the notion of feature in order to define it more precisely. In later sections, the individual steps are discussed.

3.1 Defining a feature

So far, we have used the notion of *feature* relatively informally throughout this chapter. We define a feature as a logical unit of behaviour that is specified by a set of functional and quality requirements. A feature generally captures a considerable set of requirements and is, as such, used to group requirements, which simplifies requirements handling. In addition, a feature represents a logical unit of behaviour from the perspective of one or several stakeholders of the product. For instance, the user of a product generally considers the product to consist of a number of functional units that are identified as different. Each such functional unit, we refer to as a feature.

We explicitly consider quality requirements to be part of features. The functionality specified by a feature can have associated quality requirements with respect to, e.g., performance, reliability, security and flexibility. These quality requirements may, however, have an effect on the overall product. For instance, the product performance when using a particular feature generally depends on the other active processes in the product. Thus, the decision to include a feature in the product will result in particular requirements, especially quality requirements, to affect the product-level requirements. The product-level requirements may then, in turn, have effects on the other features.

So far, we have considered features to be atomic units that can be put together in a product without difficulty, except for the quality requirements of some features that frequently affect other features. However, features are generally not independent and several types of relations can exist between them. The first and most basic type of relation is the 'depends-on' relation, i.e. the source feature in this relation requires the presence of the sink feature in order to be useful. A second type of relation, this one bi-directional, is 'mutually exclusive'. The semantics of this relation is that the two related features can never be present simultaneously in a product since this would lead to logical inconsistencies. Mutually exclusive features generally specify incompatible functional behaviour. Finally, the directional relation of 'conflicting' can be used. Conflicting features are not logically incompatible, but rather exhibit conflicting quality requirements. In the first part of the book discussing software architectural design, we considered several examples. However, one can state, for instance, that real-time predictability generally conflicts with run-time flexibility. Features imposing conflicting quality requirements on the overall product will require the software architect to spend effort on reconciling the differences. For instance, in the aforementioned example, the resulting product may be designed such that real-time predictability is ensured, but a number of dimensions of flexibility have been included. The software architect, in this example, would, for instance, need to incorporate checks on all points where the flexibility can be used to make sure that the real-time characteristics are not compromised.

Finally, we have presented features as logical units of behaviour specification which are included as 'black-boxes' in products. This may not be accurate in all types of product families. Especially in families where the products exhibit a low-end to high-end range, low-end products often include the same features as high-end products, but the low-end products only incorporate the basic aspects. In the cases that we have studied this has, where possible, been achieved by setting parameters in the components implementing the features, meaning that the low-end products include the same component, but the more advanced aspects have been disabled. In the cases where this was not possible, multiple versions of components are present, using one version for low-end and another for high-end products.

3.2 Candidate product selection

The first step in scoping is obtaining an understanding of what products potentially could be included in the product line. The way to conduct this step depends considerably on whether the product line is initiated for an existing set of products or for a new set. In the case of an existing set of products, selecting the candidate products is a straightforward activity. In the case where the intention is to take an evolutionary approach, i.e. to start with a small set of products and gradually to include more products, we need, at some point, to decide what products to start with. For now, however, we include all products as candidates.

When initiating a product line in a new domain, selecting candidate products is considerably less easy since there are no real-world examples within the organization. The candidate products need to be defined based on the strategic plan for the organization and based on existing examples developed by others, e.g. competitors.

Particularly in the case of an existing set of products, it is important to aim for the next generation of products rather than naïvely and directly defining the candidate products based on the current versions of the existing products. The rationale for this is straightforward. First, the initiation of the product line will take a, potentially considerable, amount of calendar time and the product line should support the instantiation of the products that will be required at that point in time, rather than currently. Second, initiating a product line represents a considerable investment and it needs to be used for a sizeable period of time in order to generate a return on this investment, generally a number of years. Consequently, it should be possible to instantiate competitive products using the product line for a period preferably longer than the time needed to repay the investment and the product line should accommodate for future products as well as today's.

However, the issue of balancing between today's and future requirements on the product-line architecture is a delicate one. Dikel *et al.* (1997) discuss this problem in more detail and point out that too strong a focus either on current or on future requirements may cause the software product line to fail.

3.3 Candidate feature selection

The second step in the activity of scoping is the selection of features that are candidates for inclusion in the product line. To select features, they first need to be identified. So, unless the candidate products selected in the previous section have a specified set of features associated with them, the features associated with each candidate product must be identified and defined.

The concept of feature has been discussed in Section 3.1, but it is important to identify the stakeholders for candidate product and to identify features from their respective perspectives. It is difficult to make general statements about the granularity of a feature, but a feature should represent a logical unit of behaviour from the perspective of the stakeholder and contain a sizeable set of requirements, i.e. there should, at least, be an order of magnitude difference between the number of features and the number of requirements for a member of a product line. In addition, the feature set should preferably be manageable without further organization. Often, features represent larger chunks of functionality in bigger products than in smaller products.

An issue to address is the case where different people perform candidate feature identification for the candidate products. In that case, the features may be unharmonized, i.e. a feature in one product covers functionality from multiple features identified in another product. If there is a direct 'part-of' relation between the identified features, this is simple to fix, but generally things are not so simple. If features from different products overlap in ways that do not allow for a simple mapping, the features need to be *harmonized*. During harmonization, the conflicts between features are resolved by redefining features. The simplest way to harmonize is to split features into smaller parts. However, this may lead to fragmented features that do not represent logical units of behaviour anymore. Therefore, it is important to perform harmonization in a careful manner. Finally, it is generally acceptable to describe the behaviour of a product by features that include more behaviour than strictly required by the product. Assuming that the features are included in the product-line architecture, the product will automatically and without additional development cost exhibit the additional behaviour when instantiated from the product line.

Once the feature set for each candidate product is identified and harmonized, it is possible to define a matrix where the candidate products and the candidate features make up the two dimensions. Each location in the matrix is marked if the feature is provided by the product. In Table 6, an example matrix is shown. Feature 1 is included in three products, feature 2 and feature 3 in two products and feature 4 only in a single product. Based on this, one can see that the inclusion of feature 1 in the product-line architecture is rather likely, whereas the inclusion of feature 4 is

Table 6　　　Example of a product and feature matrix

Product/feature	F1	F2	F3	F4	...
S1	X				
S2		X	X		
S3	X	X		X	
S4	X		X		
...					

relatively unlikely. Feature 4 would typically be included in the product-specific features of product 3.

It depends on the number of candidate products and features how selective one should be at this point with respect to excluding features. As long as the sets are still manageable, it may be beneficial to incorporate all or most features. However, for larger sets, straightforward set reductions are those that exclude all features only implemented by a single or a few products.

The result of this step is a set of candidate features with associated information with respect to the products that implement the features.

3.4 Feature graph specification

Features are not necessarily atomic building blocks, but may have, as discussed earlier, relations between them. When performing the actual product line scoping, discussed in the next section, it is important to understand these relations, so that conflicts and incompatible requirements are avoided, or at least managed, as much as possible. A useful tool to achieve this understanding is the use of a *feature graph*.

A feature graph provides a graphical representation of the relations between features. The feature graph may use relations of several types. The 'depends-on' relation between two features is obviously useful when scoping the product line since it avoids the situation where a feature is excluded from the product line while other features depend on it. However, it also allows for checking the correctness of the product/feature matrix. Some core feature may not have been identified as part of a product since no stakeholder uses it directly, and consequently nobody identifies it is a feature, even though it is a necessary part of the product.

The 'mutually exclusive' relation, in principle, implies that of the related features only one is present in a product. However, in some cases this is not feasible and the software architect will be forced to spend explicit effort on resolving the issue. The relation encourages the incorporation of the mutually exclusive features as pure alternatives, allowing each product to be instantiated using one of the alternatives and being able to exchange the alternatives without manipulating the rest of the product.

The 'conflicting' relation between features is primarily concerned with quality attributes. Thus, the inclusion of both features will lead to conflicting quality attributes that will require the explicit attention of the software architect in order to resolve the conflict. If the conflicts between the components cannot be resolved or it is not beneficial to do so, one can treat the relation as a 'mutually exclusive' relation as well. However, this requires that none of the quality attributes have such effects on the product-line architecture such that even when the feature is not included, the architecture still conflicts with the other feature.

3.5 Product-line scoping

At this point all information needed for performing the actual selection of products and features for the product line is present. The step of product-line scoping is concerned with selecting those products and features which optimally support the overall goals identified in the business case.

The ultimate goal of the product line is that the instantiation of products which are part of the product line is optimal in terms of development effort, time-to-market or some other factor. This leads to the interesting situation that the exclusion of a feature from the product line does not automatically allow the software architect to ignore it. Even for the product requiring the feature excluded from the product line, it should be possible to be instantiated from the product line and extended with a product-specific implementation of the feature against reasonable effort and time demands. This requires that the feature requirements be added to the functionality provided by the derived product-line architecture without having to redesign the derived architecture. Finally, it is clear that it is important that products in the product line have no fundamentally conflicting requirements that affect the architecture as a whole since even features excluded from the product line may cause conflicts.

Once the products included in the product line have been selected from the candidates, the next step is to select the features included in the product line. Basically, one can identify two extreme approaches, i.e. the minimalist and the maximalist approaches. The minimalist approach only incorporates those features in the product line that are used by all products. All remaining features are handled as product-specific features. A disadvantage of the minimalist approach is that the benefits of the product-line approach are not exploited to the full extent due to the overly conservative approach. However, it minimizes the risk involved in adopting a product line since all functionality that is invested will be used by all products. Software product-lines resulting from minimalist approaches are frequently referred to as platforms.

The maximalist approach includes all features in the product line. Product instantiation is then performed by excluding parts of the product line. The prototypical example where this approach is used is the fire-alarm product line by Securitas Larm. The product-line architecture and components have an associated tool that automates and supports the instantiation of products based on the product line.

As usual, the general case is somewhere in between the two extremes. Features used by most products are included whereas features used by few products are excluded and handled differently. Although some research exists that defines economic models for scoping a product line (e.g. De Baud and Schmid, 1999), scoping remains, in most cases, a qualitative decision process based on the strategic plans for the organization.

3.6 Specification of product-specific requirements

Once the scope of the product line has been defined, it becomes possible to define a clear boundary between functionality provided by the product line and functionality that is product-specific. At this point, the product-specific requirements need to be defined because the software architecture for the product line needs to be designed such that the product software architectures in the family can easily be instantiated. Whereas architecture assessment, as discussed in the previous part of the book was primarily concerned with the quality attributes that the product needs to provide, in the context of software product lines, a second main aim with assessment is to determine whether the product-line architecture sufficiently supports the instantiation of the products in the family.

4   Product and feature planning

At this point, the product-line scope has been defined. However, the scope only specifies the currently planned feature and product set of the software product line. Since we know that incorporating expected changes is generally considerably less expensive than unexpected changes since the software can be designed to easily accommodate expected changes, it is a worthwhile activity to construct a plan with respect to the products and features that are intended to be included in future versions. In some companies, as we have seen in the case of Symbian, these plans are referred to as (technical) 'roadmaps'.

Planning the supported products and features is a natural activity when using the evolutionary approach to introducing a product line, since the intention is to gradually expand the scope of the software product line. However, even in case of the revolutionary approach, where all relevant existing products and features are replaced, it is generally desirable to consider future developments in the domain of the product line.

Feature and product planning is a logical extension of the scoping activity discussed in the previous section. The features and products that were considered but not included during scoping are likely candidates for being included in the planning. In addition, an analysis of expected future developments outside the control of the organization, e.g. available technology, market developments, etc., may provide useful suggestions with respect to potential future features and products.

The feature graph is extended with the features considered as future extensions as well as with the relations between the selected and the potential future features. An interesting issue that should be considered at this point is the presence of conflicts between selected features and features that may be included in the future. Depending on the estimated likelihood that the feature is selected, the conflict may either be addressed or ignored. If the conflict is addressed, it is handled as described in the previous section on scoping. Even if it is ignored, it is important to explicitly document the conflicts associated with incorporating the potential future feature.

The feature and product planning activity extends the artefacts defining the product-line scope with requirements concerning the relative ease of incorporating of new features and products. During the design of the product-line architecture, these requirements can be used as a tool to verify the evolveability of the product-line architecture. In addition, the requirement specifications of the individual products are extended with requirements that indicate potential new features to be included in the product. These requirements are used as described earlier.

5 Product-line architectural design

The design of software architectures has been discussed extensively earlier in the book, thus, in this section we only address the issues that are specific to the design of a software architecture for a product line.

One can identify a number of different approaches to using a product-line architecture. At one extreme, the software architecture defined for the product line can be used 'as-is' for the products in the family. The difference in the implementation between the products is expressed using the variability of the components. At the other extreme, the product-line architecture is only used as part or core of the product architecture. The software architecture of the product may extend and potentially even make, generally minor, changes to the product-line architecture. Several alternative approaches can be defined in between the two extremes. For instance, the product-line architecture may be used for all products, but products may have their own component implementations. In general, our experience is that the product architectures virtually always use the same archetypes and make relatively modest extensions to the product-line architecture. Changes to the product-line architecture are small and relatively infrequent since major changes often prohibit the use of product-line components. This requires product-specific component implementations, which are expensive and invalidate many of the benefits of the product-line approach.

A second difference between the design of a software architecture for a product line and an architecture for an individual product is that product-specific features need to be considered even when designing the product-line architecture. The product-line architecture affects the design and implementation of product-specific features. If product-specific features are not considered, typical consequences may be concerned with quality attributes where design decisions made for the product-line architecture make it impossible for specific products to implement their features. However, even functional requirements defined in product-specific features may be hard or impossible to implement if not considered during product-line architectural design.

In the following sections, the product-line-specific aspects of software architectural design are discussed. We use the structure of our architectural design method, i.e. functionality-based design, architectural assessment and architecture transformation.

5.1 Functionality-based architectural design

Functionality-based architectural design, as described in Chapter 4, is concerned with the definition of the product context, the identification of archetypes and the description of product instantiations. When designing a product-line architecture, most of the activities are equivalent, but some extensions to the activity are needed.

The method assumes that we start from the functional requirements and ignore the quality requirements for the time being. However, the features defined and scoped earlier contain both functional and quality requirements. Consequently, the first step is to define a requirement specification for the product-line architecture that combines the functional requirements for each feature in one set of functional requirements. We perform a similar grouping activity for the quality requirements. Finally, since we will evaluate the product-line architecture with respect to its suitability for the products in the product-line scope, the reorganization of features into a set of functional and a set of quality requirements is also performed for each product. This includes the potential future features identified during feature planning.

Defining the product context

In the case of developing a software architecture for a product line, the contexts in which the software architecture has to operate are much more diverse than for a single product. The products that are part of the product line may be very diverse in terms of their context, in terms of the underlying hardware, the external products that it communicates with and the user interface. To give an example, the fire-alarm product-line architecture covers, in principle, the complete range of products. At the low end, a product for an individual household is stand-alone and consists of a few sensors, an actuator and a user interface consisting of a few LEDs and a button. High-end fire-alarm products may cover sites consisting of multiple buildings, thousands of sensors, hundreds of actuators and an advanced graphical user interface. These products consist of multiple distributed processors communicating through a network and, in addition, generally interface with other building automation products. The product-line architecture for the fire-alarm product should, consequently, cover widely diverse contexts.

The contexts in which products that are members of the product line operate are not necessarily specified for the product line as a whole. Instead individual products often distinguish themselves in terms of the supported context. The issue that has to be addressed by the software architect is whether the product-specific aspects of product contexts must be addressed by the product-line architecture or whether these aspects can be added modularly to the product software architecture. Some product context aspects, e.g. the distribution in the fire-alarm product, are fundamental and lead to product-wide effects if not addressed in the product-line architecture from the start. Other aspects are highly modular and have minimal effect on the architecture as a whole and can thus be handled just for the particular product covering that context aspect.

Generally, several product context aspects are not incorporated in all, but rather in a subset of the products. Handling these aspects for each product independently is not desirable since this would decrease reuse between products. The alternative approach is to incorporate those aspects in the product-line architecture. Although this does not suffer from the redundancy problem, it may cause overheads for the products which do not incorporate that aspect of the context. The appropriate approach depends, obviously, on how hard or easy it is to exclude the aspect, what overheads it causes for the products not using the aspect and what overheads the handling of duplicates causes in case the aspect is excluded from the product line.

An alternative approach is to define a hierarchy of product families where the higher levels cover more products but fewer features and the lower levels cover fewer products but provide support for more features. Assuming that there is a predominant dimension along which the set of products in the product line can be decomposed into smaller, more focused sets, this is a feasible approach. For instance, Axis Communications employs such an approach, as described in the previous chapter. However, this approach complicates the organization and management of the product-line assets. In addition, in many cases there may be more issues than just the product context aspects that would require an alternative hierarchy, in case the technique was employed.

Identifying archetypes

The next step in functionality-based software architectural design is the identification and definition of archetypes. This task is also described in Part I of the book, but there are aspects specific to the design of a software architecture for a product line. The archetypes represent the core concepts used for modeling the software architecture and for describing the product instantiations.

The archetypes are particularly relevant for product-line architectures since the commonality between the products in the product line is represented to a large extent through the archetypes. Archetypes provide the core abstractions on which the product line is defined and the fundamental concepts in the components are defined in terms of archetype instances.

Identifying the archetypes that are optimal for the product-line architecture is more difficult than for a software architecture for a single product, especially because the archetypes should be based not only on the product-line requirements, but at least on the primary product-specific requirements as well.

Depending on the amount of product-specific features compared to the amount of product-line features, it may be necessary to identify product-specific archetypes in addition to the product-line archetypes. The product-specific archetypes should uniformly extend the product-line archetypes. Overlap between archetypes should be removed where possible since it undermines the underlying approach by reducing the conceptual integrity of the software for the product.

Once the archetypes have been selected, the relations between them need to be defined in a similar fashion to that described in Chapter 4. The issues specific to the product line which need to be considered are primarily concerned with the consistency of archetype sets for each product. For instance, if an archetype X is dependent on an archetype Y that is excluded for a particular product, then the architecture for that product will be inconsistent and consequently explicit effort is required from the software architect to address this.

Describing product instantiations
The final step in functionality-based architectural design is describing product instantiations. The goal of this step is to verify the suitability of the selected archetypes and the ability of the current architecture to represent all variations of the product.

In the case of a product-line architecture, the range of products covered by the architecture is obviously much larger than for a single product. Consequently, the described product instantiations need to cover all products at the extremes. For instance in the case of the fire-alarm product line, there are low-end products with highly restricted resources and high-end products that are distributed and handle large numbers of sensors and actuators, but also have access to large amounts of resources in terms of computing power and memory. The product-line architecture should, in this case, allow for a cost-effective implementation of the low-end products without restricting high-end products in terms of the features and performance that these products should provide. Similarly, as in the case of Symbian, the features required from EPOC by communicators should not invalidate EPOC's usability for smartphones.

Finally, the description of product instantiations allows for studying and addressing the conflicts between features that are remaining after the scoping activity. Although scoping intends to integrate and reorganize conflicting features, there often remain some conflicts especially for the least typical products in the architecture. As we stated earlier, these conflicts require explicit attention from the software architect during the architectural design. However, it does not necessarily need to be addressed during the design of the product-line architecture. It may be possible to delay the handling of the conflict until the design of the product containing the conflict. It is, however, important to identify potential conflicts and, for each conflict, to establish that it is possible to defer the resolution of the conflict until product design.

5.2   Architecture assessment

In Chapter 5, we have described the process of architecture assessment for its quality requirements in considerable detail. Three techniques for assessing a software architecture were identified, i.e. using scenarios, simulation or mathematical models. All techniques make use of scenario profiles, i.e. a set of scenarios, generally with some relative importance associated with each scenario.

When designing a product line, the techniques for architecture assessment presented in Chapter 5 can, to a large extent, be used as presented. However, there is an important distinction: the qualities of the product-line architecture are not relevant in themselves, but rather the way these qualities translate to the software architecture of the products that are part of the product line. In addition, the product-line architecture needs to be assessed for the intended context, in terms of hardware, networks, other communicating products, user interface, etc. However, the context is generally different for each product in the product line. For instance, in the case of EPOC, smartphones are generally equipped with GSM functionality, with a relatively low data communication bandwidth, but wide range. Especially future communicators will, most likely, support the Bluetooth standard, providing high bandwidth, but a small range. These differences will put pressure on the software architecture of the product line to incorporate certain design solutions. However, despite the fact that each of the products has its quality requirements, the product-line architecture should enable each product in the family to fulfil its requirements.

To assess the product-line architecture for its quality requirements, a straightforward approach would be to assess each of the product instantiations developed during functionality-based architectural design. Each of the product instantiations has its own specified context and the product-line architecture fulfils the assessed quality requirement if each of the assessments was successful. However, performing an assessment is an expensive and time-consuming activity and repeating the process for each member of the product line is generally not cost-effective.

Two alternatives can be identified for achieving cost-effective architecture assessment, i.e. using a reference context and assessing the products at the extremes. The reference context provides a number of constants with respect to the hardware, the communication bandwidth, the number of devices that the product communicates with, etc. In addition, a reference product is defined. The reference product is not necessarily an actual member of the product line, but it should contain the critical features present in the product line. The intention is that the reference context and product are defined such that the results of architectural assessments will be valid for all products in the product line. As discussed in Chapter 8, Symbian uses this approach for each of its device families.

An alternative approach is to assess a subset of the products in the product line. Typically, the products describing the extremes are selected. For instance, in the case of the fire-alarm product, the smallest, most low-end, and the largest, most high-end, product would be assessed. If the product-line architecture fulfils the requirements of the selected products, then it is assumed that it fulfils the requirements of all products.

There are cases where it is not appropriate to select the products at the extremes. For instance, for a family of products, it may be preferable to assess the product-line architecture for the products that they contain are expected to sell in the largest quantities. For those products it is most important that they contain the minimal amount of resources needed by the context to fulfil the requirements. By minimizing the amount of provided resources while fulfilling the quality requirements, the cost of the product is minimized and, consequently, profit increased. In such cases, the consequence may be that the products at the extremes, e.g. the low- and high-end products, have resources in excess. However, if the benefits of the product line exceed the cost of unneeded resources for some products in the family, this is an acceptable situation.

Next to fulfilling the features and quality requirements of the products currently part of the family, an important activity is the assessment of the product-line architecture for the inclusion of future features and products. The goal of the step of feature and product planning was to formulate what features and products are likely to be included in future versions of the product line. This information is used as input to the assessment of the evolvability (or maintainability) of the product-line architecture.

Generally, the most appropriate technique to assess maintainability is scenario-based assessment. To apply this technique, a maintenance profile is required. This scenario profile should be based on the aforementioned feature and product-planning information. Depending on the number of features and products that are considered for future inclusion, the software architect can either define a complete profile, i.e. include all features and products, or a selected profile, i.e. a representative subset of the considered features and products. In either case, each scenario should be augmented with a relative priority, indicating the likelihood and the importance of inclusion. Performing the assessment of maintainability using the specified profile is described in more detail in Section 3 of Chapter 5.

5.3 Architecture transformation

Architecture transformation is concerned with improving the quality attributes of a software architecture. In Chapter 6, four types of architecture transformations are introduced, i.e. imposing an architectural style, imposing an architectural pattern, applying a design pattern and converting quality requirements to functionality. Often a combination of transformations is required for the architecture to fulfil its quality requirements.

The transformations discussed in Chapter 6 are applicable to the design of a product-line architecture as well. In addition to these general transformations for improving quality attributes, product-line architectures may require transformation for achieving three aspects, i.e. variants, optionality and conflicts. These aspects are discussed below in more detail.

Variants

Some architectural solutions, such as architectural patterns, may not satisfy the requirements of all members of the product line. Instead, it is necessary to use two or more solutions for subsets of the product line. For example, low-end fire-alarm products use an application-level scheduler for achieving concurrency, and are relatively static, thus requiring no additional operating product support. High-end fire-alarm products exhibit more complex behaviour and consist of much smaller series, allowing for the use of a real-time kernel. In that case, the product-line architecture should support these variants. To present an example from Axis: in the storage product line, the CD-ROM products only support a read-only file system, whereas the Jaz drive products support read-write file systems. Due to the large amount of differences between read-only and read-write file systems, these have been implemented as variants of the file system component.

Typical transformations that support variants are the layered style, allowing the variant to be encapsulated as a layer, the broker architectural pattern, since it can be used to reduce the coupling between stable and varying pieces of software, and a number of design patterns, e.g. *abstract factory, strategy* and *mediator.*

Optionality

The second aspect typical for a product-line architecture is the optionality of parts of the architecture. For some products in the product line, certain components are excluded. Architecture transformations may be needed that reduce the dependency on optional components while maintaining the possibility of accessing these components if present. An example of optional functionality in the Symbian case is the user interface of the EPOC devices. Communicators generally employ a keyboard and a pointing device, whereas smartphones lack a keyboard and, in some cases, even the pointing device. The functionality associated with these interface devices has, to a large extent, been implemented as optional functionality, allowing many of the components to be used in all types of information devices.

Typical transformations that support optionality are the blackboard architectural style, since components depend only on the blackboard, not on other processes, and design patterns such as the *proxy* pattern, providing a placeholder controlling access, and the *strategy* pattern, allowing components to behave differently in different contexts.

Conflicts

Finally, a third aspect that may occur in a product-line architecture concerns conflicts between components or parts of the product-line architecture, which is optimized for the most important members of the product line, and product-specific components that are needed to fulfil the requirements on particular products. Other sources of conflicts may be the incorporation of legacy software or third-party software that is not designed to match the product-line architecture. Typical examples of such conflicts are mismatches in control flow assumptions, multiple representations of the same state and mismatches in provided and required interfaces. In, for instance, Garlan *et al.* (1995) several sources of architectural mismatches are examined. As mentioned, conflicts between the product-line architecture and the requirements of individual products should be identified during the design of the product-line architecture. Whether a conflict is handled in the product-line architecture or whether its resolution is delayed until product development is up to the software architect to decide.

If the conflict is handled in the product-line architecture, transformations are required to handle mismatches or other conflicts. Although architectural mismatches may exist between the product-line architecture and legacy or third-party software, architectural styles and patterns are generally not at the right level to address the mismatches. Generally, small-scale solutions, such as the use of design patterns, are needed to address the concrete locations where the conflicts appear. Examples of design patterns that may prove useful in resolving conflicts are *adapter, proxy* and *mediator.*

6 Component requirement specification

The result of the product-line architectural design process is a software architecture consisting of a set of related components. The software architecture assumes, for each component in the set, that it implements a certain required behaviour. Since the next development phase is the design and implementation of the components that make up the product line, it is necessary to specify the requirements of each of the components. The aim of this activity is to develop the requirement specifications for the components. There are several aspects that need to be defined in the component requirement specification, i.e. interfaces, functionality, quality attributes and variability. Below, each aspect is discussed in more detail.

- **Interfaces.** The architecture defines the relations the component has with other components. Each relation defines an interface that the component should support. This interface can either be a provided interface, through which the component offers functionality to other components, or a required interface, through which the component requests functionality from other components that it requires for its own correct functioning. The component requirement specification should define the provided and required interfaces that the component should support. In addition, there is a third type of interface, i.e. the configuration interface, used for handling the variability of the component. This interface is discussed below.

- **Functionality.** The component should provide certain functionality on its provided interfaces. Some of that functionality can be fulfilled by functionality that the component obtains through its required interfaces, but generally a considerable part is implemented inside the component. The component functionality should be specified as part of the component requirement specification. To maintain the encapsulation of the component and not expose its internals, it is usually preferable to specify the requirements in a black-box manner, i.e. in terms of expected behaviour at the interfaces.

- **Quality attributes.** Although software architectural design is concerned with organizing the functionality such that the quality requirements put on the architecture are fulfilled, no architecture will be able to avoid the need to distribute part of the quality requirements to the components as well. Unless the components provide certain performance, reliability, flexibility and maintainability properties, the architecture as a whole will be unable to fulfil its requirements. Consequently, it is important to specify the quality attributes that the component should fulfil.

- **Variability.** Finally, since the identified components are used in a variety of software architectures, i.e. the product architectures derived from the product-line architecture, the components generally need to be configured to handle the differences between the products. The required points of variability, i.e. aspects of the functional or quality requirements that need to be variable, are specified in the component requirement specification. It is important to note at this point that incorporating variability in a component is a costly activity which complicates the structure of the software. Therefore, only the required variability should be specified and implemented.

7 Validation

As discussed in Chapter 7, introducing a product line and converting software development from the one-at-a-time approach to a reuse-based approach represents a major strategic decision and investment. The product line will have a major impact on the organization for several years to come. Therefore, it is important to validate that the product line supports all features defined during scoping, that it can be easily instantiated for each of the products in the product line and that planned new features can be easily incorporated.

The product-line architecture represents the main design decisions and, once the complete product line is in place, changing any of these decisions will be very hard. Thus, it is justified to perform an explicit evaluation of the software architectural designed for the product line, rather than delaying the evaluation until the complete product line is in place.

Since the product-line architecture is designed by a software architect or a team of architects, these persons are generally not suitable to perform an evaluation to verify the successful achievement of all requirements. Instead, an evaluation performed by representatives of the stakeholders would provide an external perspective that will identify weaknesses of the product-line architecture more easily.

The evaluation is generally organized as a meeting, sometimes over several days, where the stakeholders present their major requirements and concerns with respect to the product-line architecture. The team of software architects presents the product-line architecture, explains design decisions and answers questions and concerns with respect to the architecture. The form of the meeting, where all stakeholders are present, allows for the identification of conflicting requirements. The team of software architects can present its approach to the handling and balancing of the conflicts and the stakeholders can jointly decide whether or not the design decisions are acceptable. The result of the meeting should be treated as a 'toll-gate', i.e. the continuation with subsequent phases in the design, e.g. component development, can only occur when the stakeholders have accepted the product-line architecture. For instance, in Kazman *et al.* (1994) a technique for architecture assessment by the stakeholders is given.

In some organizations, stakeholder meetings may be infeasible, undesirable, or both. For instance, companies developing mass-market products may find it difficult to select representatives for the product users. Therefore, some companies have instantiated architecture assessment teams which, either by invitation or proactively, evaluate software architectural designs developed by the software architects in project teams. The intention is similar to aims discussed earlier: to identify weaknesses in a software architecture for an individual product or a product line, before the product implementation is started. Through this evaluation, identified weaknesses can be addressed at a fraction of the cost of addressing these weaknesses later in the development process.

8 Conclusion

The focus of this chapter is the first main phase in the conversion to a software product-line approach to the development of software products, i.e. the design of a software architecture for the product line. The design of this architecture is a complex activity since, on the one hand, it should support the easy instantiation of products and, on the other, it should, preferably, not conflict with any of the product-specific requirements. Weaknesses in the product-line architecture which are identified once the product line has been developed are generally very costly to address.

The design process of the product-line software architecture consists of six main steps, i.e. business case analysis, scoping, feature and product planning, product-line architectural design, component requirement specification and verification. Each of the steps is briefly summarized below.

- **Business case analysis.** This is concerned with establishing, at a sufficient level of certainty, that the product-line approach represents a cost-effective and superior approach. In addition, the analysis provides data for deciding on a revolutionary or evolutionary path for the conversion from a products-based to a software product-line-based organization.

- **Scoping.** This activity determines the products and the product features that are included in the product line. It may not be beneficial or even desirable to include all products and features in the product line, especially not from the start.

- **Product and feature planning.** The focus of this step is on identifying the characteristics of subsequent versions of product-line architecture. Since there will be continuous development of the product-line architecture in terms of the features and products it supports and incorporating new, but anticipated, features is generally considerably easier than other features, it is important to develop a plan for feature incorporation.

- **Product-line architectural design.** The main step in the process is the design of the software architecture for the product line. Software architectural design,

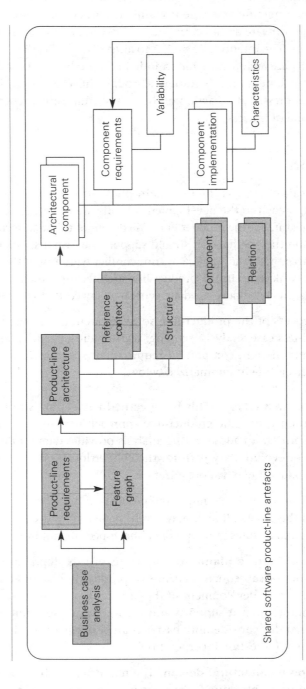

Shared software product-line artefacts

Figure 47   Artefacts developed during the design of the product-line architecture

however, has been discussed at length in Part I of the book, so in this chapter we have only addressed the activities which are specific to designing a software architecture for a product line.

- **Component requirement specification.** The software architecture dictates a set of components that implement the required behaviour. This activity is concerned with specifying the requirements for each of the components. The requirement specification defines the interfaces, the functionality, the quality attributes and the variability that each component should support.

- **Verification.** Finally, before entering the next activity, i.e. component development, it is important to verify that the product-line architecture supports the requirements specified by the stakeholders. This can be established either by a stakeholder meeting or by architecture assessment teams that perform an external evaluation.

Finally, in Fig. 47 the artefacts developed during this phase in the adoption of a software product-line approach are presented as grey boxes. The design of the product-line architecture is concerned with the majority of the groundwork for the software product line as a whole.

9 Further reading

The design of a product-line architecture is also discussed in Jacobson *et al.* (1997), though it is referred to as application family engineering, and in Weiss and Lai (1999). De Baud and Schmid (1999) discuss the issues of software product-line scoping. Dikel *et al.* (1997) discuss the problems of focusing too much on either the current or the future requirements during the development of the software product-line assets.

CHAPTER 10

Developing components: traditional

Part I of the book discusses the design of software architectures. A software architecture, once defined, specifies the components that are part of the architecture and, for each component, its provided and required interfaces and its functional and quality specifications. In addition, the software architecture generally defines design rules and constraints that need to be followed by the architectural components.

However, what is a component, exactly? One workshop series on component-oriented programming defined a component as follows: 'A software component is a unit of composition with contractually specified interfaces and explicit context dependencies only. A software component can be deployed independently and is subject to composition by third parties.' (Weck *et al.*, 1997 and 1998 and Bosch *et al.*, 1999).

Although the above definition contains many useful aspects, we believe that the second part especially is too strong to cover all cases where, in our experience, one can use the term software component. For instance, in the case of product-line architectures, the component is not composed by third parties, but rather by the organization itself, for the various products. In addition, the above definition assumes that components are composed in a 'LEGO-brick' manner, i.e. without having to adapt component instantiations to their context. In our experience, components generally do need to be adapted to suit their context and configuration interfaces are used for this purpose. In addition, the above definition does not address the quality attributes of the component. In our experience, the applicability of a component is determined to a considerable extent by the quality attributes it exhibits, especially in embedded systems. Therefore, we will use the following definition: a software component is a unit of composition with explicitly specified provided, required and configuration interfaces and quality attributes.

Developing reusable components is a fairly constrained process in that the software architecture, of which the component will be a part, defines to a considerable extent the way the component is to be developed, the functionality encompassed by the component and the required quality of the component. In addition to the software architecture, there are, however, several other factors which affect component development, such as the intended reusability of the component and the presence of legacy code.

The intended reusability of a component is of high importance for component development, because it has a considerable effect on the design, implementation and deployment of the component. One can identify three levels of component reuse:

- **System versions.** The lowest level of reuse is to use components over subsequent versions of a software system. The component needs only to fulfil the product requirements and be prepared for future system requirements. This type of reuse – though some authors, e.g. Poulin (1997), do not consider this to be reuse – has been used for decades and the software engineering industry is well able to exploit this.

- **Software product line.** The second level of reuse is where components are used for subsequent product versions and for a family of products containing related, but not identical, functionality. A component should, in this context, be prepared to easily incorporate new requirements for subsequent versions, but also cover the differences in component requirements between the various products. The latter is generally referred to as *variability*. Although several publications exist (e.g. Jacobson *et al.*, 1997) this level of reuse is definitely not part of the industrial practice. However, several companies have recently adopted or are slowly converting to this level of reuse (see e.g. van der Linden, 1998).

- **Third-party components.** The highest level of reuse is the use of components over product versions, a family of products and within different organizations. This is also referred to as commercial off the shelf (COTS) technology. Although the use of components such as operating systems and database management systems is generally accepted, the use of COTS components in the core application domain, e.g. fire-alarm or dialysis-system functionality, is very limited. Except for very restricted domains, e.g. Visual Basic components or third-party libraries for Mathematica application packages, the software engineering industry as a whole is nowhere near this level of reuse maturity.

The above discussion of reuse levels suggests that the software engineering industry is currently in the early phases of adopting the second reuse level, i.e. reuse based on software product lines. We believe that the identified reuse levels define an evolutionary scale where each organization has to evolve through each level before adopting the next level. Consequently, we suggest, where relevant, that software development organizations focus on achieving software product-line-based reuse of components, rather than trying to achieve COTS-based reuse in one step.

In this part of the book, we discuss, among other matters, the development of reusable components. In this chapter, we discuss the development of components in general, whereas the next chapter is concerned with the use of object-oriented frameworks as reusable components in products. Object-oriented frameworks, in our experience with several companies employing product-line architectures, form a highly suitable concept for software product-line components.

The remainder of this chapter is organized as follows. In the next section, the process associated with component development is discussed. The notion of domain and its relation to components is discussed in Section 2. The provided and required interfaces of components are examined in Section 3, and the variability supported by components is the topic of Section 4. Since components may fail to fulfil all application requirements, Section 5 is concerned with component adaptation. The incorporation of aspects, constraints and rules resulting from design decisions during architectural design is discussed in Section 6 and the chapter is concluded in Section 7.

1 Component development process

The development of reusable components, as mentioned earlier, is a difficult process since it is constrained by several factors. As shown in Fig. 48, the software architectural design process results in component requirements, both functional and quality requirements, but also several constraints and design rules that the component should obey. Examples of these are the means of communication, e.g. pipes, events or messages, the concurrency model and the transaction model. In addition, often legacy code exists that should be incorporated even when developing based on a newly designed architecture. Even when it is decided to develop the next generation of a particular product of a software product line and the software architecture for the new generation is designed without constraints, the investment needed to develop all components from scratch often is prohibitively high. In addition, legacy code represents past investments whose return needs to be maximized. Finally, since the organization most likely did not change domain altogether, legacy code does contain relevant domain functionality. Consequently, wherever possible, legacy code often needs to be incorporated in components. Finally, since the component that is to be developed is supposed to be reusable, there often is an interest in maximizing the applicability of the component. For instance, in the case of a product-line architecture, the component may be developed to suit even products or systems that are not part of the product line. In any case, an explicit analysis of the variability required from the component is needed to develop a successful component.

Based on the above, we can deduce that the design of a reusable component is a rather constrained process. However, that is not necessarily negative since it also

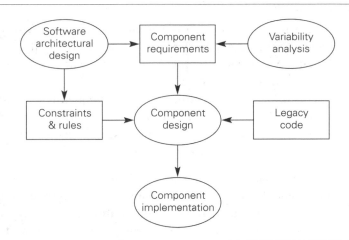

Figure 48   Component development: activities and deliverables

limits the number of design decisions that have to be taken by the component designer. Once the component is designed, it is implemented so that it can be used for its intended purpose.

2   Components and domains

Whereas product or product-line architectures cover all functionality required for the products, the components are often associated with 'technical' domains. A component domain is, generally, a logical and recognized field of functionality. The notion of domain is somewhat confusing with respect to products and components. The customers of the products or systems generally refer to the product as a whole as being part of a particular domain. For instance, the fire-alarm systems introduced in Chapter 3 are, by their customers, considered as part of the domain of building automation systems. However, the developers of fire-alarm systems consider such systems to consist of functions from a number of domains, such as communication protocols, graphical user interface, device management, etc. In the software of the system, each of these domains is represented by one or more components. Our experience is that frequently a domain is represented by one primary component and several secondary, smaller components. The secondary components generally handle the variation in functionality required from the component.

2.1 Domains

To distinguish between the various domains, we will use the term *application domain* for customer-level domains, such as the building automation or medical domain. A software system is typically associated with an application domain. We will use the term *software domain* to refer to domains that are identified by software engineers as such. As mentioned earlier, frequently a component covers a software domain. Obviously, the definition of these terms is unsatisfactory with respect to their precision and generality, but lacking better alternatives, we will use these in the remainder of this part of the book.

We have so far ignored an important aspect of domains, i.e. domains are hierarchical, thus higher-level domains can recursively be decomposed into lower-level domains. For instance, the domain of communication protocols can be decomposed into several layers of protocol domains, see e.g. the OSI layer model presented in Fig. 28 of Chapter 6. One can view the *software domain*, defined earlier, as the top-level domain, incorporating all software-related domains. This domain can, recursively, be decomposed into lower-level domains, until it reaches the level of concepts. A *concept*, in our terminology, is an atomic domain that can be represented by a single entity in a software system, e.g. a class. The concept is atomic in that further decomposition will no longer lead to meaningful parts. Consequently, a domain consists of concepts and, possibly, lower-level domains. These concepts and lower-level domains have relations to each other. These relations can also be viewed as concepts.

The domain of software can be decomposed further into software application domains and software service domains. Software service domains cover the domains traditionally studied by computer science, including communication protocols and techniques for lexing, parsing, persistence and transactions. Software application domains are related to application domains in that these domains contain representations of application (or real-world) domains that are directed for use in software systems. Examples of these can, among others, be found in the sciences, e.g. medicine, organizational science, chemistry, manufacturing, etc.

There are few accepted standards on taxonomies for domains, be it software application or service domains. The most notable exception is probably the work by special interest groups within OMG (for URL see end list of references) on defining standards for vertical (software application) domains, such as business objects, electronic payments and medical facilities. A domain standard identifies the primary concepts in the domain and defines interfaces for these concepts. The standard, once defined, can be used as a contract for the interfaces of component implementations in that domain. The actual content of an interface is discussed in the next section, but one should not underestimate the difficulties of inter-operating components, even in the presence of standards. Even for the basic CORBA facilities, e.g.

brokering and communication, different implementations of the CORBA standard are often not capable of interacting.

2.2 Components

The relation between domains and components was briefly discussed in the introduction to this section, i.e. components implement domains. However, as can be deduced from the discussion about domains, it is not always clear what a domain is, there are no generally accepted definitions, nor is it obvious at what level of granularity a component should implement a domain, considering the fact that domains are hierarchically decomposed into lower-level domains.

There is, as one may expect, no simple answer to this question, mainly since the granularity of a component should be balanced by two conflicting forces:

- small components are more likely to be reused than large components because small components cover a smaller domain, or even just a concept, and consequently there is a larger chance that a small domain suits the product that the software engineer is constructing, without the need to exclude, potentially large, parts of the component functionality;

- when reused, large components give considerably more leverage than small components. Although often underestimated, there is a cost associated with reusing a component, consisting of the effort required to find the component, analyze its suitability, etc. Although the general rule of thumb, according to Poulin (1997), is that the reuse cost is about 20 per cent of the development cost, this percentage increases for small components, although this depends on the type of component. Thus, below a certain size threshold, the cost of reusing a component may exceed the cost of developing the component from scratch.

Although the notion of a component, as presented in the literature (e.g. Szyperski, 1997), is close to the class concept in traditional object-oriented languages, useful components are generally considerably larger than individual classes. Thus, where classes represent concepts in the domain, components represent domains. The size of components differs considerably, from a small number of classes, covering a sensor including its calibration and variation points, to complete communication protocol implementations which may consist of 80 KLOC or more.

Since components implement domains and domains are organized hierarchically, it is possible for components to be organized in hierarchies as well. Sometimes, the term 'component framework' (Szyperski, 1997) is used to refer to aggregating components. In the next chapter, we discuss object-oriented frameworks as a means to implement more coarse-grained components with considerable amounts of variability.

One can identify different types of intended uses for a component. The most basic, and commonly exercised, type is the use of a component for subsequent versions of a particular product or system. This has become so common that many do not consider this reuse. At the second level, a component is used both for subsequent versions of a product and for the various products or systems developed by an organization. Several either ongoing or recently finished research efforts by large industrial organizations, e.g. the ARES Esprit project (van der Linden, 1998), are trying to employ this approach, i.e. product-line architectures, for concrete product lines. The third level is the use of a component for subsequent product versions, for various products and within several organizations. Except for a number of small and specialized domains, the current state of practice in the software industry has not been able to adopt this approach.

To conclude, defining the boundaries and deciding upon the granularity of components is not a simple task and requires, among other things, careful analysis of the domain, the contexts in which the component is to be reused and the goals of the organization with respect to component reuse. It is important to be realistic about the possibilities and risks of component-based software development and not aim for too ambitious goals. Instead, especially for organizations inexperienced with respect to reuse, an evolutionary, iterative approach is appropriate to minimize risk and to avoid disappointment due to overly optimistic expectations.

3 Component interfaces

Components, as the term implies, are not isolated entities, but interact with their environment. For most components, the environment primarily consists of other components. The components invoke other components with requests for data or actions to be performed or to inform about relevant events. However, components are developed independently and are intended to be freely combined with other components. That requires that component implementations be unrelated to each other. This leads to an interesting dilemma: on the one hand components need to interact with each other and on the other hand components may not depend on other components.

The solution to the dilemma is the use of interfaces. An *interface* defines a contract between a component requiring certain functionality and a component providing that functionality. The interface represents a first-class specification of the functionality that should be accessible through it. The interface specification is, ideally, independent of the component or components implementing that interface.

Components interact with other components and entities and, as discussed earlier, there are good reasons, such as decreased coupling, to explicitly define the interactions of a component at its encapsulation boundary. In Section 3.1, we will discuss the problems of traditional interfaces. However, when developing a reusable component, what interfaces should be defined and implemented for the component? Generally, one can identify three types of interfaces that need to be supported by a component, i.e. provided, required and configuration interfaces.

The provided and required interfaces are intended for the interaction with other components, whereas the configuration interfaces are intended for use by the user of the component. When constructing an application or system based on reusable components, each component needs to be instantiated and configured. The configuration consists of defining, for each variation point supported by the component, what concrete variation should be used in this component instance. Each configuration interface provides access to a variation point and allows the software engineer to control it. In Section 4, we discuss component variability in more detail.

The remainder of this section is organized as follows. In the next section, we present the basic notion of interfaces and discuss its limitations. Section 3.2 discusses the notion of provided interfaces whereas required interfaces are discussed in Section 3.3. Configuration interfaces are discussed in Section 4.

3.1   Issues with interfaces

The basic representation of an interface is provided in the form of an application programming interface (API) that contains a list of operations, generally including argument types and the type of entity returned. This type of interface has, for instance, been included in the Java programming language (for URL see end list of references). A class may state that it implements a particular interface, whereas another class may declare a reference to an object implementing that interface. When both classes are instantiated, the later object, once it has a reference to the first object, may invoke operations on that object that are declared by the interface. The object providing that interface may support operations not declared by the interface, but those cannot be accessed by the calling object. The use of interfaces decreases the coupling between classes in the Java system, as well as decreasing the coupling between components.

Although the basic representation of an interface presented above has its merit and its support in commercial programming languages is a considerable step forward, there still are remaining problems. First of all, the basic interface model assumes that all operations on the interface are accessible at all times. This is, obviously, an incorrect assumption. For instance, a buffer component buffering items cannot provide items to calling components when the buffer is empty, nor can it accept new items when the buffer is full. Thus, the state of the component generally affects the interface. As a consequence, a component compliant with the interface and invoking a component claiming to implement that interface may still cause an exception.

A second issue is that the basic interface model assumes a single-call model of interaction. Thus, each interaction between two components consists of a single request-reply pair. Although several interactions fit this model, many interactions do not and assume some kind of *protocol* to dictate the communication between components. For instance, a component representing a *file* will assume that it will be opened, then accessed zero or more times for reading or writing and subsequently be closed again. The interface model provides no means for describing these additional ordering requirements.

The issues discussed above lead to a third issue that we have identified especially for larger components: The actual interface of a component does not just exist of a set of operations, but also of a set of abstract classes that are visible to users of the component. For instance, a communication protocol component may support an operation to open a connection, returning a smaller component instance (or rather, a reference to it) representing the actual connection. Once the connection is opened, the calling component will interact with the connection component rather than with the API of the communication protocol component. If the protocol component is implemented as an object-oriented framework, the API would declare an abstract class as the return type of the *open_connection* operation. The connection component returned to the caller is an instance of a concrete subclass of the abstract class implementing the actual behaviour required for the protocol at hand, e.g. TCP. Thus, especially for large components, the component interface may consist of an API and a set of abstract entities (basic interfaces).

Finally, although interfaces define a contract between components requiring and providing functionality, this contract and its verification defines really nothing more than a set of names, i.e. a syntax. The actual semantics of the interaction is not necessarily the same for the components with the provided and required interfaces, respectively. Automatic verification of interfaces is performed using name matching, not based on the component semantics. Especially when third-party components or components from different parts in the organization are used, explicit effort is required to verify that syntactically equivalent interfaces also are semantically equivalent.

In summary, although the use of interfaces is a beneficial and necessary part of software development in general, and for component-based software development in particular, the definition of interfaces requires more than just an API specification. Considerable amounts of additional documentation is required to define the state-based aspects, implicit protocols and nested interfaces or abstract classes that are part of the externally visible behaviour of the component.

3.2 Provided interfaces

During the design of a software architecture, the components that make up the architecture are identified as well as the relations between the components. This often results in the situation where a component is related to two or more other components. A relation between a component A and another component may represent a required interface, a provided interface or a combination. In the latter case, the relation should be decomposed or reorganized such that the resulting relation(s) are purely provided or required for component A.

Based on the above, one can deduce that the aforementioned component A can have more than one provided interface. Each relation to another component where A provides functionality to that component should be represented as a provided interface, unless the other component requires the identical interface. Thus, for each type of interaction, there should be a provided interface, although multiple components can make use of the same provided interface.

To define the contents of an interface, we first need to define a few terms. First, we define the term *basic type* as referring to any of those data or object types that are supported by the language or are considered to be global within the software architecture. Examples include integers, characters, strings, etc. Second, we define a *basic interface* as an interface consisting of a list of operations, where each operation only uses basic types as arguments and as return type. Finally, an interface is defined as consisting of an identifier, a list of operations and a list of interface identifiers. The operations in the interface may use basic types or the interface identifiers as arguments and return types, but no other types, classes or interfaces. This is to ensure that a component has explicitly defined interfaces only. Even though current commercial languages do not support the interface concept as defined here, we assume interfaces to be defined as first-class entities, independent of the components that implement the interfaces.

Concluding, a component has at least one, but potentially more, provided interfaces that it implements. The provided interfaces publicize interface identifiers that refer to other defined interfaces, but a component may only publicize interface identifiers that it either defines internally or that it obtains through a required interface.

3.3 Required interfaces

Each interface provided by a component is, upon instantiation of the component, bound to one or more required interfaces. There is no one-to-one relation between provided and required interfaces since a component providing an interface may service multiple components. A required interface consists of the same elements as a provided interface, with the difference that the interface is required rather than

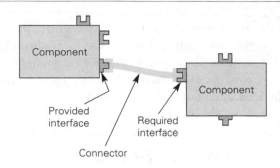

Figure 49   Components and connectors

provided by the component. Since interfaces are defined independently of components, a required interface is specified by referring to the interface identifier only.

When using components in an application or product, there may be syntactic mismatches between provided and required interfaces, even when the semantics of the interfaces match. This requires adaptation of one or both of the components or an adapting connector to be used between the components to perform the translation between the components. Adaptation can even be used to solve minor semantic mismatches.

In Fig. 49, the notion of provided and required interfaces, as well as that of connectors, is presented graphically.

4 Component variability

The notion of a reusable component requires the component to be applicable in more than one context, since it would not be reusable otherwise. The, somewhat naïve, traditional view of component-based software engineering is often presented as analogous to LEGO bricks. The components have connecting points and products are composed by connecting the components at these points.

Industrial experiences with components has shown that the so-called 'as-is' reuse described above is relatively unlikely to occur. In most situations, at least one of the assumptions about the context made by the component developer does not hold and the component needs to adjust to the context in which it is instantiated.

Adjusting a component can be achieved in two ways, viz. through variability mechanisms and through component adaptation. Variability refers to the points where the behaviour of a component can be changed. These variation points have been decided upon and incorporated during component design and represent the understanding of the component developer with respect to the variability required of the component.

Component adaptation is concerned with 'after-the-fact' changes to the component. Adaptation is required when the available variability is not sufficient for a particular instantiation of the component. The assumptions of the component developer with respect to the required variability of the component turn out to be, at least, incomplete. This is, however, a typical situation since, especially for components intended for third-party composition, it is generally impossible to predict all the ways in which the component will be used. Therefore, reusable components generally go through an iterative development process where adaptations that were necessary for earlier versions of a component are incorporated by adding variation points to the component.

The remainder of this section is organized as follows. We first discuss the various mechanisms for implementing variability in a component. Subsequently, we present the notion of a configuration interface, which is, in addition to the provided and required interfaces, the third type of component interface.

4.1 Variability mechanisms

Reuse of components generally requires the components to be configured by providing the appropriate functionality or settings at the variation points of the component. To achieve this, one can make use of a number of mechanisms. The mechanisms are briefly discussed below.

- **Inheritance.** Assuming that the component is implemented as a class in an object-oriented language, inheritance can be used as a white-box technique to specialize the component for its context. Using inheritance, the component (re)user can define a subclass and add the application-specific behaviour to the component behaviour. Depending on the object-oriented language that was used to implement the component, different mechanisms may be available to control the specialization of component behaviour. By defining operations as *abstract*, the component developer can require the component user to extend those operations. Similarly, by defining operations as *final*, the component developer can block the component user to extend behaviour that would potentially lead to inconsistencies. Inheritance has a number of associated disadvantages, especially due to the fact that functionality that forms a logical entity is divided over multiple components. This may, among others, complicate the understandability and testing of components.

- **Extensions.** An extension is a variation point where the component user provides one out of several variants of some behaviour. The strategy design pattern (Gamma *et al.*, 1994) is a typical example of using extensions. The underlying idea is to factor out functionality that may vary from stable functionality and to model the variable functionality as an independent entity. The different instances of variable functionality are implemented as variants and the component user can either select an existing variant or develop a new variant.

■ **Configuration.** A third approach to handling variability is to include all variants at all variation points into the component and to provide an interface to the component user. This interface allows the user to set parameters that select particular variants at the variation points. Through the use of, for instance, procedure parameters, components can even be configured for the invoking component.

■ **Template instantiation.** Components, at times, need to be configured with application-specific types. A typical example is a list-handling or queue component that needs to be configured with the type of element that is to be stored in the list or queue. A useful technique, present in several programming languages, is the use of *templates*, i.e. component definitions that can be instantiated for particular types. Templates are particularly useful for performing type adaptation.

■ **Generation.** The final type of variability mechanism to be discussed here is the notion of a *component generator*. The typical use of this approach is that the component user prepares a specification in some language, e.g. a domain-specific or component-specific language. This specification is taken as input by a generator, or high-level compiler, that translates the specification into, generally, a source-code-level component that can be incorporated into the product or application that the component user is concerned with. Typical examples of this approach can be found in graphical user interfaces where either a graphical or textual specification is used to generate a source-code component that implements the desired functionality.

A component generally employs several variability mechanisms. Often, for the most typical uses, configuration through parameter setting or templates is used and for more complicated, and consequently less typical, variation specifications, harder to use variability mechanisms such as inheritance are used. The latter is harder to use because it requires considerably more understanding of the internal workings of the reused component.

4.2 Configuration interface

A component, as discussed earlier, supports three types of interfaces, i.e. provided, required and configuration interfaces. In Section 3, provided and required interfaces have been introduced and discussed. In this section, we present the configuration interfaces.

A component contains a set of variation points, i.e. points where the behaviour of the component can be altered. At each variation point, a mechanism for configuring the variation point is used. In the previous section, several mechanisms were presented. With each variation point, a component configuration interface is associated. The configuration interface provides a point of access for the component user to configure the component instance according to the requirements.

The configuration interface generally consists of a documentation part and a technical part, but the balance between these two parts depends on the mechanism that is used. For instance, for parametrized configuration, the documentation consists of a specification of the semantics of each parameter and the possible settings for each parameter. The technical part consists of one or more operations on the component interface that allow the product software to test, set and change the parameters at run-time.

In summary, the component supports a set of configuration interfaces where each configuration interface is related to a variation point. Each configuration interface consists of a documentation part and a technical part. The configuration interfaces are used, upon component instantiation, to configure the component for the particular context and set of requirements for which it is used.

5 Component adaptation

In the previous section, we discussed the notion of component variability, i.e. the variations in component behaviour that have been identified by the component developer and for which a configuration interface exists. However, the provided component variability may not be sufficient for certain component instantiations, requiring the component to be changed beyond the available variability. The process of incorporating unintended changes in a component for use in a particular application is often referred to as *component adaptation*.

Over time, research in software engineering and programming languages has developed a number of techniques for adapting components. These component adaptation techniques can be categorized into white-box and black-box adaptation techniques. White-box techniques require the software engineer to adapt a reused component either by changing its internal specification or by overriding and excluding parts of the internal specification. Black-box techniques reuse the component as it is, but adapt at the interface of the component. A typical example of a black-box adaptation technique is wrapping. A wrapper encapsulates the adapted component such that all interaction with the adapted component passes the wrapper. This allows the wrapper to monitor, adjust and reject communication to and from the component. Black-box adaptation only requires the software engineer to understand the interface of the component, not the internals.

Obviously, the above division is somewhat oversimplified and in practice, e.g. inheritance often requires the understanding of only part of the internal functionality whereas wrapping may require more understanding of the component than just its interface specification. In the remainder of this section, we first present the requirements that a component adaptation technique should fulfil. Subsequently, the conventional techniques are presented and evaluated with respect to the requirements.

5.1 Requirements for component adaptation techniques

Before discussing conventional component adaptation techniques, we present the general requirements that a component adaptation technique has to fulfil. These requirements provide a framework that can be used to evaluate conventional component adaptation techniques. In the following sections, these requirements are discussed in more detail.

Black-box
The adaptation of a component and the component itself are, ideally, two separate entities. This requires that the adaptation technique requires no access to the internals of the component, but that access is limited to the interface of the component. The black-box requirement is relevant for several reasons. First, it supports the composability and reusability requirements discussed below. Second, the software engineer developing a component adaptation always has to develop some mental model of the functionality of a component. This model should, however, be kept as small and simple as possible. The black-box requirement allows, to a large extent, the software engineer to limit him or herself to the component interface only. Although a mental model of the behaviour of the component is still required, it generally needs to be less extensive and does not need to represent the actual implementation of the component. Finally, black-box component adaptation allows the reusing product to incorporate new versions of a component, provided that the part of the component interface used by the product is supported by the new version. White-box component adaptation requires the software engineer to repeat the adaptation for all versions of the component since the component internals are changed and the component code and the adaptation code are mixed.

Transparent
The adaptation of the component should be as *transparent* as possible. Transparent, in this context, means that for a component A adapted with some adaptation component X and interacting with a component B, components A and B need not change their behaviour for the adaptation to occur. Nor are the components A and B able to detect the adaptation component X. For instance, *wrappers* (discussed below) typically do not fulfil this requirement, although some techniques exist for resolving this. The user of the adapted component is forced to invoke the wrapper

rather than the original component and is thus aware of the adaptation. In addition, the transparency requirement demands that aspects of the component that do not need to be adapted be accessible without explicit effort on the part of the adaptation component. Wrapping a component, for instance, requires the wrapper to forward all requests to the component, including those that need not be adapted.

Composable

The composability requirement has three relevant aspects. First, the adaptation technique should be easily composable with the component on which it is applied, i.e. no redefinition of the component should be required. Ideally, when instantiating a component, one adds the adaptation specification and the composition is generated as an instance in the system. Second, the adapted component should be as composable with other components as it was without the adaptation. Thus, the software engineer or the system should not need to distinguish between an adapted component and an unadapted component. Communication and binding between components should be similar. Finally, the adaptation should be composable with other adaptations. In the situation where default adaptation types are available, it may be that the component needs to be adapted using multiple types of adaptation. This requires the various adaptations to be composable. Thus, when a component, for example, should be adapted for changing the interface and for adding monitoring, these adaptations can both be applied to the component without affecting each other (or at least, minimal and predictable interference). The ordering of the adaptations does matter in this context.

Reusable

In our experience, adaptations often consist of a generic part, e.g. renaming operation names, and a specific part, e.g. the actual operation names. A problem of traditional adaptation techniques is that neither the generic nor the specific part are reusable. Since the two aspects are so heavily intertwined, the generic part cannot be separated from the specific part and, consequently, the software engineer is forced to reimplement the adaptation over and over again. A new technique should provide reusability of the adaptation type and particular instances of the adaptation type, i.e. both the generic and the specific part.

Configurable

Adaptation generally consists of a generic and a specific part. For example, as we mentioned earlier, an adaptation requiring the renaming of operations has a generic part, i.e. replacing the selector in the message with another name and a specific part, i.e. which selectors should be replaced with what names. For the adaptation technique to be useful and reusable, the technique has to provide sufficient configurability of the specific part.

5.2 Adaptation techniques

When using a conventional programming language, the software engineer has three component adaptation techniques that can be used to modify a reused component, i.e. *copy-paste*, *inheritance* (in the case of an object-oriented language) and *wrapping*. In the next sections, each technique is described and subsequently evaluated with respect to the identified requirements.

Copy-paste

When an existing component provides some similarity with a component needed by the software engineer, the most effective approach may be to just copy the code of that part of the component that is suitable to be reused in the component under development. After copying the code, the software engineer will often make changes to it to make it fit the context of the new component and additional functionality will be defined or copied from other sources. Samentinger (1997) refers to this technique as *code scavenging*.

Although the copy-paste technique provides some reuse, it obviously has many disadvantages, among others the fact that multiple copies of the reused code exist and that the software engineer has to intimately understand the reused code. However, from our discussions with professional software engineers and students, we were surprised to see how often this technique is applied, especially when time pressure or other factors may force a 'quick-and-dirty' approach.

With respect to the aforementioned requirements, the evaluation of the copy-paste technique can be summarized as follows:

- **Transparent.** Since the reused code and new code are merged into a new component, there are no problems associated with transparency. Both the reused component and the client of the adapted component notice no difference between the reused code and the code for adaptation.

- **Black-box.** Since there is no encapsulation boundary between the component code and the adaptation code, the black-box requirement is not fulfilled at all.

- **Composable.** Due to the merging of code, composability of adaptation functionality with the reused component is very low. In cases where one would want to compose several types of adaptation behaviour, the software engineer has to merge all code manually.

- **Reusable.** Since the adaptation behaviour has no first-class representation and is intertwined with the code of the reused component, no reuse of either the component or the adaptation behaviour is possible, except through the same copy-paste behaviour.

- **Configurable.** Adapting a component through copy-paste does not represent the adaptation behaviour as a first-class entity, thus no configurability is available.

Inheritance

A second technique for white-box adaptation and reuse is provided by inheritance. Inheritance as provided by, e.g. C++ and Java, makes the state and behaviour of the reused component available to the reusing component. Depending on the language model, all internal aspects or only part of the aspects become available to the reusing component. For instance, in Smalltalk-80 (Goldberg and Robson, 1989) all methods and instance variables defined in the superclass become available to the subclass, whereas in C++, it depends on use of the *private* and *protected* keywords what methods and instance variables become available to the subclass. Inheritance provides the important advantage that the code remains in one location. However, one of the main disadvantages of inheritance is that the software engineer generally must have detailed understanding of the internal functionality of a superclass when overriding superclass methods and when defining new behaviour using behaviour defined in the superclass.

With respect to the requirements, the evaluation of inheritance can be summarized as follows:

- **Transparent.** Since the subclass implicitly forwards messages to the superclass, inheritance is transparent. The reused component, i.e. the superclass, and client objects using instances of the introduced subclass notice no difference.

- **Black-box.** Whether inheritance is black-box depends primarily on its implementation in the language model. In Smalltalk-80, all instance variables and methods become available to the subclass, leaving no boundary between the reused component and the adaptation code. Other language models, e.g. C++ and Java, allow for private instance variables and methods, thus being able to separate the component from the adaptation behaviour.

- **Composable.** Although the adaptation behaviour is specified in a subclass and thus separated from the component, it is still difficult to compose the adaptation behaviour with another component or to associate multiple adaptation behaviours with a class. Even though some languages would allow for simple changing of the name of the superclass for an adaptation type, the problem is still that the generic and specific parts of the adaptation are merged and are difficult to separate.

- **Reusable.** Despite the fact that inheritance facilitates the representation of the adaptation type as a class, it may prove difficult to reuse it since the name of the adapted component is hard-wired in the class and because it cannot be configured.

- **Configurable.** As mentioned, although the adaptation behaviour is represented as a first-class entity, i.e. a subclass, inheritance provides no means to configure the specific part of the adaptation behaviour.

Wrapping

Wrapping declares one or more components as part of an encapsulating component, i.e. the wrapper, but this component only has functionality for forwarding, with minor changes, requests from clients to the wrapped components. There is no clear boundary between wrapping and aggregation, but wrapping is used to adapt the behaviour of the enclosed component whereas aggregation is used to compose new functionality out of existing components providing relevant functionality. An important disadvantage of wrapping is that it may result in considerable implementation overheads since the complete interface of the wrapped component needs to be handled by the wrapper, including those interface elements that need not be adapted. For instance, Hölzle (1993) reports on experiences with using wrapping; among other things, he mentions excessive amounts of adaptation code and serious performance reductions.

The evaluation of wrapping with respect to the requirements is the following:

■ **Transparent.** Since the wrapper completely encapsulates the adapted component, clients of the component cannot send messages to the component directly but always need to pass the wrapper. This requires the wrapper to handle all messages that could possibly be sent to the component, including those messages that do not need to be adapted. However, in cases where late or run-time binding between components is used, it may be possible to achieve transparency of the wrapper.

■ **Black-box.** Since the component is accessed by the wrapper in the same way as any other client, i.e. through the interface, the wrapping technique is blackbox. The wrapper has no way to access or depend upon the internals of the adapted component.

■ **Composable.** Wrapping is, in contrast to the other conventional techniques, composable. A wrapper and its wrapped component together form a component that can be wrapped by another wrapper. This process can be repeated recursively. However, since the wrappers are not transparent, each wrapper needs to implement the complete interface of its wrapped component in order to be used in all cases where the unadapted component could be used.

■ **Reusable.** The wrapper can be reused in those cases where exactly the same adaptation behaviour is required. For some types of adaptation behaviour, the wrapper may provide a configuration interface that allows for specifying the specific part of the adaptation behaviour. However, several types of component adaptation cannot be handled through this configuration interface. For instance, the aforementioned example of renaming operation names is generally hard to configure in this way. For those types of adaptation, every difference from the original case makes as-is reuse impossible and requires either the wrapper to be edited or the combination of wrapper and component to be adapted by a new wrapper.

■ **Configurable.** Although the adaptation behaviour is represented as a first-class entity, i.e. a wrapper, generally no means to configure the specific part of the adaptation behavior are available. For instance, when the wrapper needs to change the name of an operation at the adapted component, it is generally not possible to configure the wrapper with the new operation name since this has to be hard coded in the wrapper.

5.3 Evaluating component adaptation techniques

In Table 7, an overview of the conventional adaptation techniques is presented that indicates how well each technique fulfils the specified requirements. From the table, one can see that some problems are dealt with well by wrapping but not so well by the white-box techniques, i.e. copy-paste and inheritance, and vice versa.

Table 7   Conventional adaptation techniques versus the identified problems and requirements

Requirement	Copy-paste	Inheritance	Wrapping
Transparent	+	+	–
Black-box	– –	–	+
Composable	–	–	+
Reusable	–	–	+/–
Configurable	–	–	–

The copy-paste technique, as well as inheritance, is transparent since the reused and adaptation behaviour are merged in a single entity. However, on the other requirements, the white-box adaptation techniques do not score so well. Wrapping is not transparent, since it encapsulates the adapted component. Wrapping is black-box by definition and wrapping is composable since a wrapped component can again be wrapped by another wrapper adapting different aspects of the original component. Configurability and reusability are not well supported by traditional techniques since no distinction between generic behaviour and component-specific behaviour is made. Due to this, it is not possible to separate the generic aspects and apply them for a different component.

In summary, none of the conventional component adaptation techniques fulfils the requirements that are required for effective component-based software engineering. Therefore, it is preferable if the variability provided by the component is sufficient to avoid component adaptation. However, occasionally component adaptation cannot be avoided and the component user is forced to use one of the techniques discussed in this section. In those situations, it is beneficial if the component user is aware of the weaknesses of component adaptation techniques. In our reserch, we have studied alternative component adaptation techniques, in particular, superimposition. See Bosch (1999b) for a more detailed discussion.

6 Aspects, constraints and rules

In earlier chapters, we discussed the design of software architectures. The software architectural design identifies a set of related components that make up the architecture. The development of reusable components typically takes place in the context of such an architecture or component framework (Szyperski, 1997). Consequently, as we noted at the beginning of this chapter, component development is a rather constrained process.

When analyzing the issues which need to be kept in mind during the development of reusable components, we identify three types of issues:

■ **Aspects.** During the design of software architectures, several design decisions are taken related to the architectural patterns that are incorporated. As discussed in Chapter 6, architectural patterns are typically concerned with solutions for, e.g., concurrency, synchronization, persistence, transactions and distribution. These and similar issues are often referred to as *aspects* (Kiczales *et al.*, 1997). Once a particular solution has been selected for one of the aspects at the software architectural level, it is generally necessary for components throughout the system to employ the same solution.

■ **Constraints.** The aspects described above and other design decisions lead to constraints on the component behaviour as well. The component needs to adhere to the constraints since violation may lead to incorrect system behaviour or, assuming components are monitored, the termination of the component. Constraints are often concerned with the amount of resources that a component may use, e.g. in terms of cycles and memory, but also with, among others, the communication with other components. For example, the application-level scheduler discussed in Chapter 6 invokes the *tick* method of active objects in a round-robin fashion. The maximum execution time of each *tick* method must be limited to a predefined maximum, otherwise the response time of the system as a whole will fall below the required level.

- ■ **Rules.** Whereas constraints specify what components are not allowed to do, rules specify how particular types of behaviour need to be achieved. A rule may, for instance, require that components should notify some monitoring component when performing certain types of activities.

During component development, it is important to comply with the restrictions specified by the aspects, the constraints and the rules. However, at least as important, the component developer should, as much as possible, try to avoid mixing the component behaviour related to the domain with consequences of design decisions with respect to aspects, constraints and rules. By separating the behaviour related to design decisions from the domain behaviour, the cost of changes to the design decisions, which are bound to occur, will be limited. In addition, one can provide variation points that allow the component user to change the design decisions without having to change the component internals. For instance, by factoring out the behaviour related to persistence, the component user can change this aspect by providing an alternative variant.

7 Conclusion

In this chapter we have examined the development of reusable components. We have adopted the following component definition: *A software component is a unit of composition with explicitly specified provided, required and configuration interfaces and quality attributes.* Subsequently, we presented the component development process and identified that it is rather constrained due to the rules and constraints imposed by the software architecture and the potential presence of legacy code that may need to be incorporated. Then we discussed the notion of domains and the relation to components.

Components, in our definition, should support three types of interfaces, i.e. provided, required and configuration interfaces. We have discussed the weaknesses of traditional API-based interface models and described the three types of interfaces in more detail.

Since the configuration interface only supports intended variability, which may be insufficient, on occasion component adaptation is required to incorporate or change behaviour in ways that the component developer failed to identify. Therefore, we have discussed the notion of component adaptation, the requirements one may put on component adaptation and the strengths and weaknesses of existing techniques for component adaptation.

Finally, we have discussed the aspects, constraints and design rules that a component must incorporate. We have stressed the importance of clear separation of behaviour related to design decisions and the domain behaviour covered by the component.

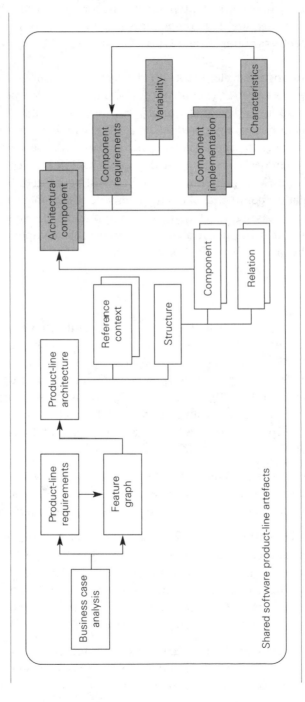

Figure 50 Artefacts generated during component development

The development of the components shared by the members of the software product line results in the generation of a number of artefacts. In Fig. 50, the generated artefacts are presented as grey boxes.

8 Further reading

Software components have been a topic of research since the article by McIlroy (1969) during the late 1960s. However, the actual concrete content of the software component has changed from functions and procedures to modules. The book by Szyperski (1997) presents an excellent overview of the state of the art as well as practice. A second book discussing software engineering using software components is Samentinger (1997). As mentioned earlier, Hölzle (1993) discusses the integration of independently developed components and addresses, among other things, the problems associated with wrapping components. The proceedings of the annual workshop on component-oriented programming are worth reading to obtain an understanding of the state of research in this domain, for example, Weck *et al.* (1997 and 1998) and Bosch *et al.*, (1999b). However, being a co-organizer for all but the first instance of the workshop, I may be biased.

In our research, we have studied, among others, the problems associated with adaptation of software components and alternative adaptation techniques (Bosch, 1999b).

CHAPTER 11

Developing components: object-oriented frameworks

One type of component not originally thought of as a component is the notion of *object-oriented frameworks*. The concept of object-oriented frameworks was developed during the second half of the 1980s (e.g. Johnson and Foote, 1988). An object-oriented framework provides an abstract design and implementation for a particular domain. Applications are constructed by using the framework as a basis and extending it with application-specific functionality. A framework consists of a framework architecture, specifying a number of abstract classes and, possibly, concrete classes inheriting from these abstract classes that provide reusable implementations. In this chapter, we use the term object-oriented framework to refer both to the framework architecture and any artefacts that support the implementation of applications based on the framework. However, some authors use the term framework only to refer to the framework architecture and use other terms, e.g. framework implementation to refer to the other aspects.

Whereas the original notion of object-oriented frameworks assumed a single framework to be used for the construction of applications, during recent years we see increasingly often the use of multiple frameworks in the construction of software systems. Each framework covers a domain and since systems tend to cover multiple domains, multiple frameworks are needed to cover the required system functionality.

When using multiple frameworks for the construction of software products, it is clear that frameworks are components, i.e. parts composed to form larger entities. However, the notion of a framework as a component does not match well with the conventional view on reusable components. In the next section, we compare the conventional view, primarily found in academia, with the industrial practice found in software development organizations.

The remainder of this chapter is organized as follows. In the next section, we compare the academic and industry view of software components. We use this comparison to justify discussing object-oriented frameworks as components in a product-line architecture. To provide a more extensive background on object-oriented frameworks, Section 2 discusses the history of frameworks and presents a number of definitions. Section 3 looks at the issues associated with composing independently developed frameworks, and Section 4 considers four alternative framework component models. The design of object-oriented frameworks is discussed in Section 5 and the chapter is concluded in Section 6.

1 Comparing the academic and industrial views

In the previous chapter, we discussed component development from a view that primarily is based on how academia and software engineers without experience in component-based software development often view components. This perspective centres around five main assumptions:

- **Black-box.** The first assumption is concerned with the black-box nature of components. Components have encapsulation boundaries that limit access to the internals of the component both for invoking components and for software engineers using the component in system construction.

- **API interface.** The second assumption based on which we defined components was that a component has a single point of access through a, relatively narrow, application programming interface (API). All component functionality can be accessed by invoking the operations of the API.

- **Little variability.** Components are supposed to have no or very few variation points that can be configured very easily through, e.g., parametrization at component instantiation.

- **Standards.** A fourth assumption that often is viewed as an ambition rather than as part of the state of practice is that there exist standardized interfaces for the components in the various domains. Since the interfaces are standardized and components implement these, components can be traded on component markets and are mutually exchangeable, with respect to the standardized interface.

- **Formal verification.** The functionality provided by the components is of primary importance, whereas the quality attributes supported by the component are not nearly as relevant, if considered at all. Since the focus is on asset functionality, the formal verification of functionality becomes an important issue.

Although the above assumptions seem very reasonable from an outsider's perspective, our experience is that the components used in industry do not match these assumptions. Instead, the components are considerably larger and less clear-cut than the assumptions we presented above. The industrial components are outlined below.

- **Size.** Components are large pieces of software (sometimes more than 100 KLOC) with a complex internal structure and no enforced encapsulation boundary. The component consists of a large number of smaller, but related entities that implement the component functionality.

- **Interface.** In addition to the component API, the interface is provided through entities internal to the component, e.g., classes in the framework. These interface entities have no explicit differences to non-interface entities.

- **Variability.** Components tend to have numerous variation points where the behaviour of the component could or should be varied. Some variation points require the addition of application-specific code, whereas others require the component user to select among a variety of alternatives.

- **Component source.** Components are primarily developed internally and include functionality relevant for the products or applications in which it is used, not with respect to domain taxonomies. Externally developed components are generally subject to considerable (source code) adaptation to match, e.g. product-line architecture requirements.

- **Quality attributes.** Obviously, components should provide the required functionality. However, the quality attributes, e.g. performance, reliability, code size, reusability and maintainability, have equal importance. A component that does not fulfil its quality requirements, e.g. lack of efficiency with respect to resources, will be rejected, even if it does provide the functionality requirements.

The conclusion that we have drawn from the above observations is that larger components are the type of components that are used in industry because the leverage provided by these components is at acceptable levels, whereas that of smaller components is not. Consequently, software products are constructed from fewer but larger components. Object-oriented frameworks represent a frequently used approach to constructing these larger components. As a result, in the remainder of this chapter, we present the notion of object-oriented frameworks and the modeling of components based on these principles.

2 Object-oriented frameworks[1]

Since its conception during the second half of the 1980s, the concept of object-oriented frameworks has attracted attention from many researchers and software engineers. Frameworks have been defined for a large variety of domains, such as user interfaces, operating systems within computer science and financial systems,

---

1 Sections 2, 3 and 5 in this chapter are adapted from Bosch *et al.* in Fayad *et al.* (1999b) *Domain-Specific Application Frameworks* and Bosch *et al.* in Fayad *et al.* (1999a) *Building Application Frameworks*. Adapted by permission of John Wiley & Sons.

fire-alarm systems and process control systems within particular application domains. Large research and development projects were started within software development companies, but also at universities and even at the governmental level. For instance, the EU-sponsored Esprit project REBOOT (Karlsson, 1995) had a considerable impact on the object-oriented thinking and development in the organizations involved in the project and later caused the development of a number of object-oriented frameworks (e.g. Dagermo and Knutsson, 1996).

In addition to the intuitive appeal of the framework concept and its simplicity from an abstract perspective, experience has shown that framework projects can indeed result in increased reusability and decreased development effort: see e.g. Moser and Nierstrasz (1996) and Mattsson (1999).

In the remainder of this section, we first present an overview over the history of object-oriented frameworks. Then we define some of the concepts and, finally, we present the lifecycle of object-oriented frameworks.

2.1 History

Early examples of the framework concept can be found in literature that has its origins in the Smalltalk environment (e.g. Goldberg and Robson, 1989) and Apple Inc. (Schmucker, 1986). The Smalltalk-80 user-interface framework, Model-View-Controller (MVC), was perhaps the first widely used framework. Apple developed the MacApp user-interface framework which was designed for supporting the implementing of Macintosh applications. Frameworks attained more interest when the Interviews (Linton *et al.,* 1989) and ET++ (Weinand *et al.,* 1989) user-interface frameworks were developed and became available. Frameworks are not limited to the user-interface domain but have been defined for many other domains as well, such as operating systems (Russo, 1990) and fire-alarm systems (Molin and Ohlsson, 1998). With the formation of Taligent in 1992, frameworks became a subject of interest in larger communities. Taligent set out to develop a completely object-oriented operating system based on the framework concept. The company delivered a set of tools for rapid application development under the name *CommonPoint* that consists of more than a hundred object-oriented frameworks (Andert, 1994; Cotter and Potel, 1995). The Taligent approach made a shift in focus from large monolithic frameworks to many fine-grained integrated frameworks.

Many object-oriented frameworks exist that capture a domain well but relatively little work has been done on general framework issues such as methods for framework usage, testing of frameworks, etc. Regarding documentation, patterns have been used for documentation of frameworks (Johnson, 1992; Huni *et al.*, 1995) and for describing the rationale behind design decisions for a framework (Beck and Cunningham, 1989). Other interesting work of general framework nature concerns the restructuring (refactoring) of frameworks. Since frameworks often undergo several iterations before even the first version is released, the framework design and code change frequently. In Opdyke (1992), a set of behaviour-preserving 'refactorings' are defined that help to remove multiple copies of similar code without changing the behaviour. Refactoring can be used for restructuring inheritance hierarchies and component hierarchies (Johnson and Opdyke, 1993).

Roberts and Johnson (1996) describe the evolution of a framework as starting from a white-box framework, a framework which is reused mostly by subclassing, and developing into a black-box framework, a framework which mostly is reused through parametrization. The evolution is presented as a pattern language describing the process from the initial design of a framework as a white-box framework, to a black-box framework. The resulting black-box framework has an associated visual builder that will generate the application's code. The visual builder allows the software engineer to connect the framework objects and activate them. In addition, the builder supports the specification of the behaviour of application-specific objects.

2.2   Definition of concepts

Most authors agree that an object-oriented framework is a reusable software architecture comprising both design and code but no generally accepted definition of a framework and its constituent parts exist. The probably most referenced definition of a framework is found in Johnson and Foote (1988):

> *A framework is a set of classes that embodies an abstract design for solutions to a family of related problems.*

In other words, a framework is a partial design and implementation for an application in a given problem domain. When discussing the framework concept, terminological difficulties may arise due to the fact that a common framework definition does not exist and because it is difficult to distinguish between framework-specific and application-specific aspects. For the discussion in the remainder of this chapter, we need to define the following terms: *core framework design, framework internal increment, application-specific increment, object-oriented framework* and *application*.

The *core framework design* comprises both abstract and concrete classes in the domain. The concrete classes in the framework are intended to be invisible to the *framework user* (e.g. a basic data storage class). An abstract class is either intended to be invisible to the framework user or intended to be subclassed by the framework user. The latter classes are also referred to as *hot-spots* (Pree, 1994). The core framework design describes the typical software architecture for applications in the domain.

However, the core framework design has to be accompanied with additional classes to be more usable. These additional classes form a number of class libraries, referred to as *framework internal increments*, to avoid confusion with the more general class library concept. These internal increments consist of classes that capture common implementations of the core framework design. Two common categories of internal increments that may be associated with a core framework design are the following:

- **subclasses** representing common realizations of the concepts captured by the superclasses. For example, an abstract superclass of Device may have a number of concrete subclasses that represent real-world devices commonly used in the domain captured by the framework;

- **a collection of (sub)classes** representing the specifications for a complete instantiation of the framework in a particular context. For example, a graphical user interface framework may provide a collection of classes for a framework instantiation in the context provided by Windows 2000.

At the object level we talk about the *core implementation* which comprises the objects belonging to the classes in the *core framework design* and *increment implementation* which consists of the objects belonging to the classes defined in the *internal increments*. Thus, an *object-oriented framework* consists of a *core framework design* and its associated *internal increments* (if any) with accompanying implementations. Unlike Roberts and Johnson (1996), who make the distinction between the framework and a component library, our interpretation of a framework includes class libraries.

Some authors categorize frameworks into *white-box* and *black-box* frameworks (e.g. Johnson and Foote, 1988), or *calling* and *called* frameworks (e.g. Sparks *et al.*, 1996). In a white-box (inheritance-based) framework, the framework user is supposed to customize the framework behaviour through subclassing of framework classes. As identified by Roberts and Johnson (1996), a framework often is inheritance-based in the beginning of its lifecycle, since the application domain is not sufficiently well understood to make it possible to parametrize the behaviour. A black-box (parametrized) framework is based on composition. The behaviour of the framework is customized by using different combinations of classes. A parametrized framework requires a deep understanding of the stable and flexible aspects of the domain. Due to its predefined flexibility, a black-box framework is often more rigid in the domain it supports. A calling framework is an active entity, proactively invoking other parts of the application, whereas a called framework is a passive entity that can be invoked by other parts of the application. However, in practice, a framework hardly ever is a pure white-box or black-box framework or a pure calling or called framework. In general, a framework has parts that can be parametrized and parts that need to be customized through subclassing. Also, virtually each framework is called by some part of the application and calls some (other) part of the application.

An *application* is composed of one or more core framework designs, each framework's *internal increments* (if any) and an *application-specific increment*, comprising application-specific classes and objects. The application may reuse only parts of the object-oriented framework or it may require adaptation of the core framework design and the internal increments for achieving its requirements.

3   Composing independently developed frameworks

Traditional framework-based application development assumes that the application is based on a single framework that is extended with application-specific code. Particularly in the domain of software product lines, however, one can identify a development where software engineers make use of multiple frameworks that are composed to fulfil the system requirements. Consequently, rather than the predominant part of an application, frameworks are used as components in a larger system that composes several frameworks.

In our experience, object-oriented frameworks, if not explicitly designed otherwise, tend to make constraining assumptions about their context. Thus, when composing two or more independently developed frameworks it is generally clear that the involved frameworks are developed for reuse by extension with newly written application-specific code and not for composition with other software components. This focus on reuse through extension causes a number of composition problems that surface when software engineers try to compose frameworks. The primary composition problems that we have identified are described below.

3.1   Composition of framework control

One of the most distinguishing features of a framework is its ability to make extensive use of dynamic binding. In traditional class or procedure libraries, the application code invokes routines in the library and it is the application code that is in control. For object-oriented frameworks, the situation is inverted and it is often the framework code that has the thread of control and calls the application code when appropriate. This inversion of control is often referred to as the *Hollywood principle*, i.e. 'Don't call us – we call you'. In Fig. 51, this inversion is graphically illustrated.

In Sparks *et al.* (1996) a distinction is made between 'calling' and 'called' frameworks. Calling frameworks are the active entities in an application, controlling and invoking the other parts, whereas 'called' frameworks are passive entities that can be called by other parts of the application, i.e. more like class libraries. One of the problems when composing two calling frameworks is that both frameworks expect to be the controlling entity in the application and in control of the main event loop.

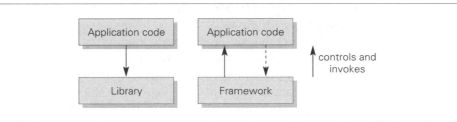

Figure 51   The inversion of control

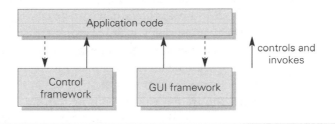

Figure 52   The problem of framework control composition

As an example, we use the composition of a control framework and a graphical user interface (GUI) framework (Fig. 52). The control framework has generally a well-defined control loop that has to be performed in real time and that reads sensors, computes, activates actuators and stores the necessary historical data. The GUI framework has a similar thread of control, though not real-time, that updates the screen whenever a value in the system changes, e.g. of a sensor, or performs some action when the user invokes a command. These two control loops can easily collide with each other, potentially causing the measurement part to miss its real-time deadlines and causing the GUI to present incorrect data due to race conditions between the activities.

Solving this problem is considerably easier if the frameworks are supplied with source code that makes it possible to adapt the framework to handle this problem. However, the control loop in the framework may not be localized in a single entity. Often it is distributed over the framework code, which causes changes to the control to affect considerable parts of the framework.

In addition to merging the framework control loops by adapting the framework code, each framework can be assigned its own thread of control, leading to two or more independently executing control loops. Although this might work in some situations, one has to be aware of, at least, two important drawbacks. First, all application objects that can be accessed by both frameworks need to be extended with synchronization code. Since classes often cannot be modularly extended with synchronization code, it requires editing all reused classes that potentially are accessed by both processes. A second drawback is that often one framework needs to be informed about an event that occurred in the other framework because the event has application-wide relevance. This requires that the control loops of the frameworks become much more integrated than two concurrent threads.

3.2 Composition with legacy components

A framework presents a design for an application in a particular domain. Based on this design, the software engineer may construct a concrete application through extension of the framework, e.g. subclassing the framework classes. When the framework class only contains behaviour for internal framework functionality, but not the domain-specific behaviour required for the application, the software engineer may want to include existing, legacy, classes in the application that need to be integrated with the framework. It is, however, far from trivial to integrate the legacy class in the application, since frameworks often rely heavily on the subclassing mechanism. For instance, since the legacy component is no subclass of the framework class, one runs into typing conflicts.

In order to illustrate the problem, a control framework is, again, used as an example. The framework handles the measurement cycle and provides for attaching a sensor, a control algorithm and an actuator by specifying the interface classes of Sensor, ControlStrategy and Actuator. Figure 53 shows the framework.

Assume that we have a library of legacy components with different types of sensors, actuators and strategies for controlling, and that we have found suitable classes that we want to use in the three places in the framework's interface. Our library sensor class is called TempSensor, and it happens to be a subclass of the class Sensor, which is an abstract class defined in our library. However, since the framework also defines a class Sensor, the usage of the library class will lead to conflicts. Even if the class name for the library superclass matches with that of the framework interface class, the class TempSensor cannot be used, because these names do not designate the same class. An alternative approach, which is used in Fig. 53, is to make use of the *adapter* design pattern (Gamma *et al.*, 1994) for class adaptation. This approach normally solves the problem, assuming no name clashes between class names in the framework and the legacy components. However, as we identified in Bosch (1998a), the *adapter* design pattern has some disadvantages associated with it. One disadvantage is that for every element of the interface that needs to be adapted, the software engineer has to define a method that forwards the call to the

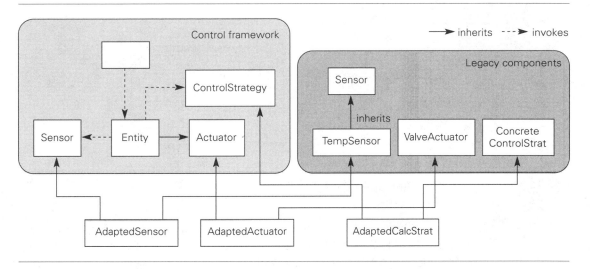

Figure 53   The control framework and associated legacy classes

corresponding method in the legacy class. Moreover, in case of object adaptation, those requests which otherwise would not have required adaptation have to be forwarded as well, due to the intermediate adapter object. This leads to considerable implementation overheads for the software engineer. In addition, the pattern suffers from the *self problem* (Lieberman, 1986) and lacks expressiveness. Finally, since behaviour of the *adapter* pattern is mixed with the domain-related behaviour of the class, traceability is reduced.

The problems related to integration of legacy components in framework-based applications is studied in more detail in Lundberg and Mattsson (1996).

3.3 Framework gap

Often when thinking about composition problems of components, the first thing that comes to mind is different kinds of overlap between the components, but there may also exist problems due to non-overlap between the components. This typically occurs when a framework is used to provide the implementation of an architectural component, but the framework does not cover all required functionality. This problem is generally referred to as *framework gap* (see e.g. Sparks *et al.*, 1996).

If the framework is a called framework, the framework gap problem may be solved with an additional framework interface including both the existing and additionally required functionality. In Fig. 54, such a 'wrapping' approach is illustrated graphically.

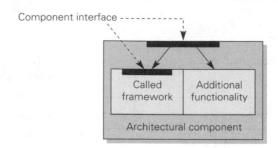

Figure 54   Extending framework to fulfil component requirements

In the case where a *calling* framework lacks functionality, mediating software is needed to alleviate the problem. This mediating software is often tricky to develop since framework A has to be informed by framework B of what has happened in framework B in terms that can be interpreted by framework A. The mediating software may also need to cut out parts of the functionality offered by the frameworks and replace these parts with application-specific code that composes the functionality from framework A and B and the functionality required for the framework gap. An additional problem is that since the mediating software becomes dependent on the current framework versions, this may lead to rather complex maintenance problems for the application when new versions of the framework beome available.

3.4 Composition overlap of framework entities

When developing a software system based on reusable components, it may occur that two (or more) frameworks both contain a representation, i.e. class, of the same real-world entity, but modeled from their respective perspectives. When composing the two frameworks, the two different representations should be integrated or composed since they both represent the same real-world entity. If the represented properties are mutually exclusive and do not influence each other, then the integration can be solved by multiple inheritance. However, very often these preconditions do not hold and there exist shared or mutually dependent properties between the representations, causing the composition of the representations to be more complex. We can identify at least three cases where alternative composition techniques are necessary. Below, these cases are discussed.

First, consider the situation where both framework classes represent a state property of the real-world entity but the entity is represented in different ways. For example, an entity in one framework contains a boolean state for its value and should be composed with a second framework which has modeled the entity using a more complex representation such as real numbers. When these two representations of the entity are composed into an integrated one, this requires every state update in one framework entity class to be extended with the conversion and update code for the state in the other framework class.

In the second case, assume that both framework classes represent a property *p* of the real-world entity, but one framework class represents it as a state and the other framework class as an operation. The value of the particular property *p* is indirectly computed by the operation. In some system, the software engineer may want to compose both actuator representations into a single entity. One actuator class may store as a state whether it is currently active or not, whereas the other class may indirectly deduce this from its other state variables. In the application representation, the property representation has to be solved in such a way that reused behaviour from both classes can deal with it.

In the third case the situation is that the execution of an operation in one framework class requires state changes in the other framework class. For instance, one of the frameworks collects history information that it requires for its continued correct operation. A message to one entity implementation may require that a state of the other framework class needs to be updated accordingly. When the software engineer combines the classes from the two frameworks, this aspect of the composition has to be explicitly implemented in the glue code.

3.5 Composition of entity functionality

Sometimes a real-world entity's functionality has to be modeled through composition with parts of functionality from different frameworks. Consider the case of a typical three-tier software architecture with three layers, each represented by a framework; at the top we have a user interface layer, in the middle an application domain-specific layer and at the bottom a persistence layer. Our real-world entity is now represented in the application domain-specific framework but some aspects of the entity have to be presented in the user interface layer and the entity also has to be made persistent for some kinds of transactions etc. Just composing the respective classes from the three frameworks or using multiple inheritance will not result in the desired behaviour. For example, changes of state caused by messages to the application domain-specific part of the resulting object will not automatically affect the user interface and persistence functionality of the objects.

Thus, the software engineer is required to extend the application domain class with behaviour for notifying the user-interface and database classes, e.g. using the *observer* design pattern (Gamma *et al.*, 1994). One could argue that the application domain class should have been extended with such behaviour during design, but, as we mentioned earlier, most frameworks are not designed to be composed with other frameworks but to be extended with application-specific code written specifically for the application at hand.

This problem occurred in the fire-alarm system, where several entities had to be persistent and were stored in non-volatile memory, i.e. an EEPROM. To deal with this, each entity was implemented by two objects, i.e. one application object and one persistence object. These two objects were obviously tightly coupled and had frequent interactions, due to the fact that they both represented parts of one entity.

4   Framework component models

There are several factors that influence the optimal approach to modeling a framework as a component in a software product line. One of the factors is the amount of product-specific behaviour that is required from the component. Secondly, a factor influencing the organization of the framework is the number of independent variation points. A framework can have several variation points, but choosing an alternative for one point restricts the choices in the other variation points. If this is the case, sets of alternatives can be grouped.

We have identified four framework component models that can be used in a software product line. Some of these models are used in the cases discussed earlier, whereas others are based on general experience. These models are discussed in more detail below.

4.1   Product-specific extension model

The traditional approach to using frameworks is by extending the framework for each instantiation that is generated. In the case of a software product line, this results in an instantiation of the framework for each of the products that include the particular component. Since the framework only covers the behaviour that is common for all products in the product line, each product adds a product-specific extension to the framework that is used when the framework is incorporated in the software for the product. In Fig. 55, this model is presented graphically. As shown, the framework exports an interface consisting of a set of operations, i.e. o_1, o_2, ..., o_n, and a set of interfaces types, i.e. i_1, i_2, ..., i_n. As discussed earlier, the operations may return references to objects of the specified interface types that are then used for the continued operation. Ideally, the interface of the framework is not affected by the product-specific extensions. However, extending or changing the interface cannot be avoided in all cases.

An example of this type of framework component model can be found in the EIKON graphical user interface framework used in the EPOC operation system

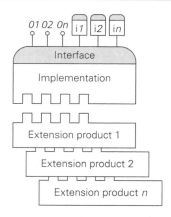

Figure 55   Product-specific extension model

developed by Symbian. Each application, e.g. an appointment manager or word processor, has its own user interface that builds upon the EIKON GUI framework, but extends it with its own GUI classes and their associated functionality.

The primary advantage of this framework component model is *simplicity*. Since only a single extension per product has to be developed and maintained as a module, a relatively simple organization of software development will be able to manage this.

The model has a number of disadvantages as well, primarily the lack of reuse between product-specific instantiations and inflexibility. Often the product-specific instantiations have common requirements for a relevant part of their behaviour. However, this model does not allow the reuse of the common parts between the instantiations. Finally, the model is inflexible in that changes to the framework will affect all instantiations.

4.2 Standard-specific extension model

The second framework component model that we have identified is the standard-specific extension model. Rather than for each product in the product line, each standard, e.g. a file-system or communication protocol standard, is implemented as an extension to the framework. Each product in the family generally incorporates one or more framework implementations, either as product variants or as configurable parts of the product. Another difference compared to the product-specific implementation model is that the common part of the framework only defines the framework interface and no, or very little, common behaviour between the framework implementations. The model is graphically represented in Fig. 56.

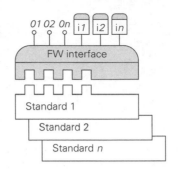

Figure 56   Standard-specific extension model

Examples of this model can be found in the product family developed by Axis Communications. Both the file-system framework and the communication protocol framework are designed in this way. The file-system framework defines an interface consisting of a number of basic concepts, such as *file* and *directory*. Each framework implementation implements a particular file-system standard, e.g. the ISO9660 CDROM format, Microsoft FAT or NTFS. In this way, the other components in the system can access the file system component without having to bother with the actual format used for the file system. Of course, there are differences between the standards that cannot be hidden behind the framework interface. For instance, the ISO9660 format is read-only since it is intended for CDROMs. Write operations on files in this format are handled through exception handling and error codes returned to the caller.

The model has as a primary advantage in that it provides a uniform interface to the other components in the architecture. Assume an architecture that consists of five fully connected components, with three possible implementations each. This would require each component implementation to be able to communicate with three versions of each of the other four components, i.e. 12 alternatives. Defining a uniform interface for each component reduces the number of required alternatives to one. Simplicity is a second advantage of this model. As long as each framework implementation adheres to the defined framework interface, it can evolve independently without dependencies on the other framework implementations.

The disadvantages of the model are lack of reuse between framework implementations, lack of product-specific extensions and decreased maintainability. The disadvantages are discussed in more detail below.

■ **Lack of reuse.** Competing standards within a particular domain generally share, despite their differences, a substantial set of domain concepts. This model, in which the common part of the component only defines the interface, does not exploit the reuse potential of object-oriented frameworks in this respect.

- ■ **Lack of product-specific extensions.** The framework component model as presented in this section does not allow for product-specific extensions. For instance, in the file-system framework case, a specific product may support a secure server that encrypts all data stored in the file system. This would require the file-system component to be extended for this particular system, which is not supported in this model.

- ■ **Decreased maintainability.** This model is notoriously unsuited for incorporating changes enforced by the client components that require changes to the component interface. Each interface change will most often require changes to each framework implementation. Since functionality common between the framework implementations is present in each implementation, rather than shared, the maintainability effort will be duplicated for all but the first implementation.

In this section, we have discussed the extreme version of the standard-specific implementation model where only the framework interface is shared between the framework implementations. It is possible to move some of the common functionality up to the framework interface part, similar to the model discussed first.

4.3 Fine-grained extension model

The models discussed up to now aim at extending the framework with a single extension that covers all variation points in the framework. These models have the advantage of relative simplicity, but suffer from lack of reuse between framework extensions and inflexibility. The fine-grained extension model discussed in this section takes the opposite approach, i.e. it aims at providing small modules of extension that only cover one or a few variation points and that themselves may be configurable. In Fig. 57 the model is presented graphically. The common framework consists of an interface and the implementation common to all instantiations. For each variation point, there is a set of generic extensions and generic extensions can be configured with product-specific extensions.

This type of framework extension model is typically more mature than the models discussed earlier because it requires a detailed understanding of the required variation points and an orthogonal definition of these points. Typical examples of this model are found in commercial graphical user-interface frameworks such as Microsoft Foundation Classes (MFC) and the VisualWorks Smalltalk-80 environment. These frameworks typically consist of an engine and a set of black-box components which can be configured with small application-specific components.

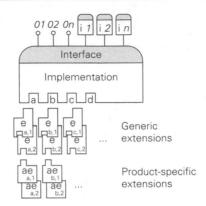

Figure 57   Fine-grained extension model

The primary advantages of this model can be found in the high flexibility of the configuration and the high reusability of extensions. Compared to the models discussed earlier, the flexibility is considerably better due to the fine-grain extension components, generally individual classes, and the independence between extension components. The user of the framework is thus free in composing arbitrary sets of extension components, although not all combinations may be semantically meaningful or even correct. Reusability of extension components is, due to their relative independence and atomicity, much higher than the extensions defined in the previous sections. A danger, however, may be inherent in the fine-grained nature of the extensions in this model. Too small extension components are not cost-effective to reuse, since understanding their functionality and place in the overall framework may take more effort than writing an extension component from scratch.

The prime disadvantage of the model is highly related to the main advantage of the models discussed earlier, i.e. complexity. Whereas the other models are relatively simple to use, this model can be very complex to use, depending on the number of variation points, the number of extension components and the number and complexity of the relations between them. A second disadvantage is that although extensions can generally be more fine-grained than one main extension component as used by the first two models, the fine-grained extension model that associates extensions with each variation point may be too fine-grained. Often, relations between extensions for different variation points exist. For instance, when selecting a particular look for a window in a graphical user interface framework, this automatically limits the choice for other widgets, such as buttons, sliders, etc., to one or a few alternatives. These relations between extensions are left implicit in this model if it is used in a straightforward fashion.

4.4 Generator-based model

The final model for using object-oriented frameworks as components in a product-line architecture is considerably different from the models earlier (Fig. 58). It is generally an extension to the fine-grained extension model discussed in the previous section. Once the suitable variation points and the useful extensions have been identified, as well as the complexity, or inconvenience, of configuring frameworks during instantiation, tool support is generally discussed as an option. Although several approaches to tool support exist (see e.g. Roberts and Johnson, 1996), these approaches can be captured as being based on some kind of generator. The two primary approaches are either a graphical configuration tool in which components are configured with available extension components or a domain-specific language (DSL) in which a configuration is specified and afterwards a matching component is generated.

An example of this approach at the product level is provided by the fire-alarm product line of Securitas Larm. The product-line architecture contains the relevant behaviour for all possible cases. A graphical configuration tool is associated with the product-line architecture. This tool is used during product instantiation to define the associations between physical devices, e.g. sensors, and their software representations and the relations between sets of sensors and sets of actuators are defined. In addition, framework functionality not used in this particular instantiation is pruned from the product. The result is a product that is a member of the product line since it represents a logical subset of the available functionality.

The advantages of this model are a combination of those of the previously discussed models, i.e. high reusability and flexibility and logical integrity of extensions. The reusability and flexibility are achieved similar to the previously discussed model since the same fine-grained extensions are used. However, since either a graphical tool or DSL compiler is used, semantic checking can be added relatively easily to these tools. Even proactive configuration can be performed by the tool: whenever a particular choice for a variation point excludes all but one choice for one or more other variation points, the tool can proactively select these exten-

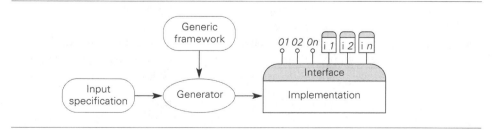

Figure 58   Generator-based model

sions. A generator-based tool considerably simplifies the, otherwise complex, use of a framework with fine-grained extensions.

Obviously, the model has a number of associated disadvantages as well. These include decreased evolvability and complication of product-specific extensions. The framework is more expensive to evolve since, in addition to the framework, a graphical or textual configuration tool has to be changed as well for each non-trivial change in the framework. Product-specific extensions are harder to incorporate than in the previous model. Although the configuration tool would normally support additional extensions, the extension has to adhere to a protocol that allows the tool to recognize the extension as of a particular type and handle it appropriately. Finally, the configuration tool does generally not allow for instantiations radically different from the ones imagined and intended by the tool designer.

5 Designing frameworks

The development of a framework is, in a way, similar to the development of a software product line, although at a lower level of abstraction. An important distinction is that the framework only has to cover the variability required for the component, whereas the product line needs to address all variability between the products in the family. We outline below the activities that are part of framework development.

- **Domain and variability analysis.** This step is concerned with identifying the domain that the framework should cover and the required variability. During the design of the product-line architecture, the software architects have performed a domain analysis at the product level. The results of this analysis that apply to the component are used as input to this phase. The framework, although it covers a particular domain, only covers a subdomain of the product-line domain. However, it needs to be studied in more detail than earlier. As a result of this activity, the requirements of the framework, the domain concepts and the relations between those concepts are established.

- **Architectural design** takes the domain analysis model as input. The designer has to decide on a suitable architectural style underlying the framework. Based on this the top-level design of the framework is made. In the first part of the book, architectural design has been discussed in detail. In addition, it is important to decide upon the framework component model that will be used for the framework, since it will influence the subsequent activities in framework development.

- During **framework design** the architectural design of the framework is refined and additional classes are designed. Results from this activity are the functionality scope given by the framework design, the framework's configuration interface (similar to the *external framework interface* described in (Deutsch,

1989)), design rules based on architectural decisions that must be obeyed and a design history document describing the design problems encountered and the solutions selected with an argumentation.

- **Framework implementation** is concerned with the coding of the abstract and concrete framework classes.

- **Framework testing** is performed to determine whether the framework provides the intended functionality, but also to evaluate the usability of the framework. It is, however, far from trivial to decide whether an entity is usable or not. Johnson and Russo (1991) conclude that the only way to find out if something is reusable is to reuse it. For frameworks, this boils down to developing applications that use the framework.

- To evaluate the usability of the framework, the **test instance generation** activity is concerned with the development of test instantiations of the product-specific components based on the framework. Depending on the particularities of the products, one can test different aspects of the framework. Based on the developed instances, testing aims, in addition to finding errors in the framework, at deciding whether the framework needs to be redesigned or is sufficiently mature for release.

5.1 Documentation

This is one of the most important activities in framework development, although its importance is not always recognized. Without a clear, complete and correct documentation that describes how to use the framework, a user manual, and design documents that describe how the framework works, the framework will be nearly impossible to use by software engineers not involved in the framework design. Although not discussed much throughout the book, the documentation of all software assets is an important activity.

6 Conclusion

Object-oriented frameworks provide an important step forward in the development of large reusable components, when compared to the traditional approaches. In addition to our own positive experiences, others (e.g. Moser and Nierstrasz, 1996 and Mattsson, 1999) have also identified that frameworks reduce the amount of development effort required for software product development in general, as well as for use as components in software product lines.

In this chapter, we have discussed the difference between the academic and the industrial perspectives on software components. The conclusion we reached was that object-oriented frameworks are a much more accurate model for reusable components in a product-line architecture than the traditional component model dis-cussed in the previous chapter.

Subsequently, an historical overview of object-oriented frameworks and a set of def-initions were presented. Since object-oriented frameworks traditionally were used individually, we discussed the composition problems that may occur when com-posing independently developed frameworks. We discussed the framework component models that we have identified, i.e. product-specific, standard-specific, fine-grained and generator-based extension models. Finally, the design of object-oriented frameworks was discussed.

7 Further reading

Over the years, an extensive body of research results has been collected on the topic of object-oriented frameworks. Two publications containing an excellent overview are Fayad *et al.* (1999) and Fayad and Johnson (1999). These books pre-sent a wide perspective on object-oriented frameworks, both from an academic and industrial perspective. The paper by Roberts and Johnson (1996) discusses the evo-lution and maturation of object-oriented frameworks and examines a number of development stages.

In our own research, we have studied object-oriented frameworks extensively. Examples include research capturing problems and experiences associated with the industrial use of frameworks (Bosch *et al.*, 1999), framework composition problems (Mattsson *et al.*, 1999) and framework evolution (Mattsson and Bosch, 1999), as well as concrete examples (Bosch, 1999a).

CHAPTER 12

Family-based
system development

Although we have invested considerable effort in developing a product-line architecture and a set of reusable components, so far we have not developed anything that actually leads to a system or product. In this chapter, we discuss the development of a product based on the reusable assets that we developed earlier.

Unlike the traditional, one-at-a-time approach to software development, the intention of using a software product-line approach is to develop as little as possible and to reuse the existing assets to the maximum extent. Any product-specific functionality is, as much as possible, developed as an extension to the product-line functionality. In addition, it is developed as generically as possible since future versions of existing products or new products may need to incorporate the functionality, at which point the functionality becomes part of the product line and is no longer product-specific.

1 Requirement specification

The requirements of products that are members of the family were addressed during the design of the product-line architecture. However, during that phase, the focus was on the commonalities between the products. The requirement specification activity during the product development phase focuses on the specifics of the product and, in particular, the functionality that is not supported by the reusable assets that are part of the family.

As discussed in Chapter 9, to simplify the handling of the requirements, we organize requirements in features, i.e. sets of related requirements that represent a logical unit of functionality for the user of the product. During the design of the product-line architecture, we defined a matrix of the products and features that are part of the family. The part of the matrix specific for the product under development is used as input to the requirement specification. In addition, the feature set defined for the product line is incorporated as input data.

The first step during requirement specification is to validate the product feature set defined during the design of the product-line architecture with respect to the actual requirements as available at that point of product development. Two main causes for differences between these specifications exist:

■ **Organizational:** the product-line architecture and assets are often not developed by the product engineering unit that develops the product, but rather by the domain engineering unit. Therefore, the requirements of the product may not be fully understood by the software architects and engineers in the domain engineering unit.

■ **Time:** generally, there is a considerable amount of calendar time between the scoping of the product-line architecture and the development of our product. In the meantime, several requirements will undoubtedly have changed and new requirements will have been added that have to be supported by the product.

Once the product-feature set has been updated and defined, the next step is to define the product-feature graph by merging the product-feature set with the feature graph for the software product line. During the merging process, the product-feature set needs to be extended with relations between the product-specific features as well as to the software product-line features. The product-feature graph should be 'pruned' as much as possible to minimize the resources needed at run-time. During the merging and pruning of the product-feature graph, several possible situations need to be addressed:

■ **Overlapping features.** A product feature may be defined in such a way that the requirements it contains overlap with requirements defined in one of the product-line features. In this case, the product feature should, where possible, be redefined to only include unique requirements. A 'depends-on' relation should be defined between the redefined product feature and the product-line feature.

■ **Superfluous features.** Once the merging is complete, it may become clear that some features are not needed for this particular product. These features should be 'pruned' from the product-feature graph. However, other features that are included in the product may depend on the features that are judged as superfluous for this particular product. The reason for such a situation may, for instance, be a design decision to optimize the implementation of some assets which are valid for most products, but not for the product at hand. A typical conflict exists between high-end and low-end products, where low-end products in a product line often need to sacrifice some resources, e.g. memory space or performance, in order to keep the family together. Although the software engineers developing the product should try to minimize such overheads, some overheads may be unavoidable and are part of the price of being part of a product line.

- **Conflicting features.** Finally, some features in the product line may plainly conflict with product features. Such conflicts may be functional in nature, e.g. the product line assumes a particular component communication model, e.g. COM, whereas the product requires another model, e.g. JavaBeans. In this case, the product needs to remove those product-line features in the product-feature graph that conflict and implement this functionality as product-specific code. If too many conflicting features exist, basing the actual product on the software product line may not be justifiable. However, for the continued discussion, we assume that the advantages of using the software product line for the product exceed the disadvantages. There is an additional cost involved that can only be justified by a majority of the products in the family using the particular conflicting feature. A second origin for this situation may be time-induced changes, such as technological revolutions. The second category of conflicting features is concerned with quality attributes. The software product line may be optimized for particular quality attributes, e.g. performance and reliability, whereas the product under development requires other qualities, e.g. security. In such cases, often additional design elements need to be added to fulfil the quality attributes for the product. In the first part of the book, we discussed the notion of software architecture transformations and generally one or more transformations are necessary to address conflicts in quality requirements. The sources of (potential) conflicts between the product requirements and the product-line requirements need to be noted for the next step, i.e. product architecture derivation.

The result of this step is a product-feature graph which includes all features required for the product and, possibly, a number of unnecessary features inherited from the product-line feature graph. In addition, a list of potential conflicts between the product line and the product under development is provided that is used during the next step.

2 Product architecture derivation

Throughout this book, we have stressed the importance of an explicit software architecture for a software product. Even a product that is part of a family is not excluded from this. However, rather than designing a software architecture from scratch, the software architecture is conceived based on the product-line architecture. We refer to this process as *deriving* a product architecture since the product-line architecture has been designed to support derivation against minimal effort.

As a first version of the software architecture of the product under development, we use the product-line architecture. The product architecture is derived from the product-line architecture through the following main steps:

- **Architecture pruning.** The first activity that the software architecture is concerned with, similar to the feature graph, is to remove the parts of the product-line architecture which are not needed for this product.

- **Architecture extension.** The second step is to extend the software architecture with the features and requirements specific to this product.

- **Conflict resolution.** The requirement specification, expressed as a feature graph, specified in the previous section is associated with a list of potential conflicts. These conflicts are, where possible, resolved in this step.

- **Architecture assessment.** Assuming that the product-line architecture provided a sufficiently strong basis for product development, the software architecture for the product should fulfil its requirements. However, to increase the confidence that the product will indeed support the requirements it may be preferable to perform a formal assessment of the software architecture as described in Chapter 5.

In the sections below, these steps are discussed in more detail. Note that the process of deriving the product architecture from the product-line architecture is different from the architectural design processes discussed in Part I of the book and in Chapter 9. The reason for this is that the main part of the architecture for the product should already be present in the form of the product-line architecture. Therefore, only a derivation rather than a complete design process is sufficient to fulfil the requirements.

2.1 Architecture pruning

The product-line architecture contains those features that are common for the products in the family. In addition, the architecture should be applicable to all family members. In practice, however, a balance needs to be achieved between the features that are common to a subset of the members in the family and consequences for the products that do not have those features. In addition, not all products in the family share the same set of quality requirements. Therefore, the product-line architecture may need to incorporate transformations required for a subset of the products in the family. Whereas functionality can frequently be handled by selective inclusion, this is often not the case for quality requirements. However, architecture transformations for achieving quality requirements are generally much harder to exclude for the products that do not require them, or may even experience them as conflicting. In this section, we address pruning the product architecture for features that focus primarily on functionality. In Section 2.3, we address the conflicts related to, among others, the conflicts between quality requirements included in the software family architecture and the product requirements.

During the design of the product-line architecture, provisions have been included in the architecture for variants and optional parts. Assuming that the product only employs a single variant, the parts that are used for the other variants need to be excluded from the architecture.

It is important to note that, even in the domain of embedded systems, it becomes more and more common to support run-time variability of products. If that is required even for the product under development, the variants not initially selected cannot be removed without further consideration. If not already present in the product-line architecture, the product architecture needs to be extended with mechanisms to select alternative variants. The unselected variants can be included in the product upon delivery or included at a later stage. In general, one can identify an increasing need for first-class representations of software architectures that are available during run-time and that can be used to dynamically replace components and possibly even change the architecture itself dynamically.

Whereas variants allow the engineer developing the software product to select one component out of a set, optionality is concerned with the actual presence of a feature or set of related requirements. Thus, in the case of optionality, the choice is to incorporate this functionality into the product or to exclude it. Excluding the functionality will then remove the involved component or components from the product architecture.

Optionality and variants are frequently used in combination. First, the software architect should decide whether the optional functionality is to be included in the product and, subsequently, the variant implementing the right version of the functionality should be selected.

For instance, in the case of Axis Communications, the software architect should first decide whether the product under development should be network-enabled or not. If it is decided that it should support a network interface, the software architect needs to decide on the protocol or protocols that should be included in the product, i.e. the variants.

2.2 Architecture extension

In the previous step, the product-line architecture was pruned to remove all parts that did not contribute to fulfilling the product requirements. The resulting software architecture does, however, not necessarily fulfil the requirements of the product. The requirements generally contain product-specific parts that are not covered by the product-line architecture. In this step, the architecture is extended to also cover the product-specific requirements.

The product-specific requirements generally consist of both functional and quality requirements. Assuming the scoping and product-line architectural design was performed as it should, the functional requirements can be handled as pure extensions to the software architecture. This may require product-specific extensions to prod-uct-line components or complete product-specific components. In the latter case, the connections between product-line components, that make up the core of the architecture, and the product-specific components need to defined as well. Ideally, these connections have been prepared for by the product-line components so that no additional effort has to be put into integrating the product-specific components.

Product-specific quality requirements may be less trivial to incorporate since these, in the worst case, may require reorganization of the complete architecture. Generally, the product-line architecture should provide for the coverage of the requirements of all products. However, as we discussed earlier, some products may be at the boundary of what can be covered by the software product line in an eco-nomical manner, i.e. without violating the requirements of the core family members. For the boundary products, architecture transformations may be neces-sary that result in considerable reorganization of the software architecture.

Reorganizing the software architecture of the product at this stage may result in the situation where the product-line components no longer match the interfaces and behaviour required by the product architecture. If this is the case, the economic benefit of being a family member is generally not present, even if the business case analysis and scoping suggested differently earlier, and the product should be devel-oped independent of the family.

If the product should remain a member of the family, some requirements need to be relaxed. For instance, in the case of a low-end family member, lower resource efficiency may be accepted because the other benefits of including the product in the family outweigh the additional cost for resources, e.g. memory or CPU power.

Finally, not all architecture transformations necessarily result in changed compo-nent interfaces. It may be possible to insert components in between product-line components. By replacing a connector with two other connectors connecting to a product-specific component, a substantial part of the component behaviour can be adapted without changing the requirements on the product-line components. Another approach is *wrapping* the product-line component with a product-specific component. For example, if encrypted communication between components in a distributed context is a requirement for just this family member, rather than incor-porating this computationally intensive requirement in the product-line architecture, wrapper components can be developed for this product that encapsu-late the product-line components.

The result of this step is a software architecture for the product that incorporates all requirements, both those supported by the family and the product-specific requirements. However, a number of conflicts may remain that need to be addressed. This is the topic of the next section.

2.3 Conflict resolution

Since the product-line architecture and the product architecture have different aims, but are strongly related, a number of conflicts may occur when deriving the latter from the former architecture. Below, a number of typical conflicts are discussed.

Conflicting, but embedded, functionality

A product-line component may, as part of its useful functionality, exhibit some behaviour which conflicts with the requirements for the product. For instance, a communication protocol component invokes an authorization component, as part of handling data packets, since this is required for the majority of the products in the family. This behaviour is embedded in the component behaviour and it is not possible to exclude it without considerable editing of the component.

One approach to handling this is by inserting a dummy authorization component that provides the required interface but exhibits no functionality related to authorization, except for returning the values to the communication protocol component that are required for its continued correct operation.

It may not always be possible to address this type of conflict by inserting some dummy component. However, conflicting functionality is generally only of concern at the point where it becomes visible at the interface of the component. Thus, some irrelevant computation inside the component is not of importance as long as the externally visible effects of it can be intercepted and handled accordingly. For instance, unproductive usage of resources should be within reasonable limits.

Missing functionality

A second type of conflict that may occur is where a product-line component fails to exhibit certain behaviour required for the correct operation of the product. For instance, in the case of the aforementioned communication protocol component, assume that it does not invoke an authorization component whereas the product requires this. Especially where the missing functionality should be inserted in between a number of units of functionality encapsulated in the component, this is hard to resolve.

There are two approaches to resolving this type of conflict, depending on the type of product-line component. If the component is white-box, i.e. intended to be extended with product-specific functionality, it may be possible to add product-specific behaviour to the component that affects the basic flow of control. If this is not possible, or if the component is intended to be used as a black-box component, the missing functionality needs to be implemented as an additional component that, in some way, needs to be connected to the product-line component. One can identify three ways of connecting to the product-line component, all requiring some form of message interception, such as wrapping. The product-specific component may intercept calls invoking the product-line component, perform the missing functionality and subsequently forward the call to the product-line component. Secondly, it may first forward the call, intercept the reply message and then perform the missing functionality. Finally, it may intercept a call by the product-line component to some other component, and perform the additional functionality at that point.

It may simply not be possible to insert the missing functionality in the product-line component in a satisfactory manner. If this is the case, the product-line component needs to be extended with this functionality in such a way that it can be excluded easily by other members of the software product line. Generally, this requires some effort since another organizational unit may be responsible for product-line components. Finally, if it is decided that it is not desirable to extend the product-line component with the functionality needed by the product, it may be necessary to implement a product-specific version of the component.

Conflicting quality attributes
Similar to conflicting functionality, the product architecture may contain inconsistencies due to conflicting quality attributes. In this case, the product-line architecture needs to be transformed to limit the effects of one or more quality requirements which are in conflict with one or more quality requirements of the product. For instance, the product-line architecture may be optimized for flexibility, including run-time flexibility, whereas the product has real-time and reliability requirements. The flexibility of the product-line architecture complicates the validation of the product requirements.

Resolving the conflicts between quality requirements has been discussed extensively in the first part of the book. There the use of architecture transformations was proposed as a means of handling the conflicts. However, in this case the product-line components have already been developed and a major reorganization of the software architecture that affects the structure of and relations between the components will be very costly.

Thus, the conflicting quality requirements should be resolved by adding design elements to the architecture and by replacing existing connections by more complicated structures that intercept certain parts of the communication between components and thus allow the quality attributes of the software architecture to be adapted. For instance, in the aforementioned example, the interfaces of the components in the architecture where run-time flexibility is handled could be intercepted by product-specific components that refuse any run-time flexibility. As a consequence, the structure and behaviour of the product architecture is more rigid, allowing for easier validation of real-time and reliability requirements.

Missing quality attribute

Some quality attribute may not be supported by the software architecture of the product line, but needs to be incorporated in the software architecture for the product. Although there is no immediate conflicting quality attribute, this may, and often will, still cause a conflict because incorporating support for the quality attribute will generally require architecture transformations, perhaps even high-level transformations, which reorganize the architecture considerably and, consequently, the requirements on the components.

One would really prefer to avoid any reorganization of the product architecture, if possible. Especially when quality attributes such as performance and real-time behaviour cannot be fulfilled by the software architecture, other than by reorganizing the software architecture, it could be an option to use more resources in terms of CPU and memory. This allows one to use the software architecture and the components without any major adaptation, against the cost of additional resources. Even in products incorporating mechanical and hardware parts, often the economies of scale reward such decisions anyhow, as can be identified in a wide range of business domains, for instance, car manufacturers such as the Volkswagen company. However, one should be careful to consider all the effects of architecture transformation or using more resources, since indirect effects may be major and difficult to handle.

If, for some reason, it is not possible to incorporate the product-specific quality attribute by adapting elements other than the software architecture, the architecture must be subjected to one or more transformations. As mentioned, the main aim, at this point, should be to incorporate the quality requirement while changing as little of the existing architecture as possible. Thus, wherever the requirement can be achieved by extending rather than reorganizing the existing software architecture, this is preferable since it allows the use of the product-line components without (major) adaptation.

Finally, for each of the conflicts requiring a resolution, it is of eminent importance to minimize the effects on the software architecture. This allows one to maximize the number of product-line components that can be used without adaptation. In some cases, this may require that for one or a few components, product-specific versions are implemented and used, rather than the product-line versions, in order to be able to use product-line versions of the other components in the product architecture.

2.4   Architecture assessment

At this point, a software architecture for a member of the product line has been derived from the software architecture of the product line, and has been extended to cover the product-specific requirements and the conflicts have been resolved. However, during these different activities, a number of 'local optimization' activities have taken place that may have had implicit effects on the other requirements. Therefore, before proceeding to the next step, it is generally advisable to perform an assessment of the architecture to make sure that all requirements are still fulfilled. The process of performing assessment and techniques that can be used for assessment have been discussed in Part 1 of the book.

3   Product-line component selection and instantiation

Once the design of the software architecture for the product has been finalized, the next step is to select a component implementation for each architectural component. Wherever we can use a product-line component rather than developing a product-specific component, this is very much preferable due to the cost-effectiveness. However, there is a constant trade-off process between the limitations and disadvantages associated with using a product-line component and the cost, both for development and maintainability, of using a product-specific version.

This step can be divided into two main activities: selection of appropriate family components, and the instantiation of each component in the context of the product architecture. In the two sections below, these activities are discussed in more detail.

3.1   Selection

The product-line assets include a set of software components that contain functionality of the architectural components in the product-line architecture. Thus, for each of the architectural components there may be zero, one or more component implementations available that can be selected for use in the product architecture. Below, the behaviour in the case of each number of implementations is discussed in more detail.

■ **No implementations.** If, during architectural design, an architectural component is identified as being relevant for the family members, but the actual implementation of the component is product-specific, it may not be feasible to implement a component at the software product-line level that will exploit the commonality between the products. In that case, the software architects and engineers of the product-line assets may decide that although the component is identified and specified as part of the product-line architecture, no implementation will be provided. Each product in the family will, consequently, implement its own version of the component.

■ **One implementation.** At the other extreme, the functionality provided by the component is common for all members of the family and no or little variation between the family members is present. In that case, it is possible to capture the functionality in one component and use variability mechanisms, discussed in Chapter 10, to handle the variations in requirements between product-line members. This approach is, obviously, the preferred approach to providing component implementations for architectural components since it provides the highest level of reuse. In our presentation of the product-line approach, we have focused on this model.

■ **More implementations.** In certain cases, there is commonality between product-line members, but the variation in requirements is such that it is not feasible to incorporate all variations in a single component implementation. In our case studies, we have identified that, among other things, quality requirements may cause conflicts that cannot be integrated in a single component implementation. In those cases, multiple component implementations are available, servicing different subsets of the software product line. Although maintaining a single implementation is very much preferable over two or more implementations, it is sometimes necessary to accept the less ideal model for practical reasons. For instance, not using multiple implementations may require considerable additional resources from some products in the family, which would not make it possible to market these products at reasonable price/benefit ratios.

For the product that is under development, we select, where possible, component implementations for each of its architectural components. If no implementation is available, we are forced to develop a product-specific component implementation, as will be discussed in Section 4. If one implementation is available then, assuming that it matches the product requirements for this architectural component, the choice easy: we take what we can get. In the case of multiple available implementations, the case is the most complex. First, we need to select the component or components out of the set of implementations that has a sufficient match with the product requirements for this architectural component.

3.2 Instantiation

If it has been shown to be possible to select a suitable component implementation from the family assets for a particular architectural component, it must be instantiated in order to fit the product requirements. In this section, we discuss the instantiation of software product-line components. However, in earlier chapters, we have discussed the development of traditional components and of object-oriented frameworks. In each case, the work required for the instantiation can be very different both in type and in amount. In the simplest case, when the component has no configuration interface, only the required interfaces need to be bound to other product components. The most extensive forms of instantiation require the development of product-specific extensions to the component or the specification of component requirements in terms of a (visual) domain-specific language that is used by a generator to generate a component implementation unique to the product at hand. Below, a number of alternatives are discussed.

Traditional component

For the purposes of instantiation, we assume that a simple traditional component has one or more provided interfaces, which will be invoked by other components in the product, one or more required interfaces, which need to be bound to components that provide the required functionality, and one or more configuration interfaces, through which the behaviour exhibited by the component can, within certain boundaries, be changed or adapted to the product-specific context. One interesting aspect is that the configuration interface may have effects on the provided and required interfaces. Thus, changing the configuration of the component may add, remove or change certain provided and required interfaces.

The instantiation of a simple traditional component is concerned with the required and the configuration interfaces. To start with the latter, configuration interfaces address the aspects in which the behaviour of the component can be changed or adapted. The aspects can be rather diverse in nature, and a few common aspects that can be configured are discussed below.

■ **Optional behaviour.** As discussed during the derivation of the product architecture, a component may need to exhibit behaviour for some products but not for others. Thus, for a particular invocation on the component, it should be configurable whether the component needs to perform the behaviour or not. This is typical optional behaviour. Frequently, selecting optional behaviour has effects on the required interfaces. For instance, optional behaviour may require to store certain requests in a logging database. If that behaviour is selected, the set of required interfaces will be extended with a required interface towards a component with logging functionality. Alternatively, when deselecting the optional behaviour, the required interface for a logging component is removed from the required interfaces that need to be bound.

■ **Variant selection.** A second type of configuration is concerned with selecting among a number of variant behaviours that are part of the component. Each variant will affect the externally visible behaviour of the component and selecting a particular variant may have effects both on the provided and on the required interfaces. For instance, selecting the variant with minimal functionality may invalidate a provided interface or operations that are part of the provided interface. In addition, some variants may, as discussed for optional behaviour, have effects on the required interfaces as well.

■ **Quality attribute selection.** Although quality attributes generally have product-wide impact on the structure of the software architecture, several quality attributes also have component-level effects in terms of behaviour that the component needs to exhibit. For instance, a security quality requirement may require the encryption of communication between components because the components may be distributed. In those cases, the component needs to provide functionality for satisfying the quality attribute, i.e. encryption/decryption functionality, that is treated as earlier under the topic optional behaviour. Note that selecting behaviour for fulfilling a particular quality attribute will have, possibly considerable, effects on other quality attributes. For instance, activating the encryption/decryption functionality will have measurable effects on the performance of the product.

The security quality attribute example can even be used to illustrate another issue, i.e. quality attribute selection may have effects on the provided and the required interfaces. For instance, the encryption/decryption unit in a component requires to communicate with a key management component, responsible for key generation and distribution, where the public key of other components can be obtained. In addition, the key management component may need to invoke components, e.g. for distributing private keys.

To summarize, even instantiating simple traditional components may be less than straightforward, especially when the configuration interface allows for variation in the provided and required interfaces.

Object-oriented framework

In Chapter 11, the design of object-oriented frameworks as components in a product-line architecture was examined. We looked at four different models of framework usage, i.e. the product-specific extension model, the standard-specific extension model, the fine-grained extension model and the generator-based extension model. The latter model will be discussed in the next section, but the first three are discussed below.

■ **Product-specific extension model.** This model explicitly assumes that the product-line component is unable to cover the product-specific requirements completely and is prepared for being extended with product-specific code. Instantiation of this component thus requires the development of a product-specific extension to the product-line component. Whereas the required and provided interfaces of the component may be affected by the product-specific code, the primary issue of concern is the configuration interface. This interface is now more like a set of classes that are to be subclassed by the product-specific extension code rather than the setting of boolean variables that was discussed for the traditional component model.

In a way, one can view the development of product-specific extensions as analogous to the development of product-line components based on the product-family software architecture. In both cases, the design freedom is restricted considerably by the context in which the software assets are supposed to operate. The product-specific extension has to fulfil the requirements of the family component in terms of the behaviour of the added subclasses. Since the subclasses may, in principle, override any operation in the superclass interface, implicit conventions present in the framework are easily violated. Therefore, the configuration interface should be defined in terms of an extension interface that specifies what classes in the framework can (or even must) be subclassed and for what operations new implementations may or should be provided.

Particularly in the case where multiple family components are frameworks employing the product-specific extension model, the product-specific extensions may need to communicate with each other, thereby extending the provided and required interfaces of the components. Since this communication is an externally visible extension of the component, one should try to avoid this type of extension where possible and rely on available interfaces.

Finally, one should not underestimate the importance of a clear interface between the product-line component and the product-specific extensions. As we will discuss in the chapter on evolution, the product-line component will evolve and it is important to be able to easily track the effects of the evolution for the product-specific extension.

■ **Standard-specific extension model.** In this model, the component has an abstract part defining the commonalties between a set of competing standards and, for each standard, a standard-specific implementation. Since these standards generally are competing alternatives, only one standard is used in a particular product. Consequently, the configuration interface basically consists of selecting the standard to be incorporated in the product under design. This is a typical example of variant selection.

In some cases, it makes sense to provide support for multiple standards in one product. For instance, networked devices like those developed by Axis generally do support multiple communication protocols and, consequently, the component incorporates multiple implementations as well. This requires that the component contains functionality for selecting the appropriate standard implementation when it is invoked.

- **Fine-grained extension model.** The fine-grained extension model has two types of extensions: generic extensions and product-specific extensions. When this model is employed generally a deep domain understanding is present in the organization developing the component. Instantiating the component for the product basically consists of a combination of the two previously discussed models. The generic extensions are selected using the previously described mechanisms for variations and optional behaviour. However, for the product-specific extensions, zero, one or more extensions may need to be developed. Not all products may need extensions, but where necessary, the intention is to develop small, focused extensions that preferably can be reused in other products as well. These extensions can, again, be incorporated in the component during instantiation using the aforementioned mechanisms.

- **Code generator.** The fourth model of framework instantiation is referred to as the generator-based model. In that model, the framework contains the domain functionality that is instantiated by the generator using an input specification. However, the domain model does not have to be specified using an object-oriented framework. Several other approaches for capturing domain knowledge in an instantiatable manner can be used, including rule-based and other high-level representations. Independent of the domain knowledge representation, the code generator will simply generate a highly specialized component, i.e. incorporating the product requirements on the component (and only those).

The generated component will have provided and required interfaces, but generally no configuration interface. The provided and required interfaces need to be bound either at product definition, instantiation or run-time in order for the component to function according to its specifications. In cases where the generated component must be able to change its functionality during the operation of the product, the component will have a configuration interface that can be invoked.

4 Develop product-specific components

The software architecture for the product we are deriving from the family consists of architectural components, most of which, in the general case, could be implemented using software product-line components. However, during the derivation of the product architecture, the architecture may have been transformed and extended with architectural components for which no component implementation exists in the family. For those components, product-specific component implementations need to be developed that provide the required functionality with the required quality attributes.

In our experience, we have frequently identified situations where components that at first were designed just for one particular product, at a later stage were generalized because the component needed to be incorporated in new products of a product line. This is part of the normal evolution of a software product line where the development of a product-specific component is actually seen as an important contributing factor for adding new products to the product line that incorporate the, up to now, product-specific component as well. Since large parts of its functionality are already available, developing a new product can be performed against a relatively small effort, compared to developing the product independently of the product line.

The consequence of this observation must be that even product-specific components should be developed as reusable components. Typically, object-oriented frameworks form, in our experience, a suitable technology for implementing components that should be generalized at a later point. The intention is not to incorporate all kinds of potentially useful requirements, but rather to perform some 'feature planning' to determine where variation points and extensions to the functionality are likely to be added. The component can then be designed such that expected evolution can be incorporated against small effort. If the component is implemented with only its immediate context of use in mind and without considering potential future uses, it may not even be feasible to use this component as a base for evolution, requiring the software engineers to start from scratch.

We have discussed the development of reusable components in earlier chapters, so we will not further address this topic here.

5   Product integration

Throughout this part of the book, we have been concerned with topics and assets that have no direct relevance to the customer of the organization developing the product. At this point we have finally reached the stage where we put all the developed parts together, i.e. product integration. The product integration step consists of three activities, i.e. collecting the instantiated product components, wiring the connections and developing the product integration code. Each activity is discussed in more detail below.

5.1   Collecting components

In the previous sections, we have instantiated the product-line components that are to be included in the product and we have developed the product-specific components. In addition, we have collected the required and provided interfaces for each of the components and have made at least a preliminary investigation of whether the required interfaces for each component can be fulfilled by the other components in the architecture. At this point, we collect all components in a single location, e.g. a product directory hierarchy. At some point all the software needs to be compiled and linked and put together in a single delivery.

5.2 Wiring connections

The second step is to instantiate the connections between the components, i.e. to provide references to components so that the required interface of one component can be bound to the provided interface of another component. The representation of the connection in the code can vary substantially and is often dictated by the architectural style chosen for the product. Below, the connectors in a number of typical architectural styles are described.

Pipes-and-filters style

As the name of the style implies, the connectors are typically pipes, i.e. directed streams of typed data. Components, referred to as filters in this style, generally have clear connection points for pipes. Typical mismatches that occur using this style are concerned with the type of data that is transported through the pipe and with the protocol for sending more complex data representations. These mismatches can generally be addressed by developing a small intermediate component that addresses the mismatches and sees to it that the expectations from both components are fulfilled.

Message-based styles

A number of architectural styles assume a message-based communication between components. The message contains information about the receiver, the invoked operation, possibly the sender of the message and the data passed to the receiving component. Instantiating the connectors for this style is primarily concerned with providing components with required interfaces with references to matching provided interfaces. The primary mismatches that may occur include incompatible operation names, incompatible data object or component reference types and cases where a single required interface needs to be serviced by two provided interfaces. In addition, protocol mismatches, i.e. the order in which two or more operations need to be invoked, may occur. Since, especially at this point in development, we need to avoid changes to component internals, the mismatches need to be solved by inserting small converter components that resolve the identified mismatches.

Event-based styles

Highly flexible systems, in particular, may employ event-based communication between components. The primary difference between message and event-based communication is that the broadcaster of an event is unaware of the receiver of the event and that communication is asynchronous, i.e. there is no reply message. (For completeness, it should be mentioned that some message-based communication approaches implement asynchronous communication as well.) Instantiating connections is primarily concerned with indicating interest in events of certain types to either the publisher of the event or the event dispatcher. Typical mismatches are, similar to message-based communication, incompatible event names, data object types and reference types. Due to the loose coupling between components in event-based systems, generally fewer assumptions are made with respect to communication protocols, so mismatches with respect to this are less common. Resolving the mismatches is performed as discussed earlier for message-based styles.

Cross-style mismatches

In addition to intra-style mismatches, a second category of mismatches is concerned with incompatabilities between the architectural styles assumed by components. For instance, one component may assume a pipes-and-filters style whereas the second assumes event-based communication. In those cases, handling the mismatches may be less trivial since the conversion that is required exceeds the cases discussed earlier generally by an order of magnitude in complexity and effort. As for the other cases, intermediate converter components will be necessary to resolve the mismatches. In Garlan *et al.* (1995) the problems associated with the composition of components based on different styles are discussed for one case.

It should be noted that in the case of a software product line, cross-style mismatches should have been prevented by the software architecting team responsible for the overall architecture. However, when incorporating product-specific third-party components, these components may indeed be based on a different style than the product architecture derived from the product-line architecture. In such cases, cross-style mismatches may occur and need to be addressed.

5.3 Product integration code

During the previous activities, often some integration code will already have been developed to handle the mismatches between components. Now the overall code for integrating all functionality in the product needs to be written. Assuming that the communication between components has been resolved in the previous activity, the functionality that remains to be developed is primarily concerned with the run-time instantiation of components, the initialization of these components and, once that part has been finished during product start-up, the handling of events external to the product by forwarding them to the appropriate components and, vice versa, the handling of events generated internally that need to have externally visible effects. Each step is discussed in some more detail below.

Run-time component instantiation

The components in the product need to be instantiated when the product is activated. However, it may not be appropriate that all components just instantiate themselves in parallel because of the dependencies between the components. For instance, if a component X that depends on a component Y is finished with instantiation before component Y is done and invokes Y, the behaviour exhibited by Y may not be what X expects. In embedded products, the actual memory locations of the data sections of components may be relevant for correct component behaviour. These and other reasons require some control over the instantiation of components. Consequently, some boot procedure is required that handles this process. For instance, in layered architectures, components are typically instantiated starting at the lowest layer, progressing upwards until the top layer is reached.

Component initialization

Besides the instantiation of components, another activity that is required is the initialization of components. Initialization is concerned with setting relevant data in the component, including component references, device names, network addresses and several other types of semi-persistent data. The instantiation and initialization processes can be sequential or intermixed in the order of execution. Thus, the product can either instantiate and initialize one component at a time or first instantiate all components and then initialize the components. Especially in the case of circular dependencies and active components, i.e. components that employ one or more concurrent threads, the latter model is preferable because it provides a higher level of control.

Binding product interfaces

The product has at least one, but generally more interfaces to other products. Examples include the underlying software and hardware, and other software systems. Analogous to a component, also the product as the top level can be considered as having provided and required interfaces. These interfaces need to be bound to other systems. This was discussed in Chapter 10. However, the provided interface of the product needs to be bound internally to components that will respond when requests are received at the product interface. Similarly, events generated by components that need to have effects external to the product need to be bound to the interfaces of these external systems.

It should be noted that some architectures, e.g. the SPLICE model described in Boasson and de Jong (1997), do not allow individual components to communicate directly. Rather, there is a central data store, i.e. a blackboard, with which all components interact. This approach decreases the dependencies between the different components.

6 Validation

The topic of this book is not about testing, but rather about software architectures. However, testing is a necessary ingredient in the development of software products that is complicated by the presence of a product-line approach. For instance, when using the product-specific extension model, the primary difficulty lies in the fact that generally, for most parts of the product, the behaviour is partially defined by the product-line components and partially by product-specific extensions to those components. This complicates the testing of components during the development of product-line assets since components are not complete without product-specific extensions. In addition, even when testing an instantiated component for one product, the test results cannot be transferred to other products since the product-specific extension for other products will be different.

This leads to the unfortunate situation that whereas we have been able to capitalize on the commonality between the products in the family with respect to software development and evolution, it seems harder to achieve similar benefits for software testing. We define three types of testing, i.e. component test, product test and field test. Field testing cannot be optimized but has to be performed for, basically, every major release of any software systems.

Component and system testing are more likely candidates for exploiting the commonality between products in the family. The amount of component testing that can be performed during the development of the reusable assets depends on the amount of variability that can be provided by the component during instantiation. If the variability is limited to a small number of settings, the component can be tested completely during component development and no component testing is required once the component has been instantiated for use in a product. At the other extreme, product-specific code is added to the component and it is not even possible to use the component without an extension. Testing the component during development must then be performed against a reference extension that, on the one hand, focuses the testing effort on the component functionality but, on the other hand, allows for testing as many features of the component as possible.

One approach to component testing is to define a set of automated tests as part of component development that are used to test the component against the reference extension, but that can also be used by the teams instantiating the component. Those teams can then use the predefined test set, extend it with their own component instantiation-specific tests and benefit at least to some extent from the commonality between the products in the family.

Supporting system testing is, of course, complicated for the same reasons that complicate component testing, but to a larger extent. In order to perform system testing independent of a particular product in the family, a reference instantiation of the product-line architecture needs to be defined, as well as reference configurations and/or extensions of all components that are part of the reference product. In that case, for those features that are not affected by the specific products, testing can be performed. Similar to component testing, rather than having the ambition to perform all testing at the product-line level, a feasible approach is to define a set of test scenarios at the product-line level that can be reused and extended for testing individual products in the software product line.

7 Packaging and release

As a final step in the instantiation of a product based on the software product-line assets, the product needs to be packaged and released. The activities required to fulfil these two aspects depend, among others, on the type of product that is being released, i.e. a product including hardware and software or a pure software product. In addition, it is relevant to distinguish between software used for first-time installation and that for upgrading already fielded products.

For instance, in the case of Axis Communications, the software for upgrading network devices already sold can generally be freely downloaded from the Axis Web site. The installation software installs a new image on the flash memory that is part of the company's products. Since Axis sells products which include difficult-to-reproduce hardware, it has no concerns with illegal copying of the software. Instead, Axis views the free distribution of software versions to its devices as a service to its customers.

8 Conclusion

The instantiation of products based on the reusable assets in a software product line has been discussed in this chapter. The instantiation phase consists of seven steps. Each of the steps is briefly summarized below.

- **Requirement specification.** Even though the requirements of the product were specified during the design of the product-line architecture, due to organizational and time reasons, it is generally necessary to reiterate over the requirements.

- **Product architecture derivation.** The product architecture is derived from the product-line architecture. Activities during derivation include pruning unneeded parts, extending the architecture with product-specific features and resolving conflicts, either functionality or quality attribute related. Finally, an architecture assessment is often suitable to increase confidence that the architecture will fulfil its requirements.

■ **Product-line component selection and instantiation.** For each architectural component in the product architecture, a product-line component is, where possible, selected and instantiated. In case of multiple alternatives, the component providing the best match with the product requirements is selected.

■ **Development of product-specific components.** For those architectural components for which no suitable product-line component could be selected, a product-specific component needs to be developed. It is important to consider the potential future generalization of the component into a product-line component when new products may require the component functionality.

■ **Product integration.** To generate the final product software, the various components and other software need to be integrated. Activities in this step include collecting the components, wiring the connections, developing system integration code and binding system interfaces.

■ **Validation.** The product and its components need to be tested to make certain that the customer receives a product of agreed upon reliability. Component testing, especially, is complicated by the fact that components often consist of generic and product-specific code. This makes it difficult to extend the advantages of a software product-line approach to testing as well.

■ **Product packaging and release.** Finally, the product needs to be packaged and released. The actual tasks in this step depend on the type of system and whether it is software for new installation or for upgrading.

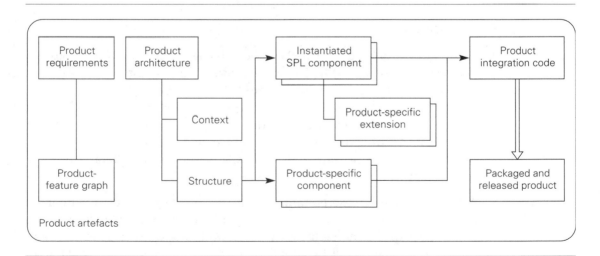

Figure 59   Artefacts generated during product instantiation

The product instantiation phase in the development of a software product line generates all the artefacts for a particular product, as shown in Fig. 59.

Finally, we have reached the point where all our efforts for developing the software product line have led to a concrete result, i.e. to a software product that can be shipped. Assuming that the problems were encountered in the process of adopting the product-line approach, the software product line can now start to generate return on investment!

CHAPTER 13

Evolving product-line assets

Although the development of software assets is an interesting and challenging activity, the true complexity of software development is often found in the evolution of the various assets. As reported in a number of publications, (see Piagoski (1996) for an overview), up to 80 per cent of the total cost of traditional software systems is spent in maintenance and as little as 20 per cent in the initial development of the system.

For software product lines, the evolution of the assets in the product line is more complex than for traditional software development, because most assets are relied upon by multiple software systems. Due to these dependencies and the fact that multiple organizational units are involved, it is difficult to maintain an overview of the status of the asset base. This easily leads to less than optimal management and use of the asset base.

In this chapter, the aim is to provide a panorama of the process of product-line evolution and to provide guidelines and techniques which can help in managing the process. To achieve this goal, we start, in the next section, by looking at the evolution of requirements and the relation between products in the product line and the reusable assets, i.e. the product-line architecture and shared software components. Then, in Sections 2 to 7, a number of different types of product-line evolution are discussed. Post-fielding and run-time evolution are discussed in Section 8. The chapter is concluded in Section 9.

1 Evolution in software product lines

The products in the software product line are used by customers. The use of the software product generally leads to new requirements. These new requirements emerge reactively, because the users require additional features, or proactively, since the marketing responsible for the product identifies new features that allow for new uses of the product or that will result in increased market share. This process occurs in parallel for all products in the product line. New requirements do no just originate from the customers, but may also result from evolution of the technology used by the software product, e.g. hardware and third-party components, new standards, etc.

Whenever new requirements emerge, the first decision that has to be taken is whether these requirements should be incorporated or whether the software product should not develop into the niche indicated by the new requirements. Once it is decided that we should incorporate the requirements, the second decision that needs to be taken is whether the requirements have, or should have, effects on the product line as a whole, or whether the effects can be restricted to the particular product at hand.

If the requirements are only relevant for the product at hand, incorporating the requirements is performed as part of the product-specific code and is similar to the ways of working in the traditional, one-system-at-a-time model. However, if we decide that these new requirements need to be incorporated in the product-line assets, several product-line assets may be affected. Changes to a shared asset will affect all products that incorporate the asset and new requirements need to be integrated carefully. One risk is that the extensions to, e.g., a software component are generally too product-specific and are not sufficiently generalized.

In Fig. 60, the evolution process, fuelled by the need to incorporate new requirements, is visualized.

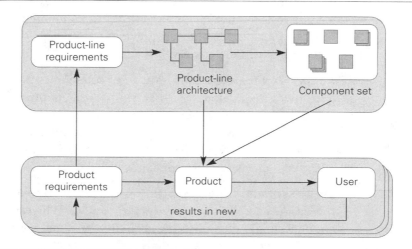

Figure 60   Requirement and product evolution in the product line

Above, we discussed the fact that the evolution of a software product line is initiated with the evolution of the requirements. These requirements can be divided into product-specific requirements and requirements on the software product line. The former can be handled as requirement evolution was handled earlier using the traditional approach, but within the latter category, we have found a number of categories of requirement evolution. Below, we present an introduction to these categories and briefly discuss the effect changes in each category can have on the product-line architecture and the product-line components. In the subsequent sections, we discuss each category in more detail.

■ **New product line.** When a new product line is introduced to the software product line, one is faced with the decision either to clone an existing product-line architecture, or to create a branch in a software product line. The decision is based on whether one can see possibilities for future commonalities that are desirable to exploit, or whether one foresees that the product lines will diverge from each other. In the former case, the decision is naturally to derive an architecture that, in much of its structure, is the same for all the product lines. In the latter case it is more suitable to split the product-line architecture into a new branch.

■ **Introduction of new product.** A new product differs from the previous members in the product line by supporting more functionality, or the same functionality in a different way. Examples that may cause this include different hardware platforms and different primary quality requirements. This is achieved by either adding a new product-specific component, changing an existing product-line component or by replacing a product-line component with a more general implementation. In some cases, the changes required are so vast that it is more cost-effective to simply rewrite the component from scratch, drawing from the experiences from the previous version, but designing to incorporate the new desired functionality.

■ **Adding new features.** This is the most common evolution of products, where the driving requirement is to keep up with the plethora of standards, user requirements, hardware advances, etc. that are available. For a product to keep its competitive edge, it must constantly raise the level of service provided to customers, and this is most easily done by supporting more functionality in addition to the existing functionality.

■ **Extend standards support.** This category is somewhat related to the former, in that the effect of the requirement is similar. Whereas adding new standards and functionality can be seen as evolution on a macro-level, to extend standard support is more on the micro level. For various reasons, it is often decided not to support a standard completely in the first release, but rather to support a subset of a standard. In subsequent releases of the product, it is a natural upgrade to extend the support until the entire standard is supported. To extend the standard support is most often concerned with changing an existing framework implementation, in order to incorporate the additional functionality.

- **New version of infrastructure.** It is not uncommon that a new version of the infrastructure, i.e. the underlying hardware and software that the product runs on, extends the support of functions. This is an example of what Lehman (1994) states: that functionality has a tendency to move from the perimeter of a product towards the centre, as the innermost layers extend and support more new functionality. To support the same requirement in two places, i.e. in the infrastructure and in the application, is not desirable, which leads to modifications in the applications to use the functionality available in the lower layers. In the extreme case, the frameworks in the interface layers will thus move from being complex processing units to become adaptors, simply forwarding the calls downwards. What this leads to is a decrease of the functionality provided by a framework implementation.

- **Improvement of quality attribute.** Basically, every type of quality attribute, as described by McCall (1994), will have a unique set of relations to the product-line architecture and the product-line components. For instance, a component implementation may need to be changed to meet more stringent performance requirements.

2 New product line

The first form of evolution that we discuss in this chapter is also the most extensive one, i.e. the introduction of a new product line based on an existing product line. This situation can occur due to a number of different circumstances. Below, we present a number of possible causes for initiating a new product line.

- **Variability too large.** A company may see an opportunity to release a set of software products on a new market or market segment based on its existing product line. However, the set of new products is different in at least one major aspect of the product behaviour. For instance, different hardware, operating system or user-interface mechanisms. In certain cases, the difference between the behaviour required by the new products is fundamentally different from the behaviour provided by the product line and the effect is that many or all components are affected by these new requirements. In that case, it may not be feasible to incorporate the requirements as variability in the components. Instead, it is required to implement specific versions of the components for the set of new products. This is a typical example of where variability requirements which are too large warrant the instantiation of a new product line.

- **Business reasons.** Particularly when products in the product line are incorporated into larger systems by the customers of the organization managing the software product line, business opportunities may occur that require the organization to initiate a new product line based on the existing one. For instance, when a new major customer is interested in incorporating a subset of the product line in its own product line, but it has strict deadlines and quality requirements, it may be wise from a business perspective to initiate a product line specific for the major customer and to, at least temporarily, accept the additional overhead and decreased reuse benefits that keeping the assets within a single product line would offer. In this case, it often is technically possible to manage the variability required by the new customer in the existing product line, but business reasons cause a new product line. At Axis Communications, this approach was taken when a new major customer was acquired with very demanding requirements regarding functionality, reliability and deadlines.

- **Incorporating independent products.** After either merging with or buying another company in the same market segment or by extending the scope of the software product line, it may be necessary to incorporate independent products into the product line. Since the products that are to be incorporated generally do not share the same architecture and components, converting these products at once may be very costly and not economically viable. In addition, these products may exhibit relevant features that currently are not included in the product line. A viable approach may then be to create a new product line within the existing product line that partially is based on the existing product line, but still maintains several of the assets of the (previously) independent product. This allows for gradual incorporation of the independent products into the product line and the evolutionary extension of the existing product line with features available in the independent (legacy) products.

- **Geographical distance.** A fourth possible reason for instantiating a new software product line is the geographical distance between the units maintaining the product line and the units maintaining a subset of the products in the product line. Due to the geographical distance, and associated communication problems resulting from, among others, different time zones, etc., it may be too complicated to maintain a highly integrated product line. A solution to this approach may then be to create a new product line within the existing product line. The new product line would use those components from the existing product line that contain no or little functionality that needs to be extended or amended with code specific for the products in the new product line. For the other components, the new product line would maintain its own versions.

■ **Cultural conflicts**. We have experienced situations at companies where the introduction of a software product line caused substantial cultural conflicts to surface between the various organizational units that were affected by the new product line. However, even when a product line is well established, problems of a non-technical nature may appear that require management to reconsider the product line approach. Often, due to reorganizations the organizational units working with product-line assets may obtain increasing levels of independence and, on occasion, the product line may restrict the agility of the individual units. For instance, one unit responsible for one product in the product line may identify an important, but tight market window for a new version of their product. However, this requires considerable adaptation of a number of components in the product line. The units responsible for the other products in the product line may not be interested to see these changes implemented in the product-line assets at the quick rate propagated by the unit that wants to exploit the market opportunity. In those cases, tension between that unit and the others will surface, causing a demand for increased independence. The unit may try to leave the product line, either officially or practically. In the latter case, it may develop product-specific versions of all but a few components. Also other scenarios may lead to cultural conflicts, such as the acquisition of companies with fundamentally different organizational cultures. When cultural conflicts appear, it is important that management takes these problems serious since failing to do so may serious cripple the progress of software development during the period of the conflict. One solution may be that the aforementioned organizational unit indeed may maintain its own version of the product-line assets for at least a limited amount of time.

The above reasons may require the introduction of a new software product line. One can identify two approaches which can be used to establish the new product line, i.e. cloning or specialization. These approaches are discussed in more detail below.

Cloning

In cases where local control and agility are the primary goals, the preferable approach is to clone the existing product line, i.e. literally to create an additional copy of all assets that are part of the product line. The organizational unit or units that demanded their own product line become responsible for the new copy of the product line. Generally, the first step is a pruning activity in which all components and architectural elements in the product line that are not necessary for the products supported by the involved unit or units are excluded from the new product line. Subsequently, often a redesign of the product-line architecture and an evolution of the software components to remove irrelevant requirements and to incorporate the new requirements is required. When deciding in favour of cloning the product line, the effort required to reorganize the new clone so that it fulfils the requirement is often underestimated. Therefore, it is generally advisable to prepare such decisions very well, since the benefits of product lines are substantial, but also somewhat subtle in that the main benefits are reaped during the evolution and the time-to-market of new products within the domain covered well by the product line.

Specialization

The second, less revolutionary, approach is to *specialize* the product line. Specialization, in this context, results in the creation of a new product line *within* the existing software product line. Analogous to object-oriented programming, the inheriting product line obtains all features and assets in the parent product line, but is able to override the existing features and assets and may extend the inherited features and assets with new functionality. If one understands that the products in the product line already exhibit a specialization relation with the product line, it is clear that a specialized product line typically is inserted in between the existing product line and a subset of the existing or new products in the product line. The specialization approach to creating new product lines is a highly viable way of working that maintains many of the advantages of a product-line approach. For instance, a typical type of evolution in hierarchical product lines is the upward movement of features in the product line, i.e. from products, to lower-level product lines up to the top-level product line.

The networked devices product line at Axis Communications is a typical example of a hierarchical product line, i.e. a hierarchy of specialized product lines. In Fig. 42 in Chapter 8, the device product line is presented graphically. At the top, a product-line architecture and a set of components are located which are shared by all products in the product line. Below that, for each organizational unit, a specialized product line is present, i.e. a specialized product line for the storage server, camera server and scanner server products. For the first specialized product line, there are again two subproduct lines, i.e. for read-only and for read-write file systems. Within each lowest-level specialized product line, a set of products has been developed and evolves constantly. These products are referred to as 'variants' within Axis.

3 Introduction of new product

The second type of evolution, and fortunately less demanding, is the introduction of a new product in the product line. The addition of a product to the product line can originate from a number of different causes. Some of the causes are discussed in more detail below.

■ **Market opportunity.** The first and most frequent reason for adding a new product to the product line is the identification of a market opportunity. The organization has identified that a certain segment in the market is not serviced by the existing product line and that there is a business case for entering the segment. Generally, the new product should exhibit much of the functionality already present in the product line, but there is one or a few features or aspects of the product that are new. A small-scale example is porting a product to a different platform, but more advanced examples exist as well. For instance, Axis had already a hard-drive-based network file server. Then it was identified that the product line could relatively easily be extended with a Jaz drive server product.

■ **Incorporate independent product.** A second scenario that leads to the extension of the product line with a product is when an independent product needs to be incorporated. One cause for adding a product is when the original decision with respect to scoping is changed by management. Management decides that a certain product should be incorporated in the product line, even if the initial decision was against incorporating the product. A second cause may be the acquisition of a company that develops a product that falls within the scope of the product line. In both cases, an existing product needs to be incorporated in the product line. It should be noted, however, that cultural conflicts, geographical boundaries and other factors may complicate the actual execution of the management decision.

■ **Extend product-line scope.** Finally, a typical scheme for adding new products to the product line is by extending the product line with products that are at the high end and at the low end of the products currently supported by the product line. The process often starts with the identification that the product line is able to support an additional product line member, if only a particular feature or feature set is added to the product line. For instance, Axis Communications has evolved its product line drastically over the years in this fashion. Initially developing printer servers, storage servers were a logical extension, as well as scanner servers and camera servers later on.

Especially this last type of adding products to the product line is frequently complicated by conflicting quality attributes. The current product line is optimized for a particular set of quality attributes, which is the result of a compromise. Since the compromise is often optimal for the products in the middle of the product line, adding products at the extremes, be it high end or low end, often requires that the software architects and engineers explicitly address the conflicts between the quality attributes in the product line and the quality requirements of the new product.

To incorporate a new product, a number of steps have to be performed. These steps are discussed in more detail below.

■ **Identify commonalities.** The first step must be to identify the commonalities between the product and product line. Since the decision has been taken to integrate the product in the product line, there must be considerable overlap between the two entities. Thus, using the feature set defined during the design of the product-line architecture, one can check for each feature whether the product implements or requires that feature as well. In the case where the feature is currently not incorporated in the product, it should be considered whether including the feature will have any negative effects for the product. If incorporating a feature in the product does not have any negative effects, but would require less variability from the components implemented in the product line, it may be beneficial to incorporate the feature.

- **Match product and product-line architectures.** Once the functionality required by the product has been identified, the software architecture for the product can be matched with the product-line architecture. Particularly when integrating an existing product, a compatible software architecture will simplify the integration process. In fact, if the software architectures are very dissimilar, it may be impossible to integrate the product. If the architectures are structurally similar, replacing product-specific components with product-line components can generally be performed at a relatively small effort. When instantiating a new product, the product architecture should be derived from the software architecture for the product line as described in Section 2 of Chapter 12.

- **Develop variation points for product-line components.** In general, an independent product that is incorporated in the product line will have variability and functionality requirements on the product-line components that are currently not supported. The components need to be extended with support for the new product as well. This can be achieved by extending the product with additional variation points that allow for the appropriate configuration of the component. If the product-specific requirements can be achieved using this approach, that is preferable. Otherwise, other approaches are required, as discussed below.

- **Develop/reengineer product-specific code.** Where the product-line assets do not facilitate the product requirements, it is necessary to implement product-specific code. This can be implemented by developing product-specific extensions to product-line components that support this, e.g. object-oriented frameworks. Alternatively, product-specific components should be developed that support the missing requirements.

In the case of an existing product being integrated in the product line, the functionality not provided by the product line is present in the code of the product. Assuming up-to-date documentation is available, the relevant parts of code need to be separated from the remaining product code. Otherwise, the existing code may need to be reverse engineered in order to document its structure. Subsequently, the parts have to be integrated into a software component and the provided, required and configuration interfaces should be specified. Finally, the component should be verified against the requirements.

- **Instantiate the product.** As the last step, the product should be instantiated based on the product-line assets and verified against the requirement specification for the product.

4 Adding new features

The third type of product-line evolution, again less dramatic than the previous type of evolution, is the inclusion of new features in the product-line assets. Typically, there exists an upward pressure in a product line in terms of the functionality in that features often are implemented first as product-specific code for a single product, then it is generalized for the most specialized product line in the hierarchy. This upward movement continues until the feature has reached the top-level product line.

Adding new features is, in our experience, the absolutely most common type of extension to the product line. The new features can originate from a wide variety of sources. Below, some typical sources of new features are discussed.

- **Market investigations.** Either passively or proactively through active research by the marketing department, demands for new features in the existing products generally appear constantly. These new features cover a wide spectrum. However, these features have in common that they originate from the perspective of the customer, i.e. the features satisfy an existing market, rather than creating a new one.

  For example, in the case of Axis Communications, the camera-server application was initially intended for individual pictures that were refreshed relatively infrequently. However, once the product was available on the market, several customers identified an interest in using the camera server for security purposes, but this requires that the camera takes pictures much more frequently than initially intended, i.e. typically every one to three seconds.

- **New technological opportunities.** With the advance of technology, new possibilities arise for products that were not available earlier. These possibilities should be exploited, but since there generally is not yet a market available for these new features, effort must be put into creating the market as well as developing products that exploit the new features.

  An illustrative example that is highly relevant at the time of writing is how the EPOC operating system developed by Symbian will exploit the opportunities of the next-generation communication standards, such as GPRS and Bluetooth.

These techniques offer the ability of being connected to the network continuously since billing is performed based on the amount of data that is transported rather than the connection time.

■ **Competitors.** Finally, a company can take the strategic decision to support a new feature throughout its product line because its competitors provide, or are expected to provide the particular feature. These features may neither be requested by its customers nor the result of technological progress, but may be necessary for maintaining or expanding market share.

The incorporation of new features in the product line is similar to traditional maintenance activities. However, one difference is that new features may not be relevant for all products in the product line, but only for a subset of the products. How such features should be incorporated is an issue that needs to be addressed explicitly by the architects and engineers working with the software product line. One of the potential problems is that extensions required to incorporate the new features may have negative effects on the products for which incorporating the new features is not relevant.

In each situation where new features are positive for one subset in the product line, but negative for the remaining products, the possibility of creating a hierarchical product line should be considered. That allows for incorporating the conflicting features in the products that need them while avoiding the negative effects for the remaining products. However, this is only feasible for features that are relatively modular in nature. For instance, quality requirements that have product-line-wide effects cannot be incorporated in this way without cloning the product line. The negative effects of the latter often outweigh other concerns and should be avoided where possible.

5 Extend standards support

As we saw in Section 1, in the first version of software products, standards are often not implemented completely, but only the part that is required for the correct operation of the product in normal modes. In addition, standards, although the name indicates stability, also evolve through the frequent release of new versions. This leads to the fourth type of product-line evolution, i.e. the extension of standard support by the products in the product line. In our work with companies, we have identified a number of types of standards that are typically implemented in an evolutionary fashion. Below, we discuss three types of standards in more detail.

■ **Network communication protocols.** These types of protocols are a typical example of standards that are extensive, evolve constantly and where the 80/20 rule applies, i.e. 80 per cent of the functionality defined in the protocol can be achieved by implementing 20 per cent of the standard. Axis Communications, in particular, has taken an evolutionary approach to supporting communication protocols in order to decrease time-to-market and staff requirements. In subsequent releases of their products, additional support for communication protocols has been provided. Axis has the advantage that its products can be updated by the customer even after acquisition by downloading new versions of the software and installing the version in the flash memory.

- **Component communication standards.** Component communication protocols such as Microsoft's COM, Sun Microsystems' JavaBeans and, especially, OMG's CORBA specify challenging amounts of details about the correct operation within their respective standard. However, for being able to operate as a component using the standard, in most cases only a limited subset of the standard is required. This allows for partial implementation in the first releases and the gradual extension of the support for the component communication standard(s).

- **File systems.** Even file systems, especially networked file systems, exhibit the property where only the core part of the functionality needs to be implemented for the product to be usable in a file-system context. For instance, in a networked file system, it is possible not to support references to other nodes. In that case, product can only be used as a leaf in the network, but for many types of products that may, at least initially, be satisfactory. For more advanced features, the file-system implementation will provide interfaces that return either error codes or other types of dummy replies.

Incorporating additional aspects of a standard is similar to the incorporation of new features, which was discussed in the previous section. We refer to the earlier sections for discussions on how to incorporate the new functionality. One difference is that standard support generally is less product-specific than features, although product lines exist in which the products distinguish themselves based on the supported standards. In addition, standards are generally well modularized and do not cause product-wide effects because of quality requirements. Consequently, there will be less tension between the products in the product line when incorporating extended standard support.

6   New version of infrastructure

The types of evolution that we have discussed up to now are primarily concerned with the incorporation of new functionality in the product line. The type of evolution discussed in this section is concerned with the opposite. In a number of cases we have identified the situation where a new version of the infrastructure, e.g.

hardware and operating systems, underlying the products in the product line implements functionality or behaviour that, up to that point, was implemented as part of the product line. In certain cases, it may be possible to ignore this fact and to continue to use the functionality as provided in the product-line assets. However, the disadvantage is that those maintaining the product-line assets remain responsible for the evolution of this functionality. In addition, the implementation provided in the infrastructure is often complete and up to date, whereas this is not necessarily the case for the implementation that is part of the product line.

Therefore, assuming the new version of the infrastructure incorporates relevant functionality, it is, in most cases and especially in the long term, preferable to make use of the functionality provided by the infrastructure and to remove the now redundant functionality from the product line. However, the disadvantage is that a potentially substantial amount of effort is required to incorporate the changes. Unlike the earlier types of evolution where functionality was added to the product line, the focus of the maintenance work is in this case not in the component providing the functionality, since this component is simply removed from the product-line asset base. Rather, all the clients of the component need to be changed in order to invoke the infrastructure interfaces instead of the original component.

Changes that affect all clients of a particular component illustrate the importance of separating the binding of required interfaces from the component specifying the interface. If the product-line architects have achieved a complete separation, then, in the simplest case, the only required change is to 'rewire' the required interfaces of the client components. However, in practice the interface provided by the infrastructure is not identical to the interface provided by the original component. In that case, either a proxy component can be introduced that converts the calls to match the infrastructure interface or all clients need to be changed in order to invoke the infrastructure appropriately.

The most complicated case is where the functionality provided by the new version of the infrastructure is not equivalent to a single component in the product, but is only part of a component or, even worse, is distributed over multiple components. In that case, the effort required to incorporate the additional infrastructure functionality is often substantial and most organizations will choose to proceed in an evolutionary manner, i.e. incorporating the functionality over the course of a number of iterations.

Finally, we discuss three categories of infrastructure that may improve and affect the product line.

■ **Hardware.** Due to Moore's law, among others, one can recognize a constant evolution of the functionality provided by hardware devices, such as microprocessors, communication devices and application-specific devices such as ASICS. In product lines that do not depend on an operating system, but implement concurrency, new features for context switching provided in the microprocessor hardware will affect the handling of concurrency in the product line. In addition, in communication-oriented processors, the lower levels of communication protocols may be implemented in hardware, freeing the product-line functionality from that task.

■ **Operating system.** Operating systems such as Microsoft Windows and the various Unix variants, such as Linux, are evolving to become more and more component-based systems, i.e. the various parts in the operating system, such as memory management, thread and process management, device management, etc. are implemented as components rather than a single monolithic entity. The set of components that is considered to be part of the operating system is constantly increasing. For instance, one of the more recent additions is the support for Internet access, but also graphical user interfaces and network protocols are additions of the last decade for most operating systems. This development has effects on virtually all product lines that run on a commercial operating system.

■ **Third-party component.** Our third example may not indicate infrastructure in the traditional sense of the word, but many product lines incorporate a number of external components that provide important functionality for the product-line members. An example is a Web-server component that allows software products to be accessed through a Web browser. Several freeware and commercial Web-server components are available that can be incorporated in the product line. However, these Web-server components are constantly improving the supported functionality and easily touch on functionality that traditionally, for instance, was considered to be database management (DBMS) functionality, such as support for various types of querying mechanisms.

It should be noted that all elements in the context of the software product line, be it hardware, operating systems or third-party components, may change in undesirable ways that may strongly affect the products in the product line. Although the use of externally developed elements is generally preferable from a cost/benefit perspective, one should be aware of the increased risk level due to reduced scope of control.

7 Improvement of quality attributes

The final type of evolution that we discuss in this chapter is not concerned with the functionality provided by the product line, but rather with the quality attributes of the product-line members and of the assets in the product line. Typical examples are the demand for improved run-time quality attributes, such as performance and reliability, and design-time quality attributes, such as flexibility and variability. A typical scenario is that the developing organization is eager to minimize the time-to-market (or delivery) for the first version of the product and in the process, attributes such as the aforementioned are sacrificed. During later versions, these attributes need to be improved in order to satisfy the users of the product, who generally complain about the less than satisfactory product properties.

As we have discussed in the first part of the book, quality requirements frequently have archiecture-wide effects on the structure of the product. Consequently, in order to improve the quality attributes, changes with architectural impact may be necessary. However, at this point we have reached the stage where changes to the product-line architecture will have effects on the software components and products that are part of the product line, i.e. architecture transformations are immensely more expensive than during the initial design of the software architecture for the product line. This is exactly the reason for spending considerable effort during the initial architectural design since all decisions taken during that stage will be very costly to revoke once the assets that are based on it are constructed.

However, although many cases exist where architectural changes cannot be avoided, there are several techniques available that are more local in their nature and that may improve the relevant quality attributes at least to a reasonable degree against a fraction of the cost of architecture redesign. We consider some examples of such techniques below.

■ **Cache.** One technique that has been used in a variety of situations is caching. By storing information in a redundant but quickly accessible form, the average delay when accessing information can be drastically decreased. Caches are typically used in microprocessors and as part of disk drivers, but also Web servers and a large variety of other applications have improved performance using a cache. The main disadvantage of using a cache is that it requires additional resources, generally memory, to improve the utilization of another resource, generally I/O bandwidth or CPU cycles. A second disadvantage is that, depending on the situation, e.g. read-only or read-write access to the information, the redundant representation can lead to inconsistencies. To avoid this, it is generally required that all access to the information is performed via the cache.

■ **Memory management.** A number of authors (e.g. Häggander and Lundberg, 1998) have indicated that especially in concurrent object-oriented applications running on parallel hardware, considerable amounts of the total computation (up to half) are spent on memory management, i.e. the allocation and de-allocation of objects. The introduction of an object pool where objects are returned after use and can be retrieved when needed has shown to increase performance drastically in those types of applications. In general, investigating the fundamental cause of performance bottlenecks and replacing some general-purpose functionality in the infrastructure with an application-specific solution can have enormous improvements in performance as a result.

- **Indirect calls.** One approach to increasing, especially run-time, flexibility is to insert a level of indirection in the communication between the components in the product. By inserting such indirection, invocations can dynamically be redirected, which improves the possibilities for dynamic replacement of components, synchronization of behaviour and the insertion of additional behaviour where necessary. The disadvantage of this approach is, obviously, run-time overhead and additional initialization code.

- **Wrapper.** The incorporation of a quality attribute may require several components to change their behaviour, which is an expensive operation to perform. In those cases where the functionality can be added before or after an operation in the component is performed, e.g. encryption and decryption, the concept of a wrapper can be a useful mechanism to achieve this. Especially when multiple components need to be extended with identical behaviour, a wrapper is effective from a development perspective, since one instance of the wrapper can be created for each component. The primary disadvantage of using wrappers is that there often is a measurable associated performance penalty. For instance, Hölzle (1993) identifies that wrapping may lead to large amounts of glue code and serious performance degradation.

8 Post-fielding and run-time evolution

The main part of this chapter has been concerned with the evolution of products at the developing organization. Although this is definitely the most typical form of evolution, evolution of product functionality may also occur at later stages in the lifecycle of the software product. One can identify four types of evolution, discussed below.

- Traditional *post-fielding evolution* where, often complex, software systems are upgraded on site after they have been installed at the customer site. However, the system is stopped during the upgrade process and needs to be restarted afterwards.

- The second type of evolution is *run-time evolution* where the system is upgraded during its normal operation. This type of evolution can be further subdivided in two types, i.e. component replacement and architecture evolution. In the former case, the architecture is static and only components are replaced, whereas, in the latter case, the architecture itself can change dynamically and adapt itself to a changing system context. Of course, this involves dynamic component adaptation or replacement as well.

■ The third type of evolution, i.e. *remote evolution*, is in between the two former ones. The system is stopped before it is upgraded, but this process can be performed remotely, using e.g. Internet-based access. Especially during recent years, one can see a development towards the latter type of system maintenance service. The rationale for this is that, among other things, it decreases the travel expenses of technicians drastically.

■ The final type of evolution is *customer-managed evolution*, where the owner of the software system is responsible for performing the upgrading of the system. The developing organization is, obviously, responsible for distributing the upgrades, but is released from performing the actual upgrading process itself.

Except for the first type of evolution, i.e. on site, traditional post-fielding evolution, software products need to be prepared for handling evolution. Run-time evolution, for instance, requires that components can be replaced under operation, which raises all kinds of interesting questions, among others, about handling the data stored in the component and replacing the references that clients have to the old component with references to the new component. Remote evolution requires a network interface that allows the inspection and change of system structure and the components that make up that structure. Finally, customer-based evolution requires very reliable upgrade modules that are able to handle a wide variety of contexts and still successfully upgrade the product or, in the worst case, leave the product in its original shape.

9 Conclusion

The evolution of assets in the product line is where the main part of the effort will be spent. Although we have spent most of the pages of this book on the design of the product-line assets, the evolution of these assets is where we will spend most of our life. However, the importance of the initial design should not be underestimated since a good design that anticipates the evolution that occurs later on in the product-line lifecycle will reduce the efforts required to evolve the product-line assets considerably. This has several positive effects, among others, the increased competitiveness due to the fact that more staff can be concerned with new development and fewer staff are needed for maintaining the existing products.

In this chapter, we have discussed a number of evolution categories that may occur within a product line. Below, these categories are briefly summarized.

■ **New product line.** A number of situations may require the introduction of a new product line, such as a too large variability for products in a new segment, business reasons, e.g. an important customer whose needs must be satisfied at all cost, the need to incorporate existing products, geographical distance between units working with different products in the product line and cultural conflicts. Two approaches are available for introducing a new product line: cloning, i.e. creating a copy of the product-line assets, and specialization, i.e. organizing the new product line as a specialization of the existing product line.

■ **Introduction of new product.** The introduction of a new product in the product line is a rather typical type of evolution in a product line. This may occur for a number of reasons: market opportunity, incorporating an existing product and extending the scope of the product line. Incorporating a new or existing product requires the product-line architects and engineers to repeat many of the steps performed during the design of the product-line assets in order to integrate the requirements and features of the new product-line member.

■ **Adding new features.** New features are generally added constantly to the product-line members. Three origins for new features can be identified, i.e. market investigations, technology opportunities and competitor-driven features.

■ **Extend standards support.** Often only a subset of the functionality defined in a standard is implemented in the first version of products. During subsequent versions, additional aspects of the existing standards and support for newer versions of standards are incorporated. Examples of standards that often are handled in this way are network communication protocols, component communication standards and file systems.

■ **New version of infrastructure.** The infrastructure based on which the products in the product line are constructed evolves as well. This may cause the situation that functionality that was implemented in the product line is available in the next version of the infrastructure. Often, it is worthwhile to remove that functionality from the product-line assets and to rely on the infrastructure. We have discussed three examples of infrastructure evolution, i.e. hardware, operating systems and third-party components.

■ **Improvement of quality attribute.** Especially due to the tough time-to-market requirements that often exist when releasing product versions, quality attributes are sacrificed in earlier versions. When developing subsequent versions, these product qualities need to be improved. Frequently appearing examples are performance, reliability and flexibility. Some techniques for improving these attributes without reorganizing the product-line architecture are the use of a cache, domain-specific memory management, indirect calls and wrappers.

Finally, we discussed the increasing importance of post-fielding and run-time evolution of products. Although these types of evolution have been common in, especially, telecommunication systems, the class of systems that requires this is increasing constantly. It is important to find cost-effective but reliable solutions for upgrading products remotely. We discussed four models: traditional post-fielding evolution, run-time evolution, remote evolution and customer-managed evolution.

10 Further reading

Maintenance and evolution of software systems in general has been the subject of extensive study by the software maintenance research community. A useful reference from that domain is Pigoski (1996). In our research, we have studied the evolution of software assets in software product lines, e.g. Svahnberg and Bosch (1999) and Mattsson and Bosch (1999).

CHAPTER 14

Organizing for software product lines

In the earlier chapters in this book, we focused on the processes which surround software product-line-based development. These processes include the design of the software architecture for the product line, the development of the software components that are part of the product line, the derivation of software products and the evolution of the aforementioned assets. However, we have not discussed the organizational structure of companies that is needed for the successful execution of these processes. It is, nevertheless, necessary to impose a structure on the individuals that are involved in the product line.

In this chapter, we will discuss a number of organizational models that can be applied when adopting a software product line approach to software development. For each model, we describe in what situations the model is most applicable, the advantages and disadvantages of the model and an example of a company that employs the model. Below, we briefly introduce the models which will be discussed in the remainder of the chapter:

■ **Development department.** When all software development is concentrated in a single development department, no organizational specialization exists with either the product-line assets or the products in the product line. Instead, the staff at the department is considered to be resource that can be assigned to a variety of projects, including domain engineering projects to develop and evolve the reusable assets that make up the product line.

■ **Business units.** The second type of organizational model employs a specialization around the type of products. Each business unit is responsible for one or a subset of the products in the product line. The business units share the product-line assets and evolution of these assets is performed by the unit that needs to incorporate new functionality in one of the assets to fulfil the requirements of the product or products it is responsible for. On occasion, business units may initiate domain engineering projects either to develop new shared assets or to perform major reorganizations of existing assets.

■ **Domain engineering unit.** This model is the suggested organization for software product lines as presented in the traditional literature, (e.g. Dikel *et al.*, 1997 and Macala *et al.*, 1996). In this model, the domain engineering unit is responsible for the design, development and evolution of the reusable assets, i.e. the product-line architecture and shared components that make up the reusable part of the product line. In addition, business units, often referred to as product engineering units, are responsible for developing and evolving the products based on the product-line assets.

■ **Hierarchical domain engineering units.** In cases where a hierarchical product line has been necessary, also a hierarchy of domain units may be required. In this case, often terms such as 'platforms' are used to refer to the top-level product line. The domain engineering units that work with specialized product lines use the top-level product-line assets as a basis upon which to found their own product line.

Some factors that influence the organizational model, but which we have not mentioned include the physical location of the staff involved in the software product line, the project management maturity, the organizational culture and the type of products. In addition to the size of the product line in terms of the number of products and product variants and the number of staff members, these factors are important for choosing the optimal model.

The remainder of this chapter is organized as follows. In Sections 1 to 4, the four aforementioned organizational models are discussed in more detail. Section 5 discusses the aforementioned factors and their effects on selecting the optimal organizational model. Finally, the chapter is concluded in Section 6.

1 Development department

The development department model imposes no permanent organizational structures on the architects and engineers who are involved in the product line. All staff members can, in principle, be assigned to work with any type of asset within the product line. Typically, work is organized in projects that dynamically organize staff members in temporary networks. These projects can be categorized into domain engineering projects and application (or product) engineering projects. In the former, the goal of the project is the development of a new resuable asset or a new version of a reusable asset, e.g. a software component. The goal is explicitly not a system or product that can be delivered to internal or external customers of the development department. The product engineering projects are concerned with developing a product, either a new product or a new version, that can be delivered to a customer. Occasionally, extensions to the reusable assets are required to fulfil the product requirements that are more generally applicable than just to the product under development. In that

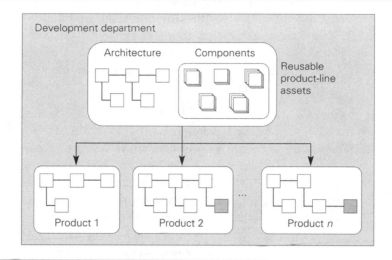

Figure 61   Development department model

case, the result of the product engineering project may be a new version of one or more of the reusable assets, in addition to the deliverable product.

In Fig. 61, the development department model is presented graphically. Both the reusable product-line assets and the concrete products based on these assets are developed and maintained by a single organizational unit. The shaded boxes indicate product-specific components.

1.1 Applicability

The development department model is primarily applicable for relatively small organizations and for consultancy organizations, i.e. organizations that sell projects rather than products to their customers. Based on our experience, our impression is that this model works for up to around 30 software-related staff members in product-based organization. If the number of staff members exceeds 30, generally some kind of organizational restructuring is required anyhow, independent of the use of a product line.

1.2 Advantages and disadvantages

The development department model has, as most things in life, a number of advantages and disadvantages. The primary advantage is simplicity and ease of communication. Since all staff members are working within the same organizational context, are knowledgeable about all parts of the product line and have contact with the customers, the product line can be developed and evolved in a very efficient manner with little organizational and administrative overheads. A second advantage is that, assuming that a positive attitude towards reuse-based software development exists within the department, it is possible to adopt a product-line approach without changing the existing organization, which may simplify the adoption process.

The primary disadvantage of this approach is that it is not scalable. When the organization expands and reaches, e.g., around 30 staff members, it is necessary to reorganize and to create specialized units. A second disadvantage is that typically within organizations, staff members are, depending on the local culture, more interested in either domain engineering or product engineering, i.e. working with a particular type of engineering has a higher status in the informal organization. The danger is that the lower-status type of engineering is not performed properly. This may lead to highly general and flexible reusable components, but result in products that do not fulfil the required quality levels, or vice versa.

1.3 Example

A company that employs this organizational model is Securitas Larm. All its product development, i.e. hardware and software, is concentrated in a single development department. This department maintains a product line in the domain of fire-alarm systems, as described in Chapters 3 and 8. The department has an engineering workforce of about 25 people, so it fits our applicability requirement. In fact, up until a few years ago, development was organized in product business units. Each product unit was responsible for sales, marketing, installation and development of the product. However, development especially did not function well in this organizational form. Generally only up to five engineers worked with the product development, which was to few to create an effective development organization. Consequently, Securitas Larm decided to reorganize development into a single development department.

2 Business units

The second organizational model that we discuss here is organized around business units. Each business unit is responsible for the development and evolution of one or a few products in the product line. The product-line assets are shared by the business units. The evolution of shared assets is generally performed in a distributed manner, i.e. each business unit can extend the functionality in the shared assets, test it and make the newer version available to the other business units. The initial development of shared assets is generally performed through domain engineering projects. The project team consists of members from all or most business units. Generally, the business units most interested in the creation of e.g. a new software component put in the largest amount of effort to the domain engineering project, but all business units share, in principle, the responsibility for all product-line assets.

Depending on the number and size of the business units and the ratio of shared versus product-specific functionality in each product, we have identified three levels of maturity, especially with respect to the evolution of the shared assets: *unconstrained model*, *asset responsibles* and *mixed responsibility*.

Unconstrained model

In the unconstrained model, any business unit can extend the functionality of any shared component and make it available as a new version in the shared asset base. The business unit that performed the extension is also responsible for verifying that, where relevant, all existing functionality is untouched and that the new functionality performs according to specification. In addition, it needs to verify that the quality attributes are not affected beyond reasonable limits.

A typical problem that companies using this model suffer from is that, especially software components, are extended with too product-specific functionality. Either the functionality has not been generalized sufficiently or the functionality should have been implemented as product-specific code, but for internal reasons, e.g. implementation efficiency or product performance, the business unit decided to implement the functionality as part of the shared component.

These problems normally lead to the erosion or degradation of the component, i.e. it becomes, over time, harder and less cost-effective to use the shared component, rather than developing a product-specific version of the functionality. Some companies, e.g. Axis Communications, have performed component reengineering projects in which a team consisting of members from the business units using the component, reengineers the component and improves its features to acceptable levels. Failure to reengineer when necessary may lead to the situation where the product line exists on paper, but the business units develop and maintain product-specific versions of all or most components in the product line, which invalidates all advantages of a product-line approach, while maintaining some of the disadvantages.

Asset responsibles

Especially when the problems discussed above manifest themselves in increasing frequency and severity, the first step to address these problems is to introduce asset responsibles. An *asset responsible* (a software engineer responsible for a particular software asset) has the obligation to verify that the evolution of the asset is performed according to the best interest of the organization as a whole, rather than optimally from the perspective of a single business unit. The asset responsible is explicitly not responsible for the implementation of new requirements. This task is still performed by the business unit that requires the additional functionality. However, all evolution should occur with the asset responsible's consent and before the new version of the asset is made generally accessible, the asset responsible will verify through regression testing and other means that the other business units are at least not negatively affected by the evolution. Preferably, new requirements are implemented in such a fashion that even other business units can benefit from them. The asset responsible is often selected from the business unit that makes most extensive and advanced use of the component.

Although the asset responsible model, in theory at least, should avoid the problems associated with the unconstrained model, in practice it often remains hard for the asset responsible to control the evolution. One reason is that time-to-market requirements for business units often are prioritized by higher management, which may force the asset responsible to accept extensions and changes that do not fulfil the goals, e.g. too product-specific. A second reason is that, since the asset responsible does not perform the evolution himself or herself, it is not always trivial to verify that the new requirements were implemented by the business unit as agreed upon. The result of this is that components still erode over time, although generally at a lower pace than with the unconstrained model.

Mixed responsibility

Often, with increasing size of the product line, number of staff and business units, a point is reached where the organization still is unwilling to adopt the next model, i.e. domain engineering units, but wants to assign the responsibility for performing the evolution assets to a particular unit. In that case, the mixed responsibility model may be applied. In that case, each business unit is assigned the responsibility for one or more assets, in addition to the product(s) the unit is responsible for. The responsibility for a particular asset is generally assigned to the business unit that makes the most extensive and advanced use of the component. Consequently, most requests for changes and extensions will originate from within the business unit, which simplifies the management of asset evolution. The other business units, in this model, no longer have the authority to implement changes in the shared component. Instead, they need to issue requests to the business unit responsible for the component whenever an extension or change is required.

The main advantage of this approach is the increased control over the evolutionary process. However, two potential disadvantages exist. First, since the responsibility for implementing changes in the shared asset is not always located at the business unit that needs those changes, there are bound to be delays in the development of products that could have been avoided in the approaches described earlier. Second, each business unit has to divide its efforts between developing the next version of

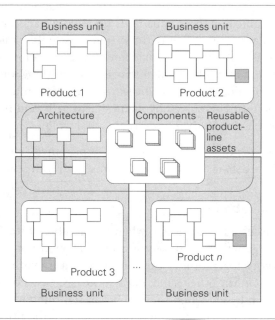

Figure 62   Business unit model

its product and of the component(s) it is responsible for. Particularly when other business units request changes, these may conflict with the ongoing activities within the business unit and the unit may prioritize its own goals over the goals of other business units. In addition, the business unit may extend the components it is responsible for in ways that are optimized for its own purposes, rather than for the organization as a whole. These developments may lead to conflicts between the business units and, in the worst case, the abolition of the product-line approach.

Conflicts

Orthogonal to the three levels of maturity above is the factor of conflict. The way a product line has come into existence is, in our experience, an important factor in the success or failure of a product line. If the business units already exists and develop their products independently and, at some point, the product-line approach is adopted because of management decisions, conflicts between the business units are rather likely because giving up freedom that one had up to that point in time is generally hard. If the business units exist, but the product line gradually evolves because of bottom-up, informal co-operation between staff in different business units, this is an excellent ground to build a product line upon. However, the danger exists that when co-operation is changed from optional to obligatory, tensions and conflicts appear anyhow. Finally, in some companies, business units appear through an organic growth of the company. When expanding the set of products developed and maintained by the company, at some point, a reorganization into business units is necessary. However, since the staff in those units earlier worked together and used the same assets, both the product line and co-operation over business units develop naturally and this culture often remains present long after the reorganization, especially when it is nurtured by management. Finally, conflicts and tensions between business units must be resolved by management early and proactively since they imply considerable risk for the success of the product line.

In Fig. 62, the business unit model is presented graphically. The reusable product-line assets are shared by the business units, both with respect to use as well as to evolution.

2.1 Applicability

As discussed in Section 1, when the number of staff members is low, e.g. below 30, the organization into business units is often not optimal since too few people are working together and the communication overheads over unit boundaries is too large. On the other hand, our hypothesis, based on a number of cases that we have studied, is that when the number of staff members exceeds 100, domain engineering units may become necessary to reduce the n-to-n communication between all business units to a one-to-n communication between the domain engineering unit and the product engineering units. Thus, with respect to staff numbers, we believe that the optimal range for the business unit model is between 30 and 100.

2.2 Advantages and disadvantages

The advantage of this model is that it allows for effective sharing of assets, i.e. software architectures and components, between a number of organizational units. The sharing is effective in terms of access to the assets, but in particular for the evolution of assets (especially true for the unconstrained and the asset-responsible approaches). In addition, the approach scales considerably better than the development department model, e.g. up to 100 engineers in the general case.

The main disadvantage is that, due to the natural focus of the business units on products, there is no entity or explicit incentive to focus on the shared assets. This is the underlying cause for the erosion of the architecture and components in the product line. The timely and reliable evolution of the shared assets relies on the organizational culture and the commitment and responsibility felt by the individuals working with the assets.

2.3 Example

Axis Communications employs the business unit model. Their storage-server, scanner-server and camera-server products are developed by three business units. These business units share a common product-line architecture and a set of more than ten object-oriented frameworks that may be extended with product-specific code where needed. Initially, Axis used the unconstrained model with relatively informal asset responsibles, but recently the role of asset responsibles has been formalized and they now have the right to refuse new versions of assets that do not fulfil generality, quality and compatibility requirements. The asset responsibles are taken from the business units that make the most extensive and advanced use of the associated assets. Within the organization, discussions are ongoing whether an independent domain engineering unit, alternatively, a mixed responsibility approach is needed to guarantee the proper evolution of assets. Whenever new assets or a major redesign of some existing asset is needed, Axis has used domain engineering projects, but 'disguised' these projects as product engineering projects by developing prototype products. The advantage of the latter is that the integration of the new asset with the existing assets is automatically verified as part of the domain engineering project.

3 Domain engineering unit

The third organizational model for software product lines is concerned with separating the development and evolution of shared asset from the development of concrete products. The former is performed by a, so-called, domain engineering unit, whereas the latter is performed by product engineering units. Product engineering units are sometimes referred to as application engineering units.

The domain engineering unit model is typically applicable for larger organizations, but requires considerable amounts of communication between the product engineering units, which are in frequent contact with the customers of their products, and the domain engineering unit, which has no direct contact with customers but needs a good understanding of the requirements that the product engineering units have. Thus, one can identify flows in two directions, i.e. the requirements flow from the product engineering units to the domain engineering unit, and the new versions of assets, i.e. the software architecture and the components of the product line, are distributed by the domain engineering unit to the product engineering units.

The domain engineering unit model exists in two alternatives, i.e. an approach where only a single domain engineering unit exists and, secondly, an approach where multiple domain engineering units exist. In the first case, the responsibility for the development and evolution of all shared assets, the software architecture and the components, is assigned to a single organizational unit. This unit is the sole contact point for the product engineering units that construct their products based on the shared assets.

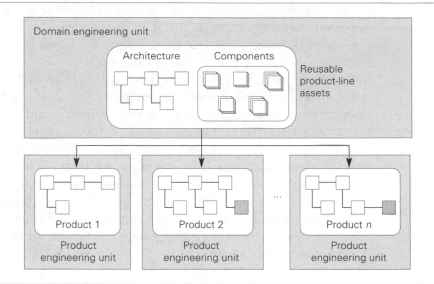

Figure 63   The domain engineering unit model

The second alternative employs multiple domain engineering units, i.e. one unit responsible for the design and evolution of the software architecture for the product line and, for each architectural component (or set of related components), a component engineering unit that manages the design and evolution of the components. Finally, the product engineering units are, also in this alternative, concerned with the development of products based on the assets. The main difference between the first and second alternative is that in the latter, the level of specialization is even higher and that product engineering units need to interact with multiple domain engineering units.

In Fig. 63, the organizational model for using a domain engineering unit is presented. The domain engineering unit is responsible for the software architecture and components of the product line, whereas the product engineering units are responsible for developing the products based on the shared assets.

3.1 Applicability

Especially smaller companies are very sceptical of domain engineering units. One of the concerns is that, just because domain engineering units are concerned with reusable assets, rather than products that are relevant for customers, these units may not be as focused on generating added value, but rather lose themselves in aesthetic, generic, but useless abstractions. However, based on our experience, our impression is that when the number of staff working within a product line exceeds around 100 software engineers, the amount of overheads in the communication between the business units causes a need for an organizational unit or units specialized in domain engineering.

Multiple domain engineering units rather than a single one become necessary when the size of the domain engineering unit becomes too large, e.g. 30 software engineers. In that case, it becomes necessary to create multiple groups that focus on different sets of component implementations within the product-line architecture. In some cases, although component engineering units exist, no explicit product-line software architecture unit is present. Rather, a small team of software architects from the component engineering units assumes the responsibility for the overall architecture.

Finally, at which point the complexities of a software product line even exceed the domain engineering unit approach is not obvious, but when the number of software engineers is in the hundreds the hierarchical domain engineering units model, discussed in the next section, may become preferable.

3.2 Advantages and disadvantages

Despite the scepticism in, especially, smaller organizations, the domain engineering unit model has a number of important advantages. First, as mentioned, it removes the need for n-to-n communication between the business units, and reduces it to one-to-n communication. Second, whereas business units may extend components with too product-specific extensions, the domain engineering unit is responsible for evolving the components such that the requirements of all products in the product line are satisfied. In addition, conflicts can be resolved in a more objective and compromise-oriented fashion. Finally, the domain engineering unit approach scales up to much larger numbers of software engineering staff than the aforementioned approaches.

Obviously, the model has some associated disadvantages as well. The foremost is the difficulty of managing the requirements flow towards the domain engineering unit, the balancing of conflicting requirements from different product engineering units and the subsequent implementation of the selected requirements in the next version of the assets. This causes delays in the implementation of new features in the shared assets, which, in turn, delays the time-to-market of products. This may be a major disadvantage of the domain engineering unit model since time-to-market is the primary goal of many software development organizations. To address this, the organization may allow product engineering units to, at least temporarily, create their own versions of shared assets by extending the existing version with product-specific features. This allows the product engineering unit to improve its time-to-market while it does not expose the other product engineering units to immature and instable components. The intention is generally to incorporate the product-specific extensions, in a generalized form, into the next shared version of the component.

3.3 Example

The domain engineering unit model is used by Symbian. The EPOC operating system consists of a set of components and the responsibility of a number of subsets is assigned to specialized organizational units. For each device family requirement definition (DFRD), a unit exists that composes and integrates versions of these components into a release of the complete EPOC operating system to the partners of Symbian. The release contains specific versions and instantiations of the various components for the particular DFRD. Some components are only included in one or a few of the DFRDs.

4 Hierarchical domain engineering units

As we discussed in the previous section, there is an upper boundary on the size of an effective domain engineering unit model. However, generally even before the maximum staff member size is reached, often already for technical reasons, an additional level has been introduced in the product line. This additional layer contains one or more specialized software product lines that, depending on their size and complexity can either be managed using the business unit model or may actually require a domain engineering unit.

In the case that a specialized product line requires a domain engineering unit, we have, in fact, instantiated the hierarchical domain engineering units model that is the topic of this section. This model is only suitable for a large or very large organization that has an extensive line of products. If, during the design or evolution of the product line, it becomes necessary to organize the product line in a hierarchical manner and a considerable number of staff members are involved in the product line, then it may be necessary to create specialized domain engineering units that develop and evolve the reusable assets for a subset of the products in the product line.

The reusable product-line assets at the top level are frequently referred to as a *platform* and not necessarily identified as part of the product line. We believe, however, that it is relevant to explicitly identify and benefit from the hierarchical nature of these assets. Traditionally, platforms are considered as means to provide shared functionality, but without imposing any architectural constraints. In practice, however, a platform does impose constraints and when considering the platform as the top-level product-line asset set, this is made more explicit and the designers of specialized product lines and product-line members will derive the software architecture rather than design it.

In Fig. 64, the hierarchical domain engineering units model is presented graphically. For a subset of the products in the product line, a domain engineering unit is present that develops and maintains the specialized product-line software architecture and the associated components. Only the components specific for the

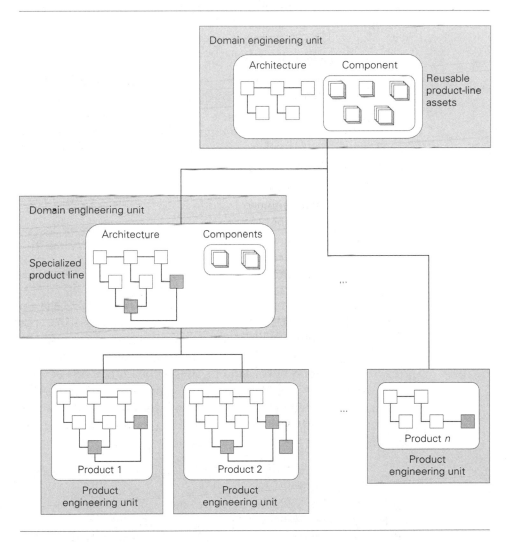

Figure 64 Hierarchical domain engineering unit model

product-line subset are the responsibility of the specialized domain engineering unit. All other components are inherited from the overall product-line asset base. The specialized domain engineering unit is also responsible for integrating the specialized with the general reusable assets.

4.1 Applicability

As mentioned in the introduction, the hierarchical domain units model becomes the preferred model when the number and variability of products in the product line is large or very large and considerable numbers of staff members, i.e. hundreds, are involved. Consequently, the model is primarily suitable in large organizations with long-lived products in the product line, since the effort and expense involved in building up this organizational model are substantial.

The complexities involved in the implementation and use of this organizational model are beyond the scope of this book, but a considerable maturity with respect to software development projects is required for this approach to succeed. This model is the fourth and most complex model that we discuss in this chapter. If the product line cannot be captured within this model, it is reasonable to assume that the scope of the product line has been set too wide.

4.2 Advantages and disadvantages

The advantages of this model include its ability to encompass large, complex product families and organize large numbers of engineers. None of the organizational models discussed earlier scales up to the hundreds of software engineers that can be organized using this model.

The disadvantages include the considerable overheads which the approach implies and the difficulty of achieving agile reactions to changed market requirements. For instance, in the case of a product part of a specialized product line that, in its turn, is part of the top-level product line, a change in a top-level component may take considerable amounts of synchronization effort. When this occurs, a delicate balance needs to be found between allowing product engineering units to act independently, including the temporary creation of product-specific versions of product-line components, versus capitalizing on the commonalities between products and requiring product engineering units to use shared versions of components.

4.3 Example

An example of an organization that has successfully adopted the hierarchical domain engineering units model is Nokia Mobile Phones. This company develops and maintains a wide variety of products in the wireless information devices domain, in particular mobile phones. The company has applied a product-line approach to its mobile phone development for several years. The software product line consists, at this point, of two levels. The top level, i.e. a 'platform', is developed and maintained by a top-level 'infrastructure' group, and consists of a product-line architecture and a set of components, which are shared by all mobile phone products and ported to different hardware platforms. For subsets of products in the product family, specialized groups exist that develop, especially, components specific to the family members in the subset. These domain engineering units have frequent contact and exchange considerable amounts of information, but are organized as independent units.

5 Influencing factors

Up to this point, we have presented the size of the product line and the engineering staff involved in the development and evolution of the product line as the primary factors in selecting the appropriate organizational model. Although, in our experience, the above factors indeed are the most prominent, several other factors exist that should be allowed to influence the selection decision as well. Below, we present some factors that we have identified in industry as relevant in this context.

5.1 Geographical distribution

Despite the emergence of a variety of technological solutions aiming at reducing the effects of geographical location, e.g. telephone, email, video conferencing and distributed document management, the physical location of the staff involved in the product line still plays a role. It simply is more difficult to maintain effective and efficient communication channels between teams that are in disparate locations and, perhaps even, time zones, than between teams that are co-located. Therefore, units that need to exchange information frequently should preferably be located closer to each other than units that can co-operate with less information.

For instance, geographical distribution of the teams developing the products in the product line may cause a company to select the domain engineering unit model because it focuses the communication between the domain engineering unit and each product engineering unit, rather than the n-to-n communication required when using the business unit model.

5.2 Project management maturity

The complexity of managing projects grows exponentially with the size of the project (in virtually any measure). Therefore, the introduction of a product-line approach requires, independent of the organizational model, a relatively high level of maturity with respect to project management. Projects need to be synchronized over organizational boundaries and activities in different projects may be depending on each other, which requires experience and proactivity in project management.

To give an example, incorporating new functionality in a product-line component at Axis Communications requires communication with the other business units at the start, during the actual execution and at the end of the project. At the start because it should be verified that no other business unit is currently including related or conflicting functionality. During the project, to verify that the included functionality and the way in which it is implemented are sufficiently general, and provide as much benefit as possible to the other business units. After the end of the project, to verify that the new version of the component provides backward compatibility to products developed by the other business units.

5.3 Organizational culture

The culture of an organization is often considered to be a hard to use concept, which is obviously the case. However, the attitude that each engineer has towards the tasks that he or she is assigned to do and the value patterns exhibited by the informal organizational groups have a major influence on the final outcome of any project. Thus, if a kind of 'hero' culture exists in which individual achievements are valued higher than group achievements, then this attitude can prove to be a serious inhibitor of a successful product-line approach that is highly dependent on a team culture that supports interdependence, trust and compromise.

For instance, at one company, which shall remain nameless, we discussed the introduction of a product-line approach. The company had extensive experience in the use of object-oriented frameworks and within each business unit reuse was widespread and accepted. However, when top management tried to implement product-line-based reuse, business unit managers revolted and the initiative was cancelled. The reason, it turned out, was that each business unit would have to sacrifice its lead architect(s) for a considerable amount of time during the development of the project. In addition, the conversion would delay several ongoing and planned projects. These two effects of adopting a product-line approach would, among other things, lead to highly negative effects on the bonuses received by, especially, business unit management. One explanation could be that these managers were selfish people who did not consider what was best for the company as a whole. However, our explanation is that top management had, over many years, created a culture in which business units were highly independent profit centres. This culture conflicted directly with the product-line approach which top management had tried to introduce.

Type of products

Finally, an important factor influencing the optimal organizational model, but also the scope and nature of the product line, is the type of products that make up the product line. Products whose requirements change frequently and drastically, e.g.

due to new technological possibilities, are substantially less suitable for large up-front investments that a wide scoped, hierarchical product-line approach may require, than products with relatively stable requirement sets and long lifetimes. Medical and telecommunication (server-side) products are typical products that have reasonably well understood functionality and that need to be maintained for at least a decade and often considerably longer.

For instance, in the introductory chapter of the second part of this book, we discussed the possibility for consultancy companies, which typically are project based, to adopt a product-line approach. Since subsequent projects often are in the same domain, the availability of a product-line architecture and a set of reusable components may substantially reduce lead time and development cost. However, the investment taken by such a company to develop these assets can never be in the same order as a product-based company with clear market predictions for new products. The consultancy company has a significantly higher risk that future projects will not be in exactly the same domain, but in an adjacent one, reducing the usefulness of the developed assets. Consequently, investment and risk always need to be balanced appropriately.

6 Conclusion

Although the processes involved in a product-line approach are the primary aspects, these processes still need to be assigned to organizational units. The structure or model of the organization developing and maintaining the product-line assets has been the topic of this chapter.

We have discussed four organizational models and discussed, based on our experiences, the applicability of the model, the advantages and disadvantages and an example of an organization that employs the particular model. Below, the four models are briefly summarized.

- **Development department.** In this model software development is concentrated in a single development department; no organizational specialization exists with either the product-line assets or the products in the product line. The model is especially suitable for smaller organizations. We have seen successful instances of this model up to 30 software engineers. The primary advantages are that it is simple and communication between staff members is easy, whereas the disadvantage is that the model does not scale to larger organizations.

- **Business units.** The second type of organizational model employs a specialization around the type of products in the form of business units. The business units share the product-line assets and evolution of these assets is performed by the unit that needs to incorporate new functionality in one of the assets to fulfil the requirements of the product or products it is responsible for. Three alternatives exist, i.e. the unconstrained model, the asset responsible model and the mixed responsibility model. The model is often used as the next model in growing organizations once the limits of the development department model are reached. Some of our industrial partners have successfully applied this model up to 100 software engineers. An advantage of the model is that it allows for effective sharing of assets between a set of organizational units. A disadvantage is that business units easily focus on the concrete products rather than on the reusable assets.

■ **Domain engineering unit.** In this model, the domain engineering unit is responsible for the design, development and evolution of the reusable assets, i.e. the software architecture and the components that make up the reusable part of the product line. In addition, product engineering units are responsible for developing and evolving the products built and based on the product-line assets. The two alternatives include the single domain engineering unit model and the multiple domain engineering units model. In the latter case, one unit is responsible for the product-line software architecture and others for the reusable software components. The model is widely scalable, from the boundaries where the business unit model reduces effectiveness up to several hundreds of software engineers. One advantage of this model is that it reduces communication from n-to-n in the business unit model to one-to-n between the domain engineering unit and the product engineering units. Second, the domain engineering unit focuses on developing general, reusable assets, which addresses one of the problems with the aforementioned model, i.e. too little focus on the reusable assets. One disadvantage is the difficulty of managing the requirements flow and the evolution of reusable assets in response to these new requirements. Since the domain engineering unit needs to balance the requirements of all product engineering units, this may negatively affect time-to-market for individual product engineering units.

■ **Hierarchical domain engineering units.** In cases where a hierarchical product line has been necessary, also a hierarchy of domain units may be required. The domain engineering units that work with specialized product lines use the top-level product-line assets as a basis upon which to found their own product lines. This model is applicable especially in large or very large organizations with a large variety of long-lived products. The advantage of this model is that it provides an organizational model for effectively organizing large numbers of software engineers. One disadvantage is the administrative cost that easily builds up, reducing the agility of the organization as a whole, which may affect competitiveness negatively.

Finally, we have discussed a number of factors that influence the organizational model that is optimal in a particular situation. These factors include geographical distribution, project management maturity, organizational culture and the type of products.

CHAPTER 15

Industrial experiences

We have presented a complete and integrated guide to the introduction and evolution of a software product-line-based approach to software development. The approach has been described using several case examples of companies described in Chapter 8, i.e. Axis Communications, Securitas Larm and Symbian. In this chapter, we describe the experiences of companies which have been using a software product-line approach for some time, in some cases more than five years. These experiences have been collected through case studies which we have carried out at Axis Communications and Securitas Larm, but also through our contacts with several other companies which employ a product-line approach.

We believe that the experiences we have collected are relevant in a wider context than just those organizations which were the subject of the case studies. The issues identified have been organized into three categories, i.e. organization, process and technology issues. The remainder of this chapter is organized according to this structure. The next section discusses organizational experiences and issues. Section 2 looks at process issues, and Section 3 discusses technological issues. The chapter is concluded in Section 4.

1 Organization

The adoption of a product-line approach to software development has implications on the business and organizational aspects of software development. In the previous chapter, we discussed a number of organizational models that can be applied, depending on the context in which the company operates. Below, a number of issues and experiences that are relevant to organizational and business units are discussed.

1.1 Background knowledge

Software engineers developing or maintaining products based on product-line assets require considerable knowledge of the rationale and concepts underlying the product line and the concrete structure of the reusable assets that are part of it. This is generally true for reuse-based software engineering, but, when using the product-line approach, the amount of required knowledge seems to be even larger. Rather than having knowledge of a component's interface, software engineers need to know about the architecture for which the asset was defined, the semantics of the behaviour of the component and the quality attributes for which the component was optimized.

For instance, new engineers starting at Axis generally require several months to get a, still superficial, overview of the product line and its assets. Only a few engineers in the organization have a deep understanding of the complete product line and it was identified that the learning process basically does not stop. Understanding the 'philosophy' behind the product-line architecture is important because new engineers should develop their software to comply with the architecture. Although architectural erosion can never be avoided completely, it should at least be minimized.

Today's software systems often are large and complex. Complexity of software is both due to the inherent complexity present in the problem domain and to less than optimal designs of software, resulting in, for example, insufficient modularization and interfaces between components which are too wide. Secondly, it is generally harder to understand abstractions than concrete entities. Thirdly, the lack of documentation and proven documentation techniques is another cause (see also Section 2.2). Finally, standard solutions, such as those available for compiler construction, are lacking in the domains in which Axis and Securitas are operating. If such standards are present, education programmes often incorporate these solutions, requiring considerably less effort for new engineers to understand the new systems, since they already have a context.

Although there are no solutions which solve this problem completely, some approaches will alleviate the problem. To begin with, a first-class, explicit representation of the product-line architecture and the architecture of the large assets should be available so that all software can be placed in a conceptual context. Second, all design and redesign of the product-line architecture and the assets should aim at minimizing the interfaces between components. Finally, although optimal documentation techniques are not available, using today's documentation techniques to provide solid documentation will be useful support.

A number of research issues can be identified. First, both for representations and for programming languages, one can identify a lack of support for high-level abstractions which capture the relevant aspects while leaving out unnecessary details. Secondly, the design and acceptance of standard solutions for domains should be stressed. It is not relevant whether the standard is formal or *de facto*, but whether it becomes part of computer science and software engineering education programmes. Finally, novel approaches to documentation are required as well as experimentation and evaluation of existing approaches to identify strengths and weaknesses.

1.2 Management support

The companies interviewed as well as other organizations that we have contact with indicate the difficulty of getting support for moving towards a product development model based on the product-line concept and away from the one-at-a-time mentality. The initial investment of a software product line will generally delay one or more products in their time-to-market, which often is considered a major problem, despite the expected future benefits. In addition, in the long term, a considerable part of the workforce will work on domain engineering rather than on engineering products, which gives an impression of ineffectiveness to non-technical folk.

To present an example, several projects in Securitas had the ambition of developing reusable assets as part of product development. As in most projects, these projects often had difficulty in keeping to their deadlines. Whenever this situation came up and a decision concerning the project had to be taken, it was decided to cancel the development of the reusable assets and focus on implementing the product functionality only. One cannot predict alternative futures, but it seems safe to assume that if Securitas had accepted a few delayed deadlines over the years, it would now have both had a larger base of reusable assets and more advanced products.

One can identify three main causes for this problem. First, senior management generally have limited technical understanding, making it difficult for them to see the benefits of a product-line-based approach. Second, the extreme focus on time-to-market does not allow for delayed deadlines that might pay off in later products. Finally, as discussed in Section 1.5 there is a lack of economic models that show the benefit of investment in product-line assets and associated documentation and tool support.

The limited technical understanding of senior management could perhaps be addressed by exposing managers more to the details and technical aspects of projects. Often, management especially does not appreciate the inherent complexities that surface with the growing size of software systems. Secondly, the development of a product-line architecture with associated software components is a strategic issue and decisions should be taken at the appropriate level. The consequences for the time-to-market of products under development should be balanced against the future returns.

The research issues relevant for this problem include, among others, the development of economic models for investment in product-line assets.

1.3 Domain engineering units

In the companies interviewed, the first instances of the reusable assets were generally developed as a separate project without an explicit product in mind. However, unlike the models described in Dikel *et al.* (1997), Macala *et al.* (1996), Jacobson *et al.* (1997), Bass *et al.* (1997) and Weiss and Lai (1999), the evolution of the assets was performed as part of product development. The explicit division between domain engineering and application engineering discussed by the aforementioned authors was not present in the companies interviewed.

The engineers interviewed were ambivalent about separate domain engineering units. The advantages of separate domain engineering units, such as being able to spend considerable time and effort on thorough designs of assets, were generally recognized. On the other hand, people felt that a domain engineering group could easily get lost in wonderfully high abstractions and highly reusable code that did not quite fulfil the requirements of the application engineers. In addition, having explicit groups for domain and application engineering requires a relatively large software development department consisting of at least several tens of people.

One can conclude that it is unclear if and, if so, in what cases an organization should have separate domain engineering units rather than performing asset development in the application engineering units. The availability of guidelines helping managers to decide on this would be highly beneficial. In the previous chapter, we formulated a number of guidelines which support the selection of the appropriate organizational model.

1.4 Time-to-market

Another important cause for the problems related to reusable assets at the companies interviewed is the time-to-market (TTM) pressure. Getting out new products and subsequent versions of existing products is very high on the priority list, thereby sacrificing other, often long-term, goals. The problem most companies are dealing with is that products appearing late on the market will lead to diminished market share or, in the worst case, to no market penetration at all. However, this all-or-nothing mentality leads to an extreme focus on short-term goals, while ignoring long-term goals. Sacrificing some time-to-market for one product may lead to considerable improvements for subsequent products, but this is generally not appreciated.

The TTM pressure is a primary cause of several of the problems discussed in this chapter. This is primarily because software engineers do not have the time to reorganize the assets to minimize dependencies or to generalize functionality. Asset evolution is often implemented as quick fixes, thereby decreasing the usability of the asset in future contexts.

To address the problems resulting from TTM pressure, it is important for software development organizations to identify that the development of a product-line architecture with associated assets is a strategic issue and decisions should be taken at the appropriate level. The consequences for the time-to-market of products under development should be balanced against the future returns. Finally, taking time out for asset redesign is necessary for a periodic 'clean up'.

Decisions related to TTM for products are based on a business case. Consequently, relevant research issues are outside the software engineering domain. However, two issues can be identified: the lack of economic models (described in the next section), and design techniques that minimize the effort required for extending assets without diminishing their future applicability.

1.5 Economic models

Reusable assets may represent investments up to several man-years of implementation effort. For most companies, such an asset represents a considerable amount of capital, but both engineers and management are not always aware of that. For instance, an increasing number of, especially implicit, dependencies between assets is a sign of accelerated ageing of software and, in effect, decreases the value of the assets. However, since no economic models are available that visualize the effects of quick fixes causing increased dependencies, it is hard to establish the economic losses of these dependencies versus the time-to-market requirements. In addition, reorganization of software assets that have been degrading for some time is often not performed, because no economic models are available to visualize the return on investment.

The lack of economic models influences several of the identified problems. In general, one can recognize a lack of forces against time-to-market pressure because no business case for sound engineering versus deadline-driven hacking of software can be presented.

2 Process

The second category of issues is formed by software process related topics. Although related to organizational issues, process issues are concerned with the flow of work activities, i.e. the dynamics, rather than the static division of the organization into units.

2.1 Information distribution

The software engineers constructing software based on or related to the product-line architecture need to be informed about new versions, extensions and other relevant information in order to function optimally. However, since so many people are involved in the process, it proves, in practice, to be very hard to organize the information distribution. If engineers are not properly informed, this may lead to several problems, such as double work, software depending on outdated interfaces, etc.

This problem was primarily identified at Axis Communications and it may be related to the organizational structure, i.e. the business units. Since potentially all business units may generate new versions of the reusable assets, software engineers have a hard time figuring out the functionality of the last version and the differences from the most recent version they worked with. Although information about an asset extension is publicized once the new version is available, during development other business units are unaware of it. This has led to conflicts on a number of occasions.

The problems associated with information distribution can be attributed to a number of causes. First, with increasing size and organization into business units, informal communications channels become clogged and more formalized communications channels are required. Secondly, a defined and enforced process for asset evolution is required so that software engineers know when to distribute and expect information. Thirdly, the business unit structure shifts focus from commonalities to differences between products, since software engineers only work with single-product categories instead of multiple ones. Finally, there are no visible differences between versions of assets, such as the unique interface identifiers in Microsoft COM (Szyperski, 1997) where an updated interface leads to a new interface identifier.

The companies interviewed do not use separate domain engineering units and are very hesitant about their usefulness. (See Section 1.3 for a detailed discussion.) However, instantiating separate organizational units responsible for reusable assets and their evolution would address several of the aforementioned causes. In either case, defining and, especially, enforcing explicit processes around asset evolution would solve some of the problems.

The primary research issue is concerned with the processes surrounding asset evolution. More case studies and experimentation are required to gather evidence of working and failing processes and mandatory and optional steps. A second research issue is the visibility of versions in software. As discussed in Szyperski (1997), although the strict Microsoft COM model has clear advantages in this respect, it does not fit traditional object models (since interfaces and objects are decoupled through a forwarding interface) and there are other disadvantages associated with the approach as well.

2.2 Documentation

Although most software is documented for maintenance purposes, documentation techniques explaining how to reuse software are still considerably less mature. (See Mattsson, (1996) for a detailed discussion.) This problem is complicated by the low priority of documentation of assets in most organizations and the backlog of most documentation, causing the software engineer to be uncertain about whether the documentation is valid for the latest version of the reusable asset. One interviewed software engineer suggested that executable code be required in the documentation so one would be able to check the correctness of a part of the documentation by compiling the associated example code.

At Axis Communications, both the protocol framework and the file-system framework have evolved considerably recently. One product, CD servers, a product in the category of storage servers, is still using an old version of the file-system framework. When investigating how to upgrade their software to use the latest version of all assets, they identified the aforementioned documentation problems.

First, documentation generally has a low priority compared to other tasks. This is reinforced by the availability of experienced engineers who know the assets well enough to answer questions which should be found in the documentation, but in many cases are not. Obviously, this approach, though it works in small development organizations, fails in larger departments. Secondly, because a documentation backlog exists, the most relevant version, i.e., the last one, is never documented. Finally, as mentioned in Section 1.1, a lack of appropriate documentation techniques for reusable assets is a known problem (Mattsson, 1996).

Defining documentation as an explicit part of the asset-evolution process, and not allowing engineers to proceed without delivering updated documentation might also alleviate the situation. Secondly, documentation as an activity has to be given a higher status, along with more support from management. Thirdly, several approaches to documenting reusable assets exist, such as example applications, recipes, cookbooks, pattern languages, interface and interaction contracts, design patterns, framework overviews and reference manuals. Despite their not being perfect, documentation using one or some of these techniques is certainly preferable to not documenting at all.

2.3 Effort estimation

Whereas the companies interviewed have obtained reasonable accuracy in effort estimation for software product development and maintenance, it has proved to be extremely hard to estimate the development of reusable assets, such as object-oriented frameworks. Among other causes, this is due to the abstract nature of the assets and the required higher levels of variability, consequently requiring iterative development. Although one iteration can be planned, it is very hard to predict the number of iterations that are required to sufficiently mature the asset.

The first version of the fire-alarm framework developed by Securitas took, despite the extensive domain knowledge of the engineers involved, several iterations before the most important abstractions were identified. Although each iteration could be planned, it was hard to know whether the framework would be sufficiently mature after a particular iteration. Maturity was very important since fire-alarm systems are highly critical systems that have to go through an extensive certification process.

The main cause of this problem is the fact that the requirements for a reusable asset are much less clear than for a concrete product. The asset should implement, at least, the common functionality of a software product line and provide sufficient configurability to include product-specific functionality. In addition, it should implement the superset of the quality requirements of the products in the software product line, since especially quality requirements are not always clear for the existing products and, obviously, are missing for future products. Thirdly, reusable assets are generally more abstract than products, and several authors (e.g., Johnson and Foote, 1988) have reported on the difficulty of developing reusable software. Finally, software engineers, being technical people, can easily get carried away in the design of reusable assets, trying to include more and more features in the design. We refer readers to Bosch (1998c) for a more extensive discussion of this issue.

The foremost solution approach is to collect and analyze the requirements of existing and especially future products in the software product line and, based on that analysis, identify conflicts and variations between products. We believe that clearer requirements lead to easier effort estimation and fewer design iterations. Secondly, staff requirements are much higher in design of reusable assets than in regular product development. Several authors (e.g. Macala *et al.* (1996) and Dikel *et al.* (1997)) report the importance of involving the most experienced engineers in these projects and warn against compromising on staff requirements.

A number of research issues can be identified. First, only very few design methods focus on design of reusable assets (e.g. Jacobson *et al.*, 1997) or on architectural design (e.g. Krasner and Pope (1988); Bosch and Molin (1999), Shlaer and Mellor (1997)). Although we have presented our approach to the design of product-line architectures, more research is still required to expand the body of knowledge. Second, effort estimation techniques generally do not incorporate variation points or variability in general. New techniques should be investigated in which these aspects are included.

2.4 When to split off products from the software product line

Another difficult issue to decide upon is when to separate a product from the software product line or when to merge a product with the product line. In the case of Axis, the printer server software was kept out of the network-server product line for three reasons, i.e., the printer server product contains considerable amounts of software specific to printer servers, traditionally the printer server software was written in C, whereas the product line software written in C++, i.e., a programming language mismatch, and, thirdly, the quality requirements for the printer server were different from the quality requirements for the other network products. In the printer server, code size was the primary requirement, with time-to-market as a secondary requirement, whereas in the other network server products, performance and time-to-market were both primary requirements. The difference in quality requirements called for a different organization of the software assets, optimizing their usability for the other network server products. Currently, however, there are discussions to merge the printer-server product software in the product-line assets.

Deciding to include or exclude a product in the software product line is a complex decision to make, involving many aspects. Guidelines or methods for making more objective decisions would be valuable to technical managers.

3 Technology

The final category of issues discussed in this chapter is related to the technology used to implement the product-line architecture, its reusable assets and the products built based on the product-line assets.

3.1 Multiple versions of assets

Product-line architectures have associated reusable assets that implement the functionality of architectural components. As discussed in the previous section, these assets can be very large and contain up to a hundred KLOC or more. Consequently, these assets represent considerable investments, multiple man-years in certain cases. Therefore, it was surprising to identify that in some cases, the interviewed companies maintained multiple versions (implementations) of assets in parallel. One can identify at least four situations where multiple versions are introduced.

■ **Conflicting quality requirements.** The reusable assets that are part of the software product line are generally optimized for particular quality attributes, e.g., performance or code size. Different products in the product line, even though they require the same functionality, may have conflicting quality requirements. These requirements may have so high a priority that no single component can fulfil both. The reusability of the affected asset is then restricted to only one or a few of the products while other products require another implementation of the same functionality.

For example, at Axis Communications, the printer-server product was left out of the product-line architecture (although it can be considered to be a product line on its own with more than 20 major variations) because minimizing the binary code size is the driving quality attribute for the printer server whereas performance and time-to-market are the driving quality attributes for the other network-server products.

Our impression is that when products in the software product line are at different points in their lifecycle, then there is a tendency to have multiple versions of assets. This is because the driving quality attributes of a product tend to change during its lifecycle from feature and time-to-market driven to cost and efficiency driven (see also Bass *et al.*, 1997).

■ **Variability implemented through versions.** Certain types of variability are difficult to implement through configuration or compiler switches since the effect of a variation spreads out throughout the reusable asset. An example is different contexts, e.g., operating system, for an asset. Although it might be possible to implement all variability through, e.g., #ifdef statements, often it is decided to maintain two different versions.

The above example of the printer server can also be used here. The different versions of assets actually implement different variability selections.

■ **High-end versus low-end products.** The reusable asset should contain all functionality required by the products in the software product line, including the high-end products. The problem is that low-end products, generally requiring a restricted subset of the functionality, pay for the unused functionality in terms of code size and complex interfaces. Especially for embedded products where the hardware cost plays an important role in the product price, the software engineers may be forced to create a low-end, scaled-down version of the asset to minimize the overheads for low-end products.

Two versions of the file-system framework have been used in Axis in different products. The scanner and camera products used a scaled-down version of the file-system framework only implementing a memory-based pseudo file system, whereas the CD-Rom and Jaz drive products used the full-scale file system implementing a variety of file-system standards. The scanner and camera products had no interest in incorporating the complete asset since it required more memory than strictly necessary, leading to increased product cost.

■ **Business unit needs.** Especially in the organizational model used by Axis, where the business units are responsible for asset evolution, assets are sometimes extended with very product-specific code or code only tested for one of the products in the software product line. The problems caused by this led to a tendency within the affected business units to create their own copy of the asset and maintain it for their own product only. This minimizes the dependency on the shared product-line architecture and solves the problems in the short term, but in the long term it generally does not pay off. We have seen several instances of cases where business units had to rework considerable parts of their code to incorporate a new version of the evolved shared asset that contained functionality that also needed to be incorporated in their product.

The aforementioned file-system framework example is also an example of a situation where business unit needs caused two versions of an asset. At a later stage, the full-scale file-system framework had evolved and the scanner and camera products wanted to incorporate the additional functionality. In order to achieve that, the product-specific code of both products had to be reworked in order to incorporate the evolved file-system framework.

3.2 Dependencies between assets

Since the reusable assets are all part of a product-line architecture, they tend to have dependencies between them. Although dependencies between assets are necessary, assets often have dependencies that could have been avoided by another modularization of the product or a more careful asset design. From the examples at the companies studied, we learned that the initial design of assets generally defines a small set of required and explicitly defined dependencies. It is often during evolution of assets that unwanted dependencies are created. Addition of new functionality may require extension of more than one asset and in the process often dependencies are created between the involved assets to implement the functionality. These new dependencies could often have been avoided by another decomposition of the architecture and have a tendency to be implicit, in that their documentation is often minimal and the software engineer encounters the dependency late in the development process. Dependencies in general, but especially implicit dependencies, reduce the reusability of assets in different contexts, but also complicate the evolution of assets within the product line since each extension of one asset may affect multiple other assets. Based on our research at Axis and Securitas, we have identified three situations where new, often implicit, dependencies are introduced:

■ **Component decomposition.** With the development of the product-line architecture, generally the size of the reusable assets also increases. Companies often have some optimal size for an asset component, so that it can be maintained by a small team of engineers; it captures a logical piece of domain functionality, etc. With the increasing size of asset components, there is a point where a component needs to be split into two components. These two components initially have numerous relations to each other, but even after some redesign often several dependencies remain because the initial design did not modularize the behaviour captured by the two components. One could, naturally, redesign the functionality of the components completely to minimize the dependencies, but the required effort is generally not available in development organizations.

To give an example from Axis: at some point, it was decided that the file-system asset should be extended with functionality for authorization access. To implement this, it proved necessary to also extend the protocol asset with some functionality. This created a (another) dependency between the file-system and the protocol assets, making it harder to reuse them separately. Currently, the access functionality has been broken out of the file-system and protocol assets and defined as a separate asset, but some dependencies between the three assets remain.

■ **Extensions cover multiple assets.** Development of the product-line architecture is due to new functional requirements that need to be incorporated in the existing functionality. Often, the required extension to the product line covers more than one asset. During implementation of the extension, it is very natural to add dependencies between the affected assets since one is working on functionality that is perceived as one piece, even though it is divided over multiple assets.

The authorization access extension to the Axis product line again provides an excellent example. At first, the access functionality was added to the file-system and protocol assets. However, the protocol framework contained the protocol user classes that were needed by the access functionality in the file-system framework, leading to strong dependencies between the two frameworks. At a later stage, the authorization access was separated from the two assets and represented as a single asset, thereby decreasing the dependencies.

■ **Asset extension adds dependency.** As mentioned earlier, the initial design of a software architecture for the product line generally minimizes dependencies between its components. Evolution of an asset component may cause this component to require information from an earlier unrelated component. If this dependency had been known during the initial product-line architectural design, then the functionality would have been modularized differently and the dependency would have been avoided.

In the protocol framework in the Axis product-line architecture, most of the implemented protocols use a layered organization to process packets which are sent up and down the protocol layers. These communication packets are nested in that each lower-level protocol layer declares a new packet and adds the received packet as an argument. At some point, the implementation of new functionality required methods of the most encapsulated packet object to refer to data in one of the packets higher up in the encapsulation hierarchy, introducing a very unfortunate dependency between the two packets.

3.3 Assets in new contexts

Since assets represent considerable investments, the ambition is to use assets in as many products and domains as possible. However, the new context differs in one or more aspects from the old context, causing a need for the asset to be changed in order to fit. Two main issues in the use of assets in a new context can be identified: mixed behaviour and design for required variability.

Mixed behaviour

An asset is developed for a particular domain, product category, operating context and set of driving quality requirements. Consequently, it often proves to be hard to apply the asset in different domains, products or operating contexts. The design of assets often hardwires design decisions concerning these aspects unless the type of variability is known and required at design time.

The main asset for Securitas is the highly successful fire-alarm system. In the near future, Securitas intends to develop a similar asset for the domain of intruder-alarm systems. Since the domains have many aspects in common, their intention is to reuse the fire-alarm asset and apply it to the intruder alarm domain, rather than developing the asset from scratch. However, initial investigations show that the domain change for the asset is not a trivial endeavour either.

Design for required variability

It is recommended best practice that reusable assets are designed to support only the variability requested in the initial requirement specification, (e.g. Jacobson *et al.*, 1997). However, a new context for a reusable asset often also requires new variability dimensions. One cannot expect that assets are designed including all possible forms of variability, but assets should be designed so that the introduction of new variability requires minimal effort.

The application of the fire-alarm framework in the intruder alarm domain can also be used here as an example. The fire-alarm and intruder-alarm systems share, to a large extent, the same operating context and quality requirements. Since the fire-alarm framework is designed for its domain and the intruder alarm domain has different requirements and concepts, one is forced to introduce variability for application domain functionality.

3.4 Tool support

The lack of tool support is a twofold issue. First, internally developed tool support requires, similar to the assets that are part of product-line architectures, an upfront investment. Because of the immediate negative effect on time-to-market of products that are currently under development, most software engineers reported that it was extremely hard to get support for tool development despite the obvious benefits. Second, both companies reported on the lack of commercial tools that were available on the market. Both develop embedded systems and even very general tools such as compilers and tools for testing were not commercially available (at least not in the required versions), causing them to either maintain proprietary tools or tool extensions or perform tasks manually that could relatively easily be automated.

For example, Securitas uses the C++ programming language because its main asset, the fire-alarm framework, extensively uses object-oriented concepts. The hardware used in fire-alarm systems contains a microprocessor for which no C++ compiler is available. Consequently, Securitas uses CFRONT for converting C++ code to C code, then a proprietary tool for making changes to the C code, then a commercial C compiler generating object code and finally a proprietary tool for rearranging the object code.

The mix of commercial and proprietary tool support described above is fairly typical. At Axis, and at other companies, we have seen similar cases. One of the causes seems to be that commercial tools generally are very much closed and users of a tool have no means to change its behaviour. A second possible cause is that either the market for such specialized tools for embedded systems is too small to make it economically viable for tool developers to develop such tools or that market mechanisms are not working optimally so that specialized tool developers are unable to get in contact with interested customers. Finally, the limited support for proprietary tool development is caused by the prioritization by management discussed earlier.

Neither the closed quality of commercial tools nor the market-related issues can be addressed by individual software development organizations. Proprietary tool development, on the other hand, is within the control of these organizations. Internal tool development should be seen as a strategic issue and treated as an investment. It is important to identify that tools generally automate tasks, allowing them to be performed by less qualified personnel thereby freeing experienced software engineers for other tasks. Considering the currently tight market for software engineers, this argument may be as important as the economic one.

Opening up tools is an important research issue that is investigated by researchers in CASE and other tools. However, these tools generally focus on general rather than embedded systems, which may have different requirements. In all, this remains a topic for further research.

3.5 Common feature core versus feature superset

An important decision that has to be taken is what to include in the product-line architecture and what to include in the product-specific and product-variation-specific code. Axis uses the more traditional commonality-based approach, where the product-line assets includes the functionality shared between the products and excludes the rest. Securitas, on the other hand, uses the 'feature superset' approach where the product-line assets encompasses the merged product functionality, thereby reducing each product to a subset of functionality provided by the product line. The advantage of the latter approach is that only a single code base has to be maintained and the products can be generated from this code base. However, this approach requires a very good understanding of the domain and the domain in itself should be rather stable. In addition, the included products should not contain functionality that conflicts with the other products. In sum, which approach to take is less than straightfoward and depends on the situation. However, the lack of decision models complicates things even further.

3.6 Early intertwining of functionality

The functionality of a reusable asset can be categorized into functionality related to the application domain, the quality attributes, the operating context and the product category. Although these different types of functionality are treated separately at design time, both in the design model and in the implementation they tend to be mixed. Because of that, it is generally hard to change one of the functionality categories without extensive reworking of the asset. The current state of practice and most authors on reusable software (e.g., Jacobson *et al.*, 1997) design for required variability only. That is, only the variability known at asset design time is incorporated into the asset. Since the requirements evolve constantly, requirement changes related to the domain, product category or context generally appear after design time. Consequently, it then often proves hard to apply the asset in the new environment.

The early intertwining of functionality is a primary cause of several of the problems discussed in the previous section. Multiple versions of assets are required because the different categories of functionality cannot be separated in the implementation and implemented through variability. Also, the use of an asset in a new context is complicated by the mixing of functionality.

Companies try to avoid mixed functionality primarily through design. For instance, the use of layers even in asset design separating operating-context-dependent from context-independent functionality avoids the mixing. Also, several design patterns (Gamma *et al.*, 1994, Buschmann *et al.*, 1996) support separation of different types of functionality and support the introduction of variability.

The primary research issue is to find approaches that allow for late composition of different types of functionality. Examples of this can be found in aspect-oriented programming (Kiczales *et al.*, 1997) and in the layered object model (Bosch, 1998a and 1998b). In addition, design solutions, such as design patterns, that successfully separate functionality should be a continuing topic of research.

3.7   Encapsulation boundaries and required interfaces

Although many of the issues surrounding product-line architectures are at the design level of software, there are language-specific issues as well. The lack of encapsulation boundaries that encapsulate reusable assets and enforce explicitly defined points of access through a narrow interface is a cause of a number of the identified problems. In Chapter 1, we discussed the difference between the academic and the industrial views on reusable assets. Some of the assets at the companies interviewed are large object-oriented frameworks with a complex internal structure. The traditional approach is to distinguish between interface classes and internal classes. The problem is that this approach lacks support from the programming language, requiring software engineers to adhere to conventions and policies. In practice, especially under strong time-to-market pressure, software engineers will access beyond the defined interface of assets, creating dependencies between assets that may easily break when the internal implementation of assets is changed. In addition, these dependencies tend to be undocumented or only minimally documented.

A related problem is the lack of *required interfaces*. Interface models generally describe the interface provided by a component, but not the interfaces it requires from other components for its correct operation. Since dependencies between components can be viewed as instances of bindings between required and provided interfaces, one can conclude it is hard to visualize dependencies if the necessary elements are missing. In Szyperski (1997) and Bosch (1998b) approaches to defining required interfaces are discussed.

The lack of encapsulation boundaries and required interfaces primarily causes problems related to component dependencies. For instance, component decomposition is complicated since the new sub-components can continue to refer to each other without explicit visibility.

As mentioned earlier, companies address these issues by establishing conventions and policies, but these tend to be broken in practice. Documentation of the assets and inspection of design documents, the implementation and the documentation of assets help to enforce the conventions and policies.

The primary research issue to address this cause is to find approaches to encapsulation boundaries that are more open than the black-box component models, but provide protection for the private entities that are part of the assets. Also, more research on the specification and semantics of required interfaces is needed. An example of an existing model is the layered object model where an 'acquaintance-based' approach is presented that allows for specifying required interfaces and binding these interfaces to other components (Bosch, 1998b).

4 Conclusion

In this chapter, the focus has been on the experiences of companies that have employed a product-line approach to software development and the issues that have been encountered by the staff at these organizations. These experiences and issues have been organized into organizational, process and technology issues.

Organizational topics that need to be addressed include, among others, the increased amount of required background knowledge by software engineers, the lack of management support for long-term goals, the questioned need for domain engineering units, the difficulty of selecting the appropriate organizational model, the time-to-market pressure against the quality of the reusable assets and the lack of economic models.

Process issues that were identified by the companies involved in the case studies include the importance and difficulty of information distribution between business units, the difficulties associated with maintaining up-to-date and accurate documentation, effort estimation problems, especially when designing reusable assets, and the scoping of the software product line.

Several issues related to technology were identified, including the need for multiple versions of reusable assets, the increasing number of implicit dependencies between components during evolution, the difficulty of using components in new contexts, the lack of appropriate tools support, feature scoping, early intertwining of functionality and the lack of encapsulation boundaries and required interfaces.

In sum, software product lines can be and are successfully applied in small and medium-sized enterprises, such as Axis Communications and Securitas Larm. These organizations are struggling with a number of difficult problems and challenging issues, but the general consensus is that a product-line approach is beneficial, if not crucial, for the continued success of the organizations interviewed.

References

Allen, R. and **Garlan, D.** (1997) 'The Wright Architectural Specification Language', Draft paper, CMU.

Alonso, A., Garcia-Valls, M. and **de la Puente, J.A.** (1998) 'Assessment of Timing Properties in Family Products' in van der Linden *Development and Evolution of Software Architectures for Product Families*.

Andert, G. (1994) *'Object Frameworks in the Taligent OS', Proceedings of Compcon 94.* Los Alamitos, CA: IEEE CS Press.

Apple Computer Inc. (1989) *MacAppII Programmer's Guide.*

Argyris, C., Putnam, R. and **Smith, D.** (1985) *Action Science: Concepts, methods, and skills for research and intervention.* San Fransisco: Jossey-Bass.

Barroça, L., Hall, J. and **Hall P.** (eds) (1999) *Software Architecture – Advances and Applications.* Springer.

Bass, L., Clements, P., Cohen, S., Northrop, L. and **Withey, J.** (1997) *Product Line Practice Workshop Report.* Technical Report CMU/SEI-97-TR-003. Software Engineering Institute.

Bass, L., Clements, P. and **Kazman, R.** (1998) *Software Architecture In Practice.* Addison-Wesley.

Beck, K. and **Cunningham, W.** (1989) 'A Laboratory for Teaching Object-Oriented Thinking', *OOPSLA'89 Conference Proceedings*, October.

Beck, K. and **Johnson, R.** (1994) 'Patterns Generate Architectures', *Proceedings of the 8th European Conference on Object-Oriented Programming*, Bologna, Italy.

Bengtsson, P.O. and **Bosch, J.** (1998) 'Scenario-based Architecture Reengineering', *Proceedings of the 5th International Conference on Software Reuse*, June.

Bengtsson, P.O. and **Bosch, J.** (1999a) 'Haemo Dialysis Software Architecture Design Experiences', *Proceedings of the 21st International Conference on Software Engineering* (ICSE'99).

Bengtsson, P.O. and **Bosch, J.** (1999b) 'Architecture Level Prediction of Software Maintenance', *The 3rd European Conference on Software Maintenance and Reengineering* (CSMR'99).

Bengtsson, P.O. and **Bosch, J.** (2000) 'An Experiment on Creating Scenario Profiles for Software Change', *Annals of Software Engineering*, Vol. 9.

Biggerstaff, T.J. and **Perlis**, A.J. (eds) (1989) *Software Reusability*, Vol. II. ACM Press.

Binns, P., **Englehart**, M., **Jackson**, M. and **Vestal**, S. (1994) *Domain-Specific Software Architectures for Guidance, Navigation and Control*. Honeywell Technical Report.

Boasson, M. and **de Jong**, E. (1997) 'Software Architecture for Large Embedded Systems', *Proceedings of Workshop on Middleware for Distributed Real-Time Software Systems*, San Francisco, December.

Boehm, B. (1996) 'Aids for Identifying Conflicts Among Quality Requirements', International Conference on Requirements Engineering (ICRE'96), Colorado, April, and *IEEE Software*, March.

Booch, G. (1994) *Object-Oriented Analysis and Design with Applications* 2nd edn. Benjamin/Cummings Publishing Co.

Bosch, J. (1998a) 'Design Patterns as Language Constructs', *Journal of Object-Oriented Programming*, 11 (2) pp. 18–32, May.

Bosch, J. (1998b) 'Object Acquaintance Selection and Binding', *Theory and Practice of Object Systems*, 4 (3), 151–68.

Bosch, J. (1999a) 'Product-Line Architectures in Industry: A Case Study', *Proceedings of the 21st International Conference of Software Engineering*, 544-54, May.

Bosch, J. (1999b) 'Superimposition: A Component Adaptation Technique', *Information and Software Technology*, No. 41, 257–73, April.

Bosch, J. (1999c) 'Design of an Object-Oriented Framework for Measurement Systems' in Fayad, M. *et al.* (eds) *Domain-Specific Application Framework*.

Bosch, J. (1999d) 'Designing Software Architectures through Evaluation and Transformation', in Barroca *et al.* *Software Architecture – Advances and Applications*.

Bosch, J. and **Molin**, P. (1999a) 'Software Architecture Design: Evaluation and Transformation', *Proceedings of the Engineering of Computer-Based Systems Conference*, August.

Bosch, J., **Szyperski**, C. and **Weck**, W. (1999b) *Proceedings of the Fourth International Workshop on Component-Oriented Programming*, Research Report 17/99, University of Karlskrona/Ronneby.

Brooks, F.P. (1995) *The Mythical Man-Month*: *Essays on Software Engineering*. Addison-Wesley Longman.

Buschmann, F., **Jäkel**, C., **Meunier**, R., **Rohnert**, H. and **Stahl**, M. (1996) *Pattern-Oriented Software Architecture – A System of Patterns*. John Wiley & Sons.

CEI/IEC 601-2 Safety Requirements Standard for Dialysis Machines.

Coplien, J.O. and **Schmidt**, D.C. (1995) *Pattern Languages of Program Design*. Addison-Wesley.

Cotter, S. and **Potel**, M. (1995) *Inside Taligent Technology*. Addison-Wesley.

Dagermo, P. and **Knuttson, J.** (1996) *Development of an Object-Oriented Framework for Vessel Control Systems*, Technical Report ESPRIT III/ESSI/DOVER Project, No. 10496.

DeBaud, J.M. and **Knauber, P.** (1998) 'Applying PuLSE for Software Product Line Development', *Proceedings of the European Reuse Workshop '98*, Madrid, November.

DeBaud, J.M. and **Schmid, K.** (1999) 'A Systematic Approach to Derive the Scope of Software Product-Lines', *Proceedings of ICSE'99*.

Deutsch, L.P. 'Design Reuse and Frameworks in the Smalltalk-80 system' in Biggerstaff, T.J. and Perlis, A.J. (eds) *Software Reusability*.

Dijkstra, E.W. (1996) A *Discipline of Programming*. Prentice Hall International.

Dikel, D., Kane, D., Ornburn, S., Loftus, W. and **Wilson, J.** 'Applying Software Product-Line Architecture', *IEEE Computer*, August, 49–55.

Fayad, M., Schmidt, D. and **Johnson, R.** (1999a) *Building Application Frameworks – Object-Oriented Foundations of Framework Design*. John Wiley & Sons.

Fayad, M., Schmidt, D. and **Johnson, R.** (eds) (1999b) *Domain-Specific Application Frameworks*. John Wiley & Sons.

Fenton, N.E. and **Pfleeger, S.L.** (1996) *Software Metrics – A Rigorous and Practical Approach*. 2nd edn. International Thomson Computer Press.

Gamma, E., Helm, R., Johnson, R. and **Vlissides, J.O.** (1994) *Design Patterns – Elements of Reusable Object-Oriented Software*. Addison-Wesley.

Garlan, D., Allen, R. and **Ockerbloom, J.** (1994) 'Exploiting Style in Architectural Design Environments', *Proceedings of SIGSOFT '94 Symposium on the Foundations of Software Engineering*, December.

Garlan, D., Allen, R. and **Ockerbloom, J.** (1995) 'Architectural Mismatch or why it's hard to build systems out of existing parts', *Proceedings of the Seventeenth International Conference on Software Engineering*, Seattle, WA, April.

Gilb, T. (1998) *Principles of Software Engineering Management*. Addison-Wesley.

Goldberg, A. and **Robson, D.** (1989) *Smalltalk-80 – The Language*. Addison-Wesley.

Gong, L. (1999) *Inside Java 2 Platform Security – Architecture, API Design and Implementation*. Addison-Wesley.

Grahn, H. and **Bosch, J.** (1998) 'Some Initial Performance Characteristics of Three Architectural Styles,' *Proceedings of the First International Workshop on Software and Performance (WOSP '98)*, pages 197–8, Santa Fe, NM October 12–16.

Häggander, D., Bengtsson, P.O., Lundberg, L. and **Bosch, J.** (1999) 'Maintainability Myth Causes Performance Problems in SMP Applications', *Proceedings of APSEC'99, the 6th Asian-Pacific Conference on Software Engineering*, Takamatsu, Japan, December.

Häggander, D. and **Lundberg, L.** (1998) 'Optimizing Dynamic Memory Management in a Multithreaded Application Executing on a Multiprocessor,' *Proceedings of ICPP'98, the 27th International Conference on Parallel Processing*, Minneapolis, August.

Häggander, D. and **Lundberg, L.** (1999) 'Memory Allocation Prevented Telecommunication Application to be Parallelized for Better Database Utilization', *Proceedings of the 6th International Austrailasian Conference on Parallel and Real-Time Systems*, Melbourne, Australia, November.

Henry, J.E. and **Cain, J.P.** (1997) 'A Quantitative Comparison of Perfective and Corrective Software Maintenance', *Journal of Software Maintenance: Research and Practice 9*, 281–97.

Hofmeister, C., Nord, R. and **Soni, D.** (1999) *Applied Software Architecture*. Addison-Wesley.

Hölzle, U. (1993) 'Integrating Independently-Developed Components in Object-Oriented Languages', *Proceedings ECOOP'93*.

Huni, H., Johnson, R. and **Engel, R.** (1995) 'A Framework for Network Protocol Software', *Proceedings of the 10th Conference on Object-Oriented Programming Systems, Languages and Applications Conference*, Austin, TX.

Jacobson, I., Booch, G. and **Rumbaugh, J.** (1998) *The Unified Software Development Process*. Addison-Wesley.

Jacobson, I., Christerson, M., Jonsson, P. and **Övergaard, G.** (1992) *Object-oriented software engineering. A use case approach*. Addison-Wesley.

Jacobson, I., Griss, M. and **Jönsson, P.** (1997) *Software Reuse – Architecture, Process and Organization for Business Success*. Addison-Wesley.

Java. URL: http://www.java.sun.com/

JavaBeans (1997) Sun Microsystems, JavaBeans 1.01 Specification. URL: http://www.javasoft.com/beans/docs/spec.html

Johnson, R.E. (1992) 'Documenting Frameworks with Patterns', *Proceedings of the 7th Conference on Object-Oriented Programming Systems, Languages and Applications*, Vancouver, Canada.

Johnson, R. and **Foote, B.** (1988) 'Designing Reusable Classes', *Journal of Object-Oriented Programming*, 1 (2), 22–5.

Johnson, R.E. and **Opdyke, W.F., Opdyke,** (1993) 'Refactoring and Aggregation', *Proceedings of ISOTAS'93: International Symposium on Object Technologies for Advanced Software*.

Johnson, R.E. and **Russo, V.F.** (1991) 'Reusing Object-Oriented Design', *Technical Report UIUCDCS 91-1696*. University of Illinois.

Jones, C.B. (1986) *Systematic Software Development using VDM*. Prentice Hall International.

Kang, K., Cohen, S., Hess, J., Novak, W. and **Peterson, A.** 'Feature-Oriented Domain Analysis (FODA) Feasibility Study', Technical Report, CMU/SEI-90-TR-021. Software Engineering Institute.

Karlsson, E.A. (ed.) (1995) *Software Reuse – a Holistic Approach*. John Wiley & Sons.

Kazman, R., Bass, L., Abowd, G. and **Webb, M.** (1994) 'SAAM: A Method for Analyzing the Properties of Software Architectures', *Proceedings of the 16th International Conference on Software Engineering.*

Kazman, R., Klein, M., Barbacci, M., Longstaff, T., Lipson, H. and **Carriere, J.** (1998) 'The Architecture Tradeoff Analysis Method', *Proceedings of ICECCS'98*, Monterey, CA, August.

Kiczales, G., Lamping, J., Mendhekar, A., Maeda, C., Lopes, C., Loingtier, J.M. and **Irwin, J.** (1997) 'Aspect-Oriented Programming', *Proceedings of ECOOP'97* (invited paper).

Kihl, M. and **Ströberg, P.** (1995) 'The Business Value of Software Development with Object-Oriented Frameworks', Master Thesis, Department of Computer Science and Business Administration, University of Karlskrona/Ronneby, Sweden, May (in Swedish).

Kotonya, G. and **Sommerville, I.** (1997) *Requirements Engineering – processes and techniques.* John Wiley & Sons.

Krasner, G.E. and **Pope, S.T.** (1998) 'A Cookbook for Using the Model-View-Controller User Interface Paradigm in Smalltalk-80', *Journal of Object-Oriented Programming*, 1 (3), August–September.

Kruchten, P.B. (1995) 'The 4+1 View Model of Architecture', *IEEE Software*, November 42–50.

Kruchten, P.B. (1999) *The Rational Unified Process: An Introduction.* Addison-Wesley.

Kruchten, P.B. and **Thompson, C.J.** (1994) 'An Object-Oriented, Distributed Architecture for Large-Scale Ada Systems', *Proceedings of the TRI-Ada '94 Conference*, November.

Lajoie, R. and **Keller, R.K.** 'Design and Reuse in Object-oriented Frameworks: Patterns, Contracts and Motifs in Concert', *Proceedings of the 62nd Congress of the Association Canadienne Française pour l'Avancement des Sciences*, Montreal, Canada, May.

Lehman, M.M. (1994) 'Software Evolution', in Marciniak, J.L. (ed.) *Encyclopedia of Software Engineering.*

Lieberman, H. (1986) 'Using Prototypical Objects to Implement Shared Behaviour in Object Oriented Systems', *Proceedings OOPSLA'86.*

Lim, W. (1996) 'Reuse Economics: A comparison of Seventeen Models and Directions for Future Research', *Proceedings of the International Conference on Software Reuse*, April.

Linton, M.A., Vlissides, J.M. and **Calder, P.R.** 'Composing User Interfaces with Interviews', *IEEE Computer*, 22 (2).

Liu, J.W.S. and **Ha, R.** (1995) 'Efficient Methods of Validating Timing Constraints,' in Son, S.H. (ed.) *Advanced in Real-Time Systems.*

Luckham, D.C., Kenney, J.J., Augustin, L.M., Vera, J., Bryan, D. and **Mann, W.** (1995) 'Specification and Analysis of System Architecture Using Rapide', *IEEE Transactions on Software Engineering*, Special Issue on Software Architecture, 21(4), 336–55.

Lundberg, L., Bosch, J., Häggander D. and **Bengtsson, P.O.** (1999) 'Quality Attributes in Software Architecture Design', *Proceedings of IASTED 3rd International Conference on Software Engineering and Applications*, October.

Lyu, M.R. (ed.) (1996) *Handbook of Software Reliability Engineering.* McGraw-Hill.

Macala, R.R., Stuckey, L.D. and **Gross, D.C.** (1996) 'Managing Domain-Specific Product-Line Development', *IEEE Software*, 57–67.

Marciniak, J.L. (ed.) (1994) *Encyclopedia of Software Engineering.* John Wiley & Sons.

Martin, R.C., Riehle, D. and **Buschmann, F.** *Pattern Languages of Program Design 3.* Addison-Wesley, 1998.

Mattsson, M.M. (1996) 'Object-Oriented Frameworks – a survey of methodological issues', Licentiate thesis, Department of Computer Science, Lund University, 1996.

Mattson, M.M. and Bosch, J. (1999) 'Stability Assessment for Evolving Object-Oriented Frameworks', *Journal of Software Maintenance*, 11 (7), March.

McCall, J.A. (1994) 'Quality Factors' in Marciniak, J.L. (ed.) *Encyclopedia of Software Engineering.*

McIlroy, M.D. 'Mass Produced Software Components' in **Naur, P.** and **Randell, B.** (eds) *Software Engineering, Report on A Conference Sponsored by the NATO Science Committee.*

Molin, P. and **Ohlsson, L.** (1998) 'Points & Deviations – A pattern language for fire alarm systems', *Pattern Languages of Program Design 3.* Addison-Wesley.

Molin, P. (1997) 'Towards Local Certifiability in Software Design', Licentiate Thesis, Lund University.

Moser, S. and **Nierstrasz, O.** (1996) 'The Effect of Object-Oriented Frameworks on Developer Productivity', *IEEE Computer*, September, 45–51.

Naur, P. and **Randell, B.** (eds) (1969) *Report on a Conference Sponsored by the NATO Science Committee 7–11 October 1968.* Garmisch, Germany: NATO Science Committee.

Neufelder, A.M. *Ensuring Software Reliability.* Marcel Dekker, Inc.

ObjectStore (1993) Documentation ObjectStore Release 3.0 for Unix Systems, December.

Ogden, W.F., Sitaraman, M., Weide, B.W. and **Zweben, S.H.** (1994) 'Part I: The RESOLVE Framework and Discipline – A Research Synopsis', *Software Engineering Notes* 19 (4), 23–8.

OMG. URL: http://www.omg.org

Opdyke, W.F. (1992) 'Refactoring Object-Oriented Frameworks', PhD thesis, University of Illinois at Urbana-Champaign.

Opdyke, W.F. and **Johnson, R.E.** (1993) 'Creating Abstract SuperClasses by Refactoring', *Proceedings of CSC'93: The ACM 1993 Computer Science Conference*, February.

Parnas, D.L. (1976) 'On the Design and Development of Program Families', *IEEE Transactions on Software Engineering*, Vol. SE-2, No. 1.

Perry, D.E. and **Wolf, A.L.** (1992) 'Foundations for the Study of Software Architecture', *Software Engineering Notes*, 17 (4), 40–52.

Poulin, J.S. (1997) *Measuring Software Reuse.* Addison-Wesley.

Pree, W. (1994) 'Meta Patterns – A means for capturing the essential of reusable object-oriented design', *Proceedings of the 8th European Conference on Object-Oriented Programming*, Bologna, Italy.

Prieto-díaz, R. and Arango, G. (1991) *Domain Analysis and Software Systems Modeling*. IEEE Computer Society Press.

The RAISE Method Group (1995) *The RAISE Development Method*. Prentice Hall.

Richardson, D.J. and Wolf, A.L. (1996) 'Software Testing at the Architectural Level', *Proceedings of the Second International Software Architecture Workshop*, San Francisco, CA, October.

Roberts, D. and Johnson, R. (1996) 'Evolving Frameworks: A Pattern Language for Developing Object-Oriented Frameworks', *Proceedings of the Third Conference on Pattern Languages and Programming*, Montecillio.

Rumbaugh, J., Blaha, M., Premerlani, W., Eddy, F. and Lorensen, W. (1991) *Object-oriented modeling and design*. Prentice Hall.

Russo, V.F. (1990) 'An Object-Oriented Operating System', PhD thesis, University of Illinois at Urbana-Champaign.

Samentinger, J. (1997) *Software Engineering with Reusable Components*. Springer Verlag.

Schäfer, S., Prieto-Díaz, J. and Matsumoto, M. (1994) *Software Reusability*. Ellis Horwood.

Shaw, M. and Clements, P. (1997) 'A Field Guide to Boxology: Preliminary Classification of Architectural Styles for Software Systems', *Proceedings of COMPSAC 97, First International Computer Software and Applications Conference*, August.

Shaw, M., DeLine, R., Klein, D.V., Ross, T.L., Young, D.M. and Zelesnik, G. (1995) 'Abstractions for software architecture and tools to support them', *IEEE Transactions on Software Engineering*, April.

Shaw, M. and Garlan, D. (1994) 'Characteristics of Higher-level Languages for Software Architecture', *CMU-CS-94-210*, December.

Shaw, M. and Garlan, D. (1996) *Software Architecture – Perspectives on an Emerging Discipline*. Prentice Hall.

Shlaer, S. and Mellor, S.J. (1997) 'Recursive Design of an Application-Independent Architecture', *IEEE Software*, January/February, 61–72.

Schmucker, K.J. (1986) *Object-Oriented Programming for the Macintosh*. Hayden Book Co.

Simos, M.A. (1997) 'Lateral Domains: Beyond Product-Line Thinking', *Proceedings Workshop on Institutionalizing Software Reuse (WISR-8)*.

Son, S.H. (ed.) (1995) *Advanced in Real-time System*. Prentice Hall.

Smith, C.U. (1990) *Performance Engineering of Software Systems*. Addison-Wesley.

Sparks, S., Benner, K. and Faris, C. (1996) 'Managing Object-Oriented Framework Reuse', *IEEE Computer*, September, 53–61.

Storey, N. (1996) *Safety-Critical Computer Systems*. Addison-Wesley.

Svahnberg, M. and Bosch, J. (1999) 'Evolution in Software Product Lines: Two Cases', *Journal of Software Maintenance*, 11 (6), 391–422.

Szyperski, C. (1997) *Component Software – Beyond Object-Oriented Programming*. Addison-Wesley.

Taligent (1995) *The Power of Frameworks*. Addison-Wesley.

Tanenbaum, A.S. (1988) *Computer Networks*. Prentice Hall.

TeleLarm (1996) Framework Design Document U00269.

Terry, A., Hayes-Roth, F. *et al.* (1994) 'Overview of Teknowledge's DSSA Program', *ACM SIGSOFT Software Engineering Notes*, October.

van der Linden, F. ed. (1998) 'Development and Evolution of Software Architectures for Product Families', *Proceedings of the Second International ESPRIT ARES Workshop, Las Palmas de Gran Canaria, Spain, LNCS 1429, Springer Verlag, February*.

van Gurp, V. and Bosch, J. (1999) 'Using Bayesian Belief Networks in Assessing Software Architectures', *Proceedings of the First BeNeLux Conference on the State-of-the-Art of ICT Architecture*, The Netherlands November.

Vlissides, J.M., Coplien, J.O. and Kerth, N.L. (1996) *Pattern Languages of Program Design 2*. Addison-Wesley.

Weck, W., Bosch, J. and Szyperski, C. (1997) 'Proceedings of the Second International Workshop on Component-Oriented Programming (WCOP'97)', *TUCS General Publication No. 5*, September 1997 Turku: Turku Center for Computer Science.

Weck, W., Bosch, J. and Szyperski, C. (1998) 'Proceedings of the Third International Workshop on Component-Oriented Programming (WCOP'98)', *TUCS General Publication No. 10*, September Turku: Turku Center for Computer Science.

Weinand, A., Gamma, E. and Marty, R. (1989) 'Design and Implementation of ET++, a Seamless Object-Oriented Application Framework', *Structured Programming*, 10 (2).

Weiss, D.M. and Lai, C.T.R. (1999) *Software Product-Line Engineering – A Family-Based Software Development Process*. Addison-Wesley.

Wilson, D.A. and Wilson, S.D. (1993) 'Writing Frameworks – Capturing Your Expertise About a Problem Domain', Tutorial notes, 8th Conference on Object-Oriented Programming Systems, Languages and Applications, Washington.

Wirfs-Brock, R., Wilkerson, B. and Wiener, L. (1990) *Designing Object-Oriented Software*. Prentice Hall.

Wirth, N. (1971) 'Program Development by Stepwise Refinement', *Communications of the ACM*, 14, 221–7.

Zhao, M., Wohlin, C., Ohlsson, N. and Xie, M. (1998) 'A Comparison between Software Design and Code Metrics for the Prediction of Software Fault Content', *Information and Software Technology*, 40, (14), 801–809.

Index

abstract factory pattern 38, 149–50
abstraction layers 62
academic perspective of architecture 11–12, 13–14, 239–40
ACID properties 137
actuators 46
ad-hoc architectural design 111–12
adaptation techniques *see* component adaptation
adaptive maintenance 43, 52
adding new features 284, 291–2, 299
aggregate relations 59
Allen, A. 59
Alonso, A. 102, 108
Althin Medical 49
Andert, G. 241
Apple Computer 49
application domains 218
application engineering 163, 164
application programming interface (API) 221, 239
application-level persistence 139
application-level schedulers 135–6
Arango, G. 33, 59
archetype identification 57–60, 69–70, 73–4
    aggregate relations 59
    bottom-up approach 58
    candidate archetypes 58–60
    conceptual integrity 59
    domain-analysis method 59
    generalization relations 59
    pipes-and-filters style 60
    recurring patterns 58, 60
    and subsystems 58
    top-down approach 58
archetype instantiations 63
architectural description language (ADL) 12
architectural patterns 38, 131–45
    concurrency 132–6
    distribution 140–2
    graphical user interfaces 142–4
    persistence 136–9
    quality attributes 132–44

rule 131
transactions 136–9
architectural styles 37–8, 116–30
    blackboard 122–4
    cross-style mismatches 276
    event-based 275–6
    implicit invocation 127–8
    layered 119–22
    merging of 115
    message-based 275
    object-oriented 125–7
    pipes and filters 117–19, 275
    wiring connections 275–6
architecture extension 262, 263–5
architecture pruning 262–3
architecture transformation 36–9, 109–58, 207–8
    categories of 110–11, 114
    conceptual integrity 111
    conflicts 208
    design patterns 38, 145–51
    distributing requirements 39, 154–5
    imposition of architectural patterns 131–45
    optionality 207–8
    process 112–16
    quality requirements to functionality conversion 39, 151–4
    selection of transformation 113–14
    styles 116–30
    variants 207
artefacts 25, 106–7, 172, 174
aspects 234
assessing architectures 79–108, 205–7, 262, 268
    artefacts developed 106–7
    experience-based 103–4
    mathematical model-based 100–2
    performing assessments 104–5
    profiles 87–91
    qualitative 80, 105–6
    quantitative 80–1, 105–6
    scenario-based 91–4
    simulation-based 95–100
    theoretical maximum 81

asset responsibles engineers 305–6
Axis Communications 176–80, 263, 308–9, 324, 328

basic interfaces 223
Bass, L. 11, 117, 157, 164, 322, 328
Beck, K. 55, 241
Bengtsson, P.O. 31, 35, 49, 85, 89, 108, 158
binding product interfaces 277
black-box frameworks 227, 228, 239, 243
blackboard style 79, 122–4, 129–30
    deviations 129–30
    maintainability 124
    performance 123–4
    reliability 124
    safety 124
    security 124
Boasson, M. 123, 277
Boehm, B. 108
Booch, G. 30
Bosch, J. 31, 35, 45, 49, 85, 89, 108, 158, 237, 247,
    258, 300, 326, 334
bottom-up approach to archetype identification 58
bottom-up reuse 161
boundary definition 56–7
broker architecture 140–1
Brooks, F.P. 59, 109, 111
Buschmann, F. 37, 38, 115, 116, 117, 143, 146, 157,
    333
business case analysis 189–90, 191–3, 286
    benefits 165
    costs 191
    current situation 192
    investment analysis 192–3
    prediction of the future 192–3
    staff competence 191
    time-to-market 191
business process reengineering 4
business units 301, 304–9, 317–18, 329

caches 296
called frameworks 244
candidate archetypes 58
candidate feature selection 196–8
candidate product selection 195–6
change profiles 34
change scenarios 28, 83
Clements, P. 117
cloning 287–8
code scavenging/salvation 161, 230
collecting components 274–5

commercial off the shelf (COTS) technology 215
commonalites between products 289–90
communication protocol components 222
compatibility 44
competitive advantage 3–4, 5
complete profiles 83–4
component adaptation 225, 227–34
    black-box technique 227, 228, 239, 243
    composability requirements 229
    configuration 229
    copy-paste adaptation 230
    evaluation of techniques 233–4
    inheritance 231
    reuseability 229
    transparency 228–9
    wrapping 228–9, 232–3
component communication standards 293
component decomposition 329–30
component domains 217–20
component frameworks 163
component initialization 277
component interfaces 220–4
component requirement specification 190–1, 208–10
component reuse 13–14
component selection 268–9, 280
component source 240
component system engineering 164
component variability 224–7
components 12–14
    concrete 144
    definition 214
    periodic 144
    product-specific 273–4
    size of 240
    third-party 215, 295
    variability 224–7, 239
    wiring connections 275–6
components development 214–37
    aspects 234
    constraints 234
    domains and components 217–20
    levels of reuse 215
    process 216–17
    rules 235
    software product line reuse 215
    system versions reuse 215
    see also object-oriented frameworks
composability requirements 229
composition of framework control 244–6
composition with legacy components 246–7

computer science domains 62
conceptual integrity 59, 111
concrete components 144
concurrency 132–6, 144
    application-level scheduler 135–6
    non-preemptive threads 134–5
    operating system processes 132–3
    operating system threads 133–4
    reliability 133
    safety 133
    security 133
configurability 43, 48, 52, 225, 229
configuration interface 226–7
conflict between business units 307
conflict resolution 262, 265–7
conflicting features 261
conflicting relations 198
constraints 234
context of the product 202–3
control systems 51
control theory 63
Coplien, J.O. 146
copy-paste adaptation 230
copyrights 169
CORBA 140
core framework design 242–3
corrective maintenance 43, 52
costs
    and business case analysis 191
    of development 5, 9, 10, 282
    of hardware 44
    of maintenance 5, 6, 10
Cotter, S. 241
cross-style mismatches 276
culture 110, 287, 316
Cunningham, W. 55, 241
current situation analysis 192
cycle for entities 47
cyclomatic complexity metric 100–1

Dagermo, P. 241
database management systems (DBMS) 136–7
De Baud, J.M. 213
de Jong, E. 123, 277
deadlines 4–5, 6
decomposing product lines 163–6
decomposing of the system 61–5, 70, 74
    abstraction layers 62
    archetype instantiations 63
    control theory 63

domain entities 61–3
entity-based decomposition 63–4
functional decomposition 63
and interfaces 61
problem-domain functionality 64
defining concepts 242–4
defining profiles 84–5
defining the system context 67–9, 72–3
delivery of systems 4–5, 6
demonstrability 43, 53
dependence on software 1–2
dependencies between assets 329–31
deployment of product-line software 166, 171–2
design of frameworks 256–7
design patterns 38, 145–51
    abstract factory 149–50
    façade 147–8
    observer 148–9
    quality attributes 146–50
    strategy pattern 37, 110, 111, 145
design process lifecycle 10–11
design of product-line architecture 189–213
    architecture assessment 205–7
    architecture transformation 207–8
    business case analysis 189–90, 191–3
    component requirement specification 190–1, 208–10
    functionally-based 202–5
    product and feature planning 190, 200–1
    scoping 190, 194–200
    validation 210–11
detector technology 43
Deutsch, L.P. 256–7
development costs 5, 9, 10, 282
development departments 301, 302–4, 317
development of product-line software 165, 168–9, 170–1
development quality 27
device family requirement definition (DFRD) 312
devices 153–4
dialysis systems *see* haemodialysis systems
Dikel, D. 196, 213, 322, 326
distributing requirements 39, 154–5
distribution 48, 140–42
divide-and-conquer principle 39, 154
documentation 257, 325
domain analysis 33, 256
domain description 42–3, 45–8, 49–51
domain engineering units 165, 302, 309–12, 318, 322

domain entities 62–3
domain extensions 56–7
domain-analysis archetype identification 59
domains 61–2, 218
    application domains 218
    and components 217–20
    software domains 218

EC-Gruppen 45, 49
economic growth 4
economic models 323
effort estimation 325–6
EIKON GUI framework 250–1
encapsulation boundaries 334–5
entities modelling 33, 55
entity functionality 249–50
entity-based decomposition 63–4
EPOC operation system 250–1
event-based styles 275–6
evolution in software product lines 166–7, 168,
    172, 282–5
experience-based assessment 36, 103–4
explicit architectural design 111
extending standards support 284–5, 292–3, 299
extensions 225–6, 262, 263–5, 330–1

façade pattern 147–8
family-based system development 259–81, 271
    component selection 268–9, 280
    instantiation 269–73, 280
    packaging and release 279, 280
    product architecture derivation 261–8, 279
    product integration 274–7, 280
    product-specific components 273–4, 280
    requirement specification 259–61, 279
    validation 278–9, 280
Fayad, M. 258
features 194–5, 259–61, 333
    adding new features 284, 291–2, 299
    graph specification 198–9
    overlapping features 260
    product and feature planning 190, 200–1
    superfluous features 260
    see also scoping
Fenton, N.E. 102
file systems 293
fine-grained extension model 253–4, 273
fire-alarm systems 3–4, 41–44
    archetype identification 69
    and concurrency 144

decomposing into components 70
defining the system context 67–9
domain description 42–3
imposition of an architectural style 129–30
interfaces 68–9
quality requirements 43–4, 153
system instantiations 71
flexibility 48, 143
Foote, B. 238, 242, 326
forecasting 192–3
formal verification 239
framework component models 250–6
    fine-grained extension 253–4, 273
    generator-based 255–6, 273
    product-specific extension 250–1, 271–2
    standard-specific extension 251–3, 272
framework gap 247–8
framework implementation 257
framework internal increments 243
framework testing 257
functional decomposition 63
functionality-based architectural design 3, 7, 25, 27,
    33, 54–78, 209, 265–6
    archetype identification 57–60, 69–70, 73–4
    culture and education 110
    decomposing into components 61–5, 70, 74
    describing system instantiations 65–9, 71, 76
    domain extensions 56–7
    interface-specific requirements 58
    separation of design 54–5
    system context definition 55–7, 67–9, 72–3
functionally-based product-line design 202–5
    context of the product 202–3
    describing product instantiations 204–5
    identifying archetypes 203–4

Gamma, E. 37, 38, 110, 115, 145, 146, 225, 247, 249,
    333
Gang of Four (GoF) book 146
Garlan, D. 37, 59, 82, 116, 125, 127, 276
generalization relations 59
generator-based model 255–6, 273
geographical distribution 286, 315
Gilb, T. 28
goal of architectural design 112
Goldberg, A. 241
Grahn, H. 108
graphical user interfaces 142–4

Ha, R. 28, 30, 35, 82, 100
haemodialysis filtration (HDF) 50

haemodialysis systems 49–53
    archetype identification 73–4
    decomposing into components 74
    defining the system context 72–3
    domain description 49–51
    quality requirements 51–3
    system instantiations 76
Häggander, D. 30, 129, 133, 196
hardware costs 44
hardware evolution 294–5
harmonization of features 197
hazard scenarios 28, 83
hierarchical domain engineering units 302, 312–15, 318
Hollywood principle 244
Hölzle, U. 237, 297
Huni, H. 241

impact analysis 92, 113
implement profiles 97
implicit architectural design 111
implicit invocation style 127–8
independently developed frameworks 244–50
indirect calls 297
individual software systems 162
industrial perspective of architecture 11–12, 13–14, 239–40
information distribution 323–4
inheritance 225, 231
initiating a product line 166–9
input data estimation 101
instantiations 204–5, 269–73, 280
    archetype instantiations 63
    describing system instantiations 65–9, 71, 76
    run-time component instantiation 277
integration code 276–7
interactivity in systems 142–3
interface-specific requirements 56
interfaces 44, 51, 55, 61, 68–9, 209, 240
    application programming interface (API) 221, 239
    basic interfaces 223
    binding product interfaces 277
    component interfaces 220–4
    configuration interface 226–7
    graphical user interfaces 142–4
    provided interfaces 223
    required interfaces 223–4
intertwining of functionality 333–4
introduction of new products 284, 288–91, 299
investment analysis 192–3
iterative product development 23–5

Jacobson, I. 29, 34, 92, 163, 164, 213, 215, 322, 326, 331, 333
JavaBeans 127
Johnson, R. 238, 241, 242, 243, 258, 326

Karlsson, E.A. 241
Kazman, R. 11, 108
Kiczales, G. 234, 334
Knutsson, J. 241
Kotonya, G. 27
Krasner, G.E. 142, 326

Lai, C.T.R. 213, 322
layered architectural style 34, 37, 119–22
    maintainability 121
    OSI seven-layer model 119–20
    performance 121
    relaxed layered style 120
    reliability 122
    safety 122
    security 122
Lehman, M.M. 285
levels of reuse 215
Lieberman, H. 247
Linton, M.A. 241
Liu, J.W.S. 28, 30, 35, 82, 100
Lundberg, L. 129, 133, 158, 247, 296
Lyu, M.R. 28, 82, 100

Macala, R.R. 322, 326
McCabe's cyclomatic complexity metric 102
McCall, J.A. 11, 27, 86, 285
McIlroy, M.D. 6, 161, 237
maintainability 43, 52
    and abstract factory patterns 149
    and application-level persistence 139
    and blackboard style 124
    and broker architecture 141
    and concurrency 132–3
    and database management systems (DBMS) 138
    and façade patterns 147
    and graphical user interfaces 143
    and implicit invocation style 128
    and layered architectural style 121
    and object-oriented style 126
    and observer patterns 149
    and pipes and filters style 118
    and redundancy 153
    and remote method invocation 142
    and self-monitoring 152
    and threads 134, 135

maintenance profiles 87
maintenance costs 5, 6, 10
man-made interfaces 44, 51
management support 321
market opportunities 288–9
Martin, R.C. 146
mass-market products 23, 25
mathematical model-based assessment 35–6, 100–2
   input data estimation 101
   predict the quality attribute 101
   representing the architecture 101
   select and abstract a model 101
Mattsson, M.M. 241, 247, 257, 258, 300, 325
measurement systems 44–9
   actuators 46
   analysis phase 46
   cycle for entities 47
   distribution 48
   domain description 45–8
   quality requirements 48–9
   real-time behaviour 47–8
   sensors 45, 46
Mellor, S.J. 326
memory management 296–7
merging of styles 116
message-based styles 275
Microsoft 7
Microsoft COM 324
mixed responsibility business unit model 306–7
model-view-controller 142, 241
module-based programming 2
Molin, P. 31, 42, 135, 158, 241, 326
monitoring threads 134
Moser, S. 241, 257
multiple versions of assets 327–9
mutually exclusive relations 198

network communication protocols 292–3
new product lines 284, 285–8, 299
new versions of infrastructure 285, 293–5, 299
Nierstrasz, O. 241, 257
Nokia Mobile Phones 314–15
non-preemptive threads 134–5

object-oriented frameworks 238–58, 271–3
   academic and industrial views 239–40
   composition of framework control 244–6
   composition with legacy components 246–7
   core framework design 242–3
   definition of concepts 242–4

   designing frameworks 256–7
   documentation 257
   entity functionality 249–50
   framework component models 250–6
   framework gap 247–8
   framework internal increments 243
   history 241–2
   independently developed frameworks 244–50
   overlap of framework entities 248–9
   subclasses 243
object-oriented languages 2, 42, 111
object-oriented style 125–7
ObjectStore 138
observer patterns 148–9
Ohlsson, L. 31, 135, 158, 241
Opdyke, W.F. 242
operating system processes 132–3
operating system threads 133–4
operating systems 295
operational quality 26
optional behaviour 270
optionality 207–8
organizational culture 110, 287, 316
organizational models *see* product-line organization
OSI seven-layer model 119–20
overlap of framework entities 248–9
overlapping features 260

packaging and release 279, 280
patterns *see* architectural patterns; design patterns
perception of software architects 109
performance
   and abstract factory patterns 149
   and application-level persistence 139
   and application-level schedulers 136
   and blackboard style 123–4
   and broker architecture 141
   of database management systems (DBMS) 138
   and façade patterns 147
   and graphical user interfaces 143
   and implicit invocation style 128
   and layered architectural style 121
   and object-oriented style 125–6
   and observer patterns 148–9
   and pipes and filters style 118
   and profiles 86–7
   and redundancy 153
   and remote method invocation 142
   requirements 43
   and self-monitoring 152
   and threads 133, 135

performance modelling 35–6, 100–1
periodic components 144
Perry, D.E. 38, 116
persistence 136–9
    application-level 139
    database management systems (DBMS) 137–8
    transaction handling 139
Pigoski, T. M. 282, 300
pipes and filters style 60, 117–19, 275
platforms 312–13
point archetypes 70
Pope, S.T. 142, 326
post-fielding 297–8
Potel, M. 241
Poulin, J.S. 30, 108, 215, 219
prediction of the future 192–3
Pree, W. 242
presentation-abstraction-control 142–3
Prieto-Díaz, R. 33, 60
problem-domain functionality 64
product architecture derivation 261–8, 279
    architecture assessment 262, 268
    architecture extension 262, 263–5
    architecture pruning 262–3
    conflict resolution 262, 265–7
product and feature planning 190, 200–1
product integration 274–7, 280
    collecting components 274–5
    integration code 276–7
    wiring connections 275–6
product lifecycle 23
product-line architecture 9–10, 11, 66, 162
    applicability of concepts 169–70
    decomposing product lines 163–6
    design of 189–213
    initiating a product line 166–9
product-line assets 282–300
    adding new features 284, 291–2, 299
    assets in new contexts 331
    dependencies between assets 329–31
    encapsulation boundaries 334–5
    evolution in software product lines 282–5
    extending standards support 284–5, 292–3, 299
    feature core versus feature superset 333
    improving quality attributes 285, 295–7, 299–300
    intertwining of functionality 333–4
    introduction of new products 284, 288–91, 299
    multiple versions of assets 327–9
    new product lines 284, 285–8, 299
    new versions of infrastructure 285, 293–5, 299

post-fielding 297–8
required interfaces 334–5
run-time evolution 297–8
splitting off products 327
tool support 332
product-line concepts 169–70
product-line organization 301–18, 319–23
    business units 301, 304–9, 317–18, 329
    development departments 301, 302–4, 317
    domain engineering units 302, 309–12, 318, 322
    economic models 323
    and geographical distribution 315
    hierarchical domain engineering units 302,
        312–15, 318
    management support 321
    and organizational culture 316
    project management maturity 315–16
    time-to-market (TTM) 322–3
    and type of products 316–17
product-line scoping 199–200
product-specific components 273–4, 280
product-specific extension model 250–1, 271–2
production technology 44
profiles 28, 34, 82–91
    complete profiles 83–4
    defining profiles 84–5
    implement profiles 97
    maintenance profiles 87
    and performance 86–7
    quality attribute profiles 86–9
    and reliability 88
    and safety 88–9
    and security 89
    selected profiles 83–4
project management maturity 315–16
protective systems 51
provided interfaces 223
pruning 262–3

qualitative assessment 80, 105–6
quality attributes 101, 132–44, 146–50, 209, 240
    assessing 34–7
    conflict resolution 266–7
    conversion to functionality 39, 151–4
    development quality 26
    family-based system development 271
    improving 285, 295–7, 299–300
    missing 267
    objectives 5–6
    operational quality 27

prediction 92–3
and production technology 44
profiles 86–9
ranking of 113
and requirements engineering 27–32
requirements specifications 43–4, 48–9, 51–3,
    153, 327–8
quantitative assessment 80–81, 105–6
quasi-experimentation 83

rate-monotonic analysis (RMA) 102
real-time behaviour 47–8, 53
REBOOT 241
recurring patterns 58, 60
redundancy 152–3
relaxed layered style 120
release and packaging 279, 280
reliability
    and abstract factory patterns 149
    and application-level persistence 139
    and blackboard style 124
    and broker architecture 141
    and concurrency 133
    and database management systems (DBMS) 138
    and façade patterns 147
    and graphical user interfaces 143
    and implicit invocation style 128
    and layered architectural style 122
    and object-oriented style 126
    and observer patterns 149
    and pipes and filters style 118
    and profiles 88
    and redundancy 153
    and remote method invocation 142
    and self-monitoring 152
    and threads 134, 135
remote method invocation 141–2
required interfaces 223–4, 334–5
requirements 25, 27–32, 259–61, 279
reuse of software 2, 6–8, 161–2
    bottom-up reuse 161
    code scavenging/salvation 161
    component reuse 16–17
reuse-oriented organizations 165
revolutionary approach to product-line initiation
    166–7
Richardson, D.J. 131
RISE (Research in Software Engineering) 10
Roberts, D. 242, 243, 258
Robson, D. 241

role of software 3–8
rules 38, 131, 235
Rumbaugh, J. 29
run-time component instantiation 277
run-time evolution 297–8
Russo, V.F. 241

safety 52–3
    and abstract factory patterns 149
    and application-level persistence 139
    and blackboard style 124
    and broker architecture 141
    and concurrency 133
    and database management systems (DBMS) 138
    and façade patterns 147
    and graphical user interfaces 144
    and implicit invocation style 128
    and layered architectural style 122
    and object-oriented style 126
    and observer patterns 149
    and pipes and filters style 118–19
    and profiles 88–9
    and redundancy 153
    and remote method invocation 142
    and self-monitoring 152
    and threads 134, 135
Samentinger, J. 230, 237
scenario-based assessment 28, 34–5, 91–5
    assigning weights 85
    change scenarios 83
    definition of categories 84–5
    effectiveness of 92
    hazard scenarios 83
    impact analysis 92
    quality attribute prediction 92–3
Schäfer, S. 33
Schmid, K. 213
Schmidt, D.C. 146
Schmucker, K.J. 241
scoping 190, 194–200
    candidate feature selection 196–8
    candidate product selection 195–6
    feature graph specification 198–9
    features definition 194–5
    harmonization of features 197
    product-line scoping 199–200
    specification of product-specific requirements 200
Securitas Larm AB 3–4, 41–4, 180–2, 304
security
    and abstract factory patterns 149
    and application-level persistence 139

and blackboard style 124
and broker architecture 141
and concurrency 133
and database management systems (DBMS) 138
and façade patterns 148
and graphical user interfaces 144
and implicit invocation style 128
and layered architectural style 122
and object-oriented style 127
and observer patterns 149
and pipes and filters style 119
and profiles 89
and redundancy 153
and remote method invocation 142
and self-monitoring 152
and threads 134, 135
selected profiles 83–4
selection of transformation 113–14
self-monitoring 152
sensors 45, 46, 55–6, 150
separation of design 54–5
Shaw, M. 37, 116, 117, 125, 127
Shlaer, S. 326
simulation-based assessment 35, 95–100
accuracy of 99–100
defining and implementing the context 96
graphical interface 100
implement profiles 97
implementing architectural components 96–7
initiate profile 97
predict quality attribute 97
and reliability assessment 98–9
simulate system 97
size of components 240
Smith, C.U. 28, 30, 35, 82, 100, 101, 108, 157
software architecture 10–12
Sommerville, I. 27
Sparks, S. 243, 244, 247
specialization 200, 288
SPLICE model 277
splitting off products 327
staff competence 191
staff numbers 307
stakeholder communication 11
standard-specific extension model 251–3, 272
standards 44, 239, 284–5, 292–3, 299
strategy design pattern 37, 100, 111, 145
structural metrics 102
styles see architectural styles
subclasses 243

subsystems 58, 116–17
superfluous features 260
Svahnberg, M. 300
Symbian 183–7, 312
system context definition 55–7, 67–9, 72–3
system instantiations 71, 76
system requirements 27
system versions reuse 215
Szyperski, C. 16, 140, 161, 163, 219, 237, 324, 334

tacit knowledge 29–30
Taligent 241
Tanenbaum, A.S. 119
TeleLarm 41, 42
temperature sensors 45
template instantiation 225
TempSensor 247
test instance generation 257
theoretical maximum assessment 81
third-party components 215, 295
threads 133–5
tick method 144–5, 234
time-to-market (TTM) 4–5, 6, 10, 191, 322–3
tool support 332
top-down approach to archetype identification 58
traditional software development 4–5
transaction handling 136–9
transformation see architecture transformation
transparency and component adaptation 228–9
type of products 316–17

ultrafiltration (UF) 50
unconstrained business unit model 305
usage profile 28
user-adapted instantiations 44

validation 210–11, 278–9, 280
van der Linden, F. 215
van Gurp, V. 108
variability of components 224–7, 239
component adaptation 225
configuration 225
extensions 225–6
generation 225
inheritance 225
template instantiation 225
variants 207, 263, 270–1
verification 239
versions 328
Vlissides, J.M. 146

Weck, W. 12, 214, 237
Weinand, A. 241
Weiss, D.M. 213, 322
white-box frameworks 243
Wilson, D.A. 34
Wilson, S.D. 34

Wirfs-Brock, R. 92
wiring connections 275–6
Wolf, A.L. 38, 116, 131
wrapping 228–9, 232–3, 264, 297

Zhao, M. 99